Early Praise for *Case Studies in Retrofitting Suburbia*

"Contentious and desirable as ever, suburbia continues to beguile and confound us. And there is no one more competent to analyze the challenges and dissect the opportunities in our sprawling communities than June Williamson and Ellen Dunham-Jones. With their new follow-up book on the past decade's best practices in retrofitting suburbia, a monumental achievement of scholarship and insight, they succeed in positioning this socio-economic phenomenon within today's predicament of converging crises when leveraging every possible transform-ative feat feels ever more urgent."

Galina Tachieva, author of *Sprawl Repair Manual*

"The most important single challenge facing the American built environment is to "retrofit" 20th century suburbs to meet 21st century goals of equity, sustainability, and community. June Williamson and Ellen Dunham-Jones not only grasp the most difficult suburban issues ranging from automobile dependence to aging populations to water and energy resilience. Their uniquely comprehensive research has enabled them to identify and to document key case studies from across North America where redesign has led to successful retrofits. At once deeply practical and deeply idealistic, this book opens up important opportunities for suburbs everywhere."

Robert Fishman, author of *Bourgeois Utopias: The Rise and Fall of Suburbia*

"June Williamson and Ellen Dunham-Jones's latest book, *Case Studies in Retrofitting Suburbia*, masterfully chroni-cles the innovative spirit of planners, developers, advocates and policy makers retrofitting American car-oriented suburbs into thriving, people-centric communities of opportunity and resilience. This book paints a loud and clear picture that our movement must address the intersectionality between urban design, racial justice, climate, economic prosperity and public health to meet the current and future challenges we face in the American suburban built environment. If you're a community innovator dedicated to reimaging America's car-centric suburbs into thriving, people-centric communities of opportunity and resilience, this book is for you!"

Christopher A. Coes, vice president of Smart Growth America and director of LOCUS: Responsible Real Estate Developers and Investors

"In 2008, *Retrofitting Suburbia* was a revelation. Why do so many suburban communities want to change their built environment, and just as importantly, *how* can they do it? It quickly became a must-read not only in the planning field, but also for residents seeking answers to seemingly immutable local challenges. By offering concrete advice that was adaptable and scalable to the many different types of places, the book quickly became the "how to" guide for retrofitting the suburbs. With *Case Studies in Retrofitting Suburbia*, June Williamson and Ellen Dunham-Jones deepen their exploration of the "why" and double down on the "how." This time, the case studies are organized by imperatives, such as public health, how to support an aging population, and social equity. Together, they cover a rich diversity of challenges in virtually every type of suburb from all corners of the U.S. Individually, the examples are fascinating reads. The discussion of Guthrie Green in Tulsa, Oklahoma, for example, delves into the history of the adjacent Greenwood neighborhood, site of the 1921 Tulsa Race Massacre. It high-lights the ways in which a wide range of Tulsans—architects and planners, community members, public health officials, educators—have come together to reshape the physical space as a contribution to much-needed healing and reconciliation, and the building of social cohesion in a deeply traumatized community. That case study and many others remind us that while the *physical* form of places typically gets most of the attention in local debates, "the suburban *social* body," as the authors call it, is the reason why we are compelled to seek change."

Don Chen, president of the Surdna Foundation

JUNE WILLIAMSON | ELLEN DUNHAM-JONES

CASE STUDIES IN
RETROFITTING
SUBURBIA

URBAN DESIGN STRATEGIES FOR URGENT CHALLENGES

WILEY

For general information about our other products and services, please contact our Customer Care Department within the United States at (800) 762-2974, outside the United States at (317) 572-3993 or fax (317) 572-4002.

Wiley publishes in a variety of print and electronic formats and by print-on-demand. Some material included with standard print versions of this book may not be included in e-books or in print-on-demand. If this book refers to media such as a CD or DVD that is not included in the version you purchased, you may download this material at http://booksupport.wiley.com. For more information about Wiley products, visit www.wiley.com.

Library of Congress Cataloging-in-Publication Data is available:

ISBN 9781119149170 (Cloth)
ISBN 9781119149187 (ePDF)
ISBN 9781119149194 (ePub)

Cover design: Wiley
Cover image: Courtesy of Ellen Dunham Jones

SKY10023290_121720

CONTENTS

INTRODUCTION

hange is everywhere in the suburbs of northern America, the built landscapes where most residents of the United States and Canada live. Speculative visions of futuristic solar suburbs powering electric cars and e-bikes make headlines at the same time that mid-century-modern ranch house renovations are all the rage. Exurban "McMansions" fill with multigenerational families while new infill housing and backyard cottages are built to meet the needs of smaller households in inner suburban neighborhoods. Established suburbs largely built for young white families are more likely to be populated today by older white faces and younger faces of color.

The shopping centers, office parks, garden apartment complexes, and highway strip corridors of the twentieth century are aging and changing too. Many are being retrofitted to meet new needs. In areas experiencing growth pressure, they're being redeveloped into more "urban" places—read: more mixed in use, walkable, and dense in building area. In communities with little to no economic growth pressure, many of these failing properties are providing lower-cost space for entrepreneurs to start or expand small, local businesses.

The growing vacancies in weaker markets make visible longstanding discrimination and structural racism in the built environment and growing societal inequalities, expressed by a shrinking middle class and increased rates of poverty in suburban populations. As the gap between rich and poor places widens, so does the ability to cope with infrastructure maintenance, adaptations to prepare for the impacts of climate change, public health pandemics and epidemics of obesity and loneliness, as well as the economic shifts presented by online shopping and the automation of labor. Based on decades of tracking a wide array of case studies, this new book adds dozens of newly documented case studies describing

how suburban places conceived and built for obsolete twentieth century paradigms are retrofitted to address the most pressing challenges of today.

We are both architects, urban designers, and academics; since first meeting in the early 1990s, together and apart we have closely tracked the transformational trends in northern American suburban areas. This scholarly and creative journey has led us to develop complementary expertise in the histories of suburbanization and its discontents, the economics of land development, the subtleties of demographic analysis, and the complex intersections of built form, culture, ecologies, and politics. Our accumulated knowledge and our shared wisdom—we think—are captured in these pages. We advance and expand arguments made in our first collaborative book-length project, *Retrofitting Suburbia: Urban Design Solutions for Redesigning Suburbs*.[1] That book was released in late 2008 and updated in 2011. This book, next in the series, contains entirely new contents and is not a revision. We conceived it to be deeply rewarding to read on its own and as a sequel that builds on the earlier book.

In Part I, we spell out newly emergent challenges manifest in suburban situations and what communities and their designers can do to address them in six thematic chapters: Disrupt Automobile Dependence; Improve Public Health; Support an Aging Population; Leverage Social Capital for Equity; Compete for Jobs; and Add Water and Energy Resilience. Each of these chapters describes the contours of the challenge and summarizes current research about how suburban development

---

[1] Ellen Dunham-Jones and June Williamson, *Retrofitting Suburbia: Urban Design Solutions for Redesigning Suburbs* (Hoboken, NJ: Wiley, 2008). An updated, paperback edition was released in 2011.

patterns have exacerbated the problems, sometimes unintentionally. These chapters set the stage by discussing a variety of retrofit solutions, available resources, and successfully employed techniques from various fields, including urban design, building and landscape architecture, urban planning, and real estate development. Our focus in these chapters is on how changes to the physical form of suburbia help communities adapt to challenges and embrace potentials to become more resilient, livable, enjoyable, equitable, and prosperous for all.

Part II features 32 case studies of a wide range of suburban retrofits in diverse market conditions in northern America. Organized from the west coast of the continent to the east, the "before" uses cover the range of typical suburban property types: suburban arterial roads and intersections, parking lots, shopping malls, strip centers, big box stores, office and industrial parks, garden apartments, residential subdivisions, auto-body repair lots, a gas station, even a decommissioned airport. They include ambitious, large-scale, resource-intensive redevelopments, more modest community-serving reinhabitations of buildings and landscapes, and impressive regreenings. Many of our favorites include aspects of all three primary retrofitting strategies: some redevelopment to connect us to the future, some reinhabitation to connect us to the past, and some regreening to connect us to nature. We selected the case studies based on how much they "raised the bar" in meeting at least one of the particular challenges outlined in Part I and how well they layered solutions to aspects of additional challenges. Each case study narrative is written to highlight replicable design strategies and policies, recognizing market constraints. Each, we hope, describes enough of the implementation process to inspire others to follow.

As authors, we can't help but hope our readers will devour every word from cover to cover. However, the book is deliberately organized with bullet point references to allow readers to focus on a particular challenge in Part I and go immediately to the most relevant case studies in Part II, and vice versa. We commissioned photographer Phillip Jones to take many of the excellent photos in the book. We encourage readers to further explore the case studies via our ample footnotes and by searching images online. Hint: our inner geeks love using the clock icon in Google Earth Pro to travel back through time and track changes while zooming in and out at the larger context.

Readers will benefit from understanding the larger context for the book, starting with how we define "suburban." We've chosen not to engage ongoing debates over how to quantitatively define suburbs.[2] We focus on built form. A property with a building surrounded by surfaces that are lawn or paved for parking we define as suburban form. If the building fronts a sidewalk and places the parking either under or behind it, that's urban form. If the road infrastructure is dendritic—branching out like a tree—that's suburban form. If the streets are networked—interconnected and walkable, with frequent intersections—that's urban form. Most instances of suburban form are located in places we generically refer to as suburbs or suburbia. There are many cities, however, that have properties within them characterizable as suburban form that are good candidates for retrofitting. And there are many suburbs with districts of good urban form that should be preserved, if not extended.

Places built with suburban form have been highly resistant to change. Land-use policies, defended by NIMBYs (neighborhood activists who protest "Not in My Back Yard"), and highway investments have directed new growth to the places of least resistance, at the ever-expanding metropolitan periphery. These developments have often come at the expense of opportunities to densify already developed properties. A shift started with a handful of private-sector-led retrofits in the late 1980s and picked up steam by the mid-2000s with the growing popularity of new urbanism, smart growth, and the "return to the city" movement. In our first book we featured case studies on redeveloping "underperforming asphalt" (developer-speak

---

[2] Despite suburbs being where the majority of US citizens live, neither the US Census Bureau or the Office of Management and Budget provide a systematic definition of the term. They distinguish and report on urban and rural, metropolitan and micropolitan (small towns). By default, the suburbs are simply those parts of a metropolitan urban area that aren't the core cities. This has prompted numerous attempts to better distinguish types of suburbs through history and in the present. A few of many sources include Ann Forsyth, "Defining Suburbs," *Journal of Planning Literature,* 5 June 2012; June Williamson, *Designing Suburban Futures: New Models From Build a Better Burb* (Washington, DC: Island Press, 2013); RCLCO, ULI Terwilliger Center, "The New Geography of Urban America: An Interactive Map for Classifying Urban Neighborhoods," 19 June 2018; Whitney Airgood-Obrycki and Shannon Rieger, "Defining Suburbs: How Definitions Shape the Suburban Landscape," Working Paper, Joint Center for Housing Studies of Harvard University, 20 February 2019, https://www.jchs.harvard.edu/research-areas/working-papers/defining-suburbs-how-definitions-shape-suburban-landscape.

for underused parking lots) into more sustainable, compact, walkable, mixed-use places.[3]

The Great Recession of 2008 hit suburbs hard and resistance to change began to fade as dead shopping centers and stalled subdivisions proliferated. An occupied or demolished building was better than a vacant one and the number of reinhabitation and regreening projects in our database of examples grew.[4] The Great Recession also prompted ambitious public planning efforts, such as the Obama administration's Partnership for Sustainable Communities and Neighborhood Stabilization Program.[5] These federal programs resulted in successful community revitalizations, demonstrating the benefits of integrating mixed travel modes, uses, and incomes—especially in suburbs.

The combination of an increasingly ambitious public sector willing to invest in public-private partnerships, ongoing vacancies due to the so-called "retail apocalypse," and a significant market shift in favor of walkable, urban lifestyles dramatically expanded the movement to retrofit suburban sprawl.[6] The market

interest in walkability aligns remarkably well with the public sector's efforts to meet the challenges of improving public health, equitable and affordable access to opportunities, a society with more people living longer, and the pressing need to mitigate climate change impacts. Our database of retrofitting examples has exploded over the past decade from 80 to over 2,000 entries. Slightly more than half we classify as redevelopments, only 2% as regreenings, and the rest comprise incomplete tallies of the vast number of reinhabitations and adopted corridor retrofit plans. This book is inspired by how complex, diverse, and creative the newest retrofits are. If the previous generation of retrofits were mostly about reducing auto dependency, these projects continue that effort but also layer on aspects of solutions to multiple challenges. We are humbled by the tremendous imagination it took to envision such change and the dedication of the numerous public- and private-sector champions without whom these projects would not have been implemented.

Will retrofitting maintain the same pace? In early 2020 the US entered another recession and numerous retail chains declared bankruptcy at the same time as a viral pandemic spread across the globe, leading to a great many deaths and unprecedented job losses. We believe these crises have increased the need and opportunities for retrofitting, although the long-term effects are unknown.

Our first book has since been joined by others engaged by the topic. We welcome their work and the growing efforts to document how well retrofits perform over time.[7] How much more sustainable are they than what proceeded them? Which performance metrics are most useful and comparable in our emerging age of big data? Where and when does retrofitting risk displacement by gentrification? What unknown new challenges lie ahead? While we and our cohort look to northern America, some answers may come from researchers

---

[3] We only track examples that, one way or another, are improving sustainability. We do not track examples where new retail replaces old retail.

[4] See the foreword to the updated edition of *Retrofitting Suburbia: Urban Design Solutions for Redesigning Suburbs* (Hoboken, NJ: Wiley, 2011).

[5] Between 2009 and 2016, the US Federal Sustainable Communities Partnership funded $240 million in planning grants and over $3.5 billion for implementation to over 1,000 communities to improve their infrastructure and rewrite their zoning to attract development in the future that would integrate more uses, more transportation choices, and more income groups. For the first time ever, grant proposals were coordinated between the US Department of Transportation, Department of Housing and Urban Development, and the Environmental Protection Agency.

[6] The significance of changing demographics driving new market preferences should be understood as communities plan for tomorrow's residents. The majority of households in the US today are one- to two-person and the proportion is expected to rise. While each local condition varies, the majority of households in suburbs overall are either empty-nester Baby Boomers or Millennials (in 2020, they aged 56–74 or 24–39 respectively). Despite their different motivations, both generations' interests have converged to drive the market to retrofit the suburbs for more urban lifestyles, contributing to the 75% rent premium that walkability now adds to real estate values. See Tracy Hadden Loh, Christopher B. Leinberger, and Jordan Chafetz, *Foot Traffic Ahead* (George Washington University School of Business & Smart Growth America, 2019). See also Arthur C. Nelson, *The Reshaping of Metropolitan America* (Washington DC: Island Press, 2013).

---

[7] The literature on suburban retrofits continues to grow but tends to be heavier on documenting design intentions than project performance. See Galina Tachieva, *Sprawl Repair Manual* (Washington, DC: Island Press, 2010); Emily Talen, ed., *Retrofitting Sprawl: Addressing Seventy Years of Failed Urban Form* (Athens: University of Georgia Press, 2015); and Jason Beske and David Dixon, eds., *Suburban Remix: Creating the Next Generation of Urban Places* (Washington, DC: Island Press, 2018). See also Build a Better Burb: http://buildabetterburb.org/.

studying diverse suburban retrofits around the world. Retrofits of superblocks in China, Soviet Khrushchevka in Eastern Europe, and shopping centers everywhere are all on the rise and deserve ever more attention. This is especially important at a time when many in the growing global middle class aspire to adopt versions of northern America suburban lifestyles. We hope that the new suburbs built for them might learn from how yesterday's models are being retrofitted today. Future researchers should have much to work on and we look forward to learning new retrofit strategies to help all of us transform suburban places to meet local and global challenges.

ACKNOWLEDGMENTS

As we look back on all of the individuals and organizations that helped this book come to fruition, we can't help but also look forward to those we hope will find the work within lights a path through uncertain times ahead. We hope the strategies this book documents to boost health, equity, and prosperity for all will be relevant as communities focus on reestablishing a more just public life in towns, cities, and suburbs across the globe.

There have been many stepping stones along the way from completing our first book together in 2008, *Retrofitting Suburbia,* to this one. Each step both deepened our lines of inquiry and expanded our grasp of the complex, diverse challenges that retrofits can and are addressing. Former HUD Secretary Henry Cisneros invited us to write a chapter on suburban retrofits for the book *Independent for Life: Homes and Neighborhoods for an Aging America*. Dr. Richard Jackson interviewed us in his documentary series "Designing Healthy Communities." We are each frequently requested to speak to issues of climate change and resilience as well as equity and affordability in suburbia. June organized the Build a Better Burb ideas competition and ParkingPLUS design challenge for the Rauch Foundation. The competition resulted in a website of the same name that's a terrific resource, hosted by the Congress for the New Urbanism (CNU) and steered by Robert Steuteville. June published the research and results in *Designing Suburban Futures: New Models from Build a Better Burb*. Ellen steadily built the database of retrofits to over 2000 entries. (She wishes there were more regreenings, and regrets that the database is not yet ready to make public.) She gave a TEDx talk on retrofitting suburbia that went viral. Ellen and June were commissioned by *AD* to write "Dead and Dying Shopping Malls, Reinhabited." Interactions with locals as we've traveled far and wide giving interviews, lectures, and workshops—many thanks to publicists Irina Woelfle and April Roberts—have enriched our understanding of the obstacles and workarounds to implementing retrofits. We are grateful for all of these opportunities, and so many others.

We learned much from shared discussions with our peers, their publications, and practices. Thanks go to John Anderson and David Kim, Allison Arieff, Barry Bergdoll, Rick Bernhardt, Scott Bernstein, Jason Beske, Peter Calthorpe, Ann Daigle, David Dixon, Victor Dover and Joe Kohl, DPZ CoDesign (Elizabeth Plater-Zyberk, Andres Duany, and Galina Tachieva), Stephen Fan, Doug Farr, Richard Florida, Ann Golob, Rachel Heiman, Jim Hughes, Amanda Kolson Hurley, Interboro (Georgeen Theodore, Tobias Armborst, and Dan D'Oca), Kaja Kühl, Robert Lane, Nancy Levinson, Mike Lydon and Tony Garcia, Liz Moule and Stef Polyzoides, Chuck Marohn, Reinhold Martin, Jana McCann and Jim Adams, Michael Mehaffy, Joe Minicozzi, Becky Nicolaides, Christopher Niedt, Nathan Norris, Brian O'Looney and John Torti, Michael Piper, Dan Reed, Duke Reiter, Lynn Richards, David Smiley, Emily Talen, Anne Tate, Marilyn Taylor, John Tschiderer, and many others.

We owe a special gratitude to the numerous colleagues and students who helped us along the way. From the City College of New York where June serves as Chair of Architecture at the Spitzer School of Architecture, we offer thanks to faculty colleagues Nandini Bagchee, Hillary Brown, Gordon Gebert, Marta Gutman, Brad Horn, and Sean Weiss, and we extend a special debt of gratitude to the late, great Michael Sorkin. He is deeply missed. We thank all the students who participated in June's suburbs-focused seminars and studios, and especially Belma Fishta, Melanie Nunez, and Mary Gilmartin for their superb help with the graphics and permissions. We offer similar thanks to students in Ellen's Retrofitting Suburbia seminar and studios at Georgia Tech, where she directs the Master of Science in Urban Design degree and benefits from ongoing conversations about retrofitting with many of the faculty. Special thanks to Steve French, Scott Marble, Julie Kim, Subhro Guhathakurta, Richard Dagenhart,

John Crittenden, Valerie Thomas, Marilyn Brown, and Michael Chang for insights into analytical methods and to the many students who have helped with the database, graphics and performance research: Liz Teston, Kyla Dowlen, Zorana Matic, Sarthak Dhingra, Animesh Shrestha, Wesley Brown, Jiaxuan Huang, Jules Krinsky, Jinxin "Angela" Xu, Yeinn "Grace" Oh, Jun Wang, Yilun Zha, Osvaldo Broesicke, Nevidita Sankararaman, and Alexandra Maxim.

From our academic perches, we are especially grateful to all those working out in the field who generously shared their stories with us for the case studies. We tried to acknowledge all the lead participants, but we recognize that complex urban design projects often involve too many consultants to name them all. We apologize for the inevitable omissions. Look for continuing work in this area at www.retrofittingsuburbia.com.

At Wiley, thanks for your talents—and considerable patience—to editors Margaret Cummins, Helen Castle, Kalli Schultea, Todd Green, Amy Odum, Indirakumari S, and Amy Handy.

Most of all, we thank our readers. The impact and popularity of our first book completely surprised us. To see how it emboldened many of you to champion for change in your own communities and practices is what inspired us to write this new book. We're sorry that we could only fit in 32 case studies!

Finally, we thank our families for putting up with our being obsessively preoccupied much longer than expected and for dragging you to visit so many off-the-beaten-track locations. To David and Theo in New York, Ellen is enormously grateful to you for embracing June in love, laughter, and productive energy. To Phil in Atlanta, June (and Ellen) still can't quite believe that you became a drone pilot just to be able to produce so many of the original photos in this book. It's been a team effort all the way through and we love you madly.

June Williamson, New York, November 2020
Ellen Dunham-Jones, Atlanta, November 2020

PART ONE
URGENT
SUBURBAN
CHALLENGES

Chapter I.1
Disrupt Automobile Dependence

Trying to cure traffic congestion by adding more capacity is like trying to cure obesity by loosening your belt.

If every place worth visiting had enough parking for all the people who wanted to visit, there would be no places left worth visiting.

Widely cited amongst traffic engineers, unknown sources

Suburban form has always been shaped predominantly by transportation. Early suburbs from the mid-nineteenth century centered on the railroad stations, while early twentieth-century streetcar suburbs were designed with row after row of narrow-lot blocks a short walk from the transit corridors. The rapid, widespread adoption of private cars enabled the emergence of late twentieth-century auto-oriented suburban sprawl, characterized by low-density urbanism, separated uses, and "leapfrog" development patterns wherein lower-cost agricultural or forested land further out on the periphery, accessible from a highway exit, was preferred for new construction over closer-in sites. Soon, many more households were in locations where private cars were the default mobility choice.

In 2016 there were 1.97 motor vehicles per US household.[1] No one knows just how many parking spaces there are nationwide, but there are some startling city-wide numbers. Des Moines, Iowa, has 19 parking spaces per household while Jackson, Wyoming, has 27. Seattle, Washington has 29 parking spaces per acre servicing a population density of 13 people per acre, while Los Angeles County has 200 square miles worth of parking spaces.[2] In the words of the US Supreme Court, car ownership is now a "virtual necessity."[3] This sense of "necessity," we believe, can be altered. We don't really require that much parking. And couldn't the land be put to better use?

Meanwhile, the growing global middle classes, in pursuit of lower-density living and the status and convenience of the private automobile, are at risk of becoming just as auto-dependent as northern Americans. That convenience comes at a staggering cost to public and environmental health, let alone the $25 per day on average that Americans pay to own a car.

Yet converging forces are increasingly disrupting conventional patterns of private car ownership and automobile dependency. These include:

- New forms of mobility such as carsharing, carhailing, electric vehicles, mobility-as-a-service models, autonomous shuttle buses, autonomous cars, and drones
- New forms of electric micromobility that help with the "first/last mile problem" such as e-bikes, e-scooters, and e-skateboards
- Increased traffic congestion in areas of growing population, reducing the convenience of travel by private car
- Increasing investments in public transit (although results in ridership are mixed)
- Apps with real-time information about transit schedules, weather, and traffic
- Online shopping and the transfer of consumer trips to delivery trips
- Increasingly crowded and crumbling highways and subways
- Younger generations' reduced interest in car ownership and increased preference for urban lifestyles and shared mobility

[1] Michael Sivak, "Has Motorization in the US Peaked? Part 9: Vehicle Ownership and Distance Driven, 1984–2015," University of Michigan Sustainable Worldwide Transportation, Report No. SWT-2017-4, February 2017.

[2] Eric Scharnhorst, "Quantified Parking: Comprehensive Parking Inventories for Five U.S. Cities," Research Institute for Housing America and Mortgage Bankers Association, May 2018. See also David Z. Morris, "L.A.'s Massive 'Crater' Shows Why Parking is the Biggest Fight in Urban Planning," Fortune, 14 January 2016.

[3] Gregory H. Shill, "Americans Shouldn't Have to Drive, but the Law Insists on It," The Atlantic, 9 July 2019.

Figure I.1-1 Nearly half of the trips in suburban areas dominated by single-family detached houses are under three miles, yet over 90% of those are made by car. More sidewalks, bike lanes, and everyday uses could dramatically reduce auto dependency. Rezoning to allow denser housing types could even make transit feasible. Source: Authors.

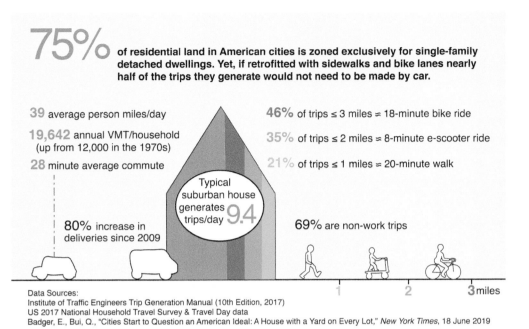

75% of residential land in American cities is zoned exclusively for single-family detached dwellings. Yet, if retrofitted with sidewalks and bike lanes nearly half of the trips they generate would not need to be made by car.

39 average person miles/day

19,642 annual VMT/household (up from 12,000 in the 1970s)

28 minute average commute

80% increase in deliveries since 2009

Typical suburban house generates 9.4 trips/day

46% of trips ≤ 3 miles ≈ 18-minute bike ride

35% of trips ≤ 2 miles ≈ 8-minute e-scooter ride

21% of trips ≤ 1 miles ≈ 20-minute walk

69% are non-work trips

1   2   3 miles

Data Sources:
Institute of Traffic Engineers Trip Generation Manual (10th Edition, 2017)
US 2017 National Household Travel Survey & Travel Day data
Badger, E., Bui, Q., "Cities Start to Question an American Ideal: A House with a Yard on Every Lot," *New York Times*, 18 June 2019

All of these disruptive factors are accelerating the trends to retrofit underperforming and vacant suburban commercial properties and excess "grayfield" parking lots that we identified in our first book, *Retrofitting Suburbia: Urban Design Solutions for Redesigning Suburbs*. Back in the 2000s, we were focused on projects that did *anything* to reduce automobile dependency. Since then, retrofits have become both more common and more ambitious at tackling the many challenges facing suburban landscapes.

Increasingly, the question isn't just "What are you doing to reduce dependence on the car?"—it's also "What are you doing for climate change, social equity, and the loneliness epidemic?" Many retrofits more directly address these social and environmental challenges by reinhabiting underperforming properties with more community-serving uses or by regreening them. However, the imperative to pursue a variety of steps to reduce automobile dependence remains fundamental because of the cascade of impacts. This isn't a war to get rid of the private car and the freedom associated with it, although the future impact of autonomous vehicles might lead in that direction. It is about expanding the freedom of transportation choices, reducing the number and length of car trips, and creating healthier and more prosperous communities at the same

time. Fundamentally, this chapter is about understanding how to better organize suburban roads, streets, and parking to achieve these goals.

ROADS, STREETS, AND STROADS

What's the difference between a road and a street? A road's primary function is *mobility*. Its job is to connect you from point A to point B at good speed with minimal interruptions. Think of a "rural road," a railroad, or a highway.

A street, on the other hand, is designed to maximize *access* to the homes, businesses, and civic institutions alongside it. It is a public space to facilitate transactions and generate both financial and social capital. It is generally part of a well-interconnected street network that distributes traffic. Some congestion on streets is a sign of a healthy economy. Streets are for getting to know one's community and for getting around: by foot, bike, bus, as well as car. Think of an "urban street"—whether Main Street (commercial), Elm Street (residential), or a grand avenue (mixed). For centuries, cities have been based on walkable streets and connected to each other by ridable roads. We still need both roads and streets.

Unfortunately, much of suburbia has been deliberately planned without good versions of either. Soon after the mass production of automobiles, visionary planners called for a dendritic "street hierarchy" to replace the urban grid and its walkable mix of uses.[4] Conceived like a tree, the highway is the trunk: large branches are the arterial roads with commercial uses; smaller branches are collector streets, often lined with higher-density residential; and the twigs are the culs-de-sac. The intent was to combine high-speed movement with the zoned separation of uses, while shielding residential neighborhoods from cut-through traffic.

In the name of safety and speed, modern reformists called for the complete separation of cars from pedestrians, even going so far as to call for the death of the street. Uses were to be disentangled from streets and separated into shopping centers, government centers, business centers, and so on, reached by high-speed roads.[5] These ideas set the pattern for the planning of modern mass suburbanization—and the acceptance of an average 100 US and 3,300 global deaths a day in car crashes as "accidents."[6]

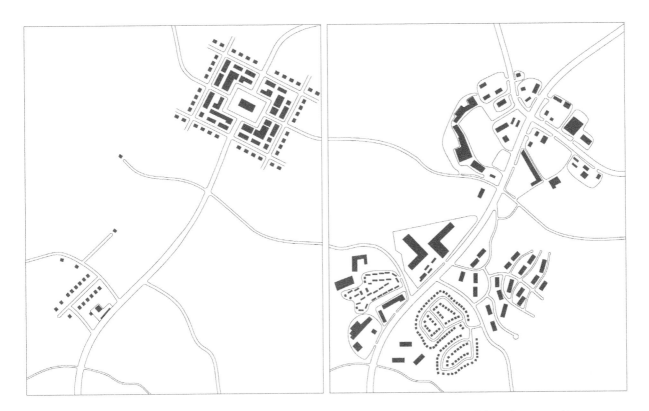

Figure I.1-2 The hypothetical image on the left distinguishes roads from streets. It shows a road through countryside connecting to the streets of a small settlement at an intersection and those surrounding a town's courthouse square. The image on the right depicts actual, by-right, development in suburban Atlanta Georgia. It shows a "stroad" lined with strip malls, fast food outparcels clustered at the major intersection, and residential subdivisions of homes and apartment complexes laid out on "faux-roads." Source: Authors.

4 See "Street Networks 101," Congress for the New Urbanism, "What We Do" tab: www.cnu.org.

5 Swiss-French modernist architect Le Corbusier first espoused this vision of modern cities and transportation in the early 1920s, culminating in *The City of To-Morrow and Its Planning* (1929) and his work on *The Athens Charter* (written in 1933, published in 1941).

6 Association for Safe International Road Travel, n.d.: https://www.asirt.org/safe-travel/road-safety-facts/

Co-benefits of Replacing Dependence on Cars with Multimodal and Transit Options

Economic	Environmental	Public Health
Reduced household transportation costs.	Less public subsidy of gasoline.	Increased physical activity and exercise.
Opportunity to invest transportation savings in equity-accruing investments, such as housing.	Nonpolluting travel, reduced contributions to greenhouse gas emissions.	Improved mental health from biophilic and social interactions—instead of stress and road rage.
Reduced municipal cost of roadway wear and tear.	Less land consumed, less asphalt and stormwater runoff per capita.	Less exposure to automobile exhaust and tire dust both inside and outside vehicles.
Tax revenue of redeveloped parking lots and spaces.	More contact with greenways leads to increased ecological awareness.	Increased mobility for nondrivers of all ages.

In addition to killing the street, suburban development also unintentionally killed the high-speed road. As growth expanded along rural roads, the property fronting the roads was typically rezoned for commercial use, buffering the residential uses behind it. Because of the roads' relatively high speed, commercial driveways were usually spaced from 150 to 250 feet apart, spreading development at low densities behind large parking lots. More residential subdivisions led to more signalized cross streets, set at minimum intervals of 1500 feet, with a half-mile recommended. The resulting pattern became anything but walkable or easily served by transit. Neighbors backing up to the commercial strips still need to get in their cars to access the businesses. Before long, the roads designed for high-speed mobility were clogged with cars also seeking access. Derogatorily referred to as "stroads," such arterials or "commercial strips" try to provide both access and mobility, but end up doing neither well.[7] Speeds along stroads barely compete with the horse and buggy for much of the day, the cost of the infrastructure and delivery of public services per household is often double that along urban streets, and the

taxes generated per acre pale in comparison to urban commercial streets.[8]

Suburban residential streets similarly evolved into a hybrid form. To distinguish them from gridded urban streets, their designs typically mimic rural roads with curves, whether or not topography calls for it. These "faux-roads" are laid out to maximize the number of residential lots in a subdivision and reduce the number of four-way intersections, both to thwart through traffic and increase safety. Yet, to further the rural image, they also deliberately lack sidewalks. Counter to the purpose of a road, their winding patterns lengthen the time it takes to get from point A to point B.

CAN'T WE DO SOMETHING ABOUT ALL THIS TRAFFIC?

In combination, the stroads, faux-roads, and lack of walkable streets produced an unloved public realm dominated by strip malls, fast food joints, and their parking lots (few of them aging well). But at the same time they produced a private realm that has been much loved by generations. The "American Dream" of the single-family home on its own plot of dirt with a car in the garage generated health and wealth, growing the white middle class.[9]

However, as the pattern has expanded it has caught communities and households in a vicious cycle of increased automobile dependency that degrades health and wealth.[10] New subdivisions and the strip malls to service them sprawl further away to outrun the traffic and offer access to an affordable, leafy, healthy, home. In addition to

---

[7] See, Charles Marohn, "The Stroad": https://www.strongtowns.org/journal/2017/10/30/the-stroad, 4 March 2013.

[8] See the many studies comparing property tax/acre in downtowns to suburbs by Joseph Minicozzi of Urban3.

[9] Racial covenants and restrictions severely limited who benefited from that wealth accumulation. See Richard Rothstein, *The Color of Law: A Forgotten History of How Our Government Segregated America* (New York: Liveright Publishing Corporation, 2017).

[10] Americans owed $1.26 trillion on auto loans in the third quarter of 2018, an increase of 75% since the end of 2009. In this period, loan originations for residents of low-income neighborhoods increased nearly twice as fast as for those in high-income neighborhoods. R.J. Cross and Tony Dutzik, "Driving Into Debt: The Hidden Cost of Risky Auto Loans to Consumers and Our Communities," Frontier Group, and U.S. PIRG Education Fund, February 2019.

chewing up the countryside, this leads to even longer trips and more emissions, runoff, car crashes, stress, and traffic.

Some have asserted that technology will soon fix the problems, allowing us to leave existing communities in the rearview mirror. We can build new "green" suburbs serviced by drone deliveries and on-demand, solar-powered private driverless cars. In MIT professor Alan Berger's vision, the cars drop off their owners so that driveways don't reduce the green space at their homes. The cars then park themselves remotely.[11] Those zero-passenger trips are what have other researchers worried. Yet Berger makes no mention of the impact that the likely doubling of trips will have on existing neighborhoods as the autonomous vehicles platoon through them.[12] Is this the same old argument for sprawl now dressed up in high-tech green drag?

New technologies aside, the more commonly applied solution to congestion is to widen the roads and highways. While intuitively it makes sense that increasing capacity should speed the efficient throughput of cars, since the 1930s study after study has shown that the benefits of road widening are remarkably short-lived. A 1998 meta-analysis found that 90% of new urban roadways in America are overwhelmed within five years and that metro areas that invested heavily in road capacity expansion fared no better in easing congestion than those that did not.[13] Why? Because more roads attract both the pent-up demand for faster trips as well as attracting more development and associated new trips. This effect is called "induced demand," and economists Gilles Duranton and Matthew Turner dubbed it "The Fundamental Law of Road Congestion."

There are countless examples, but Houston's Katy Freeway is one of the most notorious. To alleviate severe traffic congestion, it was widened from 2008 to 2011 from 11 to 18 lanes (26 lanes at its broadest point). Yet travel times between 2011 and 2014 got 30% longer in the mornings and 55% longer in the evenings.[14] Despite such compelling data, the politically expedient solution has been to build even more roads. As a result, auto dependency measured in the number of miles cars travel in the US has outpaced population growth since 1969.[15]

What happens when authorities take the opposite approach, removing rather than widening roads and highways—and investing in transit and improved connectivity? This happens more often than one might think, especially in downtowns.[16] Often cheaper than trying to repair aging infrastructure, removing highways results in a wide range of community benefits. The City of Milwaukee, Wisconsin, tore down one mile of the elevated and underused Park East Freeway, replaced it with a boulevard that is fully connected to the existing street grid, and freed up 24 acres that has been redeveloped with over $1 billion of private investment in the downtown. Traffic is more distributed, reducing concentrated air pollution and traffic congestion.[17] Other cities with more heavily used highways have replaced them with tunnels in addition to surface boulevards and expanded transit. One of the most dramatic replacements is Cheonggyecheon in Seoul, South Korea, where a 3.6 mile-section of an 18-lane elevated highway was removed and the polluted stream underneath it was restored. Now a popular public space, the stream provides numerous public benefits, including a much-improved transportation and transit network. Two years from demolition, total downtown traffic volume actually decreased 6%.[18] It was soon followed by the retrofit of another of Seoul's elevated highways into Skygarden, a pedestrian linear park. This is induced demand in reverse: trips dissipated or transitioned to non-car modes.

[11] See Alan Berger, "The Suburb of the Future, Almost Here," *New York Times*, 15 September 2017.
[12] Michael W. Levin and Stephen D. Boyles, "Effects of Autonomous Vehicles on Trip, Mode, and Route Choice," *Transportation Research Record*, 2493:1 (2015). See also Peter Calthorpe and Jerry Walters, "Autonomous Vehicles: Hype and Potential," *Urban Land*, 1 March 2017, "With private AVs on the road, the US VMT total is expected to increase by 2 trillion to 3 trillion miles over the next 30 years, according to author calculations based on several data sources—more than five times the increase over the past 30 years when auto use rose dramatically due to suburbanization, women entering the workforce, and inexpensive gasoline."
[13] Donald Chen, "If You Build it, They Will Come: Why We Can't Build Ourselves Out of Congestion," *Surface Transportation Policy Project Progress* 7:2 (March 1998).
[14] Joe Cortright, "Reducing Congestion: Katy Didn't," *CityCommentary* at *City Observatory*, 16 December 2015.
[15] Chen, ibid.
[16] See Congress for the New Urbanism, "Freeways Without Futures," www.cnu.org, 2019.
[17] "Park East Corridor", City of Milwaukee, Wisconsin, Department of City Development, n.d.: https://city.milwaukee.gov/Projects/ParkEastredevelopment.htm#.Xk3e5C2ZP_R.
[18] "Seoul Urban Regeneration: Cheonggyecheon Restoration and Downtown Revitalization," www.seoulsolution.kr, 11 August 2014, updated 21 April 2017. See also Alexander Robinson and Myvonwynn Hopton, "Cheonggyecheon Stream Restoration Project," *Landscape Performance Series*, Landscape Architecture Foundation, 2011.

There are several lessons suburbs can learn about reducing auto dependency by eliminating entire urban highways or just a few lanes of a suburban corridor. The latter, referred to as "road diets," reduce excess car lanes in order to make room for dedicated transit or bike/multimodal lanes. Even an entity that is as pro-car as the US Federal Highway Administration states, "Road Diets are an innovative roadway reconfiguration that improves safety, increases livability, and can advance the area's economic growth."[19] Narrowing lanes so as to carve out space for alternative modes has similar results: an increase in placemaking amenities; environmental performance; and economic development. For most of the twentieth century, wider lanes were believed to be safer because they were more forgiving of slight veering. However, recent studies comparing crash rates and lane widths have confirmed that narrower lanes result in less aggressive driving and the ability to slow or stop over a shorter distance to avoid a collision.[20] Road diets coupled with reduced speeds reduce the amount of space needed between cars, allowing greater throughput. They do not generally reduce congestion, but they make it significantly easier to live with and generate wealth from it.

See these case studies:

- II.1. Aurora Avenue North, Shoreline, Washington
- II.6. The BLVD, Lancaster, California

High-occupancy vehicle lanes and toll lanes can reduce induced demand on highways, but the only proven way to reduce traffic and auto dependency throughout a community is the addition of carefully planned mass transit and associated transit-oriented development (TOD) or "transit villages."

The 2.5-mile Rosslyn-Ballston corridor in Arlington County, Virginia, is an award-winning example.[21] Low-density neighborhoods were preserved and property taxes kept low, while dense TODs with limited parking on just 11% of county land absorbed so much growth at the

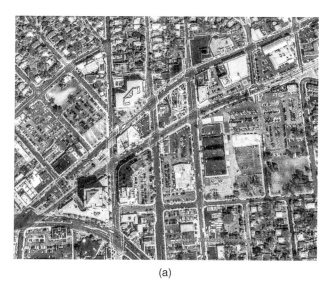
(a)

(b)

Figure I.1-3 Orthophotos from 2000 (a) and 2011 (b) of TOD redevelopment at the Clarendon Station on the Rosslyn-Ballston corridor show how allowing density on former parking lots triggered redevelopment. The zoning regulations control massing in ways that shape public space and gracefully transition to the low-rise residential areas while diversifying housing options. Source: Authors using Google Earth, 2000, © Maxar Technologies and Google Earth, 2011, © Commonwealth of Virginia.

[19] FHWA's reports particularly endorse conversion of four-lane roads to three-lanes. See Federal Highway Administration, "Debunking Road Diet Myths," safety.fhwa.dot.gov, March 2016.
[20] Dewan Masud Karim, "Narrower Lanes, Safer Streets," CITE Conference Regina, June 2015.
[21] For a deeper dive and focused study on the Clarendon Station sector plan see Susan Weaver, Weaver Research and Consulting Group, "Large Community Case Study: Rosslyn-Ballston Corridor, Arlington, Virginia," *Long Island Index*, January 2011.

stations that congestion was reduced from 6 to 23% on seven out of nine main arterials between 1996 and 2011. In the same time period, transit trips of all forms increased by a third.[22] One of the keys to transitioning the population from car trips to transit trips was charging for parking in the TODs.

PARKING, PARKING. . .AND PARKING

Economists are the first to point out that suburbia's provision of free parking, like free highway access, is another example of induced demand.[23] Why pay for transit or a taxi if parking is free? Similarly, the more off-street parking that's required by zoning, the more land it's likely to take up, making the area less conducive to walking or transit, and further increasing reliance on cars. And all that land devoted to parking tends to go underused for long stretches of a time.

What to do? Replacing parking minimums with parking maximums in zoning codes—or getting rid of parking requirements altogether—is a good place to start so long as its combined with a parking management strategy. The Victoria Transport Policy Institute maintains a long list of management techniques and their effectiveness.[24] Shared parking is at the top of their list. This generally involves clustering uses that distribute parking demand across different times of day to make better use of parking resources and therefore minimize spaces needed and costs. Particularly useful on Main Streets or mixed-use projects, these strategies often pair residents' or entertainments'

night-time parking needs with the needs of office or retail uses during the day.[25]

Another trend is unbundling parking spaces from multiunit housing and instead requiring developers of new housing to pay "in lieu" fees into a fund that builds parking facilities where they can be shared by many users. In addition to helping provide parking where it can be used more efficiently, such "parking districts" allow households who own fewer or no cars to pay for only as many parking spaces as they desire. On-site car share can make up the gap.

See these case studies:

- II.5. Parkmerced, San Francisco, California
- II.10. The Domain, Austin, Texas
- II.11. ACC Highland, Austin, Texas

Donald Shoup, a widely recognized expert in parking theory, recommends increasing the cost of parking in accordance to market demand, especially on-street parking. His landmark 2005 book *The High Cost of Free Parking* and 2018 follow-up edited book *Parking and the City* focus on three interdependent prescriptions.

First, cities should charge the price for parking that will leave approximately 15% of spaces available at any time.[26] This will eliminate the 30% of congestion that his studies attribute to cars cruising for parking.[27] Second, to make paid parking more palatable, revenue from parking meters should be designated for public service improvements in the areas in which they're collected (often to great effect, as in the revitalization of Downtown Pasadena). Third, cities should eliminate requirements for off-street parking, enabling property owners to right-size parking and redevelop excess.

22 Arlington County, VA, "FY 2015–FY 2024 Proposed Capital Improvement Plan; County Board Worksession—Transportation," 18 June 2014, as linked from Canaan Merchant, "As Arlington Booms, Traffic Drops," www.ggwash .org, 30 June 2014.

23 Several studies confirm that the higher the parking supply and the lower the cost to park, the higher the chance of someone owning a car and/or choosing to drive for their transportation. These are referenced in Alejandro Henao and Wesley E. Marshall, "The impact of ride hailing on parking (and vice versa)," *Journal of Transport and Land Use,* 12:1 (2019).

24 "Parking Management: Strategies for More Efficient Use of Parking Resources," updated 28 November 2018, *TDM Encyclopedia*, Victoria Transport Policy Institute, n.d.: https:// www.vtpi.org/tdm/tdm28.htm

25 There are many shared parking resources and calculators available online. See in particular Mary Smith, *Shared Parking*, Urban Land Institute, 2005 and Smart Growth America and the Department of City and Metropolitan Planning, University of Utah, "*Empty Spaces: Real Parking Needs at Five TODs,*" Smart Growth America, January 2017.

26 Shoup's proposals have been validated by ParkDC, a demand-based pricing parking pilot that began in 2014 and reduced congestion. See Kittelson & Associates, Inc. and Conduent, Inc., "ParkDC: Penn Quarter/Chinatown Pricing Pilot," District Department of Transportation, January 2019.

27 Donald Shoup, "Cruising for Parking," *Access* 30 (Spring 2007). A worldwide survey of 20 cities found drivers spent an average of 20 minutes looking for parking. See "IBM Global Parking Survey: Drivers Share Worldwide Parking Woes," IBM News Release, 28 September 2011.

(a)

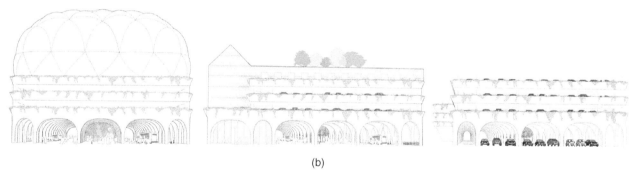

(b)

Figure I.1-4 For their project Civic Arches, featured in the ParkingPLUS design challenge sponsored in 2013 by the Long Island Index, Utile proposed replacing extensive commuter parking lots alongside the Long Island Rail Road elevated tracks and station in Rockville Centre, New York, with a series of retrofittable concrete parking decks (right elevation). Each structure is designed to be convertible short term, such as a high-ceilinged ground level that could be a covered market on weekends, and a rooftop bubble would allow for tennis (left elevation and rendering). In the longer term, flat floor plates and removable ramps allow the structures to be retrofitted to other uses (middle elevation). Source: Courtesy of Utile, Inc.

Shoup's ideas have successfully been put into practice in San Francisco, Seattle, and many other congested cities, but he sees them also having broad applicability in overparked suburban settings.

So do we. Building on underused parking lots was one of the earliest and most prevalent forms of suburban retrofitting, and has gained even more traction as parking demand has dropped in response to increased use of ride-hailing services like Uber and Lyft.[28] While such Transportation Network Companies (TNCs) have exacerbated congestion and vehicle miles traveled (VMT) by

---

[28] Henao, op cit.

cruising and contributed to lower transit usage, their impact on parking is much more positive. Airports, hotels, event venues, restaurants, and bars are particularly impacted. This allows redesign of parking space for pick-up/drop off and/or redevelopment for revenue and tax-producing uses.

Driverless cars promise to accelerate these trends in the future. Investors are already exploring a variety of alternatives to conventional parking, given some estimates of up to a 90% reduction in demand due to shared AV fleets.[29] There is considerable research on how self-parking cars might double parking capacity in existing garages. The thinking is that by dropping passengers off before entering garages, cars would no longer need room for opening doors or unloading trunks, which would allow for garages with more closely spaced spots and reduced floor-to-floor heights. Experts put the space reduction at as much as 60%. To test this, in 2015 automaker Audi announced a partnership with the City of Somerville, Massachusetts, and the developer of Assembly Row to test a fleet of self-parking cars at a parking garage in the retrofit of Assembly Square.[30]

A growing number of parking garage designers are taking a different approach, configuring new structures to be retrofitted to office or housing in the future. Providing better-reinforced flat decks with removable ramps and higher floor-to-floor dimensions costs more initially but is a form of future-proofing likely to pay off over time. Some designers are hedging their bets by employing removable stacking systems as a means to increase capacity. Similarly, if the market cannot yet fully support higher densities, surface parking lots are increasingly being designed to be retrofittable into future building sites. This typically involves placing utility lines under tree-lined parking lot drive lanes so that they can eventually be easily converted to streets between new buildings on top of the parking lots.

See this case study:

■ II.12. Mueller, Austin, Texas

Figure I.1-5 The "Pavement to Plazas" movement uses low-cost interventions—paint, café tables, and planters—to reclaim excess asphalt for social use while slowing traffic, as in this example implemented by the Memphis Medical District Collaborative in partnership with the city and the Downtown Memphis Commission. The highly visible improvements complement the organization's job programs and have succeeded in attracting redevelopment to the Opportunity Zone. Source: Courtesy of the Memphis Medical District Collaborative.

WALK, PEDAL, HAIL, AND SCOOT

A major factor behind the abundance of redeveloped parking lots is developers' embrace of the market attracted to lively, walkable streets. And while many people continue to be skeptical about why anyone would choose to walk instead of drive, Jane Jacobs's descriptions of "the sidewalk ballet" and the virtues of diversity of all kinds in 1950s Greenwich Village in New York City have been rediscovered and embraced by a generation bored with life on the stroad.[31]

Christopher Leinberger has set out to determine just how much economic and social equity value all this walkability adds to income-producing real estate. He and his co-authors have produced a series of reports distinguishing regionally significant walkable urban places, which he calls WalkUPs. They found that 761 WalkUPs in the 30 largest US metros command the following rent premiums when compared to nearby drivable suburban space: 105%

[29] Wenwen Zhang, Subhrajit Guhathakurta, Jinqi Fang, and Ge Zhang, "Exploring the Impact of Shared Autonomous Vehicles on Parking Demand: An Agent-Based Simulation Approach," *Sustainable Cities and Society*, 19 (2015).

[30] The partnership was announced by Audi in 2015, and generated many news and blog articles, but it is not clear when or if the ideas will ultimately be implemented. Audi press release, "Audi brings automated parking to the Boston area," 17 November 2015.

[31] Jane Jacobs, *The Death and Life of Great American Cities* (New York: Random House, 1961).

Figure I.1-6 Buford Highway, a stroad north of Atlanta, Georgia, is home to many strip malls and a diverse immigrant community with low car-ownership and one of the state's highest pedestrian fatality rates. To improve the area's safety and mobility, Canvas Planning is working with We Love BuHi, a nonprofit, to provide additional, safer, and more pleasant walking routes by connecting the walkways in front of the many strip malls with painted sidewalks and encouraging restaurant owners to hang lanterns reflecting their culture. Source: Courtesy of Canvas Planning Group.

for office, 121% for retail, and 61% for rental multifamily.[32] Such premiums are driving the urbanization of suburbia where market demand is strong and developers can profit despite the complexities. The report's Social Equity Index results indicate that the higher rents are significantly compensated for by the reduced transportation costs for households earning 80% of average median income, but that there is still need for aggressive affordable housing programs to allow low-income households to live in WalkUPs. The 2019 report says there is potential demand for an additional 472 WalkUPs and they "would create a new economic foundation for the US economy, one far more resilient than the economic foundation resulting from building drivable suburbs."[33]

In addition to the public, social and economic health benefits of walking that accrue to individuals, walkable master-planned communities and mixed-use redevelopments reduce traffic congestion due to what traffic engineers call high "internal trip capture" rates. That is, a measure of

efficiency through the elimination of separate car trip segments when two or more destinations are co-located.

Time and again, studies observing actual behavior in either suburban retrofits or greenfield projects character-ized by compact, gridded, mixed-use, and mixed-income design have found that such projects capture 22 to 40% of trips internally that would have otherwise burdened nearby streets.[34] Yet, the projected internal trips of such projects tend to be underestimated by the Institute of Transportation Engineers' Trip Generation standards, leading to unnecessary road widenings and traffic signals, thus increasing rather than reducing auto dependency.[35]

Trip Generation standards can't catch up quickly enough to help communities responsibly plan for the rapidly expanding multimodal revolution. Shared rides, such as carsharing, carhailing and autonomous shuttle buses, are on the rise and reducing rates of private car ownership. The number of people riding bicycles, e-bikes, e-scooters, e-mopeds, e-wheelchairs, hoverboards, single-wheel Segways, golf carts, and other short-trip vehicles have also increased and vastly expanded personal mobility options. Admitting to possible dorkiness, the *Wall Street Journal* recommends reviving rollerblading given the new three- and four-wheel designs.[36] These modes are often ideal for "first/last mile" connections to transit. They are also highly suitable for the 46% of trips in the US that are three miles or less. But only if the streets can accommo-date them safely. The Complete Streets movement and the National Association of City Transportation Officials (NACTO) have made great strides in recent years establishing guidelines for reallocating space in the public

[32] Tracy Hadden Loh, Christopher B. Leinberger, and Jordan Chafetz, "Foot Traffic Ahead: Ranking Walkable Urbanism in America's Largest Metros," George Washington University School of Business and Smart Growth America, 2019.
[33] Ibid.

[34] A 1995 study of Mizner Park, a redevelopment of a dead mall discussed in *Retrofitting Suburbia*, found it captured 40% of trips internally, and the average for mixed-use development in Florida was 36%. See Brain S. Bochner, Kevin Hooper, Benjamin Sperry, and Robert Dunphy, "Enhancing Internal Trip Capture Estimation for Mixed-Use Developments," NCHRP Report 684, Transportation Research Board, 2011. See also Asad J. Khattak and Daniel Rodriguez, "Travel Behavior in Neo-Traditional Neighborhood Developments: A Case Study in USA," *Transportation Research Part A: Policy and Practice*, 39:6 (July 2005).
[35] Jerry Walters, Brian Bochner, and Reid Ewing, "Getting Trip Generation Right: Eliminating the Bias Against Mixed Use Development," *Planning Advisory Service Memo*, American Planning Association, May 2013. See also Donald Shoup, "Problems with Trip Generation Rates," in *The High Cost of Free Parking* (2005), 42–53.
[36] Jesse Will, "Redesigned Rollerblades Worth Lacing Up," *Wall Street Journal*, 23 April 2019.

Figure I.1-7 El Camino Real is Silicon Valley's 45-mile long commercial arterial. In a bold vision to address the area's acute housing shortage and affordability crisis, planner Peter Calthorpe has proposed installing AV shuttles in dedicated lanes along El Camino Real and changing the commercial zoning to allow higher-density housing. His analysis shows this could accommodate more than 250,000 housing units whose residents could live without a car. Source: Courtesy of HDR/Calthorpe.

right-of-way to better accommodate pedestrians, bikes and transit. With the new electrified modes, there's growing interest in redesigning streets according to vehicle speed. What were "bike lanes" are increasingly being reconsidered and renamed LIT lanes (light individual transport), slow lanes, or local lanes.[37]

See these case studies:

- ▪ II.2. Hassalo on Eighth and Lloyd, Portland, Oregon
- ▪ II.5. Parkmerced, San Francisco, California
- ▪ II.32. Assembly Square, Somerville, Massachusetts

AUTONOMOUS URBANISM?

But are all these changes worth it if autonomous vehicles (AVs) are right around the corner? Won't AVs just make

the status quo a lot easier to live with? Yes, in many respects they probably will. But, we argue, existing suburbs have both the most to lose and the most to gain from AVs. Do they want to see AVs exacerbate suburban sprawl and the continued migration of wealth outward? Or might existing communities leverage AVs to spur reduced levels of private car ownership, enhanced walkability and shared rides by redeveloping excess parking lots and reallocating excess vehicle lanes on aging commercial strip corridors? Both scenarios are plausible, although it's difficult to plan for a still-evolving technology.[38]

We recommend that communities plan for three approaches: AV shuttles on dedicated routes (requiring relatively little machine learning and already operating in over 80 communities worldwide, albeit with a safety driver); AV taxi fleets (a few fleets are being piloted by

---

[37] See Andrew Small, "Let's Rethink What a 'Bike Lane' Is," *CityLab*, 24 August 2018; Gabe Klein, "How Slow Lanes Can Speed Up New Mobility (And Save Lives)," *Forbes,* 4 December 2018; and Dan Sturges, *Bounce* (forthcoming).

[38] See *Blueprint for Autonomous Urbanism*, National Association of City Transportation Officials, Module 1, Fall 2017, and 2nd ed., 2020. Also see Zachary Lancaster, Neerja Dave and Ellen Dunham-Jones, *Best Practices for Improving User Experience in AV Shuttles*, Georgia Institute of Technology, 2020.

large companies on limited routes testing mobility-as-a-service business models), and privately owned AVs (as of this writing most manufacturers have pushed delivery dates into the 2030s at the earliest).[39] Austin, Texas, is proposing autonomous shuttles in dedicated lanes as part of its Project Connect Vision Plan with a stop at ACC Highland, although Mueller, another of Austin's retrofits, was one of the first test beds for Google cars in 2015. The good news within the confusion is that the same strategies that improve transit access, walkability, micromobility, and carhailing today will enable communities to better take advantage of AVs tomorrow.

Communities should also consider how these strategies best apply when activities go online and vehicle trips decrease. Remote modes of working, education, and medicine reduce traffic and parking and also free households from having to locate near a job, school, or hospital. Suddenly, the quality of life that a place affords when residents unplug from their screens—whether access to great nature, to great urbanism, or both—becomes more important in distinguishing the value of one place over another. Retrofitting streets and neighborhoods to support social gathering rather than social isolation will likely become even more beneficial to ward off loneliness and sedentary behaviors when people work from home.

URBAN DESIGN TACTICS FOR DISRUPTING AND REDUCING AUTOMOBILE DEPENDENCE

With so many moving parts—pun intended—it's difficult to know how to best make use of suburban retrofits to meet the challenge of disrupting automobile dependence. To summarize the discussion above and prioritize the design interventions we hope our readers will act upon, we propose six recommended tactics. Most of them target the 46% of trips that are three miles or less. Others operate at a regional scale. In combination, they reduce the need for automotive travel.

1. **Improve connectivity for all modes of travel.** Start by adding sidewalks, bike lanes, street trees, street lights, murals, and possibly liner buildings on routes to everyday destinations. Then, look for ways to transform a dendritic road pattern into an interconnected street network. Are there dead ends that can be extended, new parallel streets that can be added, parking lanes that can be made into streets to reduce block sizes to no more than an 1800-foot perimeter? Where new streets aren't feasible, consider high-visibility or raised crosswalks, pedestrian paths and multiuse trails to allow for more direct routes.
See these case studies:

   - II.15. Baton Rouge Health District, Baton Rouge, Louisiana
   - II.19. Technology Park, Peachtree Corners, Georgia
   - II.25. White Flint and the Pike District, Montgomery County, Maryland

2. **Introduce a mix of uses into predominantly single-use areas**. The best way to minimize the need for travel by car is to introduce diverse, everyday destinations within a 10-minute walk (½ mile) or 10-minute bike or e-bike ride (2 or 3 miles).
See these case studies:

   - II.10. The Domain, Austin, Texas
   - II.21. Downtown Doral, Doral, Florida
   - II.23. The Mosaic District, Merrifield, Virginia
   - II.32. Assembly Square, Somerville, Massachusetts

3. **Right-zone property near transit or along corridors to allow higher-density, mixed-use, transit-feasible nodes at major intersections and minimal-access uses in-between.** In order to compete with online shopping, retailers increasingly have to be part of a larger set of attractive experiences, such as shopping in a lively public realm where food, fitness, and communal activities are part of the draw. These amenities similarly benefit office and residential tenants. Consider using transfer-of-development rights to higher-density nodes from underperforming retail sites to encourage them to be reinhabited, regreened, or where appropriate, redeveloped with urban housing.
See these case studies:

   - II.11. ACC Highland, Austin, Texas

---

[39] Automation promises to eliminate 50–85% of the operating cost that goes to pay the bus driver, enabling replacement of big buses with multiple smaller shuttles that run more frequently. By November 2019 they were operating on limited routes in over 80 pilot projects around the world. The same economics apply to AV taxis and carhailing and is why GM, Waymo, Ford, and others are preparing to shift from selling individual cars to selling "mobility as a service" through AV taxi fleets at significantly reduced fares.

- II.25. White Flint and the Pike District, Montgomery County, Maryland
- II.26. The Blairs, Silver Spring, Maryland

4. **Reallocate capacity in the right-of-way for multimodal travel and retrofit stroads.** Road diets should be feasible where average daily traffic counts fall below 10,000 vehicles per lane. To narrow lanes, NACTO recommends 10-foot lanes in urban areas and 11-foot outer lanes for dedicated transit or truck routes. To fix stroads, consider separating their street and road functions by converting them into multi-way boulevards with higher-speed "roads" in the center and local-serving low-speed "streets" on the sides. Wherever pedestrian activity is being encouraged, look for opportunities to convert pavement to plazas and remember "20 is plenty" for street speed (in miles per hour).
See these case studies:

- II.1. Aurora Avenue North, Shoreline, Washington
- II.5. Parkmerced, San Francisco, California
- II.6. The BLVD, Lancaster, California
- II.16. Uptown Circle, Normal, Illinois
- II.24. South Dakota Avenue and Riggs Road, Washington, DC
- II.25. White Flint and the Pike District, Montgomery County, Maryland

5. **Leverage parking for all modes to improve the neighborhood.** Design parking to serve additional community needs such as farmers markets or renewable energy (geothermal wells, solar canopies, or wind turbines). Invest parking meter and public garage revenue to support these and other local improvements. Build on excess parking lots. Encourage efficient management of parking through unbundling it, shared parking agreements, parking districts, and dynamic curb management of deliveries, carhailing pick-up and drop-off, and micromobility parking. Finally, design parking to be retrofittable.

See these case studies:

- II.2. Hassalo on Eighth and Lloyd, Portland, Oregon
- II.6. The BLVD, Lancaster, California
- II.13. Promenade of Wayzata, Wayzata, Minnesota

6. **Encourage shared mobility.** In the face of affordability and loneliness crises, communities should do all they can to increase access to shared transit of any form and to elevate the quality of the experience of getting to and waiting for transit. Make bus stops and rail stations into neighborhood and community hubs with pop-up market days, community billboards, and "adoption" by local businesses. Conduct "walkshops" with local residents to assess improvements needed to improve the pedestrian and micromobility user experience along major routes to the stops.
See these case studies:

- II.5. Parkmerced, San Francisco, California
- II.26. The Blairs, Silver Spring, Maryland
- II.32. Assembly Square, Somerville, Massachusetts

We encourage communities to be ambitious, but not daunted by these tactics. Sometimes, all it takes to get started is a bucket of paint and a group of volunteers dedicated to change. [40] While there's obviously a big role for public sector entities, they aren't always in the lead. Private sector leaders in business/community improvement districts often play a significant role in funding suburban retrofit planning studies and infrastructure improvements. Disrupting auto dependence is most effective when all perspectives and interests are working together.

---

[40] The Street Plans Collaborative, *Tactical Urbanist's Guide to Materials and Design: Version 1.0*, tacticalurbanismguide.com, December 2016.

Improve Public Health

Our bodies, our health and buildings are forever connected. The links between architecture and well-being are richer than merely affording safety from injury; buildings can be, should be, agents of health—physical, mental and social health. Good buildings and urban plans do precisely that. . .Humanity faces powerful challenges, a "perfect storm" of colliding dangerous forces, namely accelerating climate change, resource depletion and population pressure, and staggering harm and costs from an inundation of chronic diseases like diabetes.[1]

Richard J. Jackson, MD MPH, FAAP

The potential of suburban retrofitting to transform people's lives begins at the most fundamental level: in their individual bodies. Exemplary suburban retrofits incorporate design elements that can improve people's physical health as well as their mental and social wellness and mitigate the aspects of conventional development that contribute to crisis levels of obesity and diabetes. Dr. Richard Jackson, public health professor at UCLA and former director of the US Centers for Disease Control's National Center for Environmental Health, reminds us of the crucial role played by designers and planners who can activate buildings and physical neighborhoods into agents of better physical, mental, and social human health.

There are many facets to the design and planning challenge of improving public health. Design changes in the built landscape can reduce the known risks to human health presented by conventional suburban built form in urbanized environments. Facets of the challenge are wide-ranging and include:

- Encouraging everyday physical activity, especially walking, stair climbing, and biking
- Incorporating tenets of biophilia, or contact with nature
- Reducing social isolation with communal gathering spaces

- Improving safety from the risks of car crashes, toxins exposure, fire, flood, and crime
- Mitigating and avoiding ill effects from polluted air, soil, and water
- Increasing access in all neighborhoods to healthy foods and routine preventative health care
- Reducing the stresses of income and resource inequality

This last facet is crucially linked to all the others.

Suburban retrofitting patterns that result in compact places, conducive to walking and biking, that are close to transit, retail, services, schools, workplaces, and other everyday amenities, are increasingly recognized as a key component to improving health. However, this recognition—and the recommendations to follow—is complicated by a paradox: Adding more compact urban patterns throughout urbanized metropolitan areas can mitigate the primary health risk factors associated with sprawling urbanization—epidemic levels of chronic diseases like diabetes linked to obesity and lack of everyday exercise—but at the same time may exacerbate the human health risks associated with pollutants produced by urban congestion. The COVID-19 pandemic is revealing that individuals with these chronic conditions are more vulnerable to serious, life-threatening complications from coronaviruses. Despite greater rates of chronic diseases compared to infectious diseases, the pandemic seems to have revivified distrust of compact urbanism. How then to best promote the generally more healthy compact patterns, while mitigating the associated risks? Many scholars, practitioners, and advocates believe this paradox can be addressed, indeed *must* be tackled, in the face of the "perfect storm" described by Dr. Jackson.

How? Through thoughtful, informed planning policies and design techniques. Many suburban areas were built around assumed use of private automobiles, which enable sedentary lives. Communities and designers can choose to

---

[1] American Institute of Architects, *Local Leaders: Healthier Communities Through Design* (December 2012): www.aia.org/localleaders.

pursue policies and adopt design strategies for introducing more compact patterns that promote physical activity at the regional and neighborhood scales. At the same time, they might introduce design elements at the neighborhood, block, and building scales to minimize human exposure to unhealthy pollutants and other health stressors.

Retrofitting the many unhealthful aspects of suburban form while avoiding introducing new ones is a worthy task, and a significant challenge for the twenty-first century. The examples that follow illustrate some of the most commendable practices and policies on the front lines of the response to the "perfect storm" onslaught.

THE BURDENS OF DISEASE

What are the primary impacts—or "burdens"—of disease in the United States today? The Global Burden of Disease (GBD) is a measure of years of healthy life lost to disability (morbidity) and premature death (mortality).[2] The Institute for Health Metrics and Evaluation maintains a regularly updated listing of GBD and other health metrics for every region and country in the world, incorporating thousands of datasets.[3] For the United States, the top ten causes of disability-adjusted life years (DALYs) in 2017 were ranked as follows: [4]

1. High body-mass index (a measure of overweight and obesity)
2. Tobacco
3. Dietary risks
4. High fasting plasma glucose (a measure of prediabetes and diabetes)
5. High blood pressure
6. Drug use
7. Alcohol use
8. High total cholesterol
9. Impaired kidney function
10. Occupational risks

Unfortunately, the rates of these DALYs are higher in the United States than other comparable nations in almost all categories and cases.

Had the methodology and data been available, we can assume this list might have looked quite different a half century ago, in the thick of the era of mass suburbanization, and even more different at the turn of the twentieth century. Who knows how they will look 50 years from now? As the rankings of risk factors shift over time, tracking changed conditions and effects, we must adjust accordingly our approaches to urban design and planning intended to mitigate these risks. Attention to mental health and chronic disease continues to grow accordingly.

Health is a multifactorial phenomenon; in other words, it is determined by many complex factors working together. Actions taken with the intent of reducing one or more burdens of disease might exacerbate others. Therefore, it is important to consider the order of burdens when assessing steps taken to improve public health in any given place. Which actions will provide the most benefit to the most people?

For example, if we were to focus primarily on reducing exposure to ambient particulate matter pollution (a risk factor that dropped off the top ten list during the 2010s but nonetheless a potent risk factor for respiratory diseases, including asthma, which tends to be worse in lower-income neighborhoods), one might argue, as some do, for dispersed, low-density settlement patterns and use separation to limit people's exposure. Low-density, car-dependent types of settlements (i.e. conventional northern American suburbs), however, have been found in many studies to be correlated with high rates of obesity and diabetes, high blood pressure, and other burdens of disease associated with physical inactivity. These burdens are currently ranked higher than air pollution.[5] We need to find solutions that reduce multiple burdens of disease at the same time and, when there are conflicts, prioritize

[2] World Health Organization global burden of disease (GBD) measures burden of disease using the disability-adjusted life year (DALY). This time-based measure combines years of life lost due to premature mortality and years of life lost due to time lived in states of less than full health. The DALY metric was developed in the original GBD 1990 study to assess the burden of disease consistently across diseases, risk factors and regions: http://www.who.int/topics/global_burden_of_disease/en/.

[3] The Institute for Health Metrics and Evaluation (IHME) is an independent global health research center at the University of Washington: http://www.healthdata.org/gbd/publications

[4] IHME health data for the United States (2017): http://www.healthdata.org/united-states.

[5] For an accessible and comprehensive overview of public health research at the intersection of public health and design, see Andrew Dannenberg, Howard Frumkin, and Richard J. Jackson, eds., *Making Healthy Places: Designing and Building for Health, Well-Being, and Sustainability* (Washington, DC: Island Press, 2011). We use this anthology, prepared by multiple authors, throughout this chapter as an up-to-date guide to the state of researched knowledge in northern America on the topic.

reductions of the highest ranked burdens, while also taking particular care of the most vulnerable.

Currently, greater impacts will be achieved by prioritizing policies that mitigate the negative effects of low-density suburban sprawl, an argument for retrofitting these places rather than building new ones. Early indicators suggest that the COVID-19 pandemic won't alter this broad conclusion, aimed at reducing epidemic rates of chronic conditions that increase vulnerability to the virus.[6] Concerns about higher population density and increased risk of exposure are shorter-term propositions, to be addressed in the context of localized outbreaks.

Cost is also a significant factor in assessing proposed solutions. Which paths forward might produce the most impact for the least cost? From 1960 to 2017 the proportion of the US gross domestic product spent on healthcare increased more than *threefold*, from 5% to nearly 18%.[7] As Dr. Jackson reminds us, "These rates of illnesses and costs cannot be addressed within the medical sector alone. It is more important than ever before to invest in preventative measures that focus on efficiency, effectiveness, and equity."[8] Indeed, only five of the thirty years of increased life span achieved in the United States by the end of the twentieth century were due to medical interventions, new medicines, and the like. Twenty-five years of longevity were due to the success of public health interventions.[9] This equates to an astonishing full quarter century of longer life. We urge that, in tandem with medical approaches, retrofitting suburban form be considered a key component of any public health policy and that suburban zoning codes renew their commitment to public health, safety, and welfare in light of new knowledge.[10]

Let us examine the statistical facts regarding risks and impacts of suburban form development patterns on public health and human safely in northern America. One good source for the current state of research on the interactions among land use, transportation, and environmental quality and their combined impact on health in the United States is a 2013 technical review issued by the then-active Office of Sustainable Communities Smart Growth Program of the US Environmental Protection Agency (EPA). With over 60 contributors and reviewers, and referencing over 340 works and scientific research papers, the technical review is impressively comprehensive. We can confidently look to it to provide useful signposts and benchmarks for guiding and assessing suburban retrofits.[11]

According to the EPA review, there are three primary categories of risk and impact: levels of physical activity, obesity, chronic disease; emotional health and degree of community engagement; and likelihood of being killed or injured in a vehicle crash.

Category 1: Physical Activity, Obesity, and Chronic Disease

The report finds, "While data are lacking to resolve whether the built environment *determines* levels of physical activity and/or obesity, nearly 90 percent of studies found a positive association," and suggests "the built environment is one of the many factors that could play a role in how much people exercise and levels of obesity."[12] Further, the report suggests, "Communities with streets designed for the safety of all users, also known as *complete streets*, can facilitate walking and biking and help residents lead healthier lifestyles." In a review of six studies, the median increase in the number of people walking and biking due to street and sidewalk improvements was found to be 35%.[13]

[6] Nadja Popovich, Anjali Singhvi, and Matthew Conlen, "Where Chronic Health Conditions and Coronavirus Could Collide," *New York Times*, 18 May 2020: https://www.nytimes.com/interactive/2020/05/18/us/coronavirus-underlying-conditions.html

[7] U.S Centers for Medicare & Medicaid Services, National Health Expenditure (NHE) Fact Sheet: https://www.cms.gov/research-statistics-data-and-systems/statistics-trends-and-reports/nationalhealthexpenddata/nhe-fact-sheet.html

[8] Richard K. Jackson, "Preface," *Making Healthy Places*, xvii.

[9] Howard Frumkin et al., "Introduction," *Making Healthy Places*, 12.

[10] This shared history is well told by Joseph Schilling and Leslie S. Linton, "The Public Health Roots of Zoning; In Search of Active Living's Legal Genealogy," *American Journal of Preventive Medicine* (2005) 28 (2S2): 96–104.

[11] US Environmental Protection Agency, Melissa G. Kramer, lead author, *Our Built and Natural Environments: A Technical Review of the Interactions Among Land Use, Transportation, and Environmental Quality* (United States Environmental Protection Administration, Smart Growth Program, June 2013): https://www.epa.gov/smartgrowth/our-built-and-natural-environments. If this link becomes inactive, please contact authors for a copy.

[12] Ibid., 71, citing Alva O. Ferdinand et al., "The relationship between built environments and physical activity: A systematic review," *American Journal of Public Health* 102, no. 10 (2012): e7–e13.

[13] Ibid., 100, citing Giles et al., "From good intentions to proven interventions: Effectiveness of actions to reduce the health impacts of air pollution," *Environmental Health Perspectives* 199, no. 1 (2011): 29–36, and Heath et al., "The effectiveness of urban design and land use and transport policies and practices to increase physical activity: A systematic review," *Journal of Physical Activity and Health* 3, no. Suppl 1 (2006): S55–S76.

Category 2: Emotional Health and Degree of Community Engagement

The report emphasizes the concept of social capital: that is, the emotional benefit individuals receive from opportunities to interact with one another as well as the benefit to communities when residents are interacting socially. "Neighborhoods with more walkable streets, more public space, and a diverse mix of land uses are associated with improved social capital. Automobile dependence, lack of public spaces, and low density tend to be associated with reduced social capital," the report states.[14]

Category 3: Likelihood of Being Killed or Injured in a Vehicle Crash

Regarding vehicle safety, the report asserts, "Car crashes are the third leading cause of death in terms of years of life lost given the young age of so many car crash victims and the number of years they would have been expected to live if they had not died in a car crash. Only cancer and heart disease are responsible for more years of life lost."[15]

WALK THIS WAY: LINKING PHYSICAL ACTIVITY TO PHYSICAL DESIGN

Regrettably, most Americans do not meet current recommendations for physical activity. This is both a deeply unfortunate state of affairs, and also presents a huge opportunity for meaningful improvement. Low levels of physical activity and high rates of obesity and chronic disease together comprise one of the primary categories of risk and impact to health. Unlike many in the popular press and media who continue to fixate on a narrative of fatty, sugary diet and poor self-control to make sense of—and to cast blame for—the trends toward expanded waistlines, the public health community

has come to consensus regarding the breadth of benefits to be gained from modest, regular physical activity, whether utilitarian (walking to "run" errands, climbing stairs at work) or recreational (playing a sport, exercising on gym equipment). Researchers assert, "Few if any other health interventions are this broadly beneficial and have so few unwanted side effects."[16] As a society, why wouldn't we do everything in our powers to reap these broad benefits?

More specifically, research demonstrates that people living near walkable destinations, in mixed-use communities, engage in more physical activity than those in residential-only communities. Also, living near parks, trails, and other places for recreation is related to more recreational physical activity, particularly when supportive programs promoting such activity are in place.[17] One study found that adults living in high-walkability neighborhoods engaged in 41 more minutes of total physical activity per week than those in low-walkability neighborhoods.[18] That's only 6 minutes on average per day, and a sizable step toward achieving the recommended goal of 150 minutes per week. In Mueller, the sizable retrofit of a decommissioned municipal airport into a new community, researchers from Texas A&M found that the total mean average of minutes walked by residents increased by over 30 minutes per week, while time spent in a private car decreased by more than an hour.[19] It appears that just a few additional minutes of activity per day can make a significant difference, and at little societal cost.

A sizable market for healthier buildings and communities has emerged following the findings of public health research studies linking characteristics of community physical design to rates of physical activity in the US population. Broadly, the findings show that certain built

[14] Ibid., 73, citing Howard Frumkin, "Cities, suburbs, and urban sprawl: Their impact on health," in Nicholas Freudenberg and Sandro Galea, Cities and the Health of the Public (Nashville: Vanderbilt University Press, 2006), 143–175.

[15] Ibid., 74.

[16] James F. Sallis, Rachel A. Millstein and Jordan A. Carlson, "Community Design for Physical Activity," Making Healthy Places, 34.

[17] Ibid., 36, 40–43.

[18] J.F. Sallis, B.E. Saelens, et al., "Neighborhood Built Environment and Income: Examining Multiple Health Outcomes," Social Science & Medicine 68 (2009): 1285–93.

[19] Xuemei Zhu, Chia-Yuan Yu, Chanam Lee, Zhipeng Lu, and George Mann, "A retrospective study on changes in residents' physical activities, social interactions, and neighborhood cohesion after moving to a walkable community, Preventative Medicine 69 (2014): 593–597. See also Xuemei Zhu, Zhipeng Lu, Chia-Yuan Yu, Chanam Lee, and George Mann, "Walkable communities: Impacts on residents' physical and social health," World Health Design (July 2013): 68–75.

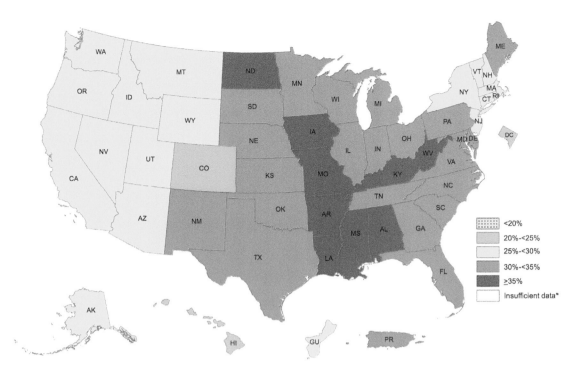

Figure I.2-1   Obesity rates in the United States are alarmingly high, as shown in this map of prevalence of self-reported obesity among US adults by state and territory in 2018, as reported by the Behavioral Risk Factor Surveillance System (BRFSS), United States Centers for Disease Control and Prevention. Note that prevalence estimates reflect BRFSS methodological changes started in 2011. These estimates should not be compared to prevalence estimates before 2011. Source: US Centers for Disease Control and Prevention, 2018.

environment attributes are associated with higher levels of physical activity. What are some built or proposed examples of how suburban retrofitting has begun to reap the benefits by raising the bar on supporting and encouraging healthy physical activity though physical design?

See these case studies:

- II.12. Mueller, Austin, Texas
- II.16. Uptown Circle, Normal, Illinois
- II.19. Technology Park, Peachtree Corners, Georgia
- II.21. Downtown Doral, Doral, Florida
- II.22. Collinwood Recreation Center, Cleveland, Ohio

Linking up residential areas to schools is particularly important everywhere. Of the United States, the 2013 EPA technical review notes: "In 1969, nearly half of students in kindergarten through eighth grade walked to school. By 2009, that figure had fallen to 13%. During that time, the percentage of students who rode a school bus stayed relatively constant, while the percentage of students who were driven to school increased. Walking or

biking to school correlates with overall levels of physical activity for children, and there is some evidence that walking or biking to school can also improve measures of physical fitness."[20] Unfortunately, many suburban school districts around the country adopted siting requirements for new schools in recent decades that led to locations far beyond walking distance for most if not all students. Even when the distances and built environment allowed it, parents became more anxious about allowing their children to walk starting in the 1980s, after the highly publicized 1979 abduction of six-year-old Etan Patz on his morning journey to school that traumatized the nation. Strategies for helping more kids walk or bike to school once again include:

- The national Safe Routes to School program
- Retrofitting state school siting standards

---

[20] US Environmental Protection Agency, *Our Built and Natural Environments*, 30.

Figure I.2-2 Before and after views of regreened Freedom Park Drive, a pilot project of Design 4 Active Sacramento to test proposed new code revisions for redesigning streets for walkability, as well as better stormwater management. Source: Photos by Judy Robinson.

- Adaptive reuse of retail and office buildings to schools in redeveloping areas
- Integration of new schools into walkable suburban retrofits[21]

Finally, one of the most important—though expensive—strategies for linking physical activity to physical design is the redesign of the right-of-way of public streets to support walkability. This was the driver for Design 4 Active Sacramento (D4AS), a countywide initiative in California. In 2013 a team from the region set out to review and learn from New York City's innovative Active Design Guidelines program. They identified several key

tenets for implementation in the lower-density Sacramento region, including:

- Walkable and bikeable streets for connectivity and accessibility
- Mixed land uses with walkable destinations
- Increasing landscape and urban forest
- Safety

The assembled team was multidisciplinary and diverse—an important factor to consider when implementing retrofits for improving public health—and included a county planner, a regional planner, a transportation engineer, the executive director of the nonprofit WALKSacramento, a neurosurgeon, a landscape architect, and the county public health officer.

Sacramento County—comprising 1.5 million residents, one-third in the City of Sacramento and the rest in surrounding suburbs—was updating various plans, making it an opportune time to review regulatory documents and

---

[21] The US Environmental Protection Agency developed school siting guidelines in 2011. See also Safe Routes to School: http://www. saferoutesinfo.org/. Montgomery County, Maryland, is encouraging the use of school prototypes that employ adaptive reuse, co-location and multilevel compact designs for better integration into communities in the White Flint redevelopment sector.

codify provisions that could improve public health outcomes. The goal of the initiative, which has garnered numerous awards, is to promote a built environment where daily walking and biking are the easy choice.[22] The greening of Freedom Park Drive, in suburban McClellan Park, is a pilot project that the new code revisions from D4AS will help to reproduce throughout the county. The two-block corridor was transformed with a landscaped median, bike lanes, two roundabouts, rebuilt sidewalks, and widened landscaped buffers that double for stormwater retention.

While it seems strange that so many Americans drive cars to places of exercise, it is important to have numerous places in all communities to support those who wish to engage in any kind of physical activity, for all ages, at a range of times, and in any type of weather.

Measuring the Health of the Built Environment

Urban planners and designers are not trained in the use of measurement and evaluative tools from epidemiology and surveillance. Real estate developers tend to treat these issues as economic externalities, unmeasured and unregulated. Conversely, public health professionals are not trained in the geographic and social contexts of disease data. A result is that public health data is often collected and analyzed at the county, city, or metropolitan scale, scales too large to be parsed relative to characteristics of the built environment at the project or neighborhood scales; also, the effects are studied on longer time frames than can be fitted to post-occupancy evaluation procedures.

HIA AND WALK SCORE

Two tools that have emerged in recent years to provide better tracking of efforts to reduce these burdens of disease in the built environment are health impact assessments (HIA) and Walk Score.

HIA is a community-based decision-making process, usually voluntary but sometimes regulatory, that is used to evaluate the potential health effects of a plan, project, or policy before it is built or implemented. HIA is applied to areas not traditionally associated with public health, such as transportation and land use. The process comprises multiple steps, from screening and scoping, to reporting and monitoring, and construction or implementation. Studies on the long-term impact of HIAs find that they can build trust between decision-makers and community residents, contribute to more equitable access to health-promoting resources, and increase protection for vulnerable communities.[23]

Walk Score's stated mission is to promote walkable neighborhoods.[24] Walk Score metrics are accessed online and through apps that rank walkability on a scale of 0 to 100 of any address in the United States, Canada, and Australia. Scores from 90 to 100 are deemed a "Walker's Paradise," while those under 50 are considered "Car-Dependent." Transit Score and Bike Score data are also provided. The methodology comprises analysis of hundreds of walking routes to nearby amenities, with the most points given for destinations within a five-minute or quarter-mile walking distance. Other walkability supporting features such as population density, block length, and intersection density are factored in.[25]

WELL BUILDING AND COMMUNITY STANDARDS FOR REAL ESTATE

Recognizing the disciplinary gaps between public health experts and real estate developers, University of Virginia medical professor Matt Trowbridge and

---

[22] Background on Design 4 Active Sacramento (D4AS) at WALKSacramento: http://www.walksacramento.org/our-work-2/d4as/

[23] For more on health impact assessments in the United States, see: https://www.cdc.gov/healthyplaces/hia.htm and https://www.pewtrusts.org/en/projects/health-impact-project

[24] Walk Score mission: https://www.walkscore.com/about.shtml

[25] For Walk Score methodology, see: https://www.walkscore.com/methodology.shtml

colleagues at the US Green Building Council and elsewhere propose greater collaboration in gathering health data at the scale of individual real estate projects and in the development of actionable health metrics. They advocate use of Walk Score, HIAs, and increased use of open data portals to which residents can be encouraged to track and post health information, such as daily physical activity.[26] One result is the International WELL Building Standard, applied to over 4,800 projects worldwide as of 2020. WELL's health and wellness metrics assess, test, and certify a property's health rating. The system measures and monitors how the design of the built environment impacts health through air, water, nourishment, light, fitness, comfort, and mind, and includes a new COVID-19 Health-Safety Rating.

ACCESS: TO GOOD FOOD, AND TO HEALTHCARE

The United States has the heaviest population in the world. With two-thirds of adults and one-third of children in the US reported to be overweight or obese, the trendlines aren't encouraging. We have no intention here to fat shame. There are a variety of factors that contribute to body weight. Studies have shown that individual-level interventions—that is, calls for heavy people to exert more self-control via changes in diet and exercise—are not slowing the national epidemic of obesity and related chronic diseases. Researchers are increasingly looking to the "food environment" of production, distribution, and marketing; efforts in this area are beginning to prove effective.[27]

This represents yet another example of the turn to ecological models of health behavior, which consider the role of the built environment and policies that promote wellness alongside treatments for illness. Farmers' markets, nearby food stores and wellness clinics, and community gardens are some of the elements that can be added to a neighborhood. Evidence suggests that involvement in community gardening, for instance, may be associated with more eating of fruits and vegetables, as well as better relations between neighbors.[28]

What might this shift toward leveraging the environment to influence healthy behavior mean for the delivery of health care? Direct clinical care, it seems, accounts for only around 10 percent of overall health outcomes. Scientific researchers increasingly study how our built environment influences health and wellness.[29]

Not surprisingly, some of the leaders in retrofitting unhealthy environments are healthcare providers. Planners collaborate with owners and operators of hospitals and medical offices located on large blocks surrounded by large parking lots to convert these areas into health districts. By improving pedestrian connectivity, transit access, planting street trees, and building on their parking lots with a mix of uses, they are providing a healthier environment for their visitors, employees, and neighbors.

And then there are medical buildings, the places people must go to receive routine clinical care. One of the more successful approaches to reviving moribund retail centers, not inappropriately, has been to insert medical clinics or to completely convert properties into medical malls. The "retailing" of healthcare services in the United States accelerated in 2010 when the Affordable Care Act created more than 22 million new "health shoppers" seeking consumer-oriented services at convenient times and locations, whether in person or online. Between 2000 and 2014, 44% of outpatient visits occurred in the evenings and on weekends, increasingly in more dispersed locations closer to homes and combined with shopping.[30]

[26] Matthew J. Trowbridge, Sarah Gauche Pickell, Christopher R. Pyke and Douglas P. Jutte, "Building Healthy Communities: Establishing Health and Wellness Metrics for Use Within the Real Estate Industry," Health Affairs, 33, no.11 (2014): 1923–1929: http://content.healthaffairs.org/content/33/11/1923.full.html

[27] Carolyn Cannuscio and Karen Glanz, "Food Environments," Making Healthy Places, 50.

[28] Ibid., 58.

[29] Bipartisan Policy Center, "Lots to Lose: How America's Health and Obesity Crisis Threatens our Economic Future," 2012 https://bipartisanpolicy.org/wp-content/uploads/sites/default/files/5023_BPC_NutritionReport_FNL_Web.pdf.

[30] Katherine G. Carman, Christine Eibner and Susan M. Paddock, "Trends in Health Insurance Enrollment, 2013–15," Health Affairs 34 (6), 2015: 1044–48.

(a)
(b)

Figures I.2-3 The Jackson Medical Mall (JMM) was first established in 1996 by pediatrician and civil rights activist Dr. Aaron Shirley in the vacant stores and empty concourses of the 1970 Jackson Mall. Partnered with local universities and colleges, the facility provides ambulatory healthcare services for the underserved, largely African American local community in a "customer-friendly" setting that includes remaining shops and restaurants, like Piccadilly Cafeteria and Save-A-Lot, as well as a thrice-weekly farmers market and a free fitness center, both operated by a nonprofit supported by the W.K. Kellogg Foundation and the USDA. The newest initiatives to the JMM incorporate arts and culture into the health and wellness mix. Source: Photos by Phillip Jones, 2019.

In addition to the 900 walk-in clinics attached to a chain of pharmacies around the country, dozens of malls have had new life breathed into them by major health clinics and medical offices, which have increased convenience to accessing healthcare.

An early example, still going strong, is the Jackson Medical Mall in Jackson, Mississippi, first established in 1996 in a 1970 mall building by a local doctor with a vision for providing holistic healthcare to underserved residents of the surrounding African American neighborhoods. In 2015 the Jackson Medical Mall Foundation was the recipient of one of six $3 million grants from ArtPlace America for community-based arts and cultural initiatives. Projects include a blues festival, a quilting project, "Truck or Treat" in the parking lot for a safe Halloween, and conversion of a former 22,000-square-foot furniture store into a multigenerational arts and cultural center. Vanderbilt University's One Hundred Oaks Medical Center, leasing the second floor of a Nashville mall, is another worthy example.

See these case studies:

- II.15. Baton Rouge Health District, Louisiana
- II.17. One Hundred Oaks Mall, Nashville, Tennessee

SAFETY: PREVENTING PREVENTABLE INJURIES

A consistent priority for public health advocates has been to make the built environment safer, especially from preventable incidents resulting in injury, and also from crime. While there are many types of injuries, the likelihood of being killed or injured in a motor vehicle crash, specifically, is one of the three primary categories of risk and impact. (The other two, as noted above, are low levels of physical activity and degrees of emotional health and community engagement.)

In 2014, motor vehicle traffic was the second leading cause of injury deaths in the US, after unintentional poisoning (which surged ahead in recent years due to opioid overdoses, a nationwide epidemic that is disproportionately impacting suburban and rural communities). For those aged 5–24 years old, traffic crashes remain the leading cause of injury death.[31] More must be done.

---

[31] Centers for Disease Control, "Leading Causes of Injury Deaths Highlighting Unintentional Injury, 2014": https://www.cdc.gov/injury/wisqars/pdf/leading_causes_of_injury_deaths_highlighting_unintentional_injury_2014-a.pdf.

0   1/2 mi   1 mi   2 mi

Figure I.2-4   Since the mid-1990s, Carmel, Indiana, a fast-growing suburb north of Indianapolis, has added over a hundred roundabouts, either through new construction or by conversion of signaled intersections on roadways both major and minor, leading to dramatic reductions in car injury rates. The roundabouts are engineered to flow traffic smoothly and save time and gas from decreased idling. They also eliminate the need for turn lanes, which has allowed longtime mayor Jim Brainerd to allocate roadway space for hundreds of miles of protected bike infrastructure. Carmel's successful economic development philosophy emphasizes investment in quality of life factors over conventional tools like tax incentives. Source: Redrawn by authors after materials from the City of Carmel, Indiana.

Communities featuring more compact designs with fewer vehicle miles traveled have been found to have lower traffic fatality rates per capita.[32] The reason seems to be simply because residents are less exposed to traffic. It follows, then, that reducing travel demand through the addition of more uses in walking distance might be an effective strategy to reducing traffic-related injuries and deaths. Indeed, studies have shown low-density sprawling patterns generate more traffic volume than higher-density compact patterns, and that traffic volume is a main determinant, or contributing cause, of traffic crashes. Therefore, suburban sprawl generates more exposure to risk of traffic-related injury or death.[33] Reducing speeds and lane widths while increasing intersection density also reduces crash incidents.[34]

One obvious strategy for lowering this risk is to prevent new sprawling developments from being built in the first place, by redirecting growth toward infill redevelopment in established suburbs. Where automobile-centric commercial

[32] David A. Sleet et al., "Injuries and the Built Environment," *Making Healthy Places,* 80, referencing R. Ewing and E. Dumbaugh, "The Built Environment and Traffic Safety: A Review of Empirical Evidence," *Journal of Planning Literature* 23:4 (2009): 347–67. See also Wesley E. Marshall and Norman W. Garrick, "Street Network Types and Road Safety: A Study of 24 California Cities," *Urban Design International* (September 2010) 15:3, 133–47.

[33] Reid Ewing et al., "Transportation and Land Use," *Making Healthy Places,* 158, referencing R. Ewing, R. Schieber, and C.V. Zegeer, "Urban Sprawl as a Risk Factor in Motor Vehicle Occupant and Pedestrian Fatalities," *American Journal of Public Health* 93 (2003): 1541–45, and T. Litman and S. Fitzroy, *Safe Travels: Evaluating Mobility Management Traffic Safety Impacts* (Victoria, BC: Victoria Transport Policy Institute, 2005).

[34] Wesley E. Marshall, Daniel P. Piatowski, and Norman W. Garrick, "Community Design, Street Networks, and Public Health," *Journal of Transport & Health* 1:4 (December 2014): 326–340.

corridors already exist, dangerous to pedestrians and cyclists as well as to drivers, they can be retrofitted, with a newly added lens on health and safely for all (not just for occupants of cars), in concert with now established principles for economic development and complete streets.

As for crime and drug dependency, an operative principle is to examine the elevated risks experienced by vulnerable populations, made vulnerable as the result of one or more circumstances. These include biological attributes such as age and disability; social constructs such as race, ethnicity, and poverty; and environmental exposures such as unsafe housing and incomplete transportation systems. Experts advise that solutions to redress the impacts of such vulnerabilities should be identified and implemented in collaboration with the populations impacted.[35]

See these case studies:

- II.1. Aurora Avenue North, Shoreline, Washington
- II.4. Phoenix Park Apartments, Sacramento, California
- II.6. The BLVD, Lancaster, California

SEEING GREEN: BIOPHILIC DESIGN AND MENTAL WELLNESS

Depression and other mental illnesses are contributors to heavy drug and alcohol use, a highly ranked burden of disease in the United States. Prevalence of these illnesses are markers of compromised emotional health and a low degree of community engagement, putting people at risk. How can retrofitting the suburban built environment contribute to improved rates of mental wellness?

Researchers have demonstrated that green settings have the capacity to alleviate mental fatigue and help restore a person's capacity to pay attention.[36] More specifically, "Evidence of cognitively rejuvenating effects has been found for a variety of natural settings, including wilderness areas, prairies, community parks, views of nature through windows, and even rooms with interior plants."[37]

This rejuvenating phenomenon is broadly characterized under the term *biophilia*, which literally means "love of life or living systems." The biophilia hypothesis, put forward by biologist Edward O. Wilson and social ecologist Stephen Kellert, asserts that humankind has an inherent tendency to affiliate with nature (here understood to include everything from other living organisms, plants and animals, to natural settings such as streams and beaches).[38] Empirical evidence supports the many benefits to be gained from designs that incorporate nature contact, from stress reduction to improvements in recovery from illness and surgery.[39] As Howard Frumkin and Jared Fox remind us, however, we still have a lot to learn about "what kinds of nature contact offer the greatest benefit, at what "dose" and frequency, and for which people."[40]

While we await further empirical results from the medical and public health researchers seeking answers to these questions, we look to designers experimenting with intuitive methods. *Biophilic design* comprises building, landscape, and urbanism strategies that seek to enhance beneficial, rejuvenating contact between people and elements of nature.[41]

What has been done to explore biophilic design and its benefits on mental wellness in suburban settings? William Sullivan of the Sustainability and Human Health Lab at the Department of Landscape Architecture, University of Illinois at Urbana-Champaign, cites studies that provide evidence that being in—or even just viewing—green space can help people recover from stressful experiences. "Analysis revealed a positive, linear association between the density of urban street trees and self-reported stress recovery. That is, the greater the density of the street trees, the faster they recovered from the stressful experience."[42] These studies suggest that it is important for suburban retrofit designs,

---

[35] Chris S. Kochtitzky, "Vulnerabilities and the Built Environment," *Making Healthy Places*, 129.

[36] William C. Sullivan and Chun-Yen Chang, "Mental Health and the Built Environment," *Making Healthy Places*, 106.

[37] Ibid., referencing Matsuoka and Sullivan 2011.

[38] Kellert, Stephen R., and Edward O. Wilson, *The Biophilia Hypothesis* (Washington. DC: Shearwater. Print, 1993).

[39] See Kaid Benfield, "The Science Is in: The healthiest neighborhoods are both walkable *and* green," Placemakers blog, 3 April 2018.

[40] Howard Frumkin and Jared Fox, "Contact with Nature," *Making Healthy Places*, 299, and Gregory N. Bateman, et al., "Nature and Mental Health: An Ecosystem Service Perspective," *Science Advances* (24 July 2019) 5:7.

[41] Terrapin Bright Green, "Economics of Biophilia": https://www.terrapinbrightgreen.com/report/economics-of-biophilia/.

[42] B. Jiang, D. Li, L. Larsen, and W.C. Sullivan, "A dose-response curve describing the relationship between tree density and self-reported stress recovery," *Environment and Behavior* (2014). Cited in William C. Sullivan and Rachel Kaplan, "Nature! Small steps that can make a big difference," *Health Environments Research & Design Journal* 9:2 (2016): 6–10.

especially when adding density, to incorporate street trees or other vegetation.

See these case studies:

- ▪ II.25. White Flint and the Pike District, Montgomery County, Maryland
- ▪ II.26. The Blairs, Silver Spring, Maryland

COMBATTING LONELINESS: THE IMPORTANCE OF SOCIAL CONNECTEDNESS

For many people in suburban settings, what's impeding their mental health may be less a lack of exposure to leafy surroundings than a lack of meaningful connections to other humans. In 2017, former US Surgeon General Vivek Murthy made headlines suggesting that the nation was experiencing a loneliness epidemic.[43] Besides depression, health consequences can include chronic inflammation, increased risks of cancer and heart disease, dementia, and shortened lifespans, equivalent to smoking 15 cigarettes a day.[44] Nearly half of all US adult age groups report sometimes or always feeling alone or left out.[45]

Leading loneliness researcher Julianne Holt-Lunstad points to the increased number of people living alone, declining marriage rates, and other factors.[46] Suburban form designed to privilege privacy might also be a contributing factor. In 1966 the Rolling Stones sang about suburban housewives' loneliness-infused drug addictions in "Mother's Little Helper."[47] Studies suggest that children raised in affluent suburban neighborhoods may be more likely to suffer from depression and abuse drugs than those in middle-class or lower-income neighborhoods.[48]

How can retrofitting the suburban built environment combat loneliness? Holt-Lunstad asserts that population-based, connection-focused interventions may have a more profound effect than interventions in individual cases.[49] She specifically cites community-level tactics such as buddy benches and infrastructure redesigned to make places walkable and safe. We might also learn from the United Kingdom, which in 2018 created a Minister for Loneliness. Parts of the comprehensive strategy are to "place community at the heart of the design of housing developments and planning" and "expand social prescribing connector schemes."[50] We may soon see doctors writing prescriptions for loneliness patients to build social capital by visiting suburban retrofits' town greens and farmers' markets, or participating in night life, intergenerational activities, and yoga classes.

See these case studies:

- ▪ II.8. Guthrie Green, Tulsa, Oklahoma
- ▪ II.23. The Mosaic District, Merrifield, Virginia

CLEANING UP: REDUCING IMPACTS OF POLLUTED AIR, SOIL, AND WATER

The professional fields of urban planning and public health both sprang from nineteenth-century battles to confront the "excesses, inequities, and perils" of urbanization in industrial cities. While the major burdens of disease in northern America shifted significantly in the ensuing decades, real concerns about pollution persist. Indeed, historian Adam Rome has linked the rise of the environmental movement in the US to observable pollution in backyard streams and bubbling up from failed septic tanks

[43] Vivek Murthy, "Work and the Loneliness Epidemic," *Harvard Business Review,* September 2017, and Vivek Murthy, *Together: The Power of Human Connection in a Sometimes Lonely World* (New York: Harper Wave, 2020).

[44] Julianne Holt-Lunstad, "The Potential Public Health Relevance of Social Isolation and Loneliness: Prevalence, Epidemiology, and Risk Factors," *Public Policy & Aging Report* 27:4 (2017): 127–130.

[45] Cigna 2018 Loneliness Index: https://www.cigna.com/assets/docs/newsroom/loneliness-survey-2018-fact-sheet.pdf.

[46] Holt-Lunstad, "The Potential Public Health Relevance."

[47] Many suburban women beat the boredom referred to by the Rolling Stones by entering the workforce in the 1970s. However, Murthy blames much of today's loneliness on workplaces that fail to build meaningful, trusting relationships while eating up more of what used to be social time.

[48] Several studies are discussed in Ron Lieber, "Growing Up on Easy Street Has its Own Dangers," *New York Times,* 9 January 2015.

[49] Julianne Holt-Lunstad, "Why Social Relationships Are Important for Physical Health: A Systems Approach to Understanding and Modifying Risk and Protection," *Annual Review of Psychology*, Vol. 69 (January 2018): 437–458.

[50] HM Government, "A Connected Society, A Strategy for Tackling Loneliness; Laying the Foundations for Change," Department for Digital, Culture, Media and Sport, October 2018: https://assets.publishing.service.gov.uk/government/uploads/system/uploads/attachment_data/file/750909/6.4882_DCMS_Loneliness_Strategy_web_Update.pdf.

in new postwar suburban neighborhoods.[51] While the primary concern was for the health of the "whole earth," activists were motivated by primal fears about tainted drinking water and other poisons finding a way into their own homes.

Fast-forward half a century, and we find the same concerns persisting, albeit exacerbated in lower-income neighborhoods, in suburban areas as much as elsewhere. Public health researchers assert that "the concept of *environmental justice* is useful for framing the convergence of the characteristics of the built environment and air pollutions exposures."[52] Simply put, vulnerable populations are more likely to experience increased exposure to environmental pollutants. Susceptible populations, however, are not limited to the vulnerable, and include many older adults, children, and people with reduced health due to diabetes, heart disease, or lung disease.

A key aspect of reducing impact and risk from various environmental pollutants is to reduce personal exposure. It is important for people, particularly those most susceptible, to avoid spending time in "microenvironments" with high concentrations of pollutants, whether in the soil, water, or air. Thoughtful, informed design policies and strategies can help, such as tree planting. In 2019 the HEAL study as part of the Green Heart Louisville project started a five-year study of the air quality and health impacts of planting 8,000 trees and shrubs in five neighborhoods near an expressway in South Louisville, Kentucky.

For polluted soils, this means brownfields remediation via capping or removal. For polluted water, this means filtering water for drinking and preventing contaminants from entering the watershed. For polluted air, particularly with regard to roads and traffic exposure, this means designing to reduce car use and idling—and hence fuel emissions—from both gas-powered and hybrid/electric vehicles. And it means managing land use, especially residential use and schools, to keep people from spending extended time in places with high concentrations of particulate matter from vehicle and other emissions.

The consensus of one public health expert is that "Residences need to be sited away from major roadways, and the design of urban areas need to preserve open space and offer walkable routes, without introducing sprawl."[53] We agree.

See these case studies:

- II.14. Maplewood Mall and Living Streets, Maplewood, Minnesota
- II.29. Wyandanch Rising, Town of Babylon, New York
- II.32. Assembly Square, Somerville, Massachusetts

WELL-EXECUTED RETROFITTING IMPROVES PUBLIC HEALTH

Suburban retrofits increasingly incorporate design elements that can improve people's physical and mental health and promote social wellness. Various empirical studies and new metrics and tools are assisting developers, designers, public health officials, planners, and others to identify which elements might be incorporated where in order to provide optimal benefits. Developers have noted a growing market for healthy urbanism, especially among the sizable Baby Boomer and Millennial generations; one group is seeking healthy aging and many in the other are seeking a healthy environment to start and raise a family. It is likely that upcoming generations may be similarly inclined toward environmental awareness and concern.

Designers of suburban retrofits assist in fighting the "perfect storm" of health-endangering forces by optimizing changes that reduce high-risk factors that are attributable to aspects of the built environment, such as dietary risks, high body-mass index, and low physical activity. They do this by, among other things, designing to support walking and physical activity, increasing street safety, adding trees and great gathering spaces, reducing exposure to pollutants, and increasing access to good food and preventative healthcare. There is still much work to be done to equitably extend these benefits to all.

[51] Adam Rome, *The Bulldozer in the Countryside: Suburban Sprawl and the Rise of American Environmentalism* (Cambridge, UK: Cambridge University Press, 2001).
[52] Jonathan M. Samet, "Community Design and Air Quality," *Making Healthy Places,* 68–69.
[53] Ibid., 74–75.

Chapter **I.3**
Support an Aging Population

Perhaps we are reaching a tipping point—a shift away from the fear of growing old and toward embracing living long. "Perennials" may just move the conversation along.[1]
Laura Carstensen, Director, Stanford Center on Longevity

In 1900, only 4% of the American population was over 65 years of age. This figure, which reached over 13% by 2010, is predicted to rise to more than 20% by 2050.[2] A generation from now, fully one-fifth of the nation's inhabitants will be "older" adults. Well over one-quarter of the population of Japan is already over 65, and many countries in Europe are not far behind. Would-be suburban retrofitters need to keep in mind the ongoing demographic shift toward a higher median age and a larger percentage of the population living to advanced age.

While some frame this as a challenge—focusing, for example, on the reduced ratio of younger adults to fund entitlements programs and provide support to frail older adults—we frame it here as a significant opportunity for new thinking about aging and the design of community in the suburban settings where most northern Americans, and an even higher percentage of older folks, are living well past their child-rearing years (if they've chosen to have children at all). Many suburban neighborhoods built around child-rearing now have fewer children in them.

A NEW NAME: PERENNIALS

What do we call this older, "post-child" population? As Stanford psychologist Laura Carstensen reminds us, language matters. Carstensen promotes the descriptor "perennials" to reference the way that, in the right environment, older adults can thrive. She writes, "The symbolism it connotes is perfect. For one, 'perennials' makes clear that we're still here, blossoming again and again. It also suggests a new model of life in which people engage and take breaks, making new starts repeatedly. Perennials aren't guaranteed to blossom year after year, but given proper conditions, good soil and nutrients, they can go on for decades. It's aspirational."[3]

Much current literature uses the term Boomers, referring to the generational cohort born from 1946 to 1964, as shorthand for the wave of adults reaching retirement age, frequently contrasted to Millennials (which, with "perennials," happens to form a nice rhyming couplet). Others refer to the "young-old" and the "old-old" as distinct groups with divergent needs; we will refer to these categories in this chapter. Gerontologists recognize that chronological age is not the best marker of either cognitive or physical functioning. While young-old and old-old might be roughly mapped to 65-plus and 85-plus groupings, they can't be strictly tied to numerical age brackets.

While no one likes to be thought of as old, we all hope to enjoy personally the twentieth-century "longevity dividend" that resulted from medical, economic, technological, and environmental advances. The cultural changes in the United States increased life expectancy at birth from 47 to 70 over the course of that century, and the benefits have persisted.[4] The longevity dividend, combined with "compression of morbidity," is allowing many more people to live longer lives in good health, with a shorter, compressed period of decline at the end.

---

[1] Laura Carstensen, "In search of a word that won't offend 'old' people," *Washington Post*, 29 December 2017.
[2] Statistics are from U.S. Census Bureau's *65+ in the United States: 2010*.
[3] Carstensen, "In search of a word."
[4] Laura Carstensen, "A Hopeful Future," in Henry Cisneros, Margaret Dyer-Chamberlain, and Jane Hickie, eds., *Independent for Life: Homes and Neighborhoods for an Aging America* (Austin: University of Texas Press, 2012), 21.

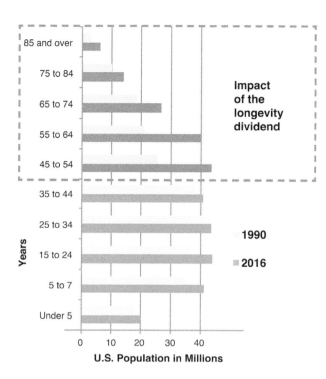

Figure I.3-1 Over the past quarter century as segments of the US population over 45 have grown significantly, the age pyramid has assumed an increasingly cylindrical shape. Source: US Census, diagram by authors.

But what do increased longevity and compressed morbidity mean for suburban neighborhoods? We are especially concerned with places specifically planned and built for families, those folks who moved to suburbs to raise children and, for the most part, still live in suburban neighborhoods, alone or with a spouse, alongside their lawn-care-demanding yards and many-bedroom houses. It isn't only the people in suburbia who are aging. So are the buildings and the infrastructure.

At the level of the individual dwelling, suburban housing can be adapted for the old-old, who are experiencing declining function or disability, by the application of "universal design" principles. These principles revolve around compensating for loss of vision and hearing, by adjusting lighting and sound levels, and compensating for physical frailty, with renovations to add grab bars, hand rails, walk-in showers, repositioned light switches, and no-step entries.[5]

THE LIFELONG COMMUNITY MODEL

Architect and planner M. Scott Ball and policy maker Kathryn Lawler assert that the outdated design of conventional suburban neighborhoods makes it more difficult for older residents to maintain good health and remain free of chronic disease as they continue to age.[6] Ball, Lawler, and their research collaborators describe the need for a profound paradigm shift to a "lifelong community" model, comprising urbanism modifications that provide particular benefit to those at advanced age. Recommendations at the neighborhood level include increased street connectivity, enhanced walkability and access to localized transit, vehicle calming, healthcare at home rather than in a clinical setting, and more frequent and convenient neighborhood retail destinations. These features would provide synergistic benefits to residents of any age.[7]

One example of this approach is unfolding in Mableton in Cobb County, Georgia. In 2011, under the auspices of the Atlanta Regional Commission (ARC), a form-based redevelopment code customized for the lifelong community model was adopted. Results to date include safer street crossings, a new town square, new community gardens and a farmers' market, and changes to zoning to permit new, aging-supportive housing types.[8]

Some of the diverse housing choices that appeal to the young-old and help combat loneliness and isolation include co-housing, accessory dwelling units, live/work flex units, and various forms of roommate-type sharing. These types of housing must be retrofitted into existing neighborhoods comprising mostly detached houses, to promote aging-in-community. Recent reports suggest that the supply of affordable, safe housing that is well connected to services

---

[5] Esther Greenhouse, "The Home Environment and Aging," in *Independent for Life*, 87–98.

---

[6] M. Scott Ball, *Livable Communities for Aging Populations: Urban Design for Longevity* (Hoboken, NJ: Wiley, 2012), 4. See also M. Scott Ball and Kathryn Lawler, "Commentary: Changing Practice and Policy to Move to Scale: A Framework for Age-Friendly Communities Across the United States," in Francis G. Caro and Kelly G. Fitzgerald, eds., *International Perspectives on Age-Friendly Cities* (New York: Routledge, 2016), 171–183.

[7] M. Scott Ball, with contributions from Susan Brecht, Kathryn M. Lawler, and Glen A. Tipton, "The Longevity Challenge to Urbanism," *Livable Communities for Aging Populations*.

[8] Laura Keyes, et al., "A Model to Move Communities from Policy to Implementation," *International Perspectives on Age-Friendly Cities*, 184–196.

Figure I.3-2 Mableton Town Square was established in 2016 in one of the first street reconfiguration projects completed after a form-based code was adopted in Mableton, Cobb County, Georgia, to implement a lifelong community redevelopment model. The 1.3-acre landscaped square, designed by Pond & Company, was created by reconfiguring a rural intersection into a one-way couplet that also enhances safe access to the adjacent Mableton Elementary School. Source: Photo by Matthew Wilder, PLA, ASLA.

Obstacles to suburban aging-in-community	Retrofitting tactics: policies and codes
Large lots become difficult to maintain; neighborhoods of large lots result in fewer activities and uses located within walking distance from home.	Revise zoning to encourage higher-density, mixed-use infill and redevelopment in targeted locations.
Houses oriented to backyards, rather than to front yards, porches, and stoops, provide fewer opportunities to receive the benefits of socializing with neighbors.	Encourage remodeling and additions to houses that engage the street. Encourage regreening of "missing teeth" parcels into neighborhood gardens.
Single-use zoning separating residential and commercial uses contributes to reliance on automobiles even for everyday trips and errands.	Allow for a mix of uses at higher densities to encourage redevelopment of underperforming properties in accessible locations.
Minimum lot sizes and restrictions on rental and multiunit housing make it difficult for residents to downsize within neighborhoods.	Allow accessory dwelling units (ADUs) and backyard cottages in residential zones. Reform zoning to allow for contextual integration of a greater range of multiunit housing types.
Wide roads and a lack of transit or sidewalks encourage speeding and discourage walking, contributing to sedentary lifestyles, poorer health, and reduced longevity.	Establish and adopt Complete Streets standards to promote safe integration of transit, walking, and biking into existing roadways.
Affordable housing for older adults on tight, fixed budgets is often located in peripheral locations, contributing to social isolation.	Preserve and produce affordable housing units within new and redeveloped walkable centers. Incorporate high-quality truly public space.

is far below the projected need.[9] Planners, developers, architects, and builders should all take note. As architecture and urbanism writer Allison Arieff cautions about the current state of housing for seniors in the United States, "Every day for the next 19 years, 10,000 people will reach age 65. That companies aren't scrambling to exploit this market is not only unfortunate for their bottom line, but almost certainly treacherous, eventually, for all of us."[10]

A BRIEF HISTORY OF RETIREMENT LIVING: SUN CITY AND THE VILLAGES OF FLORIDA

To think through the present-day urban design and planning challenge of retrofitting suburbia for perennials, it is instructive to learn from the historical development stages and evolving design protocols of Sun City, Arizona, and The Villages of Florida, two of the most prominent retirement communities in the United States.[11] Since Sun City's celebrated grand opening in 1960, millions of Americans, mostly but not exclusively middle-class and white, have migrated to vast and fast-growing age-restricted developments in the Sunbelt south. It is

---

9 Joint Center for Housing Studies at Harvard, "Projects and Implications for a Growing Population: Older Households 2015–2035 Housing," 16 December 2016.
10 Allison Arieff, "A Housing Crisis for Seniors," *New York Times*, 28 January 2017.

11 Sun City and Sun City West had a combined 2010 population of 62,000 while the population of The Villages—spanning three counties—recently passed the 120,000 mark and as of the last census was considered the fastest-growing micropolitan area in the country. Each has ~97% non-Hispanic white residents.

estimated that the current size of this niche market is fully 18% of retirees seeking new homes.[12] The marketing literature for age-restricted master-planned communities is dominated by images of leisured golden years in the sun, playing golf, living independently, and being free of the drudgery of shoveling snow.

The basic contours of the history of Sun City are well known.[13] In 1959, a highly successful contractor and developer based in Phoenix named Del E. Webb, weighing contradictory marketing and academic research, embarked on a fast-tracked new development partnership on a 20,000-acre (31 sq. mi.) area of cotton fields about 15 miles northwest of the downtown, at the time about one hour's drive away. Given the distance from employment centers, Webb and his colleagues settled on housing for retirees. They set out to copy the nearby age-segregated development of Youngtown, which had made a big media splash in the mid-1950s. The early houses at Sun City were modest modern ranches, affordable to working-class retired couples with modest savings.[14] They paid in cash.[15] Community facilities were constructed at the outset, along with five model houses. When it opened, Sun City amenities included a near-complete 9-hole golf course, the Hiway House Motor Hotel, the Sun City Shopping Center, and a community center for active recreation (crafts, pool, shuffleboard, lawn bowling, croquet, and horseshoes).

By 1980 three phases of new construction at Sun City were almost complete, comprising seven recreation centers and thousands of dwelling units, a combination of detached houses of an increasingly diverse array of models, condominiums, and rental apartments. Sun City was described by the builder as the largest development of its kind in the history of this country, its 25,000 units far surpassing iconic Levittown, New York's 14,000.[16]

The range of dwelling types on offer and the provision of innovative amenities—golf courses, pools, and recreation centers—supported the emergent concept of the "active adult" lifestyle.[17] The street morphology of the neighborhoods, anchored by recreation and shopping areas, evolved from the curving network of streets typical of early postwar planned communities and subdivisions to a distinctive pattern that debuted in 1969: concentric streets, arrayed around central nodes. Land in the spaces between the circles was devoted to golf. Sun City popularized golf-course amenities, which soon spread to suburban middle-class residential communities across the continent that were not restricted by age. (Golf is losing popularity, and at least 135 of courses are now being redeveloped or regreened, into suburban farms, urban forests, and other more ecologically productive land uses.)

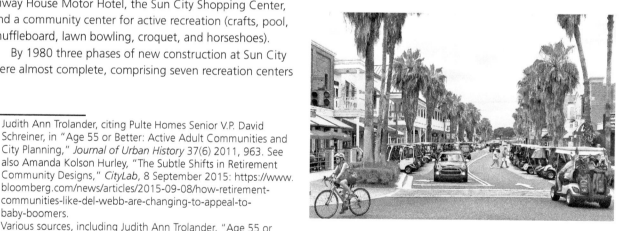

Figure I.3-3   Residents walk, bike, and drive cars and golf carts through Lake Sumter Landing, one of three themed town centers in The Villages of Florida, a massive and fast-growing age-restricted development between Orlando and Ocala. What lessons from successful "active-adult" communities—about amenities, infrastructure, and social life—can we integrate into the lifelong community model? Source: Photo by June Williamson, 2018.

[12] Judith Ann Trolander, citing Pulte Homes Senior V.P. David Schreiner, in "Age 55 or Better: Active Adult Communities and City Planning," *Journal of Urban History* 37(6) 2011, 963. See also Amanda Kolson Hurley, "The Subtle Shifts in Retirement Community Designs," *CityLab*, 8 September 2015: https://www. bloomberg.com/news/articles/2015-09-08/how-retirement-communities-like-del-webb-are-changing-to-appeal-to-baby-boomers.

[13] Various sources, including Judith Ann Trolander, "Age 55 or Better"; John Findley, "Sun City, Arizona: New Town for Old Folks," in *Magic Lands: Western Cityscapes and American Culture after 1940* (Berkeley: University of California Press, 1992), 160–213; Bret McKeand and the Sun Cities Area Historical Society, *Images of America: Sun City* (Charleston, SC: Arcadia Publishing, 2011); and the many resources, including oral histories, on the website of the Sun Cities Area Historical Society Del Webb Sun Cities Museum: http://www.delwebbs uncitiesmuseum.org.

[14] Trolander, "Age 55 or Better," 955.

[15] Melanie Sturgeon, oral interview with former DEVCO president John Meeker, 6 March 1996, Sun Cities Area Historical Society Del Webb Sun Cities Museum: http://www.delwebbsuncities museum.org/John-Meeker.php.

[16] Ibid.

[17] Ibid. John Meeker credits Sun City head of advertising Bob Garland with coining the term "active adult" and the phrase "an active new Way-of-Life."

The history of The Villages of Florida is less well known.[18] More known, perhaps, is the *fake* history of The Villages. But let's start with the real history. The Villages is located 50 miles northwest of Orlando, over an hour's drive from the airport, built on vast tracts of cattle ranch land. Comprising numerous "village" subdivisions that range in size from 100 houses to 1550, the current developed land area is approximately 23,000 acres (32 sq. mi.), a figure similar to the initial land area secured for Sun City. The Villages began in the early 1970s as a rural mobile home park called Orange Blossom Gardens, the operation of Harold Schwartz and partner Al Tarrson, land subdividers from Michigan. It was the success of just such small, scattered mobile home parks, and their appeal to elderly migrant "snowbirds," that helped convince the Del Webb organization to proceed with the first Sun City.[19]

By the early 1980s, Schwartz and Tarrson had sold only around 400 plots for mobile homes in the still rural area of central Florida. Tarrson was bought out by Schwartz's son H. Gary Morse, an advertising executive from Chicago, who set about buying up yet more land and devising plans to add amenities—a well-appointed recreation center complete with a resort-style pool with waterfall and tiki bar, and a neighborhood shopping center—thus transforming the modest mobile home park into a fully fledged active-adult community.

In 1992, the new name of The Villages of Florida was launched. Morse commissioned plans for a walkable town center. Spanish Springs Town Center first opened in 1994 and was completed in increments, to designs by Gary Mark, who was poached from the Toronto-based theme park designers Forrec, known for Universal Studios. The town center was inspired by historic St. Augustine, and heavily incorporated the theme of Ponce de Leon's mythical

Fountain of Youth.[20] A two-block-long Main Street with restaurants, boutiques, a bank, and insurance offices terminates in a pedestrian plaza, featuring fountains, of course, and a central gazebo programmed with music and dancing every night.

Here, we start to encounter the "fake" history. Many of the building facades, in a pastiche Spanish colonial style, feature plaques referencing a lively ersatz back history in which the town was settled in 1792 and populated by generations of eccentrics.[21]

Morse constructed dedicated infrastructure for golf carts and biking, most notably a golf cart bridge spanning over US Route 441, completed in 1993 to connect Orange Blossom Gardens to the rest of The Villages as it was expanded to the west and south. The clunky bridge was aged—unconvincingly—with trompe l'oeil to look like masonry and stucco. The golf cart infrastructure has become more extensive and complex with each new phase of development, now consisting of 100 miles of dedicated paths and many grade-separated intersections. Two new town centers followed, Lake Sumter Landing and Brownwood, each with a different historical theme expressed in the building facade treatments, scenographic decorative features, street names, and backstory told in faux historical plaques.

The design shift from the modernist sensibilities of Sun City to the traditionalist pastiche theming of The Villages' three town centers provokes intriguing questions, particularly since today's retirees are increasingly unlikely to have personal memories of such settings from their youth; many grew up and raised families in modern postwar drivable suburbs, rather than in walkable small towns.

The rate of growth of The Villages since the mid-1990s has been phenomenal. The Villages development arm claims to sell 200 new houses a month, with a resale monthly rate of about 200 houses. In 2020 The Villages was rated the top-selling master-planned community in the United States for the fourth year in a row; it shows no sign yet of slowing down.[22]

---

18 Sources for this history include personal author knowledge and observations gleaned from dozens of visits since 1998. Other sources are Stephen Nohlgren, "Retirement Boom Town," *St. Petersburg Times,* 14 May 2000: http://www.sptimes.com/News/051400/Floridian/Retirement_boom_town.shtml; Stephen A. Duncan, "Harold Schwartz – H Gary Morse – The Villages," Southwest Florida – Social Diary Blog, 14 March 2014: http://www.byduncan.com/2014/03/14/harold-schwartz-millionaire-h-gary-morse-billionaire/; April Warren, "Villages developer H. Gary Morse dies at 77," *Ocala StarBanner,* 30 October 2014: http://www.ocala.com/article/20141030/.ARTICLES/141039985/0/search?p=1&tc=pg; and Deane Simpson, *Young-Old: Urban Utopias of an Aging Society* (Zurich: Lars Müller Publishers, 2015).

19 Trolander, "Age 55 or Better."

20 The Villages Florida, "May 2014 Vmail - Spanish Springs 20th Anniversary," YouTube: https://youtu.be/87XRNGa3bfc.

21 June Williamson, "Sounding the Home Town Theme," *Thresholds: Journal of the MIT Department of Architecture,* 20, 2000: 56–61.

22 RCLCO Real Estate Advisors annual reports on top-selling master planned communities.

LEARNING LESSONS FROM RETIREMENT COMMUNITIES

What is the nature of the appeal of residentially segregated retirement communities? What lessons can we learn for retrofitting suburbia? Writing in the mid-'80s, geographer Patricia Gober argued that they had three characteristics:

- They were noninstitutional.
- They provided a relatively independent lifestyle.
- They were largely self-contained places.

Further, she argued three primary reasons for retirement migration to the Sunbelt:

- The structure of typical households and families moved away from intergenerational living.
- There was increased propensity to relocate among older Americans.
- Distinct communities evolved within larger metropolitan areas, a phenomenon she called "urban mosaic culture."[23]

This last was not confined to older people; young families also had a tendency to self-segregate, if they could afford it, in new suburban developments that provided amenities that catered to them, like playgrounds and new schools.[24]

In the future, we can expect to see more of the same approach to planned communities for retirees, still age-restricted and concentrated in the Sunbelt, and perhaps broadened to attract a greater range of demographic niches by, for example, catering to race, ethnicity, or sexual orientation, along with age (see, for example, the BOOM proposals by architects Hollwich Kushner, for Palm Springs and the Costa del Sol).

But we also discern seeds of a shift away from age-restricted communities and toward the retrofitting and cultivation of existing suburbs to more robustly, and affordably, support aging-in-community. These retrofitting efforts incorporate lessons from the test bed of purpose-built retirement communities. The golf course amenities represent both a commitment to open space, serving as a buffer between neighborhoods, and a commitment to

keeping residents healthy and active in the outdoors. These characteristics can be reproduced in retrofits at a more granular scale and updated to more ecologically productive uses for open space, such as pockets of urban forest that sequester carbon and parks that also function as storm drainage basins. The golf cart infrastructure suggests willingness, even eagerness, to explore alternates to car dependence. This could be tapped elsewhere to support local use of neighborhood electric vehicles (NEVs) to ferry passengers or goods. Perhaps the most important lesson retrofits should learn from Sun City and The Villages is the attention paid to making older adults feel part of a community.

What portion of the market for homes in age-restricted retirement communities could be redirected into suburban retrofits?

SOCIAL SUPPORT: REINHABITING GHOSTBOXES AND PARKING LOTS INTO AMENITIES

Planned retirement communities have long relied on the panoply of amenities, recreational facilities, and services that cater to the target 55-plus housing market. These same uses are popping up in reinhabitation-type retrofits of so-called ghostboxes, or vacant big box stores. Just as suburban malls and big box stores were once dominated by uses catering to the perceived needs of young families—Home Depot, Toys-R-Us, countless fast food franchises—we now see many of these buildings reused as community-based medical clinics, wellness facilities, and senior activity centers.

In Wisconsin Rapids, a former Walmart anchor store at the Rapids Mall was converted into the 68,000-square-foot Centralia Center. Vierbicher Associate Architects added large skylights and windows throughout to illuminate the box, which is programmed for education, senior services, and adult day care.[25] A unique feature is an indoor walking path with a spongy tiled surface to reduce impact on

---

[23] Patricia Gober, "The Retirement Community as a Geographic Phenomenon: The Case of Sun City, Arizona," *Journal of Geography* 84 (5, 1985): 189–198.

[24] Findley also makes this point, "Sun City, Arizona," 170.

---

[25] Altmann Construction Company, Inc.: http://www.altmannconstruction.com/projects/municipal-government/senior-resource-center-wisconsin-rapids-wi/.

joints.[26] More energetic walkers were able to extend their route into the adjacent mall, until it closed in early 2018. The local YMCA and Boys and Girls Club are the new owners; the two groups will convert the mall into a new community health and fitness center, and perhaps will restore the walking connection.[27] The Collinwood Recreation Center in Cleveland, Ohio, is a similar big box retrofit example.

In a contribution to *Independent for Life: Houses and Neighborhoods for an Aging America*, we wrote about an incremental accumulation of retrofits around the Northgate Mall, to serve the needs of the aging populations living in suburban subdivisions in north Seattle and adjacent suburbs.[28] The mall, designed by architect John Graham and opened in 1950, is arguably the first example of the classic "dumbbell" mall type (anchor store at each end, one in the middle, plus a food court, with the "mall" configured as a narrow open-air concourse of in-line stores, easily roofed over later, as Northgate was in 1979).[29] The retrofits include Aljoya Thornton Place, built on overflow mall parking, which includes 143 units of independent living apartments facing a linear park that is also a stormwater collection and filtration basin, and the Northgate Community Center and Northgate Branch public library. The latter were built around a small park on the former site of a Goodyear Tire store affiliated with the mall.

Soon, older residents will be able to catch a light rail to downtown Seattle from a northern terminus at Northgate, scheduled to open in 2021. A pedestrian bridge will link over the Interstate to the nearby regional hospital and a community college offering continuing education courses. The historic mall itself is now demolished; the site will be intensively redeveloped into several walkable blocks of housing, offices, and a National Hockey League training facility.

Residents have grown old in their nearby mid-twentieth-century neighborhoods and desire to age-in-community. In the US Census tract that includes Northgate, the percentage of residents over 65 more than doubled from 1970 to 2010.[30] Northgate is located at the center of three active "senior villages": Northwest Neighbors Network, PNA Village, and North East Seattle Together (NEST). Each is part of the national Village to Village Network, an organization formed in 2010 to maximize the growth, impact, and sustainability of individual senior villages. A senior village is defined by the network as "nonprofit, grassroots, membership organizations that are redefining aging by being a key resource to community members wishing to age in place. Villages are a social support network for their members that provide necessary services (such as transportation, technology assistance, running errands to the pharmacy and grocery store), community engagement activities and other important resources crucial to aging interdependently."[31] Members pay a fee to benefit from the services.

The Arlington Mills Community Center is an example of a place supportive of intergenerational activities, located along the 3.5-mile corridor retrofit of Columbia Pike in Arlington County, Virginia. A historic toll road evolved into a commercial strip, it is being incrementally transformed under the auspices of a form-based code, first adopted in 2003. Low-rise commercial buildings, set back behind parking lots, are being replaced at several key nodes along the pike by mid-rise, mixed-use buildings. Local commercial real estate tax revenue is supporting improved transit services. Access to senior services emerged as a top priority. A vacant Safeway grocery store was replaced with the light-filled, five-level Arlington Mills Community Center and Senior Center, designed by DCS Design.[32] The neighborhood is very diverse, as are many suburban areas; the residents are two-thirds non-white and 40% foreign born. The gym is designed for a contemporary vision of intergenerational exercise, supporting basketball for the younger set, and for the older, Pickleball (a game somewhere between tennis and ping pong). The rear part of the

---

[26] Wisconsin Rapids Lowell Center: https://www.lowell-center.org/.

[27] Caitlin Shuda, "Take a final look inside Rapids Mall in Wisconsin Rapids," *Wisconsin Rapids Tribune*, 31 January 2018: https://www.wisconsinrapidstribune.com/story/money/2018/01/31/rapids-mall-take-final-look-inside-wisconsin-rapids-mall/1082771001/.

[28] Ellen Dunham-Jones and June Williamson, "Retrofitting Suburbs," in *Independent for Life: Homes and Neighborhoods for an Aging America*, 179–196.

[29] Meredith L. Clausen, "Northgate Regional Shopping Center: Paradigm from the Provinces," *Journal of the Society of Architectural Historians* 43 (1984): 144–61.

[30] From 7.85% to 17.52% in Census Tract 12, King County, Washington. Source: Social Explorer and US Census.

[31] Village to Village Network: http://www.vtvnetwork.org/content.aspx?page_id=274&club_id=691012.

[32] Dunham-Jones and Williamson, "Retrofitting Suburbs," in *Independent for Life*, 187–188. See also DCS Design: http://dcsdesign.com/arlington-mill-community-center.html.

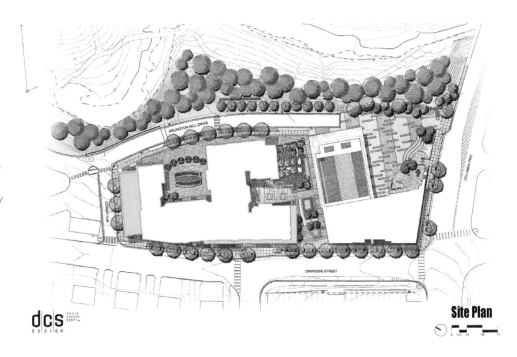

Figure 1.3-4 At a key intersection, or "node," along Columbia Pike in a diverse area of Arlington County, Virginia, a stand-along grocery store site was redeveloped as an apartment building and the Arlington Mills Community Center and Senior Center by DCS Design. A full array of programming is enjoyed by both seniors and teens. Source: Courtesy of Davis, Carter, Scott Ltd.

Site Plan

Figures 1.3-5 Tucked into the sloped site, the gym at the Arlington Mills Community Center features a wood court that can be alternately used by teens for basketball and by older folks for pickleball, a fast-growing sport similar to tennis but played on a half-size court, with slower-moving wiffleballs. Source: Photo © Eric Taylor, www.EricTaylorPhoto.com.

HOUSING CHOICES: AGING-IN-COMMUNITY AT MALLS, STRIP CENTERS, AND OFFICE PARKS

The desire to downsize one's household, casting off the baggage of working and family life, is one of the primary appeals of moving to a planned retirement community. Suburban retrofits are being tooled to address this desire, while also meeting the needs of those who want to remain embedded in their existing local social and family networks. The many failed and underutilized commercial properties dotting suburban neighborhoods provide opportunity. In *Retrofitting Suburbia*, we documented examples of housing for seniors and empty nesters included in shopping mall retrofits, specifically at Park Forest Plaza, Illinois; Willingboro, New Jersey; Belmar, Colorado; and Northgate, Washington, as noted above. This trend has, if anything, expanded.

site contains a 122-unit, 100% affordable housing building, designed by KGD Architecture, with 12 barrier-free units, and 13 units for formerly homeless individuals and families.[33]

See these case studies:

- II.22. Collinwood Recreational Center, Cleveland, Ohio
- II.27. La Station – Centre Intergénérationnel, Nuns' Island, Verdun, Quebec

---

[33] Arlington County news release: https://newsroom.arlingtonva.us/release/arlington-mill-wins-excellence-in-housing-development-award/.

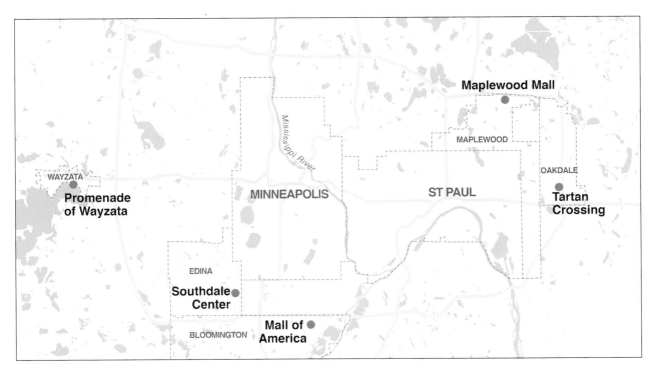

Figures I.3-6 Metropolitan Minneapolis–St. Paul is home to two of the most noteworthy enclosed shopping malls: Victor Gruen's historic Southdale Center and the gargantuan Mall of America. Two area malls, in the suburbs of Wayzata and Oakdale, have been redeveloped into seniors housing. At Maplewood Mall, a motel on an outparcel was reinhabited into memory care housing. Source: Authors.

For example, the metropolitan area of Minneapolis–St. Paul is awash in retrofits providing suburban housing for older adults. At the Maplewood Mall, a former two-story budget Days Inn motel was converted to the 115-apartment Maple Hill Senior Living. The local branch library is across the arterial. The crosswalk was enhanced to make it easier to walk there. The former Oakdale Center mall is now called Tartan Crossing. The derelict mall was demolished in 2011; the retrofit includes a large grocery store and a seniors housing complex. An interesting aspect is a landscape of cascading, stepped stormwater biofiltration ponds on the edge of the property, adjacent to the housing, that doubles as a small park. And the Wayzata Mall was also demolished, and replaced with The Promenade of Wayzata, a mixed-use center of five blocks over an underground parking deck, which includes 326 units of seniors housing.

Many office parks are experiencing high rates of vacancy in the New York metropolitan area, in Westchester County, New Jersey, and Long Island. These locations, often designed as campuses, are often more remote from existing built fabric than many shopping centers and malls.

Nevertheless, they are candidates for retrofits that cater to perennials wishing to downsize and relocate while remaining proximate to their former homes and neighborhoods. New 55-plus housing at the high end of the market is being built on corporate campus grounds, as at Bell Works in Holmdel, New Jersey.

A co-housing community consisting primarily—though not exclusively—of older adults was established in 2005 at Eastern Village Cohousing (EVC) in Silver Spring, Maryland. In an example of adaptive reuse design, EDG Architects remodeled a four-story 1950s office building into 56 units, with an array of aging-supportive features. EVC is legally structured as condominiums, with units ranging from one-bedroom flats to three-bedroom lofts. The LEED Silver project has many green features, including geothermal wells and a vegetative roof, while the former parking lot became a garden courtyard.[34] Older members formed a

---

[34] Bradley H. Winick and Martin Jaffe, "Planning Aging-Supporting Communities, American Planning Association PAS Report #579, June 2015. See also: https://buildingdata.energy .gov/project/eastern-village-cohousing-condominium and http:// www.cohousing.org/Eastern%20Village%20Cohousing.

(a)   (b)

Figure I.3-7 Before (a) and after (b) views of Eastern Village Cohousing. Lush plantings now populate the former parking court of the four-story office building converted to apartments by EDG Architects in 2005. On a recent visit, the balconies were barely visible through the mature greenery. Source: Courtesy of EDG Architects.

social group called the Sages. They plan an active social calendar of outings and activities to keep them feeling connected, to take "the edge off the loneliness," as one member in her 70s said.[35]

See these case studies:

- II.13. Promenade of Wayzata, Wayzata, Minnesota
- II.14. Maplewood Mall and Living Streets, Maplewood, Minnesota
- II.28. Bell Works, Holmdel, New Jersey

ECONOMIC AND WELLNESS FACTORS: EVOLUTION OF THE "GRANNY FLAT" AND THE HOUSEHOLD MODEL

Another tactic for accommodating aging is to encourage the construction of accessory dwelling units (ADUs). These secondary units, carved out of existing detached houses with partitions and new plumbing for the required kitchen

and bathroom, or constructed as additions, attached or detached, are not typically allowable in R-I zones. And so, the first act of retrofitting is to change codes to allow for these units. We advocate for allowing accessory units in residential zones everywhere.

The moniker "granny flat" suggested that an older parent to the dwelling's primary residents would inhabit the unit. Increasingly, however, it might be the aging parent or parents who are in the main residence, with an unrelated adult or couple in the flat. The renters might be from the same perennial cohort as the main residents, or they might be Millennials or younger. The arrangement benefits the homeowner, who receives rental income that can offset high property taxes and other expenses while using excess space in a house designed for a larger household. It also benefits the renter, by providing a more affordable rental option in neighborhoods otherwise bereft of housing diversity.

ADUs suggest squeezing additional units out of existing suburban housing fabric. Existing large houses can also be subdivided into smaller units, while appearing relatively unchanged from the outside. Such retrofits at the level of a large dwelling might support the household model of supportive care for old-old adults. In this model, an alternative to nursing homes pioneered by nonprofits such as the Green House Project, bedrooms and bathrooms for eight to twelve adults are grouped together around a

---

[35] Emily Codik, "Why DC Residents are Moving to Cohousing Communities," *Washingtonian,* March 2015: https://www.washingtonian.com/2015/03/19/why-dc-residents-are-moving-to-cohousing-communities/.

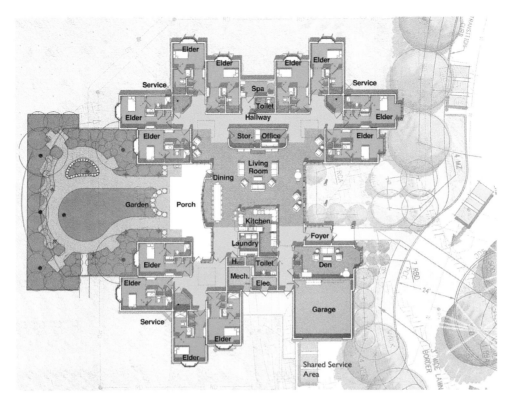

Labels in figure: Elder, Elder, Elder, Elder, Service, Spa, Service, Toilet, Elder, Elder, Hallway, Elder, Elder, Stor., Office, Elder, Living Room, Dining, Porch, Garden, Kitchen, Foyer, Laundry, Den, Elder, H., Toilet, Mech., Elder, Elec., Service, Garage, Elder, Elder, Shared Service Area

Figure I.3-8   Typical floor plan showing the household model for supportive collective living for elders. Each resident has a private bedroom, clustered on one level around a shared open plan living room, kitchen, and dining area, like a big house. This example is from White Oak Cottages in Westwood, Massachusetts, designed by EGA Architects. While this example is new construction, older buildings could be retrofitted into households. Source: Courtesy of EGA, P.C.

shared living, cooking, and eating area and comprise a social unit for caregiving.[36]

Increasing numbers of older adults are experiencing dementia as they age. Memory care housing and adult day care centers cater to the specialized needs of this population. The Promenade of Wayzata includes memory care units that residents can move to if the need arises. Pioneering models for providing a safe and stimulating daily life setting that maximize privacy and resident autonomy have been developed in the Netherlands, such as the Hogewey dementia village in Weesp, an Amsterdam suburb. In addition to grouping the 150 residents together into 27 households organized by cultural lifestyle (there are

seven different themes), the ground floor and courtyards of the complex include amenities that support everyday real-life routines, such as a supermarket and restaurant. Active participation in familiar routines produces a sense of normalcy that reduces anxiety and agitation, preserves dignity, and eases the burden on caregivers. Architects Jennifer Sodo and Max Winters of Perkins Eastman assert, "Hogewey works because of its total commitment to the vision of normalcy for older adults with dementia."[37] They cite how "the community supermarket sticks wine and incontinence supplies side by side" as evidence of a design pattern of "blurring front and back of house" to help create a setting that really functions like Main Street.[38]

---

[36] See Paula Span, "A Better Kind of Nursing Home," *New York Times,* 22 December 2017. For more information on the Green House Project, see: https://www.thegreenhouseproject.org/. For architectural models, see Perkins Eastman, *Building Type Basics for Senior Living,* 2nd ed. (Hoboken, NJ: Wiley, 2013).

[37] Jennifer Sodo and Max Winters, "Missing Main Street: Reconnecting Older Adults with Dementia to the Fabric of Authentic Living," Perkins Eastman White Paper, 23 October 2019.

[38] Ibid.

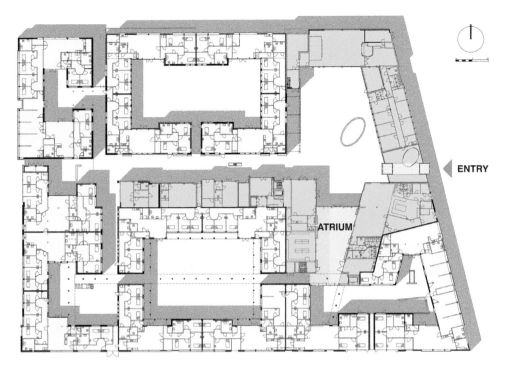

Figures I.3-9 Ground floor plan of Hogewey dementia village in Weesp, Netherlands. Around 150 residents are grouped into households arranged around courtyards that fulfill a vision of normalcy for those living with dementia. A series of outdoor and indoor spaces (shaded in orange) on the ground level comprise a shared public realm, designed for easy wayfinding, maximum independence, and fullness of self. Source: Courtesy of Molenaar & Bol & VanDillen architecten b.v., with annotations by authors.

While Hogewey dementia village was built as new construction, we think a portion or all of selected dead and dying shopping malls and strip centers in northern America could, and should, be retrofitted to a model that similarly promotes dementia-friendly normalcy, either for day visits or, if housing is added, for full-time residents. Gerontological environmental designer Emily Roberts and colleagues have designs to do just that at a dead mall in Oklahoma City.

A specific challenge of retrofitting garden apartment complexes is the obligation to rehouse older lower-income residents who may not wish to—and should not be forced to—relocate far away from their longtime social networks. The Modern at Art Place in the Fort Totten TOD in Washington, DC, has taken this on admirably.

See these case studies:

- II.21 Downtown Doral, Doral, Florida
- II.24. South Dakota Avenue and Riggs Road, Fort Totten, Washington, DC

Figure I.3-10 The public atrium of Hogewey provides access to Hogeweyk Super, the market where both household staff members and residents shop regularly, in a clear example of a deinstitutionalizing approach to senior living design and policy. It's not a novelty add-on or stage set, but the facility's *actual* central storage place for its food and supplies. Source: Photo by Jennifer A. Sodo, 2017.

POST-CAR LIFE FOR PERENNIALS?

As a culture, northern Americans have long been in denial about aging. The "perennials" framing, proposed by Laura Carstensen, is helpful in repositioning conversations about long life. Planners and developers have tried to address it with discrete, specialized projects and development "products," customized along a continuum of specialized care. Instead, what is needed are communities designed and retrofitted for lifelong needs, especially as many older adults will live past their capacity to drive safely and are more likely to live alone and be at risk of loneliness. Many younger people also can't or don't wish to drive, and may experience feelings of isolation, particularly if they live alone. Many people, not just the most vulnerable older adults, would benefit from suburbs retrofitted to provide support for the shared needs of all.

Chapter I.4
Leverage Social Capital for Equity

America's history of racial exclusion repeats and deepens itself as low-income people of color are displaced from newly chic neighborhoods, shut out of all but the lowest-wage jobs, and isolated in aging, disinvested communities—these days, in the suburbs.[1]

Angela Glover Blackwell, Founder of PolicyLink

Despite lingering depictions of outdated cultural stereotypes, recognition is finally gaining that suburbs are not physically homogenous, nor are suburbanites all the same in terms of socioeconomics, race, or ethnicity. However, built landscapes within metropolitan regions remain highly fragmented and segregated; they have been structured that way through codes and laws over decades of growth cycles, and supported by entrenched systems of racialized control and policing. The barriers to decreasing segregation and inequality stubbornly persist.

The task of confronting this challenge is vital at a time when poverty in suburbia has increased in many neighborhoods while awareness of these changes and their causes is not yet widespread.[2] As leading US equity activist Angela Glover Blackwell informs us, people who are newly displaced from gentrifying urban areas may find themselves in suburban communities that have become disinvested in over time, as their former neighborhoods once were. There they may join the newest immigrants and longtime residents who find themselves in communities with struggling schools, a lack of gathering places, and access to fewer well-paying jobs. The number of suburban census tracts with high levels of poverty is growing; many governments are caught off-guard in a vicious spiral of reduced revenues, increased maintenance costs, and obsolete, discriminatory policies. Yet, while poor places get poorer, many rich places get richer, and the uneven playing field gets more inequitable.

Not only are suburbs not homogeneous, but there will be no singular fix to make them more equitable. Jason Schupbach, expert on the role of arts and design in making better communities, reminds us why mindful design matters, asserting, "Inequity will die from a thousand cuts, not a silver bullet."[3] It is imperative for designers to contribute to vanquishing inequity by leveraging social capital to promote urban and suburban justice, delivering one small but significant cut at a time.

Social capital is defined as networks of civic trust and social cohesion, based in shared norms and values that facilitate co-operation, both within groups and between them. Networks of relationships are formed among people who live and work in a particular society, enabling that society to function effectively. These connections provide pathways for individuals to increase happiness and wellbeing and to access economic opportunity. In the case of social capital, these networks are made from literal, real-world social ties between individuals.

Within the context of suburban retrofitting, we frame social capital as the introduction or enhancement of *social infrastructure* within a project. This is especially needed in suburbs that were designed to maximize privacy and center social life primarily around schools, yet today have aging populations, smaller households, and fewer children. A strengthened social infrastructure, often integrated with greater accessibility and environmental quality, builds urban resilience: the capacity to survive, adapt, and even grow in the face of both chronic and acute stresses and shocks, whether economic, climactic, political, or all three.

In the spirit of Peter Newman's, Timothy Beatley's, and Heather Boyer's inspirational volume *Resilient Cities*, we

---

[1] Angela Glover Blackwell, "The Case for All-In Cities," in Toni Griffin, Ariella Cohen, David Maddox, eds., *The Just City Essays* (Philadelphia: Next City, 2015), 154.

[2] Michelle Chen, "Why Are America's Suburbs Becoming Poorer?" *Nation*, 22 June 2017.

[3] Jason Schupbach, "Why Design Matters," *The Just City Essays*, 226.

Figure I.4-1 Walala Pump & Go is a 2019 art installation by Camille Walala marking the entrance to downtown Fort Smith, Arkansas. Embracing hope, the French artist took over an abandoned 1950s gas station with colorful painted patterns. The contemporary art installation is one of several commissioned since 2015 by the cultural project The Unexpected, curated by Justkids, to exuberantly invigorate vacant lots and buildings in Fort Smith, and encourage people to gather. Source: Camille Walala for The Unexpected, photo by Nick Gibson, 2019.

advocate for embrace of hope in the face of fear in responding to stresses and preparing for shocks to the suburban polis.[4] To paraphrase their cri de coeur, suburbs of fear make short-term, panicky decisions, driven primarily by divisive competition, while suburbs of hope plan for the long term, guided by visions for future change formed through consensus and cooperation. Suburbs of fear see threats, while suburbs of hope seize on periods of crisis as opportunities to seek continuous improvement.[5]

How can retrofits address the challenges of leveraging social capital to promote equity and justice and of building social infrastructure that increases resilience? To summarize a few of the ways:

- Reinhabitation retrofits of commercial spaces in all suburbs including "ethnoburbs" (that is, places where recent immigrant populations have concentrated) can support the flourishing of locally owned businesses.
- Redevelopment retrofits can add and preserve jobs, housing affordability and choice.

- Regreening retrofits can provide equitable access to an enhanced civic realm of public and shared green spaces and help assert a "right to the suburb."

These strategies can and should be employed both in communities with high rates of poverty where needs are greatest, but also in more prosperous places with greater access to opportunity. The scale of operations for leveraging suburban social capital is varied, from the very local, at the level of a neighborhood or even a single block; to the larger metropolitan region in which suburban jurisdictions and areas of suburban form are embedded. Each scale of engagement depends on defining and locating the target community or communities that stand to benefit.

CONCEPTUAL FRAMEWORKS FOR INCREASING EQUITY THROUGH SOCIAL CAPITAL

Social capital at the suburban neighborhood scale has conventionally been understood in terms of socioeconomic homogeneity. The more similar the housing and lot types

---

[4] Peter Newman, Timothy Beatley, and Heather Boyer, "Urban Resilience: Cities of Fear and Hope," *Resilient Cities, Second Edition: Overcoming Fossil Fuel Dependence* (Washington, DC: Island Press, 2017), 1–14.

[5] Ibid., 6.

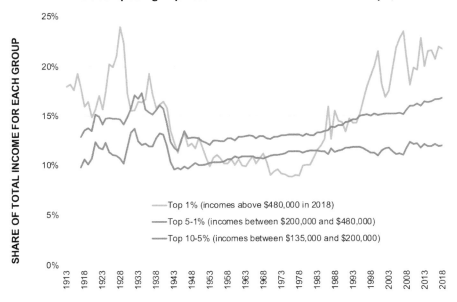

Decomposing Top 10% U.S. Income Share into 3 Groups, 1913-2018

Top 1% (incomes above $480,000 in 2018)
Top 5-1% (incomes between $200,000 and $480,000)
Top 10-5% (incomes between $135,000 and $200,000)

Source: Piketty and Saez, 2003 updated to 2018. Series based on pre-tax cash market income including realized capital gains and excluding government transfers.

Figure I.4-2 Income distribution in the US, 1913–2018, tracking the top decile of income share into three groups. While the shares accruing to both the top 10–5% and 5–1% have increased at a slight, steady rate since the end of World War II, the top 1%, beginning in the 1970s, began accruing a vastly disproportionate share of overall income, attaining levels not seen since the 1920s.
Source: From Piketty and Saez, 2003 updated to 2018. Series based on pre-tax cash market income including realized capital gains and excluding government transfers. © 2013 International Monetary Fund

are, the more likely the neighbors will come from similar backgrounds and will trust each other and build social ties. Urbanism scholar Emily Talen argues that lived experience, including social media, is so much more complex than that. She revalidates the concept of the "neighborhood," proposing an expanded notion of the *everyday neighborhood* that includes diverse uses, diverse users, and well-connected places (rather than enclaves). She argues that such an approach can foster a sense of ownership and caring without relying on social homogeneity.[6]

Shifting to the metropolitan scale, sociologists Manuel Pastor and Chris Benner synergistically advocate the active development of *diverse and dynamic epistemic communities*:

> It's a clunky term, we know, but *epistemic community* actually has an intuitive meaning: it's what you know and who you know it with. While the evidence is still tentative. . .our research suggests that such communities—ones that are diverse in their membership and sources of knowledge, and dynamic in their ability to withstand shocks, continuously learn, and adjust over time—can actually help construct and sustain regional social norms that facilitate the achievement of growth, resilience, and inclusion. In short, our ability to grow together may be fundamentally rooted in our ability to know together.[7]

Pastor and Benner propose the cultivation of metropolitan governance models and regional cultural "norms"—the

---

[6] Emily Talen, *Neighborhood* (New York: Oxford University Press, 2018). Recognizing that a neighborhood is easily reduced these days to a shaded area on a map, understood at a remote distance, through data and statistics, Talen suggests a new focus on the ways residents themselves relate to their neighborhoods as spatial units. This is vital, she asserts, for how so many people live now, navigating through the relatively undefined, overlapping, and sometimes noncontiguous expanses of space and time produced by contemporary urbanism and online social life.

[7] Manuel Pastor and Chris Benner, *Equity, Growth, and Community: What the Nation Can Learn from America's Metro Areas* (Oakland: University of California Press, 2015), 2–3.

means to "know together"—that produce not just growth, "but *just* growth—that is, economic expansion that weds prosperity and inclusion," along with the recreation of a sense of the commons and of the common good.[8] This novel framework is useful for thinking beyond zero sum-arguments, which assert that suburbs prosper at the center city's expense, and vice versa. For example, inequality is associated with a decline of faith in institutions and an erosion in the sense that different racial groups share common interests, as measured by several national surveys.[9] As Pastor and Benner note, it makes intuitive sense to relate the marked and sustained rise in inequality since the 1970s with preferences for gated residential subdivisions and the continued geographic concentration of racial and ethnic minorities and people living in poverty.[10]

To redress these trends, Pastor and Benner highlight specific diverse metro regions as models of success at balancing growth and equity, including: Salt Lake City, Utah, as shaped by the Envision Utah planning framework; Raleigh, North Carolina, where networks around the knowledge economy are floating many boats; and San Antonio, Texas, where a culture of conflict (made manifest in gated subdivisions) is responding to concerted transformation efforts, and a new culture of collaboration is emerging.

Both conceptual frameworks—Talen's local neighborhood-as-lived and diverse, and Pastor and Benner's dynamic epistemic communities that operate across large and diverse metropolitan areas—rely on social capital networks with an emphasis on so-called "weak ties," to increase equity and mitigate the stressful effects of the drastic levels of inequality that characterize northern American societies now.[11] Such informal ties have been shown to help build community resilience and faster recovery from disasters.[12]

The built environment cannot force people to get to know each other. But it can either facilitate or impede the development of weak ties. In this book we celebrate instances of suburban retrofits and retrofitting tactics that leverage suburban social capital to promote equity and justice, strengthen everyday neighborhood ties, provide more affordable housing and transportation options, increase access to economic opportunity, and sustain social diversity. At the same time, we recognize that the overall challenge is systemic and formidable. It will require sustained focus and force on multiple fronts throughout northern American societies to make truly equitable, lasting change.

DEMOGRAPHIC TRENDS IN SUBURBS AS DRIVERS OF CHANGE

The lived experience of residents in suburbia is, and always has been, diverse and complex. Suburban historians Becky Nicolaides and Andrew Wiese aptly summarize social transformations in the late modern era, since 1970, in US suburbs:

> Sweeping changes in the economy and society—the shift from a manufacturing- to service-based economy, the aging of baby boomers, profuse immigration, changing family structures, and the culmination of diverse movements for civil rights, among others—played out on the suburban stage. The result was a striking diversification of the suburban population. Suburbanites now included young singles, one-parent families, empty-nesters, retirees, gays and lesbians, and a growing share of African Americans, Latinos, and Asian Americans. By 2016, middle class white families with a male breadwinner and a stay-at-home mom—the stereotype of 1950s suburbia—were the minority. Suburbia looked more and more like America as a whole. And, of course, the reverse was also true.[13]

The suburbs of large metropolitan areas in the US and Canada are now home to the majority of their ethnic and racial minorities and immigrants. In 2010, people reporting African, Latinx, and Asian heritage comprised 28% of the suburban US population, up from 10% a

---

8 Ibid., 9.
9 Eric Uslaner, "Income Inequality in the United States Fuels Pessimism and Threatens Social Cohesion," Center for American Progress working paper, December 2012: http://www.american-progress.org/wp-content/uploads/2012/12/Uslaner.pdf. Uslaner used data from the American National Election Studies surveys between the years 1966 and 2008, the General Social Survey (1972–2010), and the Pew Values Surveys (1987–2009). See also Emmanuel Saez, "Striking It Richer: The Evolution of Top Incomes in the United States (Updated with 2017 final estimates)," UC Berkeley working paper, 2 March 2019: https://eml.berkeley.edu//~saez/
10 Pastor and Benner, *Equity, Growth, and Community,* 8–9.
11 The sociological concept of weak ties proposes the power of informal acquaintances and loose affinities to bridge to new networks.
12 Daniel P. Aldrich, *Building Resilience; Social Capital in Post-Disaster Recovery* (Chicago: University of Chicago Press, 2012).

---

13 Becky Nicolaides and Andrew Wiese, *The Suburb Reader,* 2nd ed. (New York: Routledge, 2016), 439.

Figure I.4-3 The commercial epicenter of the South Asian community in New Jersey, Oak Tree Road runs through the towns of Iselin and Edison. Shopfronts and strip malls are filled with jewelers, sari stores, restaurants, and specialty food markets. Source: Photo by Belma Fisha, 2018.

generation earlier.[14] During the same period, foreign-born Americans rose to 13% from less than 5% of the population, with around half of the foreign born settled in suburbs. The top three countries of origin shifted from Italy, Canada, and Germany in 1970 to Mexico, China, and India today.[15]

Asian Americans, in particular, have concentrated in suburbs; the geographer Wei Li coined the term "eth-noburb" to describe the new type of largely immigrant suburb, found in places often, but not always, associated with the high-tech economy: southern California's San Gabriel Valley and Silicon Valley; North Austin, Texas; Research Triangle Park in North Carolina; the Dulles corridor near Washington, D.C.; Johns Creek, Georgia; central New Jersey; and Toronto suburbs such as Brampton and

Markham.[16] While the primary driver of suburban growth in Latinx and Asian American populations was immigration, the sizeable demographic shifts also reflect the rise of a second-generation, American-born middle class.[17]

By 2010 approximately 40% of Black Americans were also settled in suburbs. Their experiences vary tremendously. Scholars have decisively demonstrated that as Black Americans achieved homeownership, they haven't realized the same home equity and wealth building gains as other groups. There is an explosion of recent scholarly literature plumbing the depths of structural racism in land planning and development in the US, with multiple voices calling for some form of reparations or legal remedy.[18] While these topics are beyond the scope of this chapter, awareness of

[14] William H. Frey, "Melting Pot Cities and Suburbs: Racial and Ethnic Change in Metro America in the 2000s," State of Metropolitan America series, no. 30, Brookings Institution, 4 May 2011; Audrey Singer and Jill H. Wilson, "Immigrants in 2010 Metropolitan America: A Decade of Change," State of Metropolitan America series, no. 41, Brookings Institution, 13 October 2011.

[15] Pew Research Center, "Modern Immigration Wave Brings 59 Million to U.S., Driving Population Growth and Change Through 2065: Views of Immigration's Impact on U.S. Society Mixed" (Washington, DC: Pew Research Center Report), September 2015. See also Mary E. Odem, "Latin American Immigration and the New Multiethnic South," in Matthew Lassiter and Joseph Crespino, eds., The Myth of Southern Exceptionalism (Oxford, UK: Oxford University Press, 2010).

[16] Wei Li, "Anatomy of a New Ethnic Settlement: the Chinese Ethnoburb in Los Angeles," Urban Studies, 35(3), 2016: 479-501; Wei Li, Ethnoburb: The New Ethnic Community in Urban America (Honolulu: University of Hawai'i Press, 2009); Wei Li and Lucia Lo, "New Geographies of Migration? A Canada-U.S. Comparison of Highly Skilled Chinese and Indian Migration," Journal of Asian American Studies 15(I), February 2012: 1–34.

[17] Singer and Wilson, "Immigrants in 2010 Metropolitan America," 8–11.

[18] Richard Rothstein summarizes the troubling history and outlines an argument for legal remedies in The Color of Law: A Forgotten History of How Our Government Segregated America (New York: Liveright, 2017). See also Bruce Mitchell and Juan Franco, "HOLC 'Redlining' Maps: The Persistent Structure of Segregation and Economic Inequality," National Community Reinvestment Coalition report (20 March 2018); University of Richmond "Mapping Inequality" project: https://dsl.richmond.edu/panorama/redlining/.

how suburbanization has been inequitably experienced by various groups over time is significant to our narrative of the need to build trust in order to leverage suburban social capital for equity.

Poverty has increased in suburbs, dramatically in some places.[19] While poverty rates remain higher in cities, the total number of impoverished Americans living in census tracts in suburbs surpassed those in cities and rural areas in 2008 and continues to increase at a faster rate, nearly three times population growth.[20] Moreover, as political scientist Scott Allard points out, "Poverty is pervasive across the suburban regions of *all* metro areas, whether they're new or old. In fact, the rates of change have been more severe in newer suburbs—those built after 1970—than in older suburbs."[21] The news isn't all bad, with many suburbs deemed likely to recover.[22]

The trends, however, demand examination. How can suburban retrofits be leveraged to increase access to decent housing and to open paths to better education and employment opportunities? How can policies and programs optimize housing stability and reduce the threat of foreclosure or eviction?

A FRAMEWORK FOR ASSERTING THE ROLE OF DESIGN IN ACHIEVING SOCIAL DIVERSITY

In northern America, especially in the United States, the geography of wealth and poverty is coarsely grained, with little mixing. While racial and ethnic diversity within neighborhoods is increasing, the same cannot be said of socioeconomic diversity—mixing by class and income. The dominant mass suburbanization processes of the twentieth century, characterized by models that grossly favored homogeneity within increments of development, had a lot to do with the current levels of social segregation. As Emily Talen and Sungduck Lee explain in *Design for Social Diversity*, "Where pre-20th century urban form accommodated social mixing, urban form after the 1920s thwarted the ability of classes to mix, even if they had wanted to. Racial prejudice complicated and accentuated the situation.. . .The consequences of failing to deliver an urban framework more supportive of social diversity have been monumental."[23]

What role, if any, can the design professions play in achieving increased social diversity? Talen and Lee assert that there are design principles that can help nurture and sustain diverse places. This is not to say that design of the built environment can create diversity, but that it can respond to evidence about the physical conditions, over which designers do have control, in which diversity is supported and may thrive. The three key design requirements Talen and Lee outline are mix, connection, and security.

How do we do it? Talen and Lee suggest:

It is a matter of reversing the rules by which social segregation occurred: allowing multi-family units where they have been excluded, and eliminating rigid building codes, minimum lot size, maximum density, minimum setbacks, and other barriers to infill development. This may also require changing lending policy, capital improvements budgeting, and the protocols of the home-building industry, which tend to favor large, single-use and single-type developments.[24]

To critics skeptical of the power of design to support social goals, Talen and Lee respond with two key points: 1) vitalization efforts are needed despite dominant gentrification narratives, as the net trend is towards more, not fewer, poor enclaves in the US; and 2) more focus is needed on measures of "neighborhood functionality" (i.e. the availability of services and amenities) rather than "social interaction," in recognition that the desire and toleration for social mix varies by cultural background. Good design

[19] Elizabeth Kneebone and Alan Berube, *Confronting Suburban Poverty in America* (Washington DC: Brookings Institution Press, 2013); Katrin B. Anaker, ed., *The New American Suburb: Poverty, Race, and the Economic* Crisis (Farnham, Surrey, UK: Ashgate, 2015). See also "American Poverty Is Moving from the Cities to the Suburbs," *Economist*, 26 September 2019.

[20] Scott Allard, *Places in Need; The Changing Geography of Poverty* (New York: Russell Sage Foundation, 2017).

[21] Interview by Tanvi Misra, "Confronting the Myths of Suburban Poverty," *CityLab*, 6 July 2017.

[22] A study of neighborhood trajectories from 1970 to 2010 in the 100 most populous US metros by Harvard's Joint Center for Housing Studies argues, "Despite increased discussions around suburban decline and suburban poverty, suburban neighbourhoods maintained a higher status than the city, were more likely to recover from reduced status and had higher frequencies of status improvement." Whitney Airgood-Obrycki, "Suburban Status and Neighbourhood Change," *Urban Studies*, 30 January 2019.

[23] Emily Talen and Sungduck Lee, *Design for Social Diversity*, 2nd ed. (New York: Routledge, 2018), 2–3.

[24] Ibid., 30.

Design for Social Diversity, adapted from Talen and Lee

MIX

In terms of *mix*, design for a built environment that sustains social diversity by including buildings of various ages (through a combination of preservation, reinhabitation, and new construction); housing of different types; zoning that allows complementary uses to be combined horizontally (side by side) or vertically (stacked in the same building); and uses that attract different people to the area at various times of day and night. These are requirements recognized to some degree by Jane Jacobs decades ago in her classic 1961 book *The Death and Life of Great American Cities*.

CONNECTION

Design for *connection* in the physical built environment by identifying and providing collective spaces and institutions and through intensifying street and path networks. Remove physical barriers, such as fences and gates, and improve roads with sidewalks, crosswalks, benches, and street trees. Permit small-scale infill and design small public plazas to allow people the opportunity to have social encounters while going about daily routines, to make eye contact with a stranger, and perhaps even strike up a conversation.

SECURITY

Providing a sense of *security* is vital to comfort. People fear crime and disorder, of course. This formulation, however, refers to the need for people to feel secure about the mixing and increased connections required in a truly diverse place. Feelings of insecurity may manifest in resistance and discomfort due to fears of displacement, on the one hand, and requests for excessive and ineffectual walls and gates due to fears of change, on the other hand. Adopt policies to provide small grants or rent stabilization programs for residents to make improvements in place. Encourage the establishment of new locations for institutions that provide support for "bridging" social capital, through formation of weak ties among people of different socioeconomic backgrounds. This can be accomplished by infill development on parking lots or by reinhabiting a dead big box store or other former retail space with this type of community-serving use. By providing shelter for groups to meet and organize, these physical home bases become local empowerment centers.[25]

can be used to channel policies and can serve as a potent catalyst for renewing attention on the civil, public realm. Conversely, inattention to design matters could undermine other efforts to increase diversity.[26]

THIRD PLACE REDUX

The sociological concept of the "third place," as introduced and popularized by Ray Oldenburg since the 1970s, continues to resonate with the suburban retrofitting agenda and is worth revisiting. To recap, a third place is not home, nor the site of work; instead it is an informal gathering place where "regulars" go to socialize in convivial company.[27] Ideally, the hosting location for such gathering is an independent, locally owned establishment—a coffee shop, brewpub, barbershop, board game cafe—although whole retail chains have sprung up that profit from fulfilling people's thirst for third places.

The classic representations of third places in popular culture are set in center city locales: the *Cheers* bar, Central Perk in *Friends,* the barbershop in *Barbershop*. Social life in popular television shows set in suburbs, from the 1970s soap drama *Knots Landing* to the 2010s sitcom *Modern Family,* tends to happen in a cul-de-sac or around an open kitchen island. Is America ready for new shows and films

---

[25] For a recent study on the role physical buildings played in nurturing radical sociopolitical movements in Manhattan by providing places to meet and organize, see Nandini Bagchee, *Counter Institution: Activist Estates of the Lower East Side* (New York: Fordham University Press 2018).

[26] Talen and Lee, *Design for Social Diversity*, 41–53.
[27] Dunham-Jones and Williamson, *Retrofitting Suburbia*, 59–60.

set in retrofitted suburban third places? We think so. (Scriptwriters: we are available to consult.)

Countless small grocery-anchored strip shopping centers have potential to be consciously reshaped into third place neighborhood anchors, with the addition of covered seating, breezeways, decent coffee, and management policies that tolerate some degree of purposeful "loitering." Public buildings, such as branch libraries, facilities for older residents, and recreation centers, are also suitable meeting places. In mild climates and good weather, people meet and congregate in outdoor public squares, gardens, and playgrounds. People sorely need places to both hang out and engage in some degree of healthy physical activity; and public and philanthropic funding can be available for suitable reinhabitations of vacant big box stores. If anything, temporary social distancing protocols instituted during virus outbreaks highlight the need. Large developers have taken note, purposefully programming third place–type areas in large redevelopment retrofits.

Oldenburg makes an important point about third places and the sociopolitical exchanges vital to the thriving of democracy: "Third places have been targeted for elimination under several monarchies and under fascist and Communist governments. Those in power fear that when citizens get together to talk, what is said may be critical of the regime and foment dissent."[28] All the more reason to advocate for their inclusion in suburban retrofits in these politically polarized times. A healthy democracy relies and thrives on good talk.

Suburban historians have documented some of the ways that suburban talk reinforced boundaries and exclusionary impulses, such as racially animated anti–school busing activism in the 1970s and 1980s, and "circle-the-wagons" defenses of low-density zoning under the guise of protecting a vaguely defined "quality of life."[29] The acronym NIMBY ("Not In My Back Yard"), a term coined around 1980, is lobbed at vocal constituencies in changing suburbs that vehemently oppose just about anything new that is proposed anywhere, and who consistently advocate for preservation of the status quo.

Yet there are powerful counter-narratives, put forward by new political coalitions seeking to offset such impulses.

The YIMBY ("Yes In My Back Yard") movement thrives in areas with extremely high housing costs, such as the Bay Area of California, Boston and Cambridge in Massachusetts, and metropolitan New York. The rallying cry is to consider the needs of future residents, not just the preferences of current residents, and promote policies that will add to the housing supply, encourage alternate-energy and green building design, and reduce auto dependency by, for example, substituting parking maximums in place of parking minimums in zoning codes.

We are eager to follow the future grassroots initiatives that will bubble up from conversations started in newly established suburban third places.

See these case studies:

- II.3. Lake Grove Village, Lake Oswego, Oregon
- II.22. Collinwood Recreation Center, Cleveland, Ohio
- II.23. The Mosaic District, Merrifield, Virginia
- II.32. Assembly Square, Somerville, Massachusetts

SOCIAL CAPITAL IN ETHNOBURBS

How is social capital being leveraged in ethnoburbs—that is, the suburbs with large numbers of residents from ethnic minorities, many of whom are first- or second-generation immigrants? Asian Americans are the fastest-growing group in US suburbs, with more than 60% living in the suburbs of the 100 largest US metropolitan areas. As urban planning scholar Willow Lung-Amam asserts in *Trespassers*, her study of Asian Americans as place makers and community builders throughout Silicon Valley in California, they are nearly as suburban as white Americans.[30]

But they are also embattled, as efforts to "weave their dreams within the valley's existing spatial fabric" are met with skepticism and even distain.[31] When new groups settle in places, they begin to impress their ideas upon the landscape, establishing networks though social connections, often formed in third places. In Silicon Valley's Fremont, as Lung-Amam documents, this happens in ethnic shopping centers, Buddhist temples, and Chinese schools.

Ethnic shopping centers are central to the lives of Asian suburbanites, who go to them to shop for specialized foods, goods, and services, and to forge bonds with the

---

[28] Ray Oldenburg, *The Great Good Place* (New York: Paragon, 1989).
[29] For one example among many, see Lily Geismer, "Good Neighbors for Fair Housing: Suburban Liberalism and Racial Inequality in Metropolitan Boston," *Journal of Urban History* 39:3 (May 2013): 454–477.

[30] Willow Lung-Amam, *Trespassers: Asian Americans and the Battle for Suburbia* (Oakland: University of California Press, 2017), 5.
[31] Ibid., 6–7.

larger Asian diaspora. Some of these malls are newly built, while many others are reinhabitations of older malls, retrofitted with new tenants, comprising a wide range of independent retailers. Asian malls are popular destinations on cultural holidays, when they play host to celebrations and festivals, and property managers schedule events with cultural themes, such as kite-making workshops and kung fu demonstrations.

While first-generation Asian immigrants do much of their shopping and socializing at ethnic malls, second-generation youths may go only occasionally, to reconnect with their ethnic heritage while also accessing feelings of being typically American.[32] The title of the Asian supermarket chain 99 Ranch Market signals the duel identity: "99" references Chinese numerology (eternity), while "ranch" references the American setting.[33]

Similarly, several older malls have been reinhabited as Hispanic-themed centers in locations where Latinx suburbanites are concentrated, as at La Gran Plaza de Fort Worth. In Canada, rezoning around Toronto's 1960s-era suburban high-rises is intended to enable local immigrants to set up small businesses in infill redevelopment. In Indianapolis, Indiana, Lafayette Square mall has been converted to the International Marketplace, where former box stores are now a Latinx grocery and butcher shop, a Latinx event center, and the International Village Welcome Center. Community activist Mary Gurnell Clark, executive director of the nonprofit International Marketplace Coalition, started out trying to keep big box businesses from leaving the surrounding 2½-square-mile area, then switched to advocating repurposing commercial buildings with locally owned businesses. Of her organization's global village approach, she says, "Our immigrant brothers and sisters aren't taking jobs, they're creating jobs."[34]

A bottom-up approach is also evident in efforts that seek to empower and advance immigrants in lower-density neighborhoods by reestablishing roots to agricultural practices. Meet Each Need with Dignity (MEND) is an antipoverty organization operating in Pacoima, a very low-income, once industrial, and now predominantly Latinx neighborhood in Los Angeles's San Fernando Valley. The organization's Growing Together Project promotes residential backyard gardens as spaces for participating families to build social capital while growing edible food. Many of the families come from agricultural backgrounds and the project not only connects them together, but it can also save them money, while empowering them to consume a healthier diet.[35]

See this case study:

- II.9. La Gran Plaza, Fort Worth, Texas

PROVIDING MORE HOUSING TYPES AND CHOICES, INCLUDING UNITS FOR RENT

While anxiety in suburbanites about upward mobility and home values has long been manifest, the foreclosure crisis of the 2008 Great Recession clearly exposed rifts.[36] The high risk of relying on a singular suburban housing "product" comprising detached houses, offered for sale rather than for rent, the only variables being dwelling size and price points, came sharply into focus. Indeed, in the recession's wake, many foreclosed detached houses entered and have remained in the rental market, with black neighborhoods in diverse metros like Atlanta disproportionately affected.[37]

The reification and protection of single-family housing—via R-1 zoning and other means—is under direct challenge by reformers. In 2019 Minneapolis, Minnesota, became the first major US city to end single-family home only zoning, a policy that, in the words of urbanism journalist Henry Grabar, "has done as much as any to entrench segregation, high housing costs, and sprawl as

[32] Ibid., 98–137.
[33] Patricia Leigh Brown, "The New Chinatown? Try the Asian Mall," New York Times, 24 March 2003.
[34] Valerie Vande Panne, "How Abandoned Big-Box Stores Can Bring Communities Together," Next City blog, 11 March 2019: https://nextcity.org/features/view/how-abandoned-big-box-stores-can-bring-communities-together.
[35] Bhavna Shamasunder, et al., "Growing Together: Poverty Alleviation, Community Building, and Environmental Justice through Home Gardens in Pacoima, Los Angeles," Environmental Justice, 8:3 (2015): 72–77.
[36] For a fine-grained anthropological study of the heady pre-recession in a New Jersey suburb, see Rachel Heiman, Driving after Class: Anxious Times in an American Suburb (Oakland: University of California Press, 2015). Heiman is now doing fieldwork in the vast new urbanist community of Daybreak, Utah.
[37] Elora Raymond, Kyungsoon Wang, and Dan Immergluck, "Race and uneven recovery: neighborhood home value trajectories in Atlanta before and after the housing crisis," Housing Studies, 31:3 (2006): 324–339, DOI: 10.1080/02673037.2015.1080821

Figure I.4-4 In a city not typically associated with suburban form, the long derelict single-story 1960s-era Far Rockaway strip shopping center with a vast parking lot in the outer reaches of Queens, New York, near a terminus of the A Train (the site once included a rail yard) is being replaced. The new Rockaway Village includes hundreds of deeply affordable apartments over new retail, community-serving amenities, and a walkable network of civic spaces. Designed by Marvel Architects, the ambitious strip mall retrofit is being developed by venerable non-profit Phipps Houses. Source: Courtesy of Marvel Architects.

the American urban paradigm over the past century."[38] Many municipalities have already become much more accepting of second units and granny flats. We expect more of this in future.

Residential development monocultures are obsolete precisely because they aren't resilient in the face of economic shocks. The residential subdivision of Windy Ridge, outside Charlotte, North Carolina, is a poignant example. Built next to industrial uses, far from transit, it was rendered "zombie" by absentee owners and multiple foreclosures, then made notorious by "The Next Slum?" a widely read 2008 article by Christopher Leinberger in *The Atlantic* magazine. The "growth machine" planning processes under which the subdivision was approved meant it was "built to fail," particularly with respect to environmental and social justice issues.[39] Revivifying such zombie subdivisions is difficult.

Protectionism of single-family house neighborhoods—against "encroachment," or erosion of visual character or quality of life, or whatever coded language is used by

NIMBYs—serves to drive up housing costs. Developers associated with groups such as LOCUS, a partner with Smart Growth America, argue persuasively that these obstructionist positions are an impediment to allowing market forces to meet real and sizable demand for other housing types and choices, preferably located in transit-served locations with walkable urban form. This includes high demand in many suburban real estate markets for units offered for rent at a range of prices; rental units can provide location mobility to those not interested in being tied to a mortgage, regardless of income.

But many northern American neighborhoods are filled with an array of older residential buildings that don't fit neatly into either category and which are only weakly encouraged, or even recognized, in typical planning and zoning regulation or typical real estate development pro forma document. These housing types—now described and categorized thanks to Dan and Karen Parolek as the *missing middle*, comprised of duplexes, fourplexes, and so on—provide an avenue for incrementally introducing more housing choices, at a greater range of prices and rents. It's a toolbox of types for urban designers and architects to play with. Cottages on Greene, in Rhode Island, is a small example of a cottage court, Wyandanch Rising on Long Island is a medium example featuring mid-rise apartments and townhouses, while Mueller in Texas is an extra-large planned community where a range of types are intentionally mixed.

[38] R-1 zoning typically limits housing to only one dwelling unit per lot and frequently requires a large minimum lot size, and sizable front, rear, and side yards. Henry Grabar, "Minneapolis Confronts Its History of Housing Segregation," *Slate* blog, 7 December 2018.

[39] Janni Sorensen, Jose Gamez, and Melissa Currie, "Windy Ridge: A neighborhood built to fail," *Applied Geography* 51 (2014): 8–25. Christopher B. Leinberger, "The Next Slum?" *The Atlantic*, March 2008.

See these case studies:

- II.12. Mueller, Austin, Texas
- II.20. Walker's Bend, Covington, Georgia
- II.29. Wyandanch Rising, Town of Babylon, New York
- II.31. Cottages on Greene, East Greenwich, Rhode Island

PROTECTING APARTMENTS UNDER THREAT

In many suburban areas there is development pressure to demolish the aging garden apartment complexes, old motels, and mobile home parks that have provided a precarious lifeline of low rents to lower-income residents. How might retrofitting protect access to housing affordability in these conditions? Based on studies of metro Baltimore, planning scholars Bernadette Hanlon and Whitney Airgood-Obrycki suggest that "suburban planners take a more active role in considering the potential direct and indirect displacement of low-income residents from redeveloped suburban spaces. This is imperative as inner-ring suburban devalorization occurs and suburban poverty grows."[40]

In recent years Fulton County, Georgia, lost over 250 one- to three-story apartment complexes containing 9,000 affordable units, approximately 9% of the local stock, mostly to obsolescence.[41] In nearby Cobb County, voters in the town of Marietta narrowly passed a controversial bond issue to fund the purchase and demolition of 1,300 units in four older apartment complexes and one strip mall on Franklin Road to build a new soccer team training facility and sports complex. The low-income renters had to find suitable housing elsewhere. The project has been both sharply criticized and celebrated with a regional redevelopment award.[42]

Nationwide, CoStar estimates that unsubsidized "utilitarian apartment buildings with minimal architectural finishes, amenities and certifications" account for three-quarters of all multifamily properties in a database of nearly 335,000 properties—calling them "Naturally Occurring Affordable Housing."[43] Recognition of their value as assets in the midst of an affordable housing crisis is growing, but so is the temptation to redevelop and densify them. One way to prevent direct displacement is by promoting and supporting the use of creative financing—usually patient capital—to devise ways of remodeling run-down structures and sites, when viable, into upgraded housing for the existing residents.

Sometimes even a small reinhabitation to benefit precarious lives can have systemic ripple effects. The efforts of Marjy Stagmeier, a renowned real estate asset manager in the Atlanta area, is instructive.[44] In 2006, on behalf of investors, her company acquired a 30-year old blighted apartment complex of 450 units in Marietta, Georgia, more than half of them burned out or filled with mold. This was housing of last resort for its transient tenants, the majority of whom were single mothers working minimum-wage jobs, whose children were struggling academically. Stagmeier made significant repairs, but the most important change was converting one apartment into a space for an after-school program. Through the students getting to know each other, so did the parents. They began helping one another out and occupancy stabilized, increasing Stagmeier's profits. By 2012 the formerly failing local elementary school had turned around too.

Stagmeier is taking the model to scale and preaching the profitability of stabilizing neighborhoods and not raising rents. Her company, TriStar, and new nonprofit, Star-C, have replicated their results with several more aging suburban apartment complexes in the worst-performing school districts around Metro Atlanta and expect further expansion.[45] In addition to fortifying social

---

[40] Bernadette Hanlon and Whitney Airgood-Obrycki, "Suburban revalorization: Residential infill and rehabilitation in Baltimore County's older suburbs," *Environment and Planning A: Economy and Space*, 50:4 (2018): 1–27.

[41] These losses, comprising approximately 9% of the total such apartments in the area, took place from 2008 to 2016. Matt Bedsole, "You'll Miss Me When I'm Gone: Garden Apartment Losses in Fulton County, 2008–2016," 27 April 2017, Georgia Institute of Technology student paper.

[42] Joe Cortright, "Why aren't we talking about Marietta, Georgia?" *City Observatory* blog, 14 July 2015.

[43] Archana Pyati, "New CoStar Data Reveal a Vast National Inventory of Naturally Occurring Affordable Housing – and an Untapped Opportunity," *Urban Land*, 24 October 2016.

[44] Jen Christensen, "Compassionate capitalist: Real estate whiz Marjy Stagmeier is changing the lives of her tenants, one apartment complex at a time," *Atlanta Journal-Constitution*, 21 August 2016: http://specials.myajc.com/compassionate-capitalist/.

[45] Indian Creek Elementary School went from being the second-worst-performing school in Georgia to winning awards from the governor's office for greatest gains three years in a row. Residents are benefitting too. Move-out rates at Willow Branch Apartments are 35% vs the national average of 70% and 40% of those who move out are doing so to become homeowners versus 11% national average. Statistics from Star-C board member Lianne Epstein, "Building from Place," presentation at CNU 27, Louisville, KY, 12 June 2019.

infrastructure within their properties with after-school and summer camp programs, community gardens, and healthcare programs, they're also building local partnerships to leverage the anticipated rise in property values for incremental, equitable improvements to the larger neighborhood—including much needed grocery stores and parks, fresh job opportunities, upgraded walkability and transit options, and greater access for the residents' voice in the community.

The Home Front at Camp Anza in Riverside, California, is another example. A long-neglected World War II–era army officer's club building was faithfully restored (winning a state preservation award) and surrounded by 30 apartments for very low-income and disabled veterans and their families.[46]

Sometimes demolition is deemed necessary for older apartments, whether due to environmental threat such as flooding or the opportunity and need for more units on sites adjacent to mass transit. In these cases, displacement can be prevented when retrofits are planned, whether by policy or choice, to rehouse former residents in the newly built apartments or nearby, as near the Fort Totten Metro station in Washington, DC, at Parkmerced in San Francisco, and in downtown Meriden, Connecticut.

As a plethora of research from the Center for Neighborhood Technology (CNT) shows, households in neighborhoods with high location efficiency—places that score high on measures of local convenience, access to goods and amenities, walkability, and transportation choice—spend significantly less on transportation than elsewhere.[47] Affordability for many may be best served by adding more housing units on sites with high location efficiency, and those with lower incomes may be best positioned to reap the affordability gains by foregoing automobile ownership and use. However, it is vital that access to the housing is maintained. In transit-rich locations, we're very likely to vote in favor of significant densification. But we also advocate strongly that rezoning of apartment building communities should require 100%

replacement affordable units to the existing tenants. This does not happen nearly enough.

See these case studies:

- II.4. Phoenix Park, Sacramento, California
- II.5. Parkmerced, San Francisco, California
- II.24. South Dakota Avenue and Riggs Road, Fort Totten TOD, Washington, DC
- II.30. Meriden Green, Meriden, Connecticut

A RIGHT TO THE SUBURB? THE PUBLIC REALM

A final aspect of leveraging suburban social capital to promote equity and justice involves redressing the public or civil realm, often an impoverished aspect of conventional suburban form. To begin, here's a quick recap of the notion of "the right to the city." French theorist Henri Lefebvre proposed the concept in 1968 as a call to claim the future city as a co-created space, produced by citizens collectively, and to counteract prevailing economic and political forces producing inequalities.[48] The concept has been reframed by some scholars to include "the right to the suburb," in recognition of a need to theorize periphery areas, not only in France's banlieues, but also in diverse and struggling suburbs elsewhere.[49]

The ways the public realm can be co-created through retrofits varies, from incorporating complete streets and more connected landscapes, to applying bottom-up, short-term "tactical urbanism" techniques to induce longer-term change, to supporting the reemergence of the commons. It's vital to understand that spaces that *look* public in form (with sidewalks, etc.) should actually afford people the rights commonly associated with public space.[50]

The idea of *complete streets* is fast becoming a "best practice" approach, through the advocacy of the National

[46] Christine Serlin, "Former World War II Base Gets New Life as Vets Housing," *Affordable Housing Finance*, 8 November 2016: https://www.housingfinance.com/developments/former-world-war-ii-base-gets-new-life-as-vets-housing_o. See also: https://www.wakelandhdc.com/home-front-at-camp-anza.html

[47] Scott Bernstein and Peter Haas, "Yes, Transit-Rich Neighborhoods Are More Affordable," *CityLab*, 29 May 2018.

[48] For a version in English, see Henri Lefebvre, "The Right to the City," in Eleonore Kofman and Elizabeth Lebas, eds., *Writings on Cities* (Oxford: Blackwell Publishers, 1996), 147–159.

[49] Genevieve Carpio, Clara Irazabal, and Laura Pulido, "Right to the Suburb? Rethinking Lefebvre and Immigrant Activism," *Journal of Urban Affairs* 33 (2011): 185–208; Dianne Harris, "The Rights to the Suburb," *The Aggregate* blog (March 2015), http://www.we-aggregate.org/piece/the-rights-to-the-suburb.

[50] June Williamson, "Protest on the Astroturf at Downtown Silver Spring: July 4, 2007," in Christopher Niedt, ed., *Social Justice in Diverse Suburbs: History, Politics, and Prospects*. (Philadelphia: Temple University Press, 2013), 54–69.

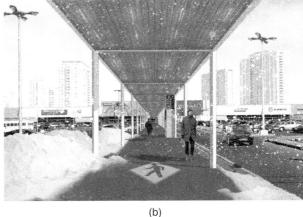

(a)   (b)

Figure I.4-5 "Knuckles and Jogs" by architect Michael Piper for Toronto Metrolink proposes a series of pedestrian paths as all-season shortcuts connecting through superblock high-rise, low-income neighborhoods in the Toronto suburbs. The paths would cut across private land as necessary to serve residents' needs for a better public realm and more direct access to transit.
Source: Michael Piper of Dub Studios, 2015.

Association of City Transportation Officials (NACTO) and others. *Complete streets* are rights-of-way designed (or redesigned) to accommodate and balance a full range of users—pedestrians, bicyclists, cars, buses, service vehicles—rather than privileging and optimizing for the drivers of private automobiles. The benefits are increased safety, but also equity in that some pedestrians, bicyclists, and bus rides are unable to drive, cannot afford it, or for other reasons don't have access to use of a private automobile.

As for the reemergence of the civic commons in the public realm, including as a space for protest, architects Andrea Woodner and Claire Weisz of the Design Trust for Public Space remind us:

> Parks as green space are not always the answer to what public space should be. (Even Olmsted believed that the sidewalks outside the rusticated walls of his Central Park were as much parkland as the acreage within.) We need to continue to imagine and invite new uses and forms for our civic commons. Problems can arise when neighborhood boundaries become barriers. When conceived as connective tissue, public space can breach neighborhood boundaries, help to ameliorate inequality, and build social cohesion locally while solving urban issues on a larger scale. This approach can tap into different budgets. Public spaces

can be platforms for a variety of exchanges, whether they are economic, social, or political. Protest is essential to preserving democracy, and it is critical that urban space and governance accommodate it.[51]

A new common town green might emerge from a former grayfield condition, where an asphalt parking lot is depaved and regreened. To best support a robust, social-capital-inducing public, designers should configure the green as a shared open common, accessible to the many, and, if resources permit, programmed with community-serving activities. While providing ecological services is an important function of increasing permeable surfaces in suburbs, the equity and justice aims are best met by providing *socially* minded services.

Toronto-based geographer Paul Hess has documented the many ways residents of that city's inner suburban master planned apartment block developments frequently subvert the restrictions of the superblock planning models and engage in "transgressive" practices to forge short cuts across private property for collective use.[52]

See these case studies:

- II.7. TAXI, Denver, Colorado
- II.8. Guthrie Green, Tulsa, Oklahoma

---

[51] Andrea Woodner and Claire Weisz, *Sharing the City: Learning from the New York City Public Space Movement 1990–2015* (New York: SharingTheCity.net, 2017).

[52] Paul M. Hess, "Property, Planning and Bottom-Up Pedestrian Spaces in Toronto's Post-war Suburbs," Mahyar Arefi and Conrad Kickert, eds., *The Palgrave Handbook of Bottom-Up Urbanism* (Palgrave Macmillan, 2019), 287–304.

RETROFITTING THE SUBURBAN SOCIAL BODY

We urge that all present and future suburban retrofitting initiatives be mindful of Angela Glover Blackwell's warning about history's penchant to repeat itself, especially at a time when the most vulnerable people are increasingly found in suburban communities, whether due to stagnant and falling incomes, social isolation, or an impoverished public realm. To raise the bar, it is no longer enough to repair the degraded and obsolete suburban built form—the suburban physical body—but it is also an imperative to nurture and support the suburban social body, for the benefit of all.

Chapter I.5
Compete for Jobs

So, rather than decentralizing the American labor pool, the rise of the internet and digital technologies had the opposite effect: It accelerated its concentration.[1]

Daniel Oberhaus, staff writer at *Wired*

The success of suburbia has long been predicated on providing good jobs with the kind of security and stability that built the middle class and enabled workers to build wealth, invest in their children's education, and support their communities. Today, many suburbs are confronting a double whammy: the shrinking middle class upon which their job base and tax revenue has historically depended and, as Daniel Oberhaus observes, a technologically enhanced generational shift away from "job sprawl" toward agglomeration, toward the advantages of urbanism.

The US middle class has been consistently shrinking from 61% of the population in 1971 to 50% in 2015.[2] Some of this is caused by new technologies that have replaced many middle-skilled routine jobs with new high- and low-skilled jobs. However, most of the blame is attributed to stagnant wages unable to support the rising cost of living.[3] From 1990 to 2018, median earnings increased 117% but the cost of housing rose 130%, medical care went up 189%, and college tuition climbed 374%.[4]

It isn't only the US whose middle class is shrinking. So are those of the 42 member countries of the Organisation for Economic Cooperation and Development, (OECD). An extensively researched OECD report says:

Middle incomes have indeed barely grown, in both relative and absolute terms in most OECD countries. Overall, over the past 30 years, median incomes increased a third less than the average income of the richest 10%. In parallel, the cost of essential parts of the middle-class lifestyle have increased faster than inflation; house prices have been growing three times faster than household median income over the last two decades. This happened in the context of rising job insecurity in fast transforming labour markets. One-in-six current middle-income jobs face high risk of automation. More than one-in-five middle-income households spend more than they earn. Over-indebtedness is higher for middle-income than for both low- and high-income households. As a result, today the middle class looks increasingly like a boat in rocky waters.[5]

The shrinking middle class is resulting in a widening wealth gap and a new geography of inequality is emerging with communities at both ends of the spectrum taking hits.[6] Lower-income suburbs, many of them former manufacturing hubs that lost their job base to offshoring in

---

[1] Daniel Oberhaus, "How Smaller Cities Are Trying to Plug the Brain Drain," *Wired*, 12 August 2019.

[2] Pew Research Center, "The American Middle Class is Losing Ground," *Social & Demographic Trends*, 9 December 2015: https://www.pewsocialtrends.org/2015/12/09/the-american-middle-class-is-losing-ground/.

[3] See Drew Desilver, "For Most US Workers, Real Wages Have Barely Budged in Decades," Fact Tank, 7 August 2018, Pew Research: https://www.pewresearch.org/fact-tank/2018/08/07/for-most-us-workers-real-wages-have-barely-budged-for-decades/

[4] More costs are discussed in: Fortune Staff, "The Shrinking Middle Class," *Fortune*, 20 December 2018.

[5] Middle-income households, defined as earning between 75% and 200% of the median national income make up, on average, 61% of the population of OECD countries. This is a decline from 64% in the mid-1980s. OECD, *Under Pressure: The Squeezed Middle Class*, (Paris: OECD Publishing, 2019): https://doi.org/10.1787/689afed1-en: 21: 15.

[6] See Enrico Moretti, *The New Geography of Jobs* (New York: Houghton Mifflin Harcourt, 2012), and Bill Bishop, *The Big Sort: Why the Clustering of America is Tearing Us Apart* (New York: Houghton Mifflin Harcourt, 2008).

Figure I.5-1 Most new jobs in the US by 2028 are projected to be in the service and medical sectors. The highest-wage, highest-growth areas are nursing, management, and software tech. All of these occupations can be expected in suburban retrofits. But will the 78% of workers in jobs earning less than $70k be able to afford new redevelopments? Source: Authors.

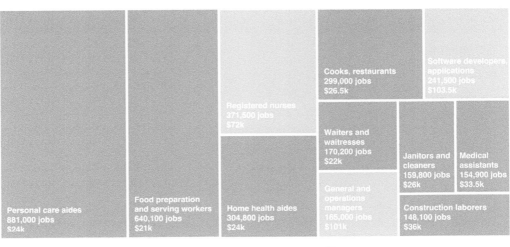

Most New Jobs in the United States
Occupation and number of new jobs (projected), 2018-2028

Source: U.S. Bureau of Labor Statistics

▪ 2018 median pay below $36,000
▪ 2018 median pay above $70,000

the 1970s and 1980s, still haven't recovered and are seeing increases in poverty. Higher-income suburbs that grew up around suburban office parks and corporate campuses are now seeing job losses as those properties start emptying out. Their TAMI tenants (technology, advertising, media, and information) are increasingly moving to "innovation districts" with "creative office" lofts in both downtowns and urbanized suburban retrofits that provide live-work-walk environments and transit access.[7] *Urbanism*—a desirable mix of uses, walkable urban form, and lively streetscapes rather than remote megastructures set in lush verdant landscapes accessible only by car—is the new amenity companies are increasingly looking for to attract the next generation of skilled employees. Suburban retrofits in suburbs of all kinds are helping communities

compete in new ways to attract and retain a diverse array of jobs.

GENERATIONAL SHIFT?

For nine straight decades before 2007, US suburban job growth outpaced that in downtowns.[8] By 2009, it is estimated that only 21% of jobs were in the 3-mile radius of a Central Business District.[9] But is this changing? During and immediately following the Great Recession of 2008 the majority of downtowns grew faster than their suburbs.[10] Many of the same high-profile corporations that fled cities for suburban office parks and corporate campuses in the 1970s and 1980s have moved back so as to better attract the digitally savvy younger workers who have flooded cities in search of urban lifestyles. Office park owners are fighting back by introducing a more walkable mix of uses and urban housing into their properties. There's even a return of

---

[7] Some examples that have made headlines: In 2010, Quicken Loans consolidated several suburban offices and started moving 8,000 employees into downtown Detroit; Motorola Mobility sold its five-building, 84-acre suburban campus outside Chicago in 2014 after it moved 2,000 employees downtown; in 2016 Weyerhauser moved from its award-winning 1971 suburban office campus in Federal Way to a new HQ in downtown Seattle; Even though it had only moved from Ohio to suburban Gwinnett County, outside of Atlanta in 2009, in 2015, NCR announced it was moving the bulk of its 4,000 employees into two new custom high-rises to be built on former parking lots in Midtown Atlanta and Georgia Tech's booming innovation district.

[8] William H. Frey, "Demographic Reversal: Cities Thrive, Suburbs Sputter," *Brookings*, 29 June 2012.
[9] Elizabeth Kneebone, "Job Sprawl Revisited: The Changing Geography of Metropolitan Employment," *Brookings*, 6 April 2009.
[10] Joe Cortright, "Surging City Center Job Growth," *City Reports*, 23 February 2015.

TECHNOLOGY

- Automation, both digital software and robotics, has replaced large numbers of routine, low-skilled jobs and may soon replace a wider variety of jobs. This has increased mid-skilled technician and engineer jobs.
- Computers and digital communication have enabled square footage per office employee to shrink. This has reduced overall office space needs (while increasing the parking ratio) and increasingly led to more collaborative, shared space, and an increased reliance on telecommuting.
- Although digital communication allows work to happen anywhere, knowledge-based industries have benefited from clustering around thick labor markets that increase productivity and have stronger access to venture capital. The effects of increased telecommuting and job losses during the COVID-19 pandemic that began in 2020 remain to be seen.

INNOVATION

- Globalization and increased competition have shifted investment away from "research" for the sake of knowledge and unforeseen inventions toward time-sensitive, market-based "innovation" to create improved products and processes.
- The sylvan corporate R&D (research and development) campus model introduced in the 1950s presumes that labs with hushed views of nature will be productive of advanced scientific discoveries. Innovation, on the other hand, is now understood to be accelerated by the knowledge spillovers that occur when groups of creative,

educated people informally interact in denser, collaborative, networking settings. Innovation benefits from urbanism, not "the park."

- Both established corporations and well-funded new start-ups have increasingly sought workspace in "innovation districts" with university affiliations. Co-working rental spaces and business incubators have also emerged to serve start-ups and "gig economy" freelancers with dynamic space needs.

MULTIPLIER EFFECT

- All jobs are not created equal in terms of economic impact. Studies show that each new "innovation job" has a multiplier effect generating from 2.5 to 5 local-serving jobs.[11] The multiplier effect for manufacturing is two and for local-serving jobs is one. The greatest growth in jobs is expected to be in local-serving, in-person services such as personal care and home health aides with low multipliers.
- Local-serving, labor-intensive businesses like restaurants and service providers may not have a high multiplier effect on job creation, but they do in terms of more of each revenue dollar going to the local payroll. It has been shown that independent small businesses keep more than three times as many dollars circulating in the local economy than chain stores do.[12]
- High-paying job clusters also tend to have a multiplier effect on nearby home values. This may be welcomed, or it may lead to tear-downs and displacement in established suburban neighborhoods.

[11] Moretti, *The New Geography*, 13, 60.
[12] The Institute for Local Self Reliance provides links and summaries to several studies in the US and Canada on the economic returns and jobs per unit of sales of independent

small businesses versus national chains. See Stacy Mitchell, "Key Studies: Why Local Matters," 8 January 2016: https://ilsr.org/key-studies-why-local-matters/#3.

58 URGENT SUBURBAN CHALLENGES

MILLENNIALS AND GEN Z

- Born between 1981 and 1996, the urban-oriented, tech-savvy Millennial generation surpassed Generation X in 2015 as the largest segment of the American workforce. It now constitutes 50% of the US workforce, largely replacing the retiring, suburban-centric Baby Boomer generation. Gen Z is the next large generation now entering the workforce.
- More college-educated than previous generations, the Millennial "digerati" are both highly mobile and highly sought after. Companies are increasingly moving to communities that are successful at attracting and retaining Millennials.
- Millennials have expressed strong preferences to live and work in walkable, urban, places—even as those owing large student debts cannot always afford them. As they began having families, many moved to suburbs with good school districts; they brought their smartphones, shared economy, and desire for a vibrant public realm with them.
- Millennials have lower rates of car ownership and higher participation in transit and bicycling than previous generations at their age. They would rather take the bus with Wi-Fi than commute by car to work, especially in conditions of high traffic, although driverless cars may change that.
- Gen Z—those born from 1997 to 2012—are the most ethnically diverse generation in the US. Early surveys of this cohort indicate their overwhelming preference for living in diverse rather than homogenous neighborhoods.[13]

RETURN OF MANUFACTURING

- Rising labor costs outside northern America, increased reliance on automation, and government incentives have led to the construction of new and revitalized manufacturing plants. Growth has been strongest in "advanced manufacturing" and perishables such as baked goods. Sometimes called "reshoring," these plants increasingly require fewer workers with more technical skills at higher wages. Job training programs are often a factor in location decisions.
- A wide variety of maker spaces, fab labs, breweries, and incubator kitchens are providing start-up space for both artisanal production and DIY hobbyists, often in older suburban office and industrial parks. Rezoning that allows retail sales and other forms of mixed-use can help businesses thrive and areas revive.
- General Electric and other manufacturers are experimenting with on-demand, custom production of consumer appliances using robotics and 3D-printers in retail shops. What other forms of manufacturing might swap centralized plants and shipping for decentralized retail on Main Street?

manufacturing jobs—large plants at the rural fringes of suburbia and more artisanal maker production in the increasingly mixed-use downtown-adjacent light industrial fringes. Post-recession, as the economy recovered, so did sprawl-building, albeit at much slower rates. But it's now accompanied by the counter-trend of a steady stream of urbanization, especially in suburban retrofits.[14]

---

[13] Consumer Trends, "Generation Z Seeks Diverse Neighborhoods in Home-Buying Decisions," *Builder*, 25 June 2019.
[14] See William H. Frey's analysis of census data, "Big City Growth Stalls Further, as the Suburbs Make a Comeback," *Brookings*, 24 May 2019. But the US Census only distinguishes urbanized areas from rural areas and does a poor job of accounting for urbanizing suburbs. In 2018, recognizing the value of more market-based distinctions between types of suburban and urban places, consumer research firm RCLCO and the Urban Land Institute developed an interactive Neighborhood Atlas that distinguishes five types of suburbs and six types of urban neighborhoods within the top 50 US metro areas. Their classification better captures the impact of retrofits. By their classification, the concentration of employment in places like Bethesda, Maryland, and Jersey City, New Jersey, qualifies them as Economic Centers, an urban classification, even though they are outside of a traditional CBD. Amongst their findings is that urban places captured 36% of new job growth between 2005-2015 and Economic Centers captured the most of any other urban or suburban neighborhood type. See, RCLCO, ULI Terwilliger Center, "The New Geography of Urban America: An Interactive Map for Classifying Urban Neighborhoods," 19 June 2018.

These dual trends reflect the sharply divergent job mix that is shaping different communities' futures. Some cities and suburbs are capturing a much higher share of the approximately 30% of jobs that are considered high-wage, "creative class," "export-oriented," or "innovation jobs." These jobs in high-tech and the energy sector are growing and have boosted the few metro economies in which these industries cluster.

But economic development officers everywhere else should note that only four of the top 20 occupations that the US Bureau of Labor Statistics projects to produce the most new jobs from 2019 to 2029 are particularly high tech.[15] Only half had salaries above $38,320, the lowest salary required to be able to buy an average home in any of the fifty states in 2018.[16] Many communities are only seeing growth in the low-wage end of local-serving, "service jobs."[17] Post-recession job growth was driven by jobs paying less than $13.33 per hour, either from fast food or short-term "gigs."[18] The wage gap between high- and low-wage jobs is manifesting in ever-deeper divides between rich and poor people and rich and poor places. As wealth is becoming more concentrated at the top, more than 60% of jobs no longer support a middle-class or better lifestyle.[19]

If middle-class jobs, long considered the staple of suburban life, are in decline, so too is the defining feature of the American Dream, upward mobility. Economist Raj Chetty's research has shown this drop-off.[20] According to the Pew Research Center, 2015 was the first time since the 1960s that the majority of Americans were not in the middle class. Their share of income fell from 62% in 1972 to 43% in 2014.[21] Middle-skill and middle-wage jobs—involving routine activities that require some post–high

school training, but not a college degree—declined from 25% of the workforce in 1985 to 15% in 2012.[22] However, with fewer young people trained to replace the aging-out machinists, lab technicians, and utility line workers, as well as the new technician jobs in automation, these jobs are predicted to be among those most needed in the future. The challenging questions for both suburbs and cities that are losing their middle class is whether they can maintain a balance between high-, middle-, and low-wage jobs. Can they protect and create new middle-class jobs? Or will they become trapped in either a cycle of rising wages and unaffordability or one of declining wages and disinvestment?

Retrofitting underperforming suburban properties cannot solve labor polarization at the national or global scale. But it is an important vehicle for addressing these questions locally. Aging office and industrial parks, as well as vacant retail sites, provide an array of opportunities, from diversifying and updating the kinds of next-generation workplaces and training offered, to better balancing the jobs-housing mix and rethinking the future relationship between the two.

RETROFITTING THE OFFICE PARK AND CORPORATE CAMPUS

In 2015, commercial real estate advisors Newmark Knight Frank found that approximately 22% of suburban office properties in the top 50 US metros were confronting obsolescence.[23] Yet in 2010 we found only a little more than a dozen approved or built plans to significantly retrofit these properties. By 2020 our database showed 205 such retrofits in process in the US.

The sites range from a few buildings on an acre or two to properties several hundred, even a thousand acres in size. They typically have some highway exposure; those that began life as industrial parks often have rail connectivity. In the late 1980s and 1990s, many of them were absorbed into "edge cities," agglomerations of auto-oriented office parks, shopping malls, and apartment complexes. The

15   "Most New Jobs," *Occupational Outlook Handbook*, US Bureau of Labor Statistics, accessed 1 November 2020.

16   This happens to be West Virginia. See "How much income you need to afford the average home in every state in 2018," How Much.net.

17   Richard Florida, "The Un-Even Growth of High and Low-Wage Jobs Across America," *CityLab*, 27 September 2013.

18   See Annie Lowrey, "Recovery Has Created Far More Low-Paying Jobs Than Better-Paid Ones," *New York Times*, April 27, 2017. See also Lawrence F. Katz and Alan B. Krueger, "The Rise and Nature of Alternative Work Arrangements in the United States, 1995–2015," National Bureau of Economic Research Working Paper No. 22667, September 2016.

19   Ryan Bhandari and David Brown, "The Opportunity Index: Ranking Opportunity in Metropolitan America," Thirdway.org, 30 October 2018.

20   See the research of Opportunity Insights, a not-for-profit based at Harvard University directed by Raj Chetty, John Friedman, and Daniel Hendren: https://opportunityinsights.org/.

21   Pew Research Center, op cit.

22   Christopher L. Smith, "The Dynamics of Labor Market Polarization," Finance and Economics Discussion Series, Federal Reserve Board, August 2013, 9.

23   Newmark Grubb Knight Frank, *Suburban Office Obsolescence; Quantifying Challenges and Opportunities*, Thought Leadership Series, September 2015.

building stock varies from light-industrial sheds to low- to-mid-rise office buildings. They are structurally solid, but their low ceilings, HVAC systems and wiring are far from current. If designed for a single tenant, the in-house amenities need to be reworked for multiple tenants. Most are flanked by surface parking lots and, in the case of headquarters or research and development campuses, elaborately groomed grounds with lakes and streams, some of which are now flooding. Their size and characteristics suggest great potential for combining strategies of redevelopment, reinhabitation, and regreening in a rich placemaking mix. However, for those same reasons they also often face steep market obstacles and community resistance.

The evolution of jobs in New Jersey is particularly revealing of these challenges. James Hughes and Joseph Seneca, professors of planning at Rutgers University, have monitored the changes extensively along with the interplay between regional economies, local politics, and demographics.[24] They note that in the 1970s and 1980s, as manufacturing plants in the state were increasingly shut down to offshoring, New Jersey was successfully transitioned to a postindustrial economy, with particular strengths in pharmaceutical companies. This happened largely by attracting corporate headquarters and their back offices out of New York City with brand new office parks and corporate campuses. Eighty percent of all the commercial office space ever built in the state was erected in the 1980s.[25] By 1988, the state surpassed New York City in total employment. But that began to change in 2004.[26] By 2015, the momentum had completely flipped. New York City regained the lead, as many of those same employers left their out-of-date suburban offices dependent on aging highways to move back into much-improved and Millennial-filled Manhattan and Brooklyn. They found a similar back-to-the-city pattern within New Jersey itself, where "for the first time in the post-World War II era the tidal wave of metropolitan expansion has begun to ebb, with the regional core outperforming the suburban ring."[27]

It's not only the jobs that have been leaving New Jersey. It's also the young people. From 2000 to 2013, the number of Millennials increased nationwide 6.8% but declined in New Jersey by 2.3%.[28] In 2012, the state ranked 47th out of 50 states for its percentage of Millennials.[29] Recognizing the importance of attracting and holding onto the next generation of workers, the state has had some success facilitating redevelopment of vacant office and industrial sites through its Transit Village Initiative, Brownfields InterAgency Work Group, and Fair Share Housing Act requirements for affordable housing. But proposals to redevelop such sites into the kind of mixed-use habitats Millennials prefer keep running into resistance.

Local community members consistently object to the multiunit housing components. The most suburbanized state in the nation, New Jersey is not known for great cities. This may partially explain why developers have had a rough time getting approvals for "urban living."[30] More crucially, New Jersey is a high-tax state and the fear of additional children attending local public schools and leading to higher taxes is rampant. The mayor of Aberdeen, however, credits the Millennial-targeted, transit-oriented, mixed-use residential redevelopments of former workplaces in his community with keeping taxes down.[31] And while some municipalities, including Montvale and Bridgewater, have used redevelopment of corporate office sites to meet their Fair Housing requirements, other elected officials have found that championing affordable housing is political suicide.[32] Lawsuits regarding redevelopment have been common and reflect the heated challenges of managing a transitioning tax base when both office and retail properties are on the wane.

See this case study:

▪ II.28. Bell Works, Holmdel, New Jersey

24 James W. Hughes and Joseph J. Seneca, *New Jersey's Postsuburban Economy* (New Brunswick, NJ: Rutgers University Press, 2014).

25 James W. Hughes and Joseph J. Seneca, "Reinventing the New Jersey Economy: New Metropolitan and Regional Employment Dynamics," *Rutgers Regional Report*, Issue Paper Number 33, December 2012.

26 Ibid.

27 James W. Hughes and Joseph J. Seneca, "The Receding Metropolitan Perimeter: A New Postsuburban Demographic Normal?" *Rutgers Regional Report*, Issue Paper Number 37, September 2014.

28 Tim Evans, "Where Are We Going? Implications of Recent Demographic Trends in New Jersey," *New Jersey Future*, September 2017.

29 Mike Maciag, "A State-by-State Look at Where Each Generation Lives," *Governing*, 31 July 2014.

30 Our research indicates that it is much easier to urbanize a suburban property if the market for "urban living" has already been proven in that metro's downtown. Santana Row, in San Jose, CA, is a rare exception.

31 Jerry Carino, "Redevelopment boom means no tax hike in Aberdeen," *App*, 31 May 2017.

32 See the examples discussed in Nick Corasaniti, "As Office Parks Empty, Towns Turn Vacancies into Opportunities," *New York Times*, 29 May 2018.

Figure I.5-2 Santana Row, San Jose, California, proves the case for urbanism as the new amenity for office use. The project's first phase retrofitted a strip mall into 11 urban blocks centered on a pedestrian-oriented street lined with upscale retail, entertainment, and upper-level residences. When some of the second-story retail space failed to lease, the owner revamped it for office. Demand exceeded expectations and more office space was added in later phases, including one million square feet across Winchester Boulevard. The ripple effects continue to expand outward and San Jose has rezoned three adjacent areas as Urban Villages. Source: Courtesy of Federal Realty Investment Trust, annotations by authors.

URBANISM AS THE NEW AMENITY

While urbanism is a hard sell in New Jersey, in Texas it's the new desired amenity for office parks. Ward Eastman, a vice president with commercial real estate services provider Cassidy Turley, credited the "live, work, play" urbanism of Legacy Town Center with setting a new standard.[33] The success of the 150-acre new urbanist town center inserted into the 3,000-acre Legacy office park in Plano, and the several similar mixed-use office parks that followed, resulted in a 22% increase in rents in the Far North Dallas submarket from 2008 to 2013.[34] The success of this paradigm shift in the design of premier suburban office real estate can be seen in the follow-up project across the Dallas North Parkway, Legacy West. Its big amenity, similar to Santana Row, is a walkable street lined with shops, cafés, and wide sidewalks. But, given its location within an enormous, spread-out office park, the street does not particularly improve walkability of the overall area as much as one might hope. Perhaps that's why the "Legacy Effect" is *only* a 22% premium.

Christopher Leinberger, professor of real estate at George Washington University, argues that the average premium nationwide for being in a regionally significant walkable urban place is 105%.[35] Several parallel studies have reinforced the value of walkability, bikeability, and access to transit to corporate America. Amazon emphasized all three in its site selection criteria for its $5 billion HQ2 before choosing Queens, New York, and Crystal City in Arlington, Virginia. While resistance in New York led Amazon to withdraw, the Arlington site, in an urbanizing suburb, is now that much better positioned to attract other major employers and their high-wage jobs.

See these case studies:

- II.10. The Domain, Austin, Texas
- II.19. Technology Park, Peachtree Corners, Georgia
- II.32. Assembly Square, Somerville, Massachusetts

It seems that every large office park and edge city is pursuing some degree of mixed-use, transit, and updated amenities to attract the next generation of workers. Just some of the more pro-active large properties include California's Bishop Ranch, Warner Center, Irvine Business Complex, and Hacienda Business Park; Pennsylvania's King of Prussia District; North Carolina's Research Triangle Park; the Bel-Red corridor outside of Seattle; Tysons and Crystal City outside of Washington, DC; Innsbrook outside of Richmond; and Atlanta's Perimeter Center. Notable trends include:

- Ten years ago, only one of these properties, Crystal City, had more than a handful of apartments. Today, all

---

[33] For more discussion of Legacy Town Center, see *Retrofitting Suburbia,* 180–183, 186.

[34] Ward Eastman, "The Legacy Effect," Cassidy Turley articles, posted 24 October 2013, citing data from Cassidy Turley's Q2 research report.

[35] Tracy Hadden Loh, Christopher B. Leinberger, and Jordan Chafetz, "Foot Traffic Ahead: Ranking Walkable Urbanism in America's Largest Metros," George Washington University School of Business and Smart Growth America, 2019.

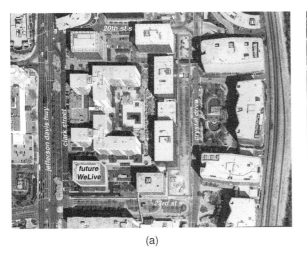

(a)   (b)

Figure I.5-3 The former parking lots fronting Crystal Drive in Crystal City, an edge city in Arlington, Virginia, are outlined in red in (a) before they were replaced in 2004 with the liner buildings and lively streetscaping shown in (b). Sources: (a) Authors using Google Earth 2003, © Maxar Technologies; (b) Courtesy of JBG Smith.

(a)   (b)

Figure I.5-4 Crystal City is targeting entrepreneurs with the conversion of Crystal Plaza 6 (a), from drab office to WeLive, 216 microunit "dorms for adults" with ample co-living and co-working spaces and colorful facade treatments. Activities like Crosshairs Garage Racing (b) are hosted by the very active Business Improvement District to build social capital. Sources: (a) Photo by June Williamson, 2018; (b) Photo by Bruce Buckley, courtesy of CXHairs.

of them either have built or are planning for hundreds if not thousands of dwelling units. Most of these are being designed in urban formats as part of mixed-use nodes within the larger properties. Whether motivated by attracting millennial employees with urbanism or by public sector efforts to improve the jobs-housing balance, their new residents are helping to dampen rush hour traffic for all by supporting more on-site, after-hours activities and businesses.

■ To further address congestion, all of them are pursuing alternatives to automobile dependence— whether walkability, bikeability, rail, or autonomous shuttle buses.[36] One study found that suburban office markets that provide walkability and transit can effectively attract talented employees and as a result have rents 42.8% higher than those that do not.[37] Bishop Ranch started offering first-last mile autonomous shuttle bus service in 2018, the first of its kind in the US to get permission to operate on public roads.

- All of these changes have required significant partnering with local municipalities. In fact, many of them have been led by public sector vision plans and removal of restrictions to new uses. In 2010, the City of Irvine, California, approved a Vision Plan and overlay zoning that enables 9,000 dwelling units to be added to the 6,000 already constructed within a more than 2,000-acre swath of the aging Irvine Business Complex, while paying for massive roadway improvements through the expected impact fees. While hardly enough to accommodate the IBC's 90,000 employees, it has enabled the Irvine Community Land Trust and Jamboree, a noted low-income housing developer, to deliver affordable housing for service workers in the area.

- Most of them have formed a business improvement district (BID) to fund and coordinate capital improvements and events. The new BID at Crystal City in Arlington County, Virginia, is successfully activating dreary public spaces with community-oriented programming and colorful art. These are important incremental steps to help Crystal City realize its ambitious plans to introduce high-density residential infill and a more walkable street grid by 2050. Will we ever know how much of a role the BID and these plans—as well as the Crystal Tech Fund's venture capital for start-ups and the DesignLab's demonstrations of full-scale reinhabitations of the "offices of the future"—swayed Amazon?

Smaller office parks have also been successful in introducing urbanism as an amenity, often by working closely with their municipalities. Prior to putting their 172-acre campus in Simsbury, Connecticut, on the market, The Hartford Insurance Company enhanced its value with a new urbanist, mixed-use form-based code. The community was able to use the process to shape its desired vision for

the site prior to adoption of the code and prior to the arrival of the new owner a year later.

See these case studies:

- II.2. Hassalo on Eighth and Lloyd, Portland, Oregon
- II.7. TAXI, Denver, Colorado
- II.21. Downtown Doral, Doral, Florida

REINHABITING AND REGREENING THE OFFICE PARK

As important as it is to grow jobs, sometimes communities can benefit from putting surplus office buildings to other uses. Given a glut of underperforming 1960s and 1970s office space and a tremendous unmet need for housing, in 2013 the United Kingdom introduced a three-year relaxation of the permission requirements that has significantly increased the conversion of office buildings to residential use.[38]

Medical-related uses have also been popular. Since 2001, almost 4.9 million square feet of general office space in New York's Westchester County has been adapted to other uses, predominantly medical clinics and labs. These renovations are now triggering residential infill and mixed-use redevelopment in the area. In Georgia, an IBM property with an 11-story L-shaped building on 56 acres was handsomely remodeled into the North Atlanta High School in 2013. Communities can encourage this type of incremental change by rezoning, updating adaptive reuse ordinances, and tax credit availability.

Sometimes, rather than redevelop or reinhabit these properties, it makes more sense to demolish the buildings and regreen them. After Aetna Insurance moved 6,400 employees from its 200-acre campus in Middletown, Connecticut, into Hartford in 2010, the company demolished their circa 1984 1.3-million-square-foot custom-designed building. They deemed it a white elephant that would make the property harder to sell. The property did not remain "regreened" for long; the strategy worked, with the site sold in 2015 for redevelopment.

---

36 By far the most ambitious in this regard is Tysons Corner. See Christopher B. Leinberger, "Retrofitting Tysons: From Edge City to Walkable Urban Place," *Development Magazine*, Summer 2018.

37 Scott Sutton, "Capital Commute: Why Investors Are Loving Suburban Office," us.jll.com, 13 February 2018.

38 The act's reduction of local control has been controversial and far more applications have been approved than have been constructed. Nonetheless, the experiment was extended through 2019.

(a)   (b)

Figure I.5-5 The Pleasant Ridge neighborhood of Cincinnati, Ohio, grew local jobs and revived the core blocks of its largely vacant Main Street by having it designated as a "Community Entertainment District"; reducing the cost of a liquor license by $25,000; securing grants and long-term loans for building restoration; working out free evening parking in daytime business's lots; and inviting veteran food truck operators to open brick-and-mortar locations, like C'est Cheese, which opened Share Cheesebar. Sources: (a) Photo by Catherine Grace Photography; (b) Photo courtesy of Emily Frank.

BOOSTING SMALL BUSINESS BY REINHABITING DEAD RETAIL

Almost half of all US private-sector jobs are in small businesses. These businesses also benefit from urbanism's easy access to networking opportunities, business services, coffee shops, fitness centers, and the like, without the employer having to provide them. While some local small businesses can afford locations in newly urbanized suburban retrofits, others are more likely to find affordable rents by reinhabiting existing buildings and contributing to neighborhood revitalization. This has the added benefit of reinforcing a sense of local community that most suburban employment centers severely lack. The older suburban Main Streets that took a hit when so many malls opened are increasingly being revived by small retail businesses as those malls die out.[39]

Back in New Jersey, for instance, the collapse of so many office parks is raising demand for office space in suburban downtowns, especially those with commuter rail access.[40] But refilling Main Street still often requires incentives and organizational help. Marlboro, New Jersey, initiated a property tax rebate called Shop Marlboro that has since been replicated by several communities. Merchants who participate in the program agree to discount their product by whatever percentage they wish in exchange for free advertising from the township. Participating locals swipe a rebate card for the discount and it is applied as a deduction to their property tax.[41]

Main Streets aren't the only areas getting refills. Auto-oriented, single-use medical districts, often full of aging medical office buildings and anchor institutions, are increasingly becoming "health districts" with safer, more walkable streets lined with diverse local businesses supported in part by buy-local procurement programs.

In addition to improving the public realm, the Memphis Medical District Collaborative (MMDC) has formed a series of successful partnerships to boost a variety of jobs in a part of town where almost half of the residents live in poverty.[42] The Work Local program hires homeless day laborers once a week at a designated location to do cleanup work on the streets, get lunch, a night's housing, and access to medical services. Hire Local 901 helps

39 See Valerie Bauerlein, "In America's Most Middle-Class City, the Mall Is Dying. Here's Why," *Wall Street Journal*, 20 December 2017.
40 Newmark Knight Frank, "Beyond Suburban Downtowns," *NJ Office Trends,* September 2017.
41 Dan Radel, "Got Taxes? Eat Pizza," *App*, 18 February 2015.
42 See Robert Steuteville, "Healing a Troubled Medical District," *Public Square*, Congress for the New Urbanism, 21 August 2019.

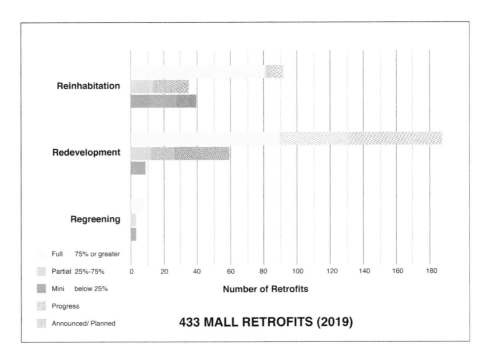

Reinhabitation

Redevelopment

Regreening

Full 75% or greater
Partial 25%-75%
Mini below 25%
Progress
Announced/ Planned

Number of Retrofits

433 MALL RETROFITS (2019)

Figure I.5-6 This analysis of retrofit proposals for enclosed shopping malls in our database as of 2019 distinguishes them according to: the retrofit strategy—reinhabitation, redevelopment, and regreening; whether it is a full, partial, or mini retrofit based on the percentage of the property affected; and whether it is completed, in progress, or planned. Of the reinhabitation retrofits, office is the most common reuse, with education and medical also frequent. The vast majority of full and partial redevelopment retrofits become mixed-use town centers or add residential and office components to the mall. The regreenings have mostly become parks with some partial examples of rooftop or raised-bed urban farming. Source: Authors.

connect neighborhood residents to training opportunities and permanent jobs in the district. In 2018 the MMDC helped 22 local small businesses sign leases at vacant storefronts and get small grants for facade improvements.[43]

Other MMDC incentive programs, including hosting the Incremental Development Alliance and identifying older buildings ripe for adaptive reuse, have kick-started a successful micro-retail incubator and a wave of new residents and larger employers to what's been rebranded as the Edge District. The safer streets and increased neighborhood employment help the hospitals' and medical schools' recruitment of higher-skilled wage-earners as well, truly connecting community and economic development.

Aging malls and strip malls have also been converted into job centers for both large and small businesses. Surprisingly perhaps, office is the most common use replacing retail in malls. Many of those

jobs are with call centers and pay low wages. Increasingly, middle-wage "eds and meds" jobs have been moving into malls but there are also examples of high-tech, higher-wage jobs.[44] Google reinhabited the Mayfield Mall in Mountain View, California, with an exploratory division called Google X, since shortened to X.[45] Smaller businesses have also done well in these

[43] Michelle Corbet, "Medical District Welcomes 22 New Businesses in 2018," *Daily Memphian,* 19 February 2019.

[44] See Ellen Dunham-Jones and June Williamson, "Dead and Dying Shopping Malls, Re-Inhabited," *Architectural Design,* no. 249, September–October 2017, 84–91.

[45] Similar examples include Google's lease of Westside Pavilion, Rackspace's headquarters in the former Windsor Park Mall in San Antonio, the Ford Motor Company's conversion of a Lord & Taylor department store to offices at the Fairlane Town Center Mall, and Under Armour put offices in adjacent black-painted former Sam's Club and Walmart as a precursor to redevelopment of Port Covington in Baltimore. 1776, a business incubator company with many locations, took over 11,000 square feet at Cherry Hill Mall in New Jersey, offering co-working space, a shared retail marketplace, programming, and classes focused on retail and e-commerce. The first mall conversion entirely to office, mostly for call centers, was Netpark Tampa Bay in 1998.

(a)   (b)

Figure I.5-7 A business incubator in a suburban strip mall? Developer Monte Anderson and the City of Desoto, Texas, converted a former hardware store into Grow Desoto Market, regreened a swath of the parking lot into a twinkle-lit networking space with food trucks and plan to build 20 loft apartments on the side. Asya L. Mitchem, shown at her co-owned business The Shoe Bar, told author Ellen Dunham-Jones, "The marketplace was a valued experience as it provided us with practical experience in operating a brick-and-mortar location with less overhead expenses and risks often associated with commercial leases." They've since moved online and we recommend checking out www.shuesq.com. Source: Photos by Phillip Jones, 2019.

spaces. An Office Depot big box store in Atlanta went from selling office furniture to renting it as co-working space. When the Bon Marche Mall in Baton Rouge, Louisiana, died in 2000, local investors converted it into the Bon Carré Technology Center, gave the mall new windows, wiring, and a facelift; attracted a state-funded high-tech business incubator with a data center; and housed 4,000 employees in 2016.[46]

However, business incubators shouldn't only focus on high tech. Too often the "innovation economy" privileges large corporations that can afford robots, and patent attorneys. Lower-tech food and farming businesses tend to be highly local and compete well against e-commerce. For example, cannabis production and sales have dramatically reduced vacancies in strip malls and warehouses in states where marijuana has been legalized.[47] As such businesses grow more corporate, communities should consider subdividing large retail spaces into "mercados" that provide launching pads for smaller entrepreneurs.

That's been the case at Grow Desoto Marketplace, a business incubator in a Texas strip mall. When the only retailer interested in occupying the vacant space was 99 Cents Only Stores, the mayor asked the owner, Monte Anderson, "Is there anything better we can do?" Together, they came up with ways to lower the barriers to entry and kick-start locally owned start-ups, many of which are eateries and most of which are Black-owned businesses. At "Pitch Mondays" entrepreneurs pitch their proposals to earn one of the 60 spots with reasonable rents, build-out construction costs included, and access to a marketing consultant. In 2019 it was 80% leased. Anderson said, "What I find in the African American community is an extreme amount of creativity and a lack of experience when it comes to access to practice business. I think it's so important that we figure out how to build wealth for local people, bottom line."[48]

Riverview Gardens in Appleton, Wisconsin, is another kind of job incubator. The organizers bought a former country club and turned the swimming pool into a

---

[46] Located in an Enterprise Zone, the project also triggered significant reinvestment in the area. However, when the tax exemption on the Bon Carré Technology Center ran out in 2017, the owners defaulted on the mortgage. As of 2019, the largest tenant, Louisiana Tech Park business incubator, is continuing to expand.

[47] See David Gelles, "A Real Estate Boom Powered by Pot," *New York Times*, 1 April 2017.

[48] As quoted in Dalila Thomas, "Former Ace Hardware is Now an Incubator for Black-Owned Businesses," *Dallas Observer*, 23 October 2018.

Figure I.5-8 Christo Rey St Martin College Prep in Waukegan, Illinois, is one of many former K-Mart stores that have been retrofitted into schools. Christo Rey is not unique in targeting such reinhabitation opportunities in under-invested areas for its network of 32 charter schools. But its four-year corporate work study program uniquely prepares students from economically disadvantaged backgrounds to develop workplace readiness skills. The Waukegan campus boasts a 98% college enrollment rate among its 400 low-income, mostly minority population. Source: Courtesy of JGMA Architects.

hydroponic greenhouse and the golf course into a farm; it provides food, jobs, and job training for the homeless and unemployed veterans.[49] Participants can earn bicycles, respect, and permanent jobs working alongside over 1,000 community volunteers. The volunteers similarly benefit from overcoming fears of the homeless and veterans by getting to know them as individuals.[50]

See these case studies:

- II.7. TAXI, Denver, Colorado
- II.9. La Gran Plaza, Fort Worth, Texas
- II.11. ACC Highland, Austin, Texas

---

[49] Other retrofits that are helping the homeless include the growing practice of reinhabiting motels with permanent housing. The Champlain Housing Trust, the Burlington Housing Authority, and Safe Harbor, took over the Ho Hum Motel in South Burlington, Vermont, from an owner who had been accepting daily state emergency vouchers for homeless stays. In addition to no longer being homeless, having a permanent address at the re-christened Beacon Apartments provides residents with a much better chance of obtaining jobs. It also has saved state funds and reduced public healthcare costs.

[50] Maureen Wallenfang, "Riverview Gardens Grows a Greenhouse," *USA Today Network-Wisconsin,* 18 April 2016.

- II.15. Baton Rouge Health District, Baton Rouge, Louisiana
- II.17. One Hundred Oaks Mall, Nashville, Tennessee

FUTURE FORECAST FOR JOBS COMPETITION

Not all of these strategies are relevant everywhere today, let alone tomorrow. Every market is unique and there will continue to be a need for much creative retrofitting of out-of-date workplaces and of job growth policies at all levels. Will cubicle farms return to fashion as office workers tire of the lack of dedicated space in today's creative offices? Will automation usher in the universal three-day work week or massive unemployment? Now that the majority of college graduates are women, will they continue to put up with suburban development patterns that exacerbate the challenges of balancing career and caregiver roles? Will homes and neighborhoods be designed to better disentangle telework's blurring of distinctions between home and work?

What is certain is that communities cannot assume that yesterday's jobs will be there tomorrow, especially not the clerical and retail jobs that accelerated suburban growth in the last half of the twentieth century. From 2007 to 2016 in the US, occupations that require postsecondary education gained 5.3 million jobs while those only requiring a high school degree lost 1.3 million jobs.[51] Many communities would be wise to focus not only on recruiting well-paying jobs and growing local entrepreneurs, but also on increasing the opportunities to learn new skills and live more affordably: allowing rentals and small-lot building types, encouraging healthy transportation modes generally and especially for access to jobs, and investing in education, especially for middle-skill jobs and life-long learning.

---

[51] US Bureau of Labor Statistics, Economics Daily, "Occupations Typically Requiring Postsecondary Education Gain 5.3 Million Jobs, May 2007–16," 26 October 2017.

Chapter I.6
Add Water and Energy Resilience

As the unparalleled costs associated with the hurricanes of the past decade demonstrate, we suppress or deny the interdependence of constructed systems, as well as their combined reliance on natural systems, at our peril.. . .What if the services provided by power plants, sewage treatment plants, and other elements of infrastructure were based on an ecological model of interdependency, instead of an industrial model of segregation?[1]

Hillary Brown, FAIA

Suburbia was not designed with climate change, sustainability, or resilience in mind. Rather, its infrastructure reflects what Hillary Brown, professor of architecture and sustainability at the City College of New York and Fellow of the Post-Carbon Institute, describes as an industrialized worldview of convenience, efficiency, and bureaucratic control. Instead of the "three-legged stool" concept used to describe sustainability, wherein environmental, economic, and social equity systems are understood as overlapping and interdependent, twentieth-century suburban development is more often described in terms of discrete "silos." In planning for new communities, engineers devised and followed standards for transportation, water, and energy systems, each optimized for a single variable.

To facilitate development on greenfield land, meandering creeks and headwaters were routinely cut off from the ecosystems they had supported and rerouted into open-air concrete drainage channels or buried in underground pipes.[2] The pipes and power lines stretching from centralized water treatment, sewer, and power plants across large metros dramatically altered local ecology and suffer from transmission loss and leakage. To pay for it all, utilities established to deliver water and power encouraged the creation of an auto-dependent, culverted landscape of detached, air-conditioned buildings surrounded by lawns, septic tanks, and parking lots.[3]

Planners similarly enacted zoning and land-use ordinances to separate uses and segregate income levels. Financing practices evolved to deliver standardized real estate products with little consideration of local climate, geography, or culture. As a consequence, suburban form has high per capita water and power consumption.

Together our habits have substantially altered our climate, polluted our air and surface waters, drained groundwater aquifers enabling saltwater intrusion, and led to soaring maintenance costs of aging infrastructure.[4] There is now far greater recognition of the damage such systems have wrought on the environment—and of how climate change is increasing flooding, droughts, sea level rise, wildfires and urban heat island impacts.

Retrofitting enables integrated approaches to these challenges:

- Designers increasingly view stormwater as a resource, not a nuisance, and locally produced energy as a smart investment.
- Regreening strategies reduce flooding and sewer overflows and provide wildfire buffers, while more compact

---

[1] Hillary Brown, *Next Generation Infrastructure: Principles for Post-Industrial Public Works* (Washington DC, Island Press, 2014).

[2] Jake J. Beaulieu, Helen E. Golden, Christopher D. Knightes, et al., "Urban Stream Burial Increases Watershed-Scale Nitrate Export," *PLoS One* 10(7): e0132256, 17 July 2015: https://doi.org/10.1371/journal.pone.0132256.

[3] Adam Rome documents the electric utilities' success at marketing "electric homes" over "solar homes" in the 1930s and '40s, as well as the growing concerns over the loss of "open space" due to suburbanization in the 1950s and '60s in *The Bulldozer in the Countryside* (Cambridge, UK: Cambridge University Press, 2001).

[4] See Patricia Buckley, Lester Gunnion, and Will Sarni, "The Aging Water Infrastructure: Out of Sight, Out of Mind?" *Issues by the Numbers,* March 2016, Deloitte Insights: https://www2.deloitte.com/insights/us/en/economy/issues-by-the-numbers/us-aging-water-infrastructure-investment-opportunities.html.

redevelopment reduces per capita demand for water and energy and reduces loss from leaks.

■ Integration of green infrastructure and water harvesting on the one hand and district energy plants and distributed renewable energy generation on the other reduce strains on existing centralized water and power systems and increase capacity for more resilient local solutions.

Such efficiency is particularly impactful given "the water-energy nexus." Most of us assume that our homes' water and power arrive through entirely separate systems. In fact, the production of all forms of energy requires a great deal of water and the distribution and treatment of water requires a great deal of energy. While percentages vary significantly across systems, approximately 40% of freshwater withdrawals in the US go to cooling thermo-electric power plants.[5] At the same time, in some municipalities up to half of the energy bill is consumed by water and wastewater utilities.[6] This interdependency compounds the risks when severe weather events occur.

When the state of California instituted water restrictions in 2015, it saved electricity and reduced greenhouse gas emissions more effectively than all the major utilities' energy-efficiency programs combined.[7] The same savings can apply at the scale of a neighborhood or home, where low-flow fixtures or photovoltaic panels provide a "twofer" benefit. The good news is that wealthy and less affluent communities alike are increasingly pursuing net-zero energy and water-neutral targets. However, most of the US has deferred maintenance on municipal water and power infrastructure, leading to a vicious cycle of dependence on continued high consumption and higher rates to cover repairs.[8] US federal regulations continue to encourage

centralized systems while local utility programs primarily encourage individuals to reduce usage.

In between these scales, new solar suburbs and community-scale net-zero energy and water strategies around the world have begun to demonstrate dramatic improvements through integrating infrastructure ecologies.[9] But upgrading the performance of *existing* suburban water and energy systems is harder and tends to be piecemeal. This is precisely where retrofits are playing a critical role delivering water and energy more efficiently and substantially improving resilience and environmental quality.

The process often starts by breaking down larger problems into individual components whose solutions can be appropriately layered. This chapter focuses on the physical changes that suburban retrofits are employing to address water quality, too much and too little water, as well as shifts to renewable energy and district-scale combined cooling, heating, and power systems.

RETROFITS TO IMPROVE WATER QUALITY: FROM GRAY TO GREEN

Numerous factors contribute to the increase in stressed water resources in northern America and around the world—and their solutions. Degraded rivers and lakes, depleted and contaminated aquifers, aging pipes, and new threats from climate change are driving efforts to improve water quality. For the most part, the design solutions represent a sea change (pun intended) from the centralized, concrete solutions that suburban places were built on.

Increasingly, gray infrastructure is being retrofitted with green infrastructure that replicates natural hydrology. Centralized water treatment plants are being augmented by decentralized efforts to manage stormwater where it falls and reduce runoff to sewers and creeks. Over 700 of the 860 communities with combined storm and sewer pipes (combined sewer overflow, or CSO issues) are retrofitting their systems so heavy storms don't flood the sewage treatment plants and dump raw sewage into rivers. Even wastewater is being treated on site. Buildings are being designed to harvest rather than shed rainwater.

[5] J.F. Kenney, N.L. Barber, S.S. Hutson, K.S. Linsey, J.K. Lovelace, and M.A. Maupin, *Estimated Use of Water in the United States in 2005* (Reston, VA: US Geological Survey, 2009).

[6] International Energy Agency, *Water Energy Nexus,* Excerpt from the 2016 World Energy Outlook (Paris), 34: https://www.iea.org/publications/freepublications/publication/.WorldEnergyOutlook2016ExcerptWaterEnergyNexus.pdf.

[7] E.S. Spang, A.J. Holguin, and F.J. Loge, "The Estimated Impact of California's Urban Water Conservation Mandate on Electricity Consumption and Greenhouse Gas Emissions," *Environmental Research Letters* 13: 1 (12 January, 2018).

[8] Danielle Ivory, Ben Protess, and Griff Palmer, "In American Towns, Private Profits from Public Works," *New York Times*, 24 December 2016; Daniel Herriges, "$3.2 Billion to Fix Tampa's Aging Pipes? From Where?" Strong Towns, 30 August 2019: https://www.strongtowns.org/journal/2019/8/30/32-billion-to-fix-tampas-aging-pipes-from-where.

[9] Arka Pandit, et al., "Infrastructure Ecology: An Evolving Paradigm for Sustainable Urban Development," *Journal of Cleaner Production* (1 October 2017): S19–S27.

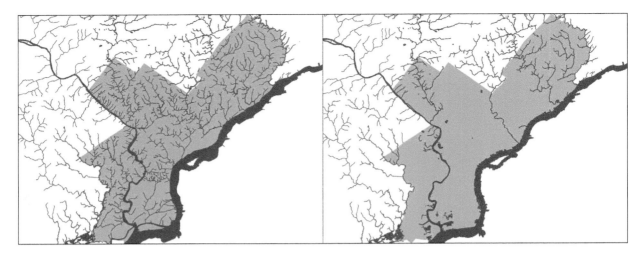

Figure I.6-1 Before the US Clean Water Act in 1972, it was normal practice to drain the wetlands and culvert the creeks for suburban development. These two maps of Philadelphia's historic streams (left) and current conditions (right) tell a very familiar story. Retrofitting provides an opportunity to daylight those creeks and improve both water quality and stream capacity. Source: Adam Levine, Historical Consultant, Philadelphia Water Department.

Generic landscapes of asphalt and lawns are sprouting native plantings in rain gardens. Culverted creeks are being daylit and a new, more localized landsape is emerging that is better able to seep, slow, and cleanse stormwater before it reaches lakes and rivers.

The Clean Water Act of 1972 and the Safe Drinking Water Act of 1974 were catalytic moments in efforts to improve water quality in the US. Why hasn't there been more progress in reducing the number of eutrophic lakes and streams in poor condition? Those laws focused on industrial pollution and the need to construct water treatment plants, and they've largely succeeded. Today, the threat has changed. The prime threat to water quality is stormwater runoff.[10] It carries sediment and fertilizers from lawns and agricultural lands; a stew of pathogens, metals, oils, and salts from roadways, parking lots and roofs; as well as sewage overflows from communities with CSOs or failing septic systems.[11] Research has shown that households in low-density suburban areas with large parking lots generate three times as much urban runoff as households living in cities with pre-1960 development patterns.[12]

For decades, suburban runoff has been directed to sewer pipes and culverted creeks before emptying into streams. Their fast-moving, sunlight-deprived discharge erodes creek beds and the plant and aquatic life that are essential to cleansing the water of harmful levels of nutrients. Today, with more extreme storms, more pavement upstream, and compacted lawns, the amount and velocity of runoff is increasing beyond the capacity of the aging pipes. This is leading to flooding and further degraded water quality.

A range of design strategies have arisen to address these problems. Their use has been accelerated in the US by the Environmental Protection Agency's (EPA) consent decrees for communities with CSOs, its mandate in 1999 for all municipal sewer systems to develop stormwater runoff management regulations, and its endorsement of green infrastructure solutions to meet these requirements in 2007. The regulations vary by state, but as of 2016 most require some form of on-site retention, typically of the first inch of rain per storm event and treatment to remove some

---

[10] This was first officially addressed in 1990 in Phase 1 of EPA's National Pollution Discharge Elimination System (NPDES).

[11] Roadways exceeding 50,000 vehicles/day typically produce more toxic pollution in highway runoff than that produced from all sewage of a typical large city. Vladimir Novotny, Jack Ahern, and Paul Brown, *Water Centric Sustainable Communities: planning, retrofitting and building the next urban environment* (Hoboken, NJ: Wiley, 2010), 35.

[12] J.P. Heaney, "Principles of Integrated Urban Water Management," in R. Field, J.P. Heaney, and R. Pitt, *Innovative Urban Wet-Weather Flow Management Systems* (Lancaster, PA: TECHNOMIC Publishing Co., 2000).

percentage of suspended solids.[13] Many require post-development groundwater recharge to match pre-development conditions, even for redevelopment projects. This can hinder redevelopment so EPA recommends that authorities incentivize on-site water management by tying it to the reduced energy demands on power plants.[14]

Meeting such requirements with fenced detention ponds isn't land-efficient (or attractive) and underground tanks aren't cheap. At the project scale, this has broadened interest in low-impact development (LID) practices to engineer natural hydrologic functions into site planning, as well as the even more nature-inspired practices of light imprint development.[15] When well designed, these practices replace detention ponds with property-enhancing landscape features that capture water where it falls and appear more like gardens or reflecting pools. At the district scale, interest has grown in open-air stormwater parks and "soft" green infrastructure solutions. In a scene playing out across the country, suburban Gwinnett County, north of Atlanta, has found that the cost of on-site stormwater infrastructure is inhibiting the redevelopment of old strip malls constructed before any such requirements were in place.[16] Instead, the county is planning a shared retention/detention facility. Charlotte Nash, chairman of the Gwinnett County Board of Commissioners says, "Public investment in district scale solutions like this will unlock tremendous private investment throughout this corridor and basin while providing an amenity and demonstrating our commitment to innovations in water technology."[17]

Even before meeting the new standards, a typical compact, mixed-use redevelopment of a suburban grayfield site improves runoff by building on the parking lots, reducing trips, and improving infiltration through the inclusion of pocket parks, tree trenches, and green gutters

in new streets. By concentrating growth compactly on already developed land, more of the watershed's soils remain undisturbed and per household runoff is dramatically reduced.[18] Retrofits that go the next step and provide permeable paving often make use of on-site demolition rubble as an underlay.

More ambitious retrofits are employing green roofs, bioswales, rain gardens, and underground filtration/infiltration basins to cleanse runoff while recycling or treating their wastewater onsite. Mashpee Commons in Cape Cod (an urbanized strip mall profiled in *Retrofitting Suburbia*) installed an on-site state-of-the-art membrane bioreactor wastewater treatment "package" plant. The electricity it uses is generated by solar collectors added to multiple roofs.[19] Cape Cod as a region struggles with water impairment from aging septic systems on large lots, with nitrogen loading impacting bays and estuaries. The Mashpee Commons facility is a model for more compact development and is a piece of the wastewater solution as the Town of Mashpee advances its Comprehensive Wastewater Management Plan.[20]

See these case studies:

- II.2. Hassalo on Eighth and Lloyd, Portland, Oregon
- II.13. Promenade of Wayzata, Wayzata, Minnesota
- II.25. White Flint and the Pike District, Montgomery County, Maryland

This brings up the question of what can be done to improve runoff in existing residential suburban neighborhoods? It isn't just a question of runoff from roads and driveways. Lawns have become less biodiverse, and more

---

13 Summary of State Post Construction Stormwater Standards, Office of Water, EPA: https://www.epa.gov/sites/production/files/2016-08/documents/swstdsummary_7-13-16_508.pdf.

14 "Spend Less Energy Managing Water," US Environmental Protection Agency: https://www.epa.gov/green-infrastructure/spend-less-energy-managing-water.

15 See Robert Steuteville, "Great Idea: Light Imprint for Walkable Green Infrastructure," *25 Great Ideas of the New Urbanism*, Congress for the New Urbanism, 15 May 2017: https://www.cnu.org/publicsquare/2017/05/15/great-idea-light-imprint-walkable-green-infrastructure.

16 Washington DC's Stormwater Retention Credit system addresses this issue by allowing properties that install green infrastructure voluntarily to sell credits to larger properties in need of them.

17 Conversation with Ellen Dunham-Jones, 15 August 2019, Sandy Springs, Georgia.

18 See "Protecting Water Resources with Higher Density Development," Office of Sustainable Communities (EPA publication 231-R-06-001, 2006), and John S. Jacob and Ricardo Lopez, "Is Denser Greener? An Evaluation of Higher Density Development as an Urban Stormwater-Quality Best Management Practice," *Journal of the American Water Resource Association* 45(3): 687–701, June 2009.

19 *Retrofitting Suburbia*, on Mashpee Commons, 95–107.

20 "Initially built as a Rotating Biological Contactor plant, the facility was rated to treat a maximum of 80,000 gallons per day. Recently, the facility was upgraded to a Membrane Bio-Reactor (MBR), a more efficient and effective treatment process that allowed for the treatment capacity to more than double without changing the footprint of the building. In addition to providing wastewater treatment to all of the Mashpee Commons commercial and residential tenants, the facility serves multiple municipal buildings (Fire Station, Police Station, Senior Center, and Library), as well as an assisted living and memory care facility on an adjacent parcel." Email from Tom Feronti and Buff Chase of Mashpee Commons to Ellen Dunham-Jones, 3 June 2018.

reliant on agrochemicals and irrigation. In cool, wet climates 20 to 40% of total household water use is applied outdoors, mostly to water lawns. That figure climbs to 60% or more in hot climates.[21] And the US Fish and Wildlife Service says homeowners use up to 10 times more chemicals per acre than farmers do.[22] Over time, as lawns become compacted, they shed more runoff than they absorb. The stormwater, pesticides, and fertilizers join the runoff in the streets heading to the sewer drains and creeks. And don't forget the surprisingly high amount of air and noise pollution caused by mowing and blowing.

In addition to the various small-lot, water-wise, prairie restoration, and food-growing strategies to minimize lawns, several municipalities have encouraged creation of vegetated bioswales and rain gardens at the edges of streets to intercept and infiltrate runoff from both lawns and roads, in both rainy and arid climates.[23] Not only do these green infrastructure features improve environmental health, the trees and diverse plantings also contribute to the mental and physical health of residents and visitors. Their shade, fine-grained textures, and beauty reward the pedestrian eye, inviting us to enjoy the physical and biophilic health benefits.

See these case studies:

- II.14. Maplewood Mall and Living Streets, Maplewood, Minnesota
- II.26. The Blairs, Silver Spring, Maryland
- II.31. Cottages on Greene, East Greenwich, Rhode Island

RETROFITTING WATER FOR RESILIENCE: TOO MUCH WATER

In addition to degrading water *quality*, suburbia's form also tends to exacerbate the problems of water *quantity*. Whether it's reimagining lawn surfaces to reduce watering,

Figure I.6-2 The first of five detention ponds at Exploration Green, a former golf course in Houston, Texas, being retrofitted into a joint flood control, recreation, conservation, and environmental project designed by SWA. When complete, the ponds and constructed wetlands are expected to protect 2000 to 3000 homes for a cost of $30 million, $28 million of which came from an $88 million bond approved by voters in 2016. Source: Photo by Joe Bibby, 2018.

reconfiguring upstream impervious surface to address flash floods downstream, creating meandering flow patterns to slow runoff, or constructing living shorelines to absorb storm surge, more and more communities are finding opportunities to build resilience by retrofitting aging suburban property types and infrastructure. This is especially significant in lower-lying, lower-income neighborhoods that tend to bear greater flood impacts.

The terms "100-year flood" and "500-year flood" entered our vocabulary in 1973 to alert us to the very real hazards of flood zones. They indicate the risk of an event in any given year (i.e. there is a 1% chance of a flood each year in a 100-year flood zone and a 0.2% chance in a 500-year flood zone based on the record of past events). The public has widely misinterpreted them to mean that such floods only occur every 100 or 500 years. Not only is this not how probability works, there is growing evidence of increased storm frequency. Perhaps not surprisingly, 10% of all occupied housing units in the US from 2011 to 2015 were in floodplains, half of them built since 1980.[24]

21 P. W. Mayer et al., *Residential End Uses of Water* (Denver, CO: AWWA Research Foundation, 1999), 167, note 19.
22 Diane Lewis, "The Toxic Brew in Our Yards," *New York Times*, 10 May 2014.
23 Seattle's pilot Street Edge Alternative, or SEA Streets program, reduced the volume of stormwater leaving the street by 99%: http://www.seattle.gov/util/EnvironmentConservation/Projects/GreenStormwaterInfrastructure/CompletedGSIProjects/StreetEdgeAlternatives/index.htm. See also the rebate incentive programs in both Tucson, AZ, and Montgomery County, MD that encourage homeowners to harvest rainwater by various means.

24 Stephanie Rosoff, Jessica Yager, "Housing in the U.S. Floodplains," Data Brief, May 2017, NYU Furman Center: http://furmancenter.org/files/NYUFurmanCenter_HousingInTheFloodplain_May2017.pdf.

Flood-prone Houston has been particularly voracious in developing its sponge-like prairie floodplains—replacing their capacity to absorb more than 8 inches of rainfall per hour compared to just half an inch for turf grass—and relying on detention ponds and channelized concrete bayous for protection.[25] The vulnerability of such practices was brutally exposed in 2017 when Hurricane Harvey dumped 40 to 60 inches of rain over several days across the metro area and caused an estimated $125 billion in damage.[26] Buying out and removing the 140,000 homes in its 100-year flood plains isn't feasible, but using eminent domain to convert a closed golf course into a stormwater detention park called Exploration Green is already proving helpful. When Hurricane Harvey hit during construction of the first pond, it retained 100 million gallons of water and has spawned the city's approval of replicating the model at the Inwood Forest Golf Course.[27] Nonetheless, shortly after Hurricane Harvey, the Houston City Council unanimously approved Meritage Homes' request to build 900 new houses on the Pine Crest Golf Club property despite being in a flood zone. The request met the city's new stricter requirement for houses to be elevated two feet above the 500-year flood elevation by deepening a drainage channel to narrow the onsite area in the floodplain and building the houses on the excavated soil.[28] But downstream from the project where Harvey damaged more than 2,300 houses and apartments, residents are worried that the new requirements do not adequately address the impacts on them.

Residents of the 250-year-old downtown of Ellicott City, Maryland, have similar worries. A mill town turned tourist destination located on the Patapsco River, the downtown has experienced many floods. However, unlike previous inundations, the devastation from the floods of 2016 and 2018 were not from rising river waters overflowing the banks. The deadly rush of water down Main Street came from extreme rainfall on the increasingly paved and developed suburban properties *uphill* and out of the floodplain.[29]

If Houston illustrates the problem of building in floodplains, Ellicott City shows that even development outside of floodplains can greatly increase downstream (or downhill) risks. Yet the extensive mapping process that the Federal Emergency Management Agency (FEMA) uses to produce floodplain maps looks backward rather than forward. It does not account for projections of changes to the built environment, sea level rise, or climate change.[30] As storms and our ability to absorb them constantly shift, the maps quickly grow out of date.[31] As confirmation, a study of 181,000 flood damage claims in Cook County, Illinois, between 2007 and 2011 found no correlation between damage payouts and federally designated floodplains.[32]

Instead of simply basing development regulations and insurance requirements on unreliable floodplains, communities should consider multiprong approaches. As previously discussed, on-site green infrastructure solutions do well at infiltrating and reusing ordinary rainfall amounts while improving water quality. But flood protection requires larger, more district-scale solutions.

Another strategy is the use of transfer of development rights (TDR) to encourage building owners in flood-prone or storm-surge areas to sell their

25 Marina Schauffler, "Enhancing Natural Protections Against Rising Waters," *Saving Land Magazine,* Land Trust Alliance, Winter 2019.

26 For a prescient discussion, see Al Shaw, Neena Satija, and Kiah Collier, "Boomtown, Flood Town," *Pro Publica*, 7 December 2106: www.propublica.org. See also Billy Fleming, "The Real Villains in Harvey Flood: Urban Sprawl and the Politicians Who Allowed It," *Guardian,* 30 August 2017.

27 Elsewhere, many golf courses have been turned into nature preserves. But increasing their biodiversity isn't quite as simple as letting nature take its course. At the Wildflower Preserve in Englewood, Florida, the Lemon Bay Conservancy employed solar aerators, artificial islands with native vegetation, water pumps, and volunteers with nets to remove the thick mats of duckweeds on the ponds that resulted from past fertilizer use and an influx of nutrients from a nearby water treatment facility used for irrigation—and has to continue working hard to keep other invasive species at bay.

28 Fauzeya Rahman, "Meritage Homes to Start Model Homes in Spring Brook Village After Houston City Council Approval," *Houston Business Chronicle*, 25 April 2018.

29 A year later, Ellicott City continued to debate options, including abandoning the historic center, spending $60 million on boring two diversion tunnels, or $85M for 18 uphill stormwater management projects.

30 Joel Scata, "FEMA's Outdated and Backward-Looking Flood Maps," Natural Resource Defense Council, nrdc.org, 12 October 2017.

31 Using higher-resolution mapping tools, research estimates that the number of US residents exposed to serious flooding is 2.6–3.1 times larger than the number calculated using FEMA flood maps. Oliver E.J. Wing, Paul D. Bates, Andrew M. Smith, et al., "Estimates of Present and Future Flood Risk in the Conterminous United States," *Environmental Research Letters* 13:3 (28 February 2018).

32 Center for Neighborhood Technology, "The Prevalence and Cost of Urban Flooding," May 2014: www.cnt.org.

development rights or trade them to move to higher ground that planners would like to see densify and urbanize. This was tried at the 536-acre Fort Washington Office Park in Upper Dublin, Pennsylvania. Built on top of a major creek and several tributaries in the early 1950s, it was 48% impervious surface by 2008. Persistent flooding, including a death in 1989, led to office vacancies. In 2013 the city established TDR sending areas in the floodplains and receiving areas on higher ground. They also received state grants to construct two upstream dry dams. However, the dams fixed the flooding problems enough that owners were no longer interested in moving or selling their TDR credits. In 2018, the city replaced the TDR zoning with a form-based code encouraging mixed-use nodes on the high ground.[33] Although the TDRs at Fort Washington only succeeded in seeding the idea of mixed-use nodes, other communities are employing them, often in conjunction with land trusts, as a way to stem the "flood, rebuild, repeat" cycle.[34]

See these case studies:

- ▣ II.18. Historic Fourth Ward Park, Atlanta, Georgia
- ▣ II.30. Meriden Green, Meriden, Connecticut

RETROFITTING WATER FOR RESILIENCE: TOO LITTLE WATER

Is the US entering the phase of "peak water," the point at which more water is consumed than is replenished? In 2013 the US Government Accountability Office found that 40 state water managers expected water shortages to occur in their states in the next 10 years. How are communities retrofitting themselves to cope with too little water?

In many respects, they're employing the same techniques already discussed but with more attention to combining water conservation, reuse, and fire prevention. Common strategies include harvesting air-conditioning condensate, closed-loop water recycling, groundwater recharge, protection of drinking water sources, xeriscaping (landscaping for arid areas with planting that use little

Figure I.6-3 Revitalizing a suburban corridor into the Fiesta District in Mesa, Arizona, involved a road diet with widened sidewalks and stormwater swales that irrigate new trees. Urban heat island effects are further mitigated by paseo pocket parks offering cooling, seating, and night lighting as shown here, with the mid-block shade and fountain at the entrance to a big box store recently renovated into high-rent office space.
Source: Photo by Ellen Dunham-Jones, 2015.

water), and water-neutral land-use planning.[35] Santa Fe, New Mexico, is an example of the latter. Instead of a more typical TDR, it has a unique Water Right Transfer Program intended to match the water demand of new developments to the acquisition of new water rights.[36] Flagstaff, Arizona, is one of a growing number of communities with a Wildland-Urban Interface (WUI) overlay zoning code intended to reduce damage to property from wildfires.[37]

At a larger scale, but less visible in terms of urbanism, water and sanitation districts in Orange County, California, have been pioneers in replenishing groundwater with highly treated wastewater. Instead of being discharged into the ocean, it is put through additional purification before

---

[33] Rebecca Heilweil, "In Fort Washington, New Life For a Historic Office Park," *Philadelphia Inquirer*, 5 March 2018: http://www.philly.com/philly/news/in-fort-washington-a-historic-office-park-new-life-20180305.html.

[34] Schauffler, "Enhancing Natural Protections."

[35] For a useful academic resource, see Yan Jiang, Yongjing Yuan, and Holly Piza, "A Review of Applicability and Effectiveness of Low Impact Development/Green Infrastructure Practices in Arid/Semi-Arid United States," *Environments* 2 (2015): 221–249: doi: 10.3390/environments2020221. For technologies related to household water conservation, see the University Municipal Water Consortium, http://www.pecanstreet.org/about/university-municipal-water-consortium/.

[36] For more tools, see the Alliance for Water Efficiency's Net Blue Toolkit, http://www.allianceforwaterefficiency.org/net-blue-landing-page.aspx.

[37] See Anna Read and Molly Mowery, "Zoning and Land-Use Tools in the Wildland-Urban Interface," *Zoning Practice* 9 (American Planning Association, September 2018).

being piped to several recharge basins, where it filters into the groundwater. The 100 million gallons of new water per day impedes saltwater intrusion and, as of 2016, meets two-thirds of the county's groundwater pumping with-drawals. More and more places, and not only in arid climates, are recycling wastewater, sometimes through centralized systems—as in Tel Aviv, Israel—and sometimes through cost-saving on-site district systems such as the Emory University WaterHub in Atlanta, Georgia.[38]

Whether by improving water quality, reducing flooding, or increasing water supply, all of these strategies increase communities' resilience to the challenges of climate change. Often used in combination, these strategies treat both stormwater and wastewater as a resource. Designers of suburban retrofits are coming up with creative new ways to integrate climate- and geography-appropriate solutions to on-site water management. In the best cases, these are opportunities to celebrate water, trees, and natural systems in beautiful public spaces that help build the social capital that is vital to community resilience.[39] At the same time, they are reducing energy usage by creating cooling microclimates and reducing water pumping. They are helping their communities adapt to and mitigate climate change.

See these case studies:

- II.5. Parkmerced, San Francisco, California
- II.16. Uptown Circle, Normal, Illinois

RETROFITTING SUBURBIA FOR ENERGY RESILIENCE

In addition to reducing dependence on central water treatment plants, suburban retrofits are increasingly

reducing energy reliance on central power plants and the grid. As with water, retrofits to suburban energy infrastructure are focused on much more localized, on-site solutions. These include a growing number of district energy heating and cooling projects, closed-loop waste-to-energy systems, and on-site renewable power generation. These strategies are driven by mandates to reduce greenhouse gas emissions (GHGs), reduce costs (average electricity rates in the US nearly doubled from 1990 to 2017), and increase reliability and resilience in the face of aging infrastructure, more frequent severe storms, power outages, fear of terrorism, and our seemingly insatiable demand for more electricity. When the grid goes down, solar panels, wind turbines, and geothermal systems can keep the power on, and increasingly at lower cost than fossil fuel options.

But there's a catch. A building may be "green," but if you have to drive to reach it, you may end up squandering all that efficiency because the energy needed for transpor-tation can be twice the amount required for building operations.[40] Research has consistently shown that total GHGs increase with distance from the urban core, largely because of the higher transportation energy consumed in low-density, spread-out areas as well as transmission loss. The other big contributor to those higher emissions is the heat loss associated with detached buildings. They have more exterior surface, much of it leaky, through which to lose thermal energy.[41]

The solution for reducing transportation energy, transmission loss, and operational energy is more compact urbanism. Smaller block sizes, a synergetic mix of uses, and the density to support them dramatically increase walkability, bikeability, and transit feasibility. At the same time, more compact building types—such as townhouses attached side-by-side or multistory

[38] Since 2010, half of Tel Aviv's agricultural irrigation comes from water reclamation. Ari Rabinovitch, "Arid Israel Recycles Waste Water on Grand Scale," *Reuters*, 14 November 2010. See also "What Is the WaterHub?" http://www.campserv.emory.edu/fm/energy_utilities/water-hub/.

[39] Smaller-scale green infrastructure projects lend themselves to community engagement and building the social cohesion that helps communities better survive natural disasters. See Betsey Russell, "Tired of Constant Flooding, Tiny Duck Hill, Mississippi Revitalized Their Community by Making It More Resilient," *Revitalization* 106 (1 September 2019). See also Daniel P. Aldrich and Michelle A. Meyer, "Social Capital and Community Resilience," *American Behavioral Scientist* 59:1 (October 1, 2014): 254–269: doi.org/10.1177/0002764214550299.

[40] Alex Wilson and Rachel Navarro, "Driving to Green Buildings," *Building Green*, 30 August 2007.

[41] Suburban homes tend to be larger than urban residences, but to the degree that they have larger households, the square footage per capita may even out this difference in per capita residential energy usage. See Christopher Jones and Daniel M. Kammen, "Distribution of US Household Carbon Footprints Reveals Suburbanization Undermines Greenhouse Gas Benefits of Urban Population Density," *Environmental Science & Technology* 48:2 (2014): 895–902. See also Jeffrey Wilson, Jamie Spinney, Hugh Millward, et al., "Blame the Exurbs, Not the Suburbs: Exploring the Distribution of Greenhouse Gas Emissions Within a City Region," *Energy Policy* 62, November 2013.

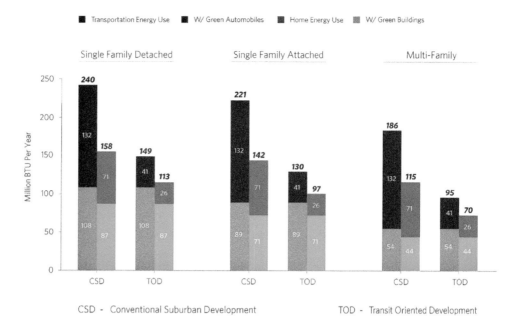

Legend: ■ Transportation Energy Use ■ W/ Green Automobiles ■ Home Energy Use ■ W/ Green Buildings

Figure I.6-4 This chart from the "Location Efficiency and Housing Type: Boiling it Down to BTUs" study of 2011 shows how much location in transit-oriented development matters. A household living in a green building with a green car in conventional suburban development still consumes more energy than one living in a not-green building, with a not-green car if the area has transit and is designed to be walkable and compact. Source: Courtesy of The Jonathan Rose Companies.

buildings—reduce per-square-foot heating and cooling demands. Their density and proximity allow for microgrids and district-scaled combined cooling, heating, and power plants (CCHP, or CHP for combined heating and power) that can provide efficiency gains of up to 80 to 90% relative to conventional separate generation of electricity and heat.[42]

Many countries, some states, and numerous communities are developing plans and retrofitting outdated policies to allow for, if not require, these kinds of systems. Canada is one of the leaders in community energy planning. QUEST, a nonprofit called Quality Urban Energy Systems of Tomorrow, documents Canada's community-scale energy retrofit and renewable energy plans, projects, and policies on its website, from harnessing tidal wave action to lake water cooling. Concerns about rising energy costs and a commitment to reduce GHGs led to federal funding in 1994 of the Partners for Climate Protection Program. It has

provided 350 municipalities with data, expertise, and tools to implement action plans and monitor the results. To meet its ambitious plans to be the greenest city, Vancouver requires large parcels to conduct a low carbon energy supply prefeasibility study and a business case of the viability of district energy systems as a condition of rezoning. Where such is not viable, the redevelopment must be designed to connect easily to any future district energy system.

In the US, the State of California has been the most aggressive about using regulations to reduce GHGs through transportation, land-use planning, and renewable energy. In 2018 it became the first state in the nation to require that all new detached houses and small apartment buildings have solar panels by 2020. Since 2008, State Bill 375 has resulted in metropolitan planning organizations (MPOs) being required to demonstrate how their regional transportation plans will meet GHG emission reduction targets. Just a few of the impacts of SB 375 are fuel cells at several wastewater plants, numerous solar/green roof programs, Los Angeles' investment in the Metro Rail system, and San Diego's socially inclusive and water-saving

---

[42] "Efficiency in District Energy," Copenhagen Centre on Energy Efficiency: http://www.energyefficiencycentre.org/energy-efficiency-accelerators/efficiency-in-district-energy.

Figure I.6-5 Vancouver, British Columbia, has designated the intersection of an existing and future subway line as a new town center. A public park lined with high-rise residential towers on the roof of the existing Oakridge Centre Mall and mid-rise office buildings along its sides have been approved. All will be serviced by a district energy system that is conceptually similar to a shared parking strategy. It will take advantage of balancing day versus night uses to efficiently distribute heating and cooling. Source: Courtesy of Henriquez Partners Architects.

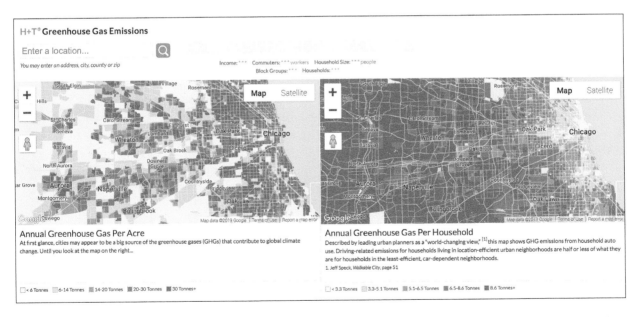

Figure I.6-6 The Housing + Transportation Affordability Index interactive map of the US allows detailed comparisons of multiple metrics related to housing location and transportation, including GHG emissions. This screen capture of Chicago reveals how GHG per acre versus GHG per household dramatically flips our understanding of the environmental, as well as monetary, costs of auto dependency. Source: Courtesy of The Center for Neighborhood Technology.

climate action plan.[43] Another important result is that several new tools have been developed to help communities everywhere understand the impact of development patterns on vehicle miles traveled, GHGs, public health, and affordability. These include Urban Footprint by Peter Calthorpe and Joe DiStefano and the Housing + Transportation Affordability Index by the Center for Neighborhood Technology.

What do these new energy policies and plans mean in terms of urban design and placemaking in the suburbs? On the one hand, it might mean business as usual. Vehicle-to-grid (V2G) technology exploits parked electric cars' batteries as storage for solar microgrids and relief for central grid peak loading. Tesla had early success leasing its SolarCity photovoltaic panels and Powerwall home battery through its electric car showrooms precisely because of the benefits of the solar-plus-storage system and how easily it is grafted onto existing single-family homes in auto-oriented suburbs.[44]

On the other hand, several of the early solar suburbs and net-zero developments laid out compact, walkable blocks and buildings to optimize solar gain or minimize heat loss. BedZed, a pioneering net-zero energy mixed-use community that opened in 2002 in a suburb of London has solar panels, a no-longer functioning waste-to energy CHP plant, rainwater harvesting, carsharing and transit access, and orients all of its homes to face south to capture solar gain. The circa 2005 BoO1 brownfield redevelopment in Malmo, Sweden's Western Harbor, is predominantly powered by a single large wind turbine capturing the North Sea winds. At the same time, its masterplan employs short, staggered east-west paths to block those winds within the development. As a demonstration project, it also employs solar panels, solar thermal collectors, a geothermal district heating system, and converts waste to biogas that runs the local buses.

More recent high-performance redevelopments have gone even further to integrate various infrastructures into closed-loop systems. Starting in the 1990s the City of Stockholm, Sweden, took the lead in redeveloping over 370 acres of truck-oriented brownfields into Hammarby-Sjostad. The project's sustainable water and transportation infrastructure is immediately evident in the mixed-use TOD with ferry and light-rail service, walkable and bikeable blocks, ample public spaces with permeable surfaces, stormwater canals, ladders, and bioswales and extensive restored wetlands. Solar panels are also abundant.

However, the "Hammarby Model" waste-to-energy eco-cycle systems are less visible, highly innovative, and very effective.[45] With a goal of producing half of all the energy it needs, the project harvests biogas and thermal energy from wastewater for district heating and cooling, feeds its combustible waste to its CHP plant, and biosolids to the wetlands, which in turn produce biofuel for the CHP plant. Underground vacuum suction chutes in each building separate combustibles, food, and newspaper waste. Block-based recycling rooms take glass, paper, plastic, and a variety of bulky items, while dangerous items are relegated to area-based waste collection. This degree of integration between waste-water-energy-transportation probably couldn't have happened without the city being the instigator and leading the coordination between departments from the very beginning.[46]

Nonetheless, the presence of CHP plants or a motivated local energy utility can spur private investment in retrofitting. Prism Capital Partners had their pick of defunct pharmaceutical campuses in New Jersey to redevelop as mixed-use. The CHP plant at the former Roche property in Nutley was a big attraction for them.[47]

Similarly, it is not a coincidence that Austin, Texas, is home to three major suburban retrofits. Its community-owned electric utility, Austin Energy, developed the first and largest green building program in the nation and has a top performing renewable energy program. Its district energy investments' revenues have exceeded expenses, helped direct growth to areas targeted by the city for

---

[43] According to the Sierra Club, over 90 cities have adopted 100% clean energy goals, and as of 2019, six have met that goal: https://www.sierraclub.org/ready-for-100/commitments.

[44] The first planned "Tesla-town," YarraBend, a redevelopment of a suburban industrial site outside Melbourne, Australia, sold out its first-phase high-end single-family homes in 2017 pre-construction. While the project plans to include higher-density condominiums as well, the sleek, future-oriented single-family homes are to include built-in Tesla powerwalls and solar panels, as well as conventional suburban front-loaded garages.

[45] See Harrison Fraker, *The Hidden Potential of Sustainable Neighborhoods: Lessons from Low-Carbon Communities* (Washington, DC: Island Press, 2013).

[46] Research has shown that Hammarby-Sjostad's integrated infrastructural systems reduce metabolic flows but is far from self-sufficient. Sofie Pandis Iveroth, Stefan Johansson, Nils Brandt, "The Potential of the Infrastructure System of Hammarby Sjostad in Stockholm, Sweden," *Energy Policy* 59 (August 2013): 716–726.

[47] Conversation between Ellen Dunham-Jones and Eugene Diaz, Principal, Prism Capital Partners, 7 March 2018, Nutley, NJ.

(a)   (b)

(c)   (d)

Figure I.6-7 Hammarby-Sjostad in Stockholm integrates (a) bike routes along restored wetlands, (b) waste-to-energy chutes at mid-rise buildings, (c) stormwater channels in public spaces, and (d) shops at transit stations, into a highly livable urbanism. While not all of the ambitious sustainability targets have been met, the return of beavers and ducks to the lake it surrounds indicates it is now cleaner than it was before the 20,000 human inhabitants arrived. Source: Photos by Ellen Dunham-Jones, 2016, 2018.

redevelopment, and have helped the utility meet its goals for electric reliability and climate protection.[48]

See these case studies:

- II.10. The Domain, Austin, Texas
- II.11. ACC Highland, Austin, Texas
- II.12. Mueller, Austin, Texas

Many of the same benefits of district systems accrue for smaller and less dense retrofits by installing renewable energy systems either in a microgrid or as independent systems. Solar power is the most popular. SOMO Village, a mixed-use retrofit of a former manufacturing facility in Sonoma County, California, relies heavily on solar and as such is the first project in North America to receive the One Planet Community ranking. Eastgate Mall in Indianapolis has been reinhabited as a data center with a 4-megawatt solar array on its roof and parking lots that provides reliability and resilience. Most often, the reasons cited for

[48] Jim Collins, "Austin Energy's District Cooling Program," Austin Energy, 13 January 2017: http://www.austintexas.gov/edims/document.cfm?id=270593

Figure I.6-8 Boulder Housing Partners redeveloped an aging mobile home community into Red Oak Park in Boulder, Colorado. As designed by Coburn Partners, the 59 energy-efficient, solar-powered "missing middle" homes are primarily rented to the former residents while increasing amenities, integration with the rest of the neighborhood, and access to transit. Source: Courtesy of Coburn Partners.

using solar are to reduce operating costs (and in some cases qualify for grants to reduce construction costs). This is particularly impactful for affordable housing, especially mobile homes, whose poor insulation leads residents to spend up to 35% of their income on energy bills, especially in cold climates like Vermont.[49] The state's first net-zero community of 14 modular homes with solar plus storage replaced an abandoned mobile home park in Waltham. The power residents sell to the utility in the summer buys them credit to get through the winter such that their electricity needs are 100% covered. There are a growing number of such examples.

Geothermal exchange technology using ground source heat pumps is another renewable source for heating and cooling buildings that is showing up in more and more retrofits. The pumps operate similar to a traditional heat pump, but leverage the earth's temperature, rather than outside air, to improve efficiency. In summer, piped liquids transfer heat from a warm interior space to the cooler earth through underground loops before entering the heat pump. The process runs in reverse in the winter. They use 25 to 50% less energy and are much quieter than conventional heating or cooling systems.

See these case studies:

- II.8. Guthrie Green, Tulsa, Oklahoma
- II.13. Promenade of Wayzata, Wayzata, Minnesota
- II.27. La Station – Centre Intergénérationnel, Nuns' Island, Verdun, Quebec

ADDING RESILIENCY BY DESIGN

Better design and planning can help us conserve more energy and water. Better design and planning can also help us both mitigate worsening climate change and adapt to it.

---

[49] Lyndsey Gilpin, "Rebuilding After the Hurricanes: These Solar Homes Use Almost No Energy," *Inside Climate News*, 4 October 2017.

But designers need to know what to plan for. There are many questions:

- Will sea level rise force coastal populations to retreat inland? Who plans for such climate refugees?
- Should communities plan for a wetter, drier, or unchanged climate?
- How will renewable energy investments perform under different climate conditions?

The Crowther Lab at the ETH in Zurich estimates that by 2050, 77% of 520 global cities' climates will resemble that of another city more than their traditional climate. Seattle's climate in 2050 will resemble what we recognize as San Francisco's climate today, London will resemble Barcelona, Madrid will resemble Marrakesh, Tokyo will resemble Changsha, and so on.[50] These analogues are useful to envisioning how to design for future water and energy needs.

The same research group made headlines in 2019 for their proposal that the biggest and cheapest way to mitigate the climate crisis is to restore one trillion of the two trillion trees that have disappeared across the globe since the start of human civilization.[51] They excluded urbanized and agricultural land to identify where reforestation could take place. But we'd like to argue that there are also tremendous opportunities and benefits to be gained from regreening underperforming asphalt everywhere.

In addition to their capacity to absorb and sequester carbon dioxide, reducing global warming, trees in urbanized areas create wind and shade microclimates that reduce Urban Heat Island effects. They stabilize soils and assist stormwater infiltration while providing much-needed habitat for numerous species. And they raise human well-being (and property values) to such an extent that the lack of trees and shade is increasingly recognized as an index of inequality and a public health concern.[52] It is heartening to see the vastly increasing number of suburban retrofits integrating town greens, pocket parks, green roofs, street trees, planted verges, bioswales, and rain gardens—as well as solar panels, geothermal systems, district energy, and waste-to-energy plants. However, only 2% of the suburban retrofits in our database are substantial regreenings such as stormwater parks, reconstructed wetlands, farms, gardens, or the kind of reforestation projects that the Crowther Lab is advocating for. We'd like to see funding and policies to support more such projects. In addition to their contributions globally, they provide cascading local benefits from triggering reinvestment, stemming blight in struggling markets, creating urban agriculture markets, reducing crime, and helping to strengthen community ties.[53]

Hand in hand with planting new trees is preserving those that already exist.[54] Large, long-lived trees with extensive root systems have more "woody biomass" in which to store carbon dioxide and through which to train water deep into the soil. Preserving existing forests and prairies from development is more important than ever and even more reason to retrofit suburbia, redirect growth back into existing communities, and reduce our water and energy consumption. In the process we get to upgrade wasteful infrastructure, make our communities more resilient, and learn to live more compactly among the trees.

---

[50] Jean-Francois Bastin, Emily Clark, Thomas Elliott, et al., "Understanding Climate Change from a Global Analysis of City Analogues," *PLoS One,* 14(7): e0217592, 10 July 2019.

[51] Jean-Francois Bastin, Yelena Finegold, Claude Garcia, et al., "The Global Tree Restoration Potential," *Science,* 5 July 2019.

[52] See Sam Bloch, "Shade," *Places Journal,* April 2019: https://doi.org/10.22269/190423.

[53] The Genesee County Land Bank based in Flint, Michigan, has a particularly impressive record of activating community groups and neighbors through its programs to convert vacant or abandoned properties into productive landscapes of trees and gardens, while improving water quality. See also the investment by Fresh Coast Capital in converting vacant lots to tree farms, in Joy Leopold, "Investment Firm Bets on Tree Farms in Formerly Industrial Midwestern Cities," *Seedstock,* 19 April 2016.

[54] Tree cover within urban land in the US is declining at the rate of 175,000 acres/year and about 36 million trees/year. David J. Nowak, Eric J. Greenfield (USDA Forest Service), "Declining Urban and Community Tree Cover in the US," *Urban Forestry & Urban Greening* 32 (2018) 32–55.

PART TWO
THE CASE
STUDIES

Aurora Avenue North

Hassalo on Eighth and Lloyd
Lake Grove Village

Phoenix Park Apartments

Parkmerced

TAXI

The BLVD

Guthrie Green

La Gran Plaza

The Domain
ACC Highland
Mueller

Figure II.0 Location map of the case studies, as found in metropolitan areas throughout northern America. Source: Authors.

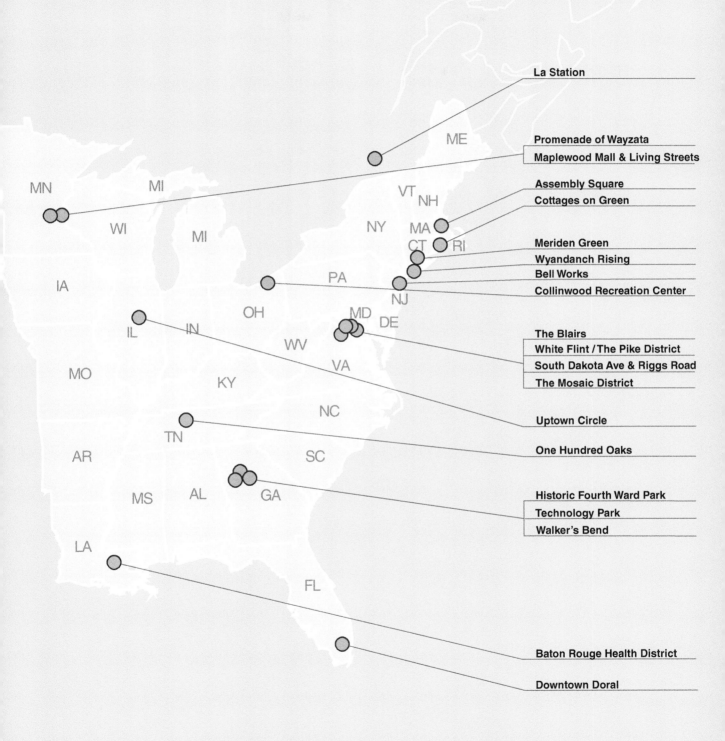

La Station

Promenade of Wayzata

Maplewood Mall & Living Streets

Assembly Square

Cottages on Green

Meriden Green

Wyandanch Rising

Bell Works

Collinwood Recreation Center

The Blairs

White Flint / The Pike District

South Dakota Ave & Riggs Road

The Mosaic District

Uptown Circle

One Hundred Oaks

Historic Fourth Ward Park

Technology Park

Walker's Bend

Baton Rouge Health District

Downtown Doral

MN

MI

WI

MI

IA

IL

IN

MO

KY

AR

MS

AL

TN

NC

SC

GA

LA

FL

ME

VT

NH

NY

MA

CT

RI

PA

NJ

OH

MD

DE

WV

VA

OVERVIEW

Following are the stories of 32 case studies, representing a wide range of suburban retrofits located in diverse contexts and conditions in northern America. They are organized from the west coast of the continent to the east, and include ambitious, large-scale, resource-intensive redevelopments, more modest community-serving reinhabitations of buildings and landscapes, and impressive regreenings. Often, these strategies are used in combination.

Aurora Avenue North
Shoreline, Washington

Challenges addressed:

- Improve public health
- Disrupt automobile dependence

One tactic toward improving public health is to prevent injuries in the first place by preventing construction of new sprawling, automobile-centric developments with their known heightened risk of crashes and poor air quality. This can be accomplished by redirecting new peripheral growth toward suburban infill redevelopment. Where automobile-centric commercial corridors already exist, dangerous to pedestrians and cyclists as well as to drivers, they can be retrofitted. These projects may apply a new lens on health and safety, in concert with now established principles for economic development, and reap the benefits of *complete streets*. Here we define complete streets, following the US Department of Transportation, as "streets designed and operated to enable safe use and support mobility for all users, including people of all ages and abilities, regardless of whether they are traveling as drivers, pedestrians, bicyclists, or public transportation riders."[1]

Three miles of Aurora Avenue North, an arterial road in suburban Shoreline, Washington, just north of Seattle, was transformed over an eighteen-year period, from 1998 to 2016, in accordance with regional goals of accommodating population growth in urban villages served by upgraded

(a)

(b)

Figure II.1-1 Before retrofitting, the Aurora Avenue North corridor near 160th Street was a typical suburban arterial road, a classic "auto mile," of car dealerships and box stores, dangerous to pedestrians (a). New crosswalks, sidewalks, greened medians, enhanced lighting, and bus rapid transit in dedicated lanes have dramatically improved the corridor's safety and performance (b). Source: Photos courtesy of City of Shoreline, Washington.

---

[1] U.S. Department of Transportation Complete Streets (2015): https://www.transportation.gov/mission/health/complete-streets.

Figure II.1-2 The Shoreline Interurban Bridge links two segments of the regional bike trail that runs parallel to the Aurora Avenue North corridor, along the old right-of-way of an interurban trolley line that ran from Seattle to Everett. The bridge, by CH2MHill Engineers, Clinkston Brunner Architects and Hough Beck Baird Inc., features public artwork by Vicki Scuri SiteWorks. Source: Photo © Brent Van Wieringen, courtesy of VS SiteWorks.

transit along major corridors.[2] At the project's inception, the commercial strip corridor had one of the highest crash rates in the United States, an average of nearly one per day, with one fatality per year. Even before completion of new landscaped medians and street trees (optimized for stormwater management), colored and scored crosswalks, buffered sidewalks, improved lighting, utilities moved underground, and bus rapid transit (BRT) service in dedicated lanes, crashes had declined by 60%. At the same time, Shoreline upgraded its segment of a 24-mile regional bike trail that runs parallel to the corridor, to make it safer and more continuous. A key component of this is a trail bridge over the corridor, accomplished with a single 50-foot long concrete girder spanning the roadway, so as not to unduly affect traffic flow during construction.

The process of financing the improvements was complex, and lengthy, requiring a creative mix of 21 different funding sources. While the transformed arterial is still dominated by auto-oriented businesses—car dealerships, chain restaurants, strip malls—the Rapid E bus line boasts King County Metro's highest daily ridership of 17,000 and abutting properties are incrementally responding to the public sector's investment, also with an eye on health.[3] New projects include two health clinics and a YMCA, an expanded farmers market, and the approved

redevelopment of the Aurora Square Shopping Center into the more bike-oriented Shoreline Place, a mixed-use village at the foot of the Interurban Trail Bridge.[4]

Similar improvements, inspired by the Shoreline retrofits, began in 2016 on a segment of Aurora Avenue North in the Licton Springs neighborhood of North Seattle, in a heavily trafficked area. The difficulties children encountered crossing the streets to get to school were cited by the Seattle DOT in the decision to fund the project.[5]

Inspired by Aurora Avenue North, Columbia Pike in Arlington County, Virginia, and other examples, the Urban Land Institute (ULI) initiated a two-year study to develop principles and a toolkit for Building Healthy Corridors. In partnership with the Rose Center for Public Leadership and the National League of Cities, ULI sponsored workshops on four automobile-centric commercial corridors: Federal Boulevard in Denver, Colorado; Vista Avenue in Boise, Idaho; Van Nuys Boulevard in the San Fernando Valley of Los Angeles, California; and Charlotte Avenue in Nashville, Tennessee.[6] While none of the case studies and demonstration projects profiled in the resultant 2016 report could be fully described as "holistically healthy," each strives in a significant way toward accomplishing noble goals of improved safety from crashes and improved health outcome from increased physical activity.

As the ULI report reminds us, 40% of children in the US walked to school in 1969, and only 13% did in 2009. Similarly, 9.9% of commuters walked to work in 1960 and only 2.8% did so in 2013. If we want to reduce car dependence and return to or exceed 1960s levels of walking, we must retrofit more streets for safety. Pedestrians on streets lacking sidewalks are 200% more likely to be involved in crashes than pedestrians on streets with sidewalks.[7] The ongoing improvements along Aurora Avenue North provide a worthy model for retrofitting many more stroads.

[2] Ryan DiRaimo, "Rezoned, Revitalized Aurora," *Urbanist,* 11 June 2018: www.theurbanist.org.
[3] Ibid.

[4] City of Shoreline, Washington, Aurora Corridor Project page and Shoreline Place Community Renewal Area: http://www .shorelinewa.gov/government/projects-initiatives/completed-projects/aurora-corridor-project and http://www.shorelinewa .gov/business/aurora-square-community-renewal-area.
[5] City of Seattle, Washington, Department of Transportation Aurora Ave N Corridor Improvements Project (update 2019): https://www.seattle.gov/transportation/projects-and-programs/ programs/neighborhood-street-fund/past-projects/aurora-ave-n.
[6] Urban Land Institute, *Building Healthy Corridors: Transforming Urban and Suburban Arterials into Thriving Places* (Washington, DC: Urban Land Institute, 2016), ULI Building Healthy Places initiative: www.uli.org/health.
[7] Ibid., 5.

Hassalo on Eighth and Lloyd
Portland, Oregon

Challenges addressed:

- Disrupt automobile dependence
- Add water and energy resilience
- Compete for jobs

Sustainability is Portland's brand. While the environmental movement spread generally in the 1970s, in Portland it coincided with urban transformations that shaped the metro. That's when freeway revolts by residents refusing to allow their neighborhoods to be demolished succeeded in redirecting transportation funding to the light rail system now known as MAX. It's also when Oregon required urban growth boundaries (UGBs) around cities so as to protect agricultural land. By 1988, instead of expanding the UGB, the city chose to redirect growth to Calthorpe Associates' plan for transit-oriented development (TOD) around the new light rail stations in the suburbs.[1] It hasn't all played out as planned, but the redevelopment of the Lloyd office district superblocks into one of Portland's late-bloomer EcoDistrict TODs, including the highly water-innovative and bike-oriented Hassalo on Eighth redevelopment, provides a glimpse into the successful brokering between ecological, economical (and sometimes equitable) strategies that the city is such a leader in exporting.

(a)

(b)

Figure II.2-1 The before photo (a) and the after rendering (b) look southwest to downtown Portland and show how construction of three new residential buildings in Hassalo on Eighth on the 700 Lloyd office building's former parking lots are urbanizing the Lloyd district. Phase 2 is expected to redevelop the block to its south, Oregon Square. Source: Courtesy of GBD Architects.

[1] See 1000 Friends of Oregon, "Making the Connections, A Summary of the LUTRAQ Project: Integrating Land-use and Transportation Planning for Livable Communities," Vol 7, February 1997.

The 410-acre Lloyd district is also a product of the 1970s. It's known for the Lloyd Center, an inward-oriented regional shopping mall and large office towers surrounded by even larger surface parking lots. Perhaps the most frequently mentioned adjective used to describe the area has been "soulless." Laid out in the 1920s with 440-foot square blocks (more than twice as big as downtown Portland's highly walkable 200-foot square blocks), it lay largely vacant until the east-west Banfield Expressway was built immediately to its south, connecting with Interstate 5, the district's western border. East of downtown and across the river, it became that part of the city where the big stuff—not housing—got built. A convention center and two arenas (now called the Rose Quarter) followed in the 1980s and 1990s.

Portland's first light-rail line opened in 1986 with stops in the Lloyd district (expanded since then to four lines). But it took several plans and organizations, the meshing of multiple agendas, and the installation of 1,000 parking meters starting in 1994 to free up the area's abundant parking lots for redevelopment.[2] Meter revenue ($1.4M in 2018), contributes to funding a new transportation management association (later named Go Lloyd), to guide change and to work alongside the newly established Business Improvement District. This strategy met the regional transit authority's interest in more riders, the property owners' interest in more development with less traffic, and the city's interest in doubling jobs and tripling housing while shifting the commute mode away from cars.[3] Rick Williams, founding director of Go Lloyd, writes, "A key factor in the success of the Lloyd District Partnership Plan was the realization by this key leadership group that transportation access was *the* critical factor underlying the economic development vision for growth in the district."[4] And it worked. In 1994, 10% of commuter trips were by transit and 1% by bike. Transit had doubled

to 21% by 1997 and more than quadrupled to 41% in 2005, with bike commuting up to almost 5%.[5]

The establishment of the Lloyd EcoDistrict in 2011 continued the collaboration between major stakeholders and the setting and monitoring of performance targets as means to gain trust and participation from the business community on issues beyond transportation.[6] One of the first EcoDistricts, it grew out of the Portland Sustainability Institute, a nonprofit set up by the city in 2009 to scale up green development beyond the individual building and export the model. EcoDistricts bring neighboring building owners and tenants together to build capacity and reap the cost efficiencies of district-scale solutions to transportation, energy, water, waste management, natural habitats, and social equity.[7] Early on, the focus for the Lloyd EcoDistrict was on reducing energy use while saving property owners' money. The Energy Action Plan and District Utility Data Tracking encourage commercial property owners to benchmark usage and learn from each other. They resulted in a 14% reduction in greenhouse gas emissions between 2010 and 2017 despite an increase in energy use.[8]

In 2012 the Lloyd was literally looped into downtown by both the extension of the downtown streetcar's route and a proposed 6-mile linear park and active transportation

2 Some of the plans that set redevelopment in motion include the 1992 Central City Transportation Management Plan that targeted the Lloyd District to capture 20,000 new jobs and 4,000 housing units by 2015, the 1997 Lloyd District Partnership Plan, and the 2001 Lloyd District Development Plan.
3 At the time, the Lloyd District was estimated to have 1,000 residents and over 20,000 employees.
4 Rick Williams, in memo to Keith Cotton, December 12, 2006, with detail of the many steps taken to achieve the target mode splits: https://www.wsdot.wa.gov/sites/default/files/2013/07/02/Lloyd_District_White_Paper.pdf,
5 Ibid.
6 In 2002, well before the formal establishment of the Lloyd EcoDistrict—and before LEED ND or SITES established neighborhood-scale rating systems—consultants Mithün and Greenworks set the stage both for the EcoDistrict protocols and for the Lloyd area in particular. They produced the Lloyd Crossing Sustainable Urban Design Plan and a set of performance metrics based on the site's "carrying capacity" as a predevelopment baseline. See "The Evolution of Performance Metrics in Practice" at mithun.com.
7 Ethan Seltzer, Tim Smith, Joe Cortright, Ellen M. Bassett, and Vivek Shandas, *Making EcoDistricts: Concepts* and *Methods for Advancing Sustainability in Neighborhoods,* 2010, Portland.
8 To meet the Lloyd EcoDistrict Roadmap's 2010 goal of no net increase in energy use by 2035 while doubling the amount of square feet, the Energy Action Plan targets upgrading existing buildings to reduce energy 33%, new buildings at 15% below Oregon's Energy Code, and on-site and off-site renewable energy generation equivalent to 20% of the district's total use. Progress is being monitored. Hassalo on Eighth claims energy reductions of 30%. In 2017, median energy use intensity for Lloyd was 67 kBtu/ft^2 compared to Portland's median of 75 kBtu/ft^2. However, this was a slight increase, not decrease, from 2010. See RWDI, *Lloyd EcoDistrict Energy Report,* 2017 and *Lloyd EcoDistrict Bi-Annual Report 2018-19.*

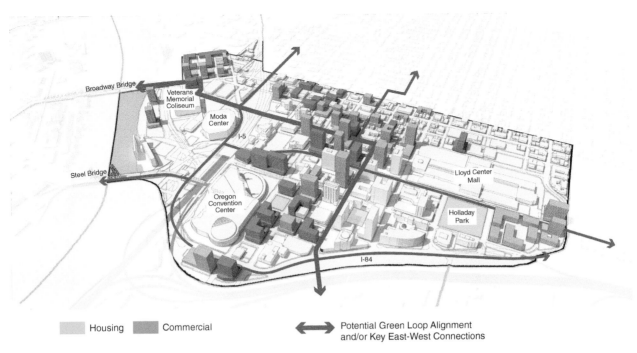

| | Housing | | Commercial | | Potential Green Loop Alignment and/or Key East-West Connections |

Figure II.2-2   The green arrows in this diagram, from Portland's Central City 2035 Plan, show the proposed bicycle-pedestrian greenways in Lloyd. The wider line is part of the proposed 6-mile Green Loop connecting the inner Eastside neighborhoods to Downtown. Implementation has started with a bike-pedestrian bridge over Interstate 84 (the southern border of the Lloyd District). The eastern face of Hassalo on Eighth fronts the Green Loop and its northern face fronts the Multnomah Boulevard bike lane heading east. Source: Courtesy of City of Portland, Bureau of Planning and Sustainability.

Figure II.2-3   The streetcar is about to pass the light rail station in this view of two of Hassalo on Eighth's new residential buildings. Designed by GBD Architects, all of the new buildings meet the street with ground-level retail. But they're deliberately differentiated in design, price point, and massing, ranging from 4 to 21 stories. Source: Photo by Lincoln Barbour.

path called the Green Loop.[9] At the convergence of all this multimodal access, American Assets Trust (AAT), a San Diego–based real estate investment trust bought 16 acres of superblocks and got to work creating urban housing for Portland's next generation of bike-loving, eco-oriented households.

AAT's first of three planned redevelopments is the 657 apartments and renovated office tower of Hassalo on Eighth.[10] They broke up the superblock and "restored" what would have been Hassalo Street and reconfigured

---

[9]   Since 2012, the Green Loop has gained traction and was endorsed by City Council in 2018. Wade Lang, vice president at AAT spoke at the May 4 hearing and stated, "The Lloyd community would be willing to work with the City to explore funding strategies and help to make the Green Loop a reality."

[10]   It was announced as one of the largest single apartment projects in Portland's history and coming at a time when the city had the second-tightest major rental market in the US. Elliot Njus, "750 apartments proposed in Lloyd District development," *Oregonian/OregonLive*, 2 March 2012.

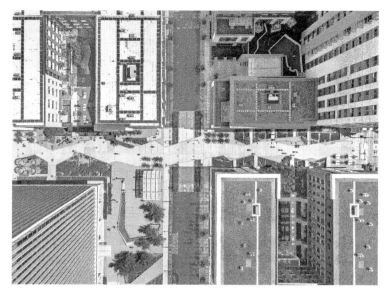

Figure II.2-4 This aerial view with north to the left shows the reconstituted Hassalo Street (running vertically), the new plaza connecting to the streetcar stop below and the car-free Eighth Street lined with rain gardens and artificial wetlands. The NORM wastewater treatment system borders the 700 Lloyd office tower, on the left. The glass-roofed elevator down to the Lloyd Cycle Station sits at the streets' intersection. Green roofs contribute to each of the new buildings' LEED Platinum status. Source: Photo by Christian Columbres.

what would have been Eighth Street as a car-free green street, increasing gathering space on the site 329%.[11] In addition to restoring the walkable scale of traditional Portland blocks, this also meant that the new buildings' scale and diverse massing relieves the monotony of the 1970s context, and is a welcome change from so many contemporary, single large-block apartment buildings.

To help proposed new on-street retail survive, AAT's local partner successfully advocated for the adjacent Multnomah Boulevard's five lanes to be reduced to three with protected bike lanes and on-street parking.[12] The EcoDistrict came up with the idea of having the bike lanes also serve as pollinator corridors with bee-friendly flowers in the protection zone's planters.[13] Within the first year, bicycle ridership on Multnomah increased by 68% while average daily vehicles dropped from 10,000 to 7,600.[14]

AAT leveraged these two trends by providing 1.8 bike parking spaces and only 0.5 car parking spaces per residential unit, significantly reducing costs.[15] AAT also collaborated with Go Lloyd on a state-of-the-art commuter-oriented 600-bike Cycle Station with secure parking, on-site mechanics, and shower facilities under the office tower. Garnering headlines for creating more long-term bike parking than any other project in the US, demand for bike parking still outstripped supply when the first building was only 80% leased.[16] Nonetheless, Bike Portland, with sponsorship from Hassalo on Eighth, wrote an in-depth three-part series on the area's unlikely transformation into what "seems likely to become the most bike-oriented high-rise neighborhood in the United States."[17]

[11] Yeinn Oh, Jun Wang, Nevedita Sankaraman, Osvaldo Broesicke, Alexandra Maxim, Yilun Zha, John Crittenden, and Ellen Dunham-Jones, "The SuRe Gap: Bridging the Gap Between Idealized and Attainable Infrastructure Sustainability and Resilience," research poster, 2019, the Brook Byers Institute of Sustainable Systems, Georgia Institute of Technology.

[12] Michael Andersen, "How Economic Growth Sold Portland Landlords on a New Bikeway," *People for Bikes*, 6 January 2013.

[13] The Lloyd EcoDistrict has since extended the pollinator corridor to Peace Memorial Park, partnered with Veterans for Peace on replanting the park with pollinator-friendly plants, and organized meetings for community input and maintenance volunteers.

[14] Christopher Monsere, Jennifer Dill, Kelly Clifton, and Nathan McNeil, "Lessons from the Green Lanes: Evaluating Protected Bike Lanes in the US," Portland State University, Transportation Education and Research Center, 2014.

[15] Hassalo on Eighth built over 800 parking spaces for the retail, reserving several hundred for a hoped-for grocery store. However, when grocer Green Zebra moved in, CEO Lisa Sedlar said, "I would have gone forward with this store without any parking allotted to us," quoted in Michael Andersen, "The four bikeways it'll take to make the Lloyd District great," *bikeport land.org*, 28 August 2015.

[16] See Amelia Taylor-Hochsberg "Portland's 'Bikescraper' breaks bike-parking record," *Archinect*, 15 January 2014. See also Michael Andersen, "The new Lloyd apartments' bike parking is already full – maybe too full," *bikeportland.org*, 15 October 2015.

[17] Michael Andersen, "Portland's next great bike neighborhood may be its most unexpected triumph yet," *bikeportland.org*, 8 July 2015.

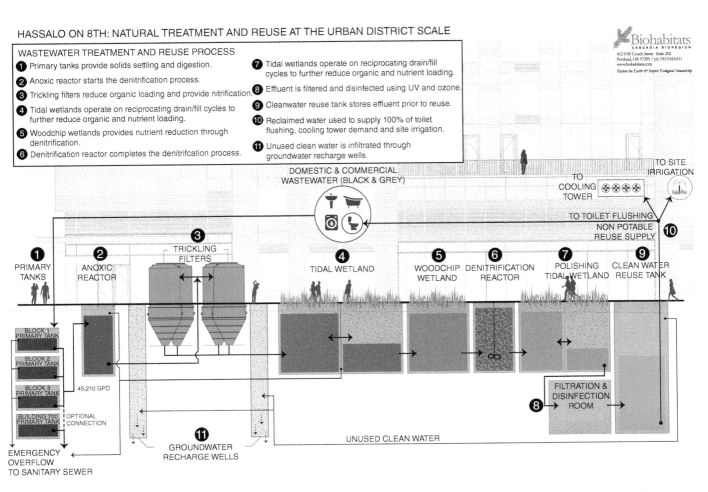

HASSALO ON 8TH: NATURAL TREATMENT AND REUSE AT THE URBAN DISTRICT SCALE

WASTEWATER TREATMENT AND REUSE PROCESS

1 Primary tanks provide solids settling and digestion.

2 Anoxic reactor starts the denitrification process.

3 Trickling filters reduce organic loading and provide nitrification.

4 Tidal wetlands operate on reciprocating drain/fill cycles to further reduce organic and nutrient loading.

5 Woodchip wetlands provides nutrient reduction through denitrification.

6 Denitrification reactor completes the denitrifcation process.

7 Tidal wetlands operate on reciprocating drain/fill cycles to further reduce organic and nutrient loading.

8 Effluent is filtered and disinfected using UV and ozone.

9 Cleanwater reuse tank stores effluent prior to reuse.

10 Reclaimed water used to supply 100% of toilet flushing, cooling tower demand and site irrigation.

11 Unused clean water is infiltrated through groundwater recharge wells.

Figure II.2-5 NORM is Hassalo on Eighth's on-site district water treatment system. It processes graywater and blackwater from all four buildings, which is then reused in the cooling tower, toilet flushing, and irrigation along the new green street. Excess clean water recharges groundwater wells. Source: Courtesy of Biohabitats.

Hassalo on Eighth's Natural Organic Recycling Machine (NORM) also made largest-in-the-nation headlines (and @PortlandNORM has its own twitter account).[18] Permitted as a water pollution control facility, it diverts up to 54,000 gallons of sewage daily from the municipal combined sewer system. Instead, the wastewater is cleaned by bacteria in a multistep artificial tidal wetland.[19] The recycled water is estimated to reduce water usage in the four buildings by half.[20] Green roofs and additional

---

[18] NORM is a new variation of the Living Machine, a wastewater treatment technology developed by Dr. John Todd in the 1980s and 1990s and successfully deployed at various scales since then. The term was since been copyrighted and Biohabitats chose to name their system NORM.

[19] Pete Munoz of BioHabitats led a team working with Glumac and PLACE landscape architects to design NORM. He points out that the green street is essential to NORM. The artificial wetlands and tanks continue underneath it, creating the district-scale infrastructure between the four buildings. Such a system is financially feasible once you get above 5,000–10,000 gallons/day. Telephone conversation with Ellen Dunham-Jones, 29 March 2017.

[20] James Cronin, "How cutting-edge technology saved Hassalo on Eighth builders $1.5M," *Portland Business Journal*, 8 February 2016.

Figure II.2-6 Walking, biking, and wastewater treatment meet in this evening view of Eighth Street from Multnomah Boulevard. It demonstrates that well-designed on-site sewage treatment doesn't smell and can even serve as an attractive amenity.
Source: Photo by Christian Columbres.

open-air constructed wetlands along the green street manage stormwater and further reduce runoff into the sewers. Kyle Andersen, principal of GBD Architects, said:

> We asked the city, "What if we treated our wastewater on site and instead of putting it into the system, we put it into the aquifer via some drywells? What if we put meters in place showing we don't have any sewage outfall? We'll use that reclaimed water for non-potable water and the rest in the aquifer." The city's Bureau of Environmental Services said, "We'll give you a 60% discount on your SDCs [System Development Charges]." That was around $1.2 million. We ran the numbers of what it'd cost to build a wastewater treatment facility and run it, do all the testing, against what we'd save in the sewer bills we wouldn't pay. It had a 2.4-year payback.[21]

Not surprisingly, Hassalo on Eighth has won several awards for sustainable design. AAT has received permission to redevelop the adjacent low-rise office building superblock known as Oregon Square with a public plaza, even taller buildings, and over 1,000 residential units to further populate and enliven Lloyd.

---

21 Brian Libby, "Hassalo on Eighth and Oregon Square: GBD's Andersen on making the Lloyd District a neighborhood," *Portland Architecture*, 5 June 2015.

Hassalo on Eighth's success has helped build the business community's trust in the Lloyd EcoDistrict vision and its director, Sarah Heinicke. She's used that trust to pivot attention to issues of climate equity and inclusion. Through greater engagement between residents and employees in volunteer activities she believes she is building the deep social capital that is strengthening community members' commitment to decarbonization and decolonization.[22] In 2017 the EcoDistrict welcomed and helped build Right 2 Dream Too, six tiny homes and three communal sleeping tents for the homeless, and saw local crime go down at the same time it increased citywide. Lloyd received Portland's largest affordable housing project in 50 years. Block 45 provides 240 units at 60% or below average median income in 12 stories with no car parking. Instead it has a large bike parking area.

Numerous other initiatives are building a more integrated community, including Lloyd Delivers. As part of the Waste Reduction Action Plan developed by the commercial property owners' stakeholder group, it provides bike delivery of office catering as well as pickup and donation of leftovers to a homeless shelter, providing almost a third of that shelter's meals while reducing food waste. Even the Lloyd Center Mall has begun renovations to be more pedestrian friendly.

Despite the dramatic physical changes, transportation mode splits in 2018 aren't that different from 2005. Drive-alone trips are down to an impressive 42%, but transit trips are also down, from 41 to 34%, bikes are only up to 6%, walking is barely up to 3%, and carpool is at 6%. The biggest change is that 9% were telecommuting in 2018.[23] How will these numbers change over time, and in particular after the Covid-19 pandemic? Are there only so many employees who can—or will—take transit to get to work in Lloyd? Will more residents mean more destinations for them to walk or bike to? In 2018 the district was renamed simply "Lloyd" to reflect its growing livability as a more complete neighborhood. Let's hope it lives up to that and continues to export lessons for the rest of us.

---

[22] Sarah Heinicke, presentation in "A Strategy to Deliver Decarbonization by 2050" at CNU 28, 13 June 2020, virtual.

[23] *Go Lloyd 2018 Annual Report*, 2019.

Lake Grove Village
Lake Oswego, Oregon

Challenge addressed:

- Leverage social capital for equity

There are many thousands of grocery-anchored shopping centers scattered throughout northern America, over 40,000 in the US alone, comprising over 55% of the shopping industry's "gross leasable area," or area that can be rented out to tenants. Almost 70,000 smaller centers are anchored by mini-marts and convenience stores.[1] Buying food is a routine chore for all households. How do reinhabitation retrofits transform these strip centers from "pop in and out" shopping centers, conceived for convenience, into places where people might actually want to spend quality time?

The owners of the Lake Grove Shopping Center in Lake Oswego, a suburb of Portland, Oregon, were inspired by La Grande Orange in Phoenix, Arizona, described in our first book.[2] They conscientiously reshaped the 39,000-square-foot strip center, built in 1963 and originally anchored by a Piggly-Wiggly supermarket, into a welcoming place for local residents, renaming it Lake Grove Village. In the reconfiguration, it's not home, and it's not work. It's a "third place" for informal hanging out, fostering community social ties, as codified in several publications by sociologist Ray Oldenburg.[3]

Beam Development worked with Works Progress Architecture and Lango Hansen Landscape Architects to "subtract" space from the building, selectively demolishing narrow segments from the longer leg of the old center's

Figure II.3-1 Flowers and produce bins spill out from Zupan's Market, through folding accordion storefront walls, into one of two new "third place" breezeway passages at Lake Grove Village connecting the front parking area to the rear. Source: Photo by Joshua Jay Elliott, 2011, courtesy of Lango Hansen Landscape Architects.

Figure II.3-2 View of Lake Grove Shopping Center before reinhabitation, circa 2010. With its heavy, banged-up aluminum awnings, stone cladding panels, and paltry seating, the 1963 center had certainly seen much better days. Source: Photo by Works Progress Architecture, courtesy of Banette Properties, LLC.

1. ICSC Research and CoStar Realty Information, Inc., "U.S. Shopping-Center Classification and Characteristics," January 2017.
2. For a description of La Grande Orange see Dunham-Jones and Williamson, *Retrofitting Suburbia*, 70–71.
3. Ray Oldenburg, *The Great Good Place: Cafés, Coffee Shops, Community Centers, Beauty Parlors, General Stores, Bars, Hangouts, and How They Get You Through the Day* (New York: Marlowe, 1997).

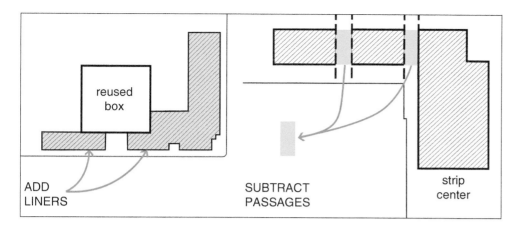

Figure II.3-3 One urban design tactic for big box stores is to add shallow liner buildings to fill up the front setback and enliven the street frontage. Another, used at Lake Grove Village, is to subtract narrow passages from strip centers, to break up the building mass, add access to the rear facade, and to provide shared area for "third place" sociability. Source: Authors.

L-shaped footprint to form two pedestrian passageways through to the rear. These selective demolitions, coupled with new storefront windows added to the back facade, produced a second "front" where once there were only dumpsters and a loading dock.

The open-air breezeways are capped with visually prominent mass timber and steel beam canopies to provide welcome and shelter from Portland's frequent rain and drizzle; the canopies have skylights to allow in dappled daylight. In order to "brim with year-round activity," the breezeways invite lounging with ample contemporary-styled seating constructed with Cor-ten steel and salvaged glulam timber, and are warmed with exterior heaters, European-style. The covered breezeway passages are animated with fresh flowers and produce that spill out from folding glass doors at Zupan's Market, the local grocer that now occupies the anchor-store spot. Taken together, these moves extend the seasonal viability of the center without enclosing the welcoming spaces.[4]

The thoughtful updates, designed with careful attention to enhancing the enduring appeal of mid-century modern style, retrofit the strip shopping center from tired and dated to lively and fresh. Deanna Bitar, an owner of the property, asserts the redevelopment was inspired by "wanting to get away from the strip mall look."[5] Yes, there is a chain café and pharmacy, but the center's other tenants comprise a curated mix of local restaurants and businesses. This is in keeping with national trends. As with enclosed shopping malls, owners of strip shopping centers are increasingly replacing retail with restaurants. In 2015, US government reports indicated that average household spending at restaurants matched that spent at grocery stores for the first time.[6]

The reinhabitation of Lake Grove Village supports the municipality's planning efforts for the Kruse Way and Boone's Ferry Road corridor, facilitated by a 2012 urban renewal plan for a 172-acre area, including 36.5 acres in the public right-of-way. The plan, permitting tax-increment financing, is codified in a zoning overlay district.[7] Bitar anticipates that more area residents will walk and bike to Lake Grove Village once $30 million in "complete streets" enhancements to the road are in place, including new medians with rain gardens, bike lanes, and crosswalks.

By one estimate, metropolitan Portland alone has 100 grocery store–anchored strip centers, plus another 700 smaller strips. Retrofits like Lake Grove Village featuring

[4] Lee Fehrenbacher, "Redevelopment of an aging strip mall offers cues for challenged submarket," *DJC Oregon*, 9 August 2012; see also the Largo Hansen project page: https://www.lango-hansen.com/projects/lake-grove-village-2/.

[5] Deanna Bitar, interview by phone with June Williamson, 17 April 2019.

[6] Eric Morath and Jeffrey Sparshott, "Wages Rise at Restaurants as Labor Markets Tighten," *Wall Street Journal*, 27 February 2015.

[7] City of Lake Oswego, *Lake Grove Village Center Urban Renewal Plan*, adopted July 2012, amended December 2015: https://www.ci.oswego.or.us/sites/default/files/fileattachments/lora/webpage/15590/lgvc_urp_first_amend_final_effective_12-3-15.pdf.

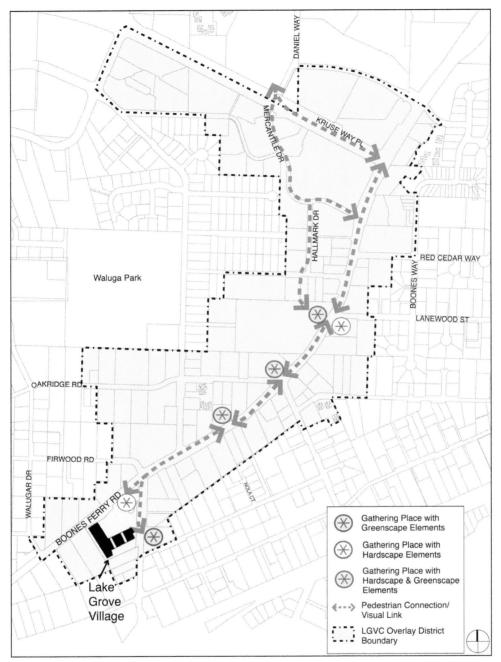

Figure II.3-4 The City of Lake Oswego envisions a series of greenscape and hardscape gathering places within the Lake Grove Village Center district, likened to a "string of pearls." Lake Grove Village is the southwestern most "pearl" on the string. Source: Redrawn by authors from City of Lake Oswego zoning code map.

Map labels: DANIEL WAY, MERCANTILE DR, KRUSE WAY PL, HALLMARK DR, BOONES WAY, RED CEDAR WAY, LANEWOOD ST, Waluga Park, OAKRIDGE RD, FIRWOOD RD, WALUGAR DR, BOONES FERRY RD, NOLA CT, Lake Grove Village

Legend:
- Gathering Place with Greenscape Elements
- Gathering Place with Hardscape Elements
- Gathering Place with Hardscape & Greenscape Elements
- Pedestrian Connection/ Visual Link
- LGVC Overlay District Boundary

restaurants and nontraditional grocery stores invite people to linger and get to know their neighbors. What a difference it would make if only 10% of these were retrofitted into third places. What if 10% of strip shopping centers in *every* northern American metro area met the growing market for welcoming third places?

Phoenix Park Apartments
Sacramento, California

Challenges addressed:

- ▨ Improve public health
- ▨ Leverage social capital for equity

In the decades after World War II, thousands of low-slung garden apartment condominium and rental complexes sprung up like mushrooms on greenfield sites dotted around fast-growing northern American cities such as Atlanta, Miami, Houston, Los Angeles, and Sacramento.[1] Designed for, and marketed to, "swinging singles" or "active seniors"—buyers and renters outside the market for detached house subdivisions nearby—many of these complexes transitioned over the decades into deteriorated housing that attracted very low-income families with few other options.[2] When well managed and maintained, the housing continues to provide vital affordable options for vulnerable people, and robust efforts should be made to preserve viable units or, in cases of redevelopment, to replace or increase the supply of affordable apartments in these neighborhoods.

Other properties, however, were sorely abused and mismanaged, suffering physical deterioration, rending tears in the social fabric, and trapping people in unhealthy places of danger and risk. When thoughtfully designed to increase safety from personal and property crime and to support wellness, reinhabitation retrofits can both improve public health outcomes and provide opportunities to residents to build social capital, for themselves and for their families' futures.

Sacramento County, California, is home to innovative reinhabitation retrofits of dilapidated garden apartment housing complexes. The Sacramento Housing and Redevelopment Agency (SHRA) created the 360-unit Phoenix Park community in the south Sacramento working-class neighborhood of Parkway up from the "ashes" of the notoriously crime-ridden Franklin Villa condominiums. To cover the $84 million budget, the SHRA marshalled 20 different sources of funding, including low-income housing tax credits (LIHTC) from the U.S. Department of Housing and Urban Development (HUD).[3] The retrofitted Phoenix Park features new swimming pools, tot lots, a gardening area, an on-site facility for young children, and a "community empowerment center" with computer workstations.

Franklin Villa, a complex of 116 four-plex condominium buildings for seniors, was a desirable place to live when built in the late 1960s. Over time, many units came under the control of absentee landlords who, though the units were designed for older couples, rented them to large, poor families creating overcrowded conditions. Without proper maintenance, units became extremely run down, and common areas suffered neglect. A dangerous drug gang (the "G-Mobb") operated freely, and crime ran rampant. Police clocked thirty homicides in the 1980s and '90s. Crime analysts suggested that the physical layout of the subdivision, with entries for half the units accessed via difficult-to-monitor rear alley garages, was conducive to gang activity that terrorized residents. It was widely considered a bad place to live.

In a four-year process, not lacking in lawsuits and controversy due to use of eminent domain powers, the

---

[1] For a history of garden apartments, co-ops, and condominiums, see Matthew Gordon Lasner, *High Life: Condo Living in the Suburban Century* (New Haven: Yale University Press, 2012).

[2] Susan Rogers, "Superneighborhood 27: A Brief History of Change," *Places* 17, no. 2 (Summer 2005); Dunham-Jones and Williamson, *Retrofitting Suburbia,* 30–35, 89–90.

[3] Donna Kimura, "Housing agency takes control of troubled neighborhood," *Affordable Housing Finance*, 1 May 2004: http://www.housingfinance.com/news/housing-agency-takes-control-of-troubled-neighborhood_o.

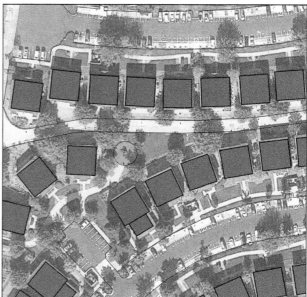

Figure II.4-1 Franklin Villa, diagrammed in 2002, was a 1960s condominium complex originally built for seniors. By the 1990s, the units were rented out by absentee landlords, and the neighborhood had become a notorious epicenter of gang activity in Sacramento, with much of the illicit activity occurring in the rear parking areas. Source: Authors.

Figure II.4-2 A current diagram of the complex, as retrofitted by Sacramento's housing agency into the Phoenix Park Apartments to house very low-income families, incorporating site design changes for improved safety. All car parking and unit entries were moved to the street-facing side, and the rear areas enclosed into shared yards, landscaped with walkways and trees. Source: Authors.

SHRA worked through homeowners' associations and with neighborhood representatives to gradually acquire all the units, including those under absentee landlord control. VBN Architects redesigned the building layouts, incorporating the rear garages as habitable area, to accommodate a greater range of sizes, from one-bedroom to four-bedroom apartments, now all rented through a central nonprofit manager to qualifying very low-income families. To deter crime, the retrofit site plan converted the wide "no-man's land" rear alleys into spaces easier for residents to claim and monitor, with fenced private gardens for residents' use, walking paths, and shared playgrounds. All parking was relocated to the front, on the streets, where people can keep their eyes on it. Gates were added to the entire complex; not a site design move we normally endorse, but it made sense for Phoenix Park. In the first three years, calls for police services fell by a third, and continued to fall in subsequent years.[4]

The state of California's redevelopment authorities (RDAs) were established at the end of World War II; in the wake of their 2011 dissolution, researchers assessing the program's more recent benefits and excesses cited Phoenix Park Apartments as a particular success story in using redevelopment powers and funding to create housing affordable to very low-income residents.[5] (The reported excesses include projects that proposed demolishing low-income housing without replacing it, thus displacing residents, in one case with the aim of expanding a shopping mall to increase sales tax revenue. Ouch.)

But all was not lost for California's inner suburbs with the demise of RDAs, and indeed new legal tools to support community revitalization and reinvestment were soon

---

[4] Bob Moffitt, "Sacramento Police Hope Approach to Crime Prevention Reduces Need for Force," Capital Public Radio, 1 October 2015: http://www.capradio.org/57352.

[5] Casey Blount, Wendy Ip, Ikuo Nakano, and Elaine Ng, "Redevelopment Agencies in California: History, Benefits, Excesses, and Closure," Working Paper, U.S. Department of Housing and Urban Development Office of Policy Development and Research (January 2014): https://ssrn.com/abstract= 2445536, http://dx.doi.org/10.2139/ssrn.2445536.

created in the state.[6] A couple of miles east of Phoenix Park, near Sacramento County's Little Saigon, Garden Village emerged from the ghost of Willow Pointe, a moldy 19-building complex built in 1977 as market-rate garden apartments. Domus Development purchased the bank-owned property in 2012 and rehabbed it for very low-income tenants, adding site amenities such as community gardens, and reconfiguring apartment layouts to add larger, three-bedroom apartments for families. Eleven of Garden Village's 195 units now house people with disabilities transitioning out of institutional care settings, in a pioneering project combining rental assistance with social and healthcare services. Funding support came from a federal HUD program that encourages collaborations between state housing and health agencies.[7]

Phoenix Park and Garden Village illustrate virtuous use of the retrofitting strategy of reinhabitation to breathe new life into the vast supply of aging garden apartment complexes found in every northern American metropolitan area, thus preserving access for many households to valued housing with low rents in inner suburban areas. They also suggest that much more work needs to be done to explore, understand, and sensitively implement urban design strategies to deter crime in low-density settings, without further endangering the very residents that the strategies are supposedly intended to safeguard.

[6] Dan Carrigg, "New Economic Development Tools Offer Opportunities for Creativity," *Western City*, March 2016: https://www.westerncity.com/article/new-economic-development-tools-offer-opportunities-creativity.

[7] Donna Kimura, "New Sec. 811 Funding Used at California Development," *Affordable Housing Finance*, 16 June 2015: http://www.housingfinance.com/developments/new-sec-811-funding-used-at-california-development_o. See also Rachelle Levitt, *Evidence Matters,* U.S. Department of Housing and Urban Development Office of Policy Development and Research (Winter 2016). Available at SSRN: https://ssrn.com/abstract=3190389, http://dx.doi.org/10.2139/ssrn.3190389.

Parkmerced
San Francisco, California

Challenges Addressed

- Add water and energy resilience
- Disrupt automobile dependence
- Leverage social capital for equity

Parkmerced is an extremely ambitious retrofit of one of the largest apartment complexes in the US. It illustrates numerous strategies; chief among them are densifying development and promoting car-free living; preserving existing affordable housing in a hyper-charged market; reducing greenhouse gas emissions; replenishing groundwater and lake water in a drought-prone region, and doing this with zero impact on existing infrastructure. Each of these is a heavy lift on its own. Doing them simultaneously is doing the heavy lifting on a tightrope. There are inherent conflicts between how much space should be redeveloped, reinhabited, regreened, or left as is. These conflicts have played out in lawsuits and financing issues that, as of this writing, have delayed ground breaking for nine years. However, even before construction begins, the debates over the priorities of preservation, conservation, and regeneration—and the surprising role of sewers in all three—provide instructive lessons and reasons for keeping an eye on this retrofit.

Built between 1941 and 1951, Parkmerced's 3,221 apartments were arranged on 152 acres in the southwest corner of San Francisco, abutting Lake Merced. Daniel Burnham's 1905 plan for the city recommended the land be preserved from development given its crucial role at the bottom of the watershed feeding the lake, San Francisco's municipal water supply from the 1880s to the 1930s. However, when the Hetch-Hetchy reservoir, 167 miles to the east, began piping water to the city in 1934, Burnham's recommendations were ignored. Soon after, Metropolitan Life Insurance (MetLife) built the complex to

Figure II.5-1 Built in the 1940s in accordance with many of the progressive ideals of the time, Parkmerced is an auto-centric master-planned apartment community that aimed to retain middle-class renters in the city by promoting "suburban living only minutes from Downtown." View circa 2013. Source: Courtesy of The Cultural Landscape Foundation.

receive a reliable income stream from returning veterans in the midst of the postwar housing shortage.[1]

Unlike later garden apartment projects that tended to omit both the "garden" and any reference to urbanism, Parkmerced's original design by architect Leonard Schultze and noted landscape architect Thomas D. Church combines Garden City-inspired low-rise perimeter blocks with Modernist "towers in the park" in a geometric plan of radiating streets reminiscent of the City Beautiful movement. Just over half of the apartments are in eleven 13-story towers. The remaining units are in 170 two-story rent-controlled townhouses that enclose communal yards with curving paths in irregular blocks. The project also included a school and a small shopping strip on its periphery but they were sold, along with several blocks of housing in the 1990s.[2] The affordable units (restricted to whites only until 1972) and mature landscape are deeply appreciated by residents and design professionals alike. The Cultural Landscape Foundation included Parkmerced in its 2008 traveling exhibition of 12 US "Marvels of Modernism" and is one of several groups advocating for its preservation.[3]

The current owner, Parkmerced LLC, an investor group led by Maximus Real Estate Partners, also hired a team of noted architects, landscape architects, and engineers and asked them how the site might again address San Francisco's extreme housing shortage as well as interest at both the city and state level in environmental sustainability.[4] Parkmerced LLC also asked for local input at over 500 community meetings. The resulting Parkmerced Vision Plan

Figure II.5-2   Not your typical suburban apartment complex, Parkmerced's rent-controlled townhouses face the sidewalk-lined streets, although the living rooms and public spaces orient to the inner courtyards, removing "eyes on the street." Source: Phil Parker Photography, 2015.

Figure II.5-3   Rendering by SOM showing the integration of livability and biodiversity into public spaces designed to absorb stormwater on site and out of sewers. Source: Skidmore, Owings & Merrill.

integrates regenerative urban and natural systems.[5] It projects a near tripling of population while reducing per capita carbon emissions, potable water consumption, wastewater, and energy consumption off the California grid by 60%. These reductions result in providing much needed

---

1   Parkmerced is one of several of the largest single-owner apartment complexes in the US, all built by MetLife at the time, including Stuyvesant Town–Peter Cooper Village in New York City and Park La Brea in Los Angeles.

2   MetLife maintained the apartments and grounds in good condition but was sued for exclusionary rental practices by Paul Trafficante, a white resident, claiming he was denied the social benefits of living in an integrated community. The Supreme Court ultimately decided in his favor in 1972, but not before MetLife sold the property. A series of new owners opened the doors to all races. In the mid-1980s the notorious "Queen of Mean" Leona Helmsley purchased Parkmerced and is said to have allowed it to deteriorate and sold off parcels to San Francisco State University before she sold the property in 1999.

3   The foundation joined ten other prominent groups including the National Trust for Historic Preservation and the Sierra Club in unsuccessfully opposing permits for redevelopment by the San Francisco Planning Department in 2011.

4   Primary consultants on the project include SOM, Woods Bagot, Fougeron Architecture, Leddy Maytum Stacy Architects, DLR Group/KwanHenmi, PAE, BKF Engineers, PWP Landscape Architecture, and Langan.

5   The City of San Francisco's board of supervisors approved the Parkmerced Vision Plan in 2011, along with the Sustainability Plan, Design Standards and Guidelines, Transportation Plan, Infrastructure Report, and a Development Agreement, all of which are available on the city planning department's website.

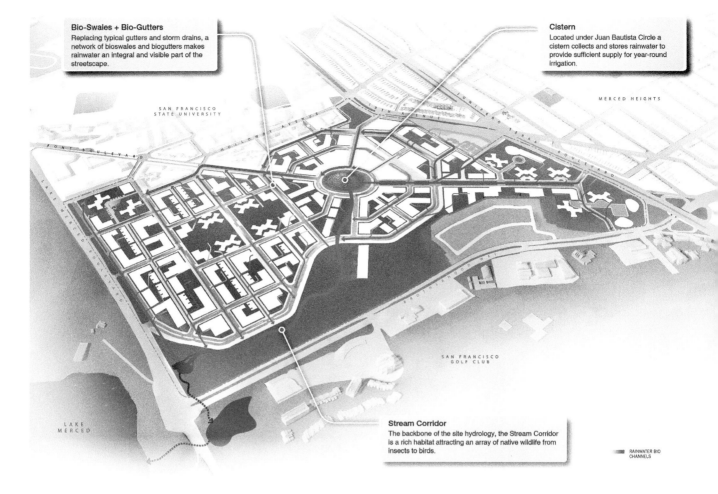

Bio-Swales + Bio-Gutters
Replacing typical gutters and storm drains, a network of bioswales and biogutters makes rainwater an integral and visible part of the streetscape.

Cistern
Located under Juan Bautista Circle a cistern collects and stores rainwater to provide sufficient supply for year-round irrigation.

SAN FRANCISCO STATE UNIVERSITY

MERCED HEIGHTS

SAN FRANCISCO GOLF CLUB

Stream Corridor
The backbone of the site hydrology, the Stream Corridor is a rich habitat attracting an array of native wildlife from insects to birds.

LAKE MERCED

RAINWATER BIO CHANNELS

Figure II.5-4 The redevelopment disconnects the downspouts and stormwater drains from the city's sewer system and mimics the site's original sloping hydrology on the flattened site through a network of biogutters and bioswales connecting through a stream corridor back to Lake Merced. Source: Skidmore, Owings & Merrill.

new housing with net-zero increases in greenhouse gas emissions, natural resource consumption, or demands on San Francisco's existing infrastructure.

Leo Chow, designer on the project for Skidmore, Owings & Merrill (SOM), said the key to the regenerative systems was to rethink water—"the conveyor belt for ecologies"—and sewers.[6] For 70 years the site's average 775 million gallons of rainfall had been directed not into nurturing the soil or Lake Merced, but into San Francisco's combined sewer system. In heavy rains, this much stormwater surging through the pipes was deemed responsible for 14% of the local system's annual overflows of raw

Figure II.5-5 Existing bus transit at Parkmerced is expected to be augmented by an approved extension to San Francisco's light rail M-line. Source: Courtesy of Maximus Real Estate Partners.

---

[6] Telephone interview between Leo Chow and Ellen Dunham-Jones, 27 March 2017.

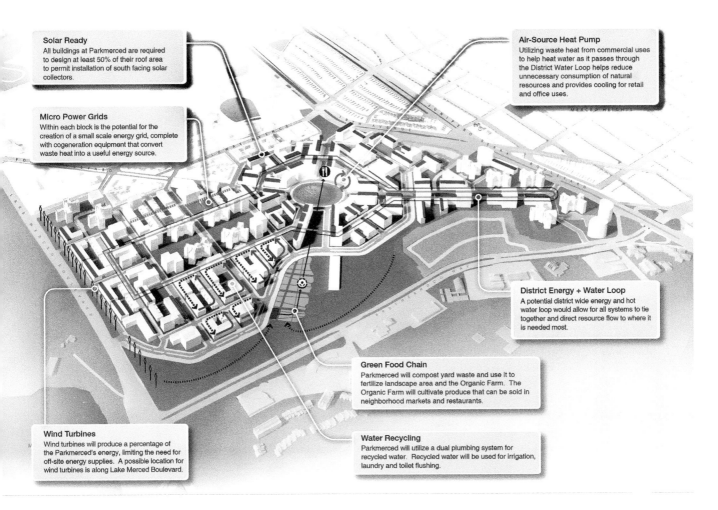

Solar Ready
All buildings at Parkmerced are required to design at least 50% of their roof area to permit installation of south facing solar collectors.

Micro Power Grids
Within each block is the potential for the creation of a small scale energy grid, complete with cogeneration equipment that convert waste heat into a useful energy source.

Air-Source Heat Pump
Utilizing waste heat from commercial uses to help heat water as it passes through the District Water Loop helps reduce unnecessary consumption of natural resources and provides cooling for retail and office uses.

District Energy + Water Loop
A potential district wide energy and hot water loop would allow for all systems to tie together and direct resource flow to where it is needed most.

Green Food Chain
Parkmerced will compost yard waste and use it to fertilize landscape area and the Organic Farm. The Organic Farm will cultivate produce that can be sold in neighborhood markets and restaurants.

Wind Turbines
Wind turbines will produce a percentage of the Parkmerced's energy, limiting the need for off-site energy supplies. A possible location for wind turbines is along Lake Merced Boulevard.

Water Recycling
Parkmerced will utilize a dual plumbing system for recycled water. Recycled water will be used for irrigation, laundry and toilet flushing.

Figure II.5-6 In addition to passive energy strategies to capture sun and block winds, the redevelopment plan proposes the integration of several active systems to reduce per capita energy consumption and greenhouse gas emissions. Source: Skidmore, Owings & Merrill.

sewage into the ocean. In the meantime, decades of overpumping of the Westside Aquifer and diversion of groundwater has reduced water levels in the lake enough to merit pumping water from the Regional Water System into Lake Merced in times of drought.

SOM's design reduces water consumption and decouples the stormwater from the municipal sewer system.[7] Water is conveyed through biogutters in alleys and streets to a constructed stream that leads from the project's central circle through a new organic farm and forest to the lake. In addition, rain gardens and new double rows of street trees in biofiltration tree wells are intended to collect and clean stormwater before it infiltrates into the ground. Lawns are largely replaced by community gardens, active playgrounds, a meadow, and water conserving plantings throughout. In keeping with recent city and state ordinances, water recycled from nearby Daly City will be used for toilet flushing and provide back-up irrigation during the dry season. The latter job will be assisted by a cistern in Juan Batista Circle, a feature at the center of Parkmerced. As a result of these multiple overlaid strategies, the site's hydrology is expected to be restored to predevelopment

---

[7] According to the Parkmerced Sustainability Plan (23 June 2011), the updating of inefficient fixtures and plumbing is expected to bring residents' usage of potable water down from 89 gallons/day to 38 gallons of potable and non-potable water/day (compared to the U.S. average of 56 gallons/day). This reduction in water consumption will similarly reduce waste water generation and the energy required to deliver both, resulting in net-zero new greenhouse gas emissions from water usage on site.

conditions, enabling eventual replenishment of the lake and aquifer and increased wildlife habitat.

Sewer separation has another significant role in the proposal. The excess capacity in the now decoupled sewer pipes determines exactly how many new apartments can tap into the existing pipes without any additional impacts on the city's sewer infrastructure: 5,679 to be exact. Added to the number of existing units, this determined the project's proposed new total of 8,900 apartments.

The proposal takes a similar approach to reducing the impacts of all of those new households on city streets. The project improves walkability throughout and adds on-site office use and neighborhood retail to reduce off-site trips. The developer is offering to contribute funds to a future M-line transit station that would anchor the retail and has established Parkmerced Labs to develop apps, fee-integrated partnerships, and technological platforms to advance shared mobility in an innovative Car-Free Living Program. Households that choose to participate will receive a $100 monthly transportation credit to use with Getaround (a peer-to-peer online car-sharing platform), Clipper (the Bay Area's all-in-one transit pass), and Uber (the ride-hailing service). In addition, all residents can use Uber Pool for a fixed rate of $5 between Parkmerced and nearby public transit stations. Unbundled parking and a free neighborhood shuttle to the Daly City BART rail station will provide further incentives to participate in the car-free program.

To further reduce strains on existing infrastructure while helping residents lower their power bills, the retrofit proposes several means to reduce per capita energy usage. Passive systems include orienting primary streets north-south so as to capture as much sunlight as possible in San Francisco's notorious fog. East-west streets are staggered and include hedgerow trees on the west side of the streets to block the ocean winds. The city-approved plan also commits to a specific level of renewable energy production and is designed to accommodate a suite of active systems to increase efficiency. These include wind turbines, photovoltaics, block-scale micro-grids, co-generation, a district energy system, and carbon offsets. What exactly will be implemented remains to be seen but three of the four first buildings permitted include co-generation plants.

The project's promise to provide 5,679 new units of desperately needed housing while helping the city meet ambitious environmental targets without straining the city's existing infrastructure swayed a 6–5 vote by the board of supervisors in its favor in 2011. But there were many counterarguments. In addition to those arguing against redevelopment on the grounds of historic preservation, opponents filed a lawsuit arguing that its environmental review was flawed and that it would unfairly displace existing residents in violation of the San Francisco General Plan's commitment to preserving affordable housing.[8] The city and the developer reassured residents that 100% of the tenants in the to-be-demolished townhouses would be offered the choice of a brand new replacement rent-controlled apartment or relocation payment benefits, as well as an interim replacement unit for long-term residents. Ultimately, judges at various levels had decided in favor of Parkmerced's redevelopment by 2014.[9]

Suburban apartment tenants have legitimate reasons to fear displacement and gentrification from retrofitting. While communities could and should require affordable replace-ment units as a condition of rezoning when allowing demolition and densification of aging garden apartment complexes, it's rare.[10] Some communities proactively seek to displace tenants from what they see as crime-ridden, low-income complexes. California law requires local housing authorities to adopt a replacement housing plan whenever the agency executes an agreement that would result in the removal of dwelling units from the housing market's very low, low, or moderate incomes.[11] In Parkmerced's case, the decision to provide 100% replacement units was negotiated through the development agreement between the city and the owners. Elizabeth Purl with San Francisco's Planning Department says that although neither state nor city law requires 100% replacement units, the project would likely not have been approved without it.[12]

[8] The city's general plan is in keeping with California's Proposition M, a 1986 state law aimed at limiting high-rise development and protecting affordable housing. In 2012, a judge acknowledged the inconsistency between the General Plan's commitment to Proposition M and CEQA, the state's Environmental Quality Act, and decided in favor of Parkmerced's redevelopment.

[9] Since then the project has been moving slowly through recapitalization and a lengthy, complex permitting process. As of early 2019, the first of five building permits has been issued, providing replacement housing for existing tenants. In addition, all buildings approved in 2015's Phase 1 are subject to the city's inclusionary requirement for 15% of units at below market rates. Subsequent phases will be subject to the city's new 20.5% inclusionary requirement.

[10] As of 2019, only seven of the 65 garden apartment complex redevelopments we're following in the US include replacement units.

[11] We would like to see more states and communities consider regulations such as CA Health & Safety Code 33413.5.

[12] Telephone interview between Elizabeth Purl and Ellen Dunham-Jones, 11 February 2019.

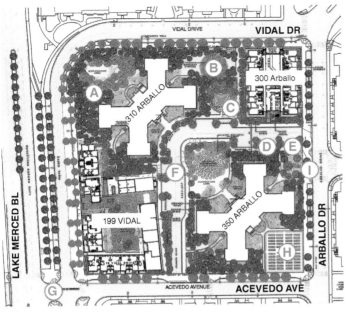

Development Block1

A. Landscaping with bioretention areas and seasonal stormwater features
B. Preserved landmark tree
C. Children's Play Area
D. Car Share Hub
E. Bike Share Pod
F. Reconfigured Driveway with dedicated drop-off and loading zones
G. New Intersection to increase permeability and pedestrian access
H. Community Gardens
I. Widened public sidewalks with landscaped buffers and bioswales

Parkmerced

Community Open Spaces, Amenities and Public Realm Improvements

(a)

(b)

Figure II.5-7 This site plan (a) and photo of the new landscaping around the existing towers (b) shows how the lawns are being replaced with community gardens and (c) infilled with new buildings, in this case housing replacement units. Source: Courtesy of Maximus Real Estate Partners.

Unlike MetLife's original investment in a low-risk, long-term revenue stream with a 3% margin, the project's redevelopment reflects how real estate financing has shifted increasingly since the 1990s toward short-term, high-profit deals with 10 to 20% margins. According to Aaron Goodman, a board member of San Francisco Tomorrow, one of the parties to the lawsuit against redevelopment, "San Francisco is so geared to this kind of flipping that you forget that you're not servicing the population you were serving before."[13]

---

[13] Quoted in Cory Weinberg, "After a $1 Billion Bet, Don't Close the Book on Parkmerced's Comeback Story," *San Francisco Business Times,* 2 December 2014.

There is little question that Parkmerced's improvements will enable its eventual 18,000 or more residents to live more resource-efficient lifestyles in a regenerative environment. Incremental implementation of the new infrastructure and buildings with gradual, block-by-block demolitions will be a challenge and hopefully provide useful lessons for all of us to learn from. But there may never be consensus on whether redevelopment was the right decision in this case. Were the sustainable water, energy, and mobility features simply put forward to greenwash the profits to be made from gentrification? Conversely, is gentrification necessary to pay for the cost of such much-needed systems? How should communities balance local fears of gentrification and displacement against global (and local) fears of climate change? Parkmerced shows us how replacement affordable units and sewers can be part of that balance.

The BLVD
Lancaster, California

Challenges Addressed:

- Disrupt automobile dependence
- Improve public health
- Compete for jobs
- Add water and energy resilience

A nine-block stretch of West Lancaster Boulevard in Lancaster, California, underwent a dramatic "road diet" in 2010, reducing four travel lanes plus a turn lane down to two. Designers and engineers placed diagonal parking in the three middle lanes, interlaced with street trees and streetlamps. They removed traffic signals from seven intersections, reduced the posted speed from 35 to 15 miles per hour, and rebranded the two-thirds of a mile length as a special place: The BLVD. Did it result in a congestion nightmare, a deathblow to already fragile shop owners? Quite the opposite. The BLVD demonstrated the multiple benefits of intelligently retrofitting wide, fast arterials with aging retail into inviting, walkable public spaces.

It helped that those nine blocks were Lancaster's historic Main Street and had "good bones." But it was also clear that its 72-foot width from curb to curb encouraged high driving speeds and was threatening to people seeking to cross on foot. The street's roots go back to the 1880s, when Lancaster started as a railroad town 70 miles north of Los Angeles in the high desert of Antelope Valley. However, the fine-grained, mostly one-story retail that thrived from the 1920s to 1950s began to lose out to strip malls and big box stores as Lancaster's growth accelerated in an increasingly suburban development pattern. The city's population grew from 48,000 residents in 1980 to 157,000 in 2010, driven by annexations and cost-conscious home buyers willing to endure hour-plus commutes into Los Angeles. In 1983 West

(a)

(b)

Figure II.6-1   These photographs before (a) and during construction (b) show how the road diet and the tree-lined central rambla retrofitted Lancaster, California's Main Street from a space to pass through into The BLVD, an attractive, flexible, and more climate-responsive destination. Source: Courtesy of City of Lancaster, California.

Lancaster Boulevard was widened from four lanes to five to try to help businesses compete with the suburban development.[1] After the Antelope Valley Mall opened in nearby Palmdale in 1990 and Sears and JCPenney closed their locations on the boulevard, there was not much meat left on the "bones."

The losses spurred several actions on the boulevard in the 1990s: construction of a new library and performing arts center; the Aerospace Walk of Honor, recognizing distinguished test pilots; and a new Metrolink rail station a block away with commuter service to Los Angeles. In 2008 the city adopted the Downtown Lancaster Specific Plan (DLSP). Produced by RBF Consulting with extensive community outreach, it included a form-based code to promote walkability and suggested the possibility of narrowing Lancaster Boulevard to two lanes.

So how did a politically conservative, working-class, and very auto-oriented community get to the point of putting their Main Street on a road diet? In just the right coalition-building way, the answer depends on who you ask. Jason Caudle, deputy city manager and then-director of the Lancaster Redevelopment Agency, sees the project as part of an economic development strategy to grow

businesses and improve the jobs-housing balance, while weaning the city off its dependence on car dealerships and gas stations for most of its tax revenue.[2] Brian Ludicke, the city's planning director, agrees but emphasizes the role of The BLVD as a pilot project to address the high fatality rate on the city's grid of one-mile spaced, 100-foot wide high-speed streets.[3] The community members who participated in shaping the DLSP gave top priorities to building a sense of community, history and heritage, and arts and culture. All three agendas—economic development, public safety, and culture—united behind the vision of a "Main Street environment," but it was the 2008 Great Recession that made it happen.

Like other communities whose economy depended largely on sprawl building, the recession hit Lancaster hard. Unemployment reached 18%, foreclosures were rampant, and construction of strip malls and subdivisions ground to a halt. The national developers quit town. But the downtown locals were still clamoring for action on their newly adopted plan. With rumors spreading that the state might soon dissolve its redevelopment agencies, Caudle was able to direct the last of California's redevelopment funds to getting the road diet on West Lancaster Boulevard

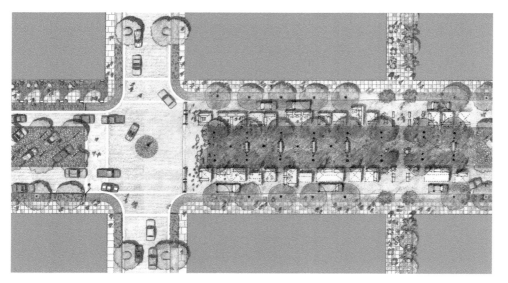

Figure II.6-2 This early partial plan shows the flexibility of the tree-lined rambla retrofit system. From left to right, it depicts a block with the rambla used for parking, a widened sidewalk for café seating under a proposed (unbuilt) arcade on the south-facing side; an intersection with no light signals; and a block with the rambla used as event space with an activated mid-block crossing. Source: Moule & Polyzoides, Architects and Urbanists.

[1] Telephone conversation between Brian Ludicke and Christy S. Dodson, March 2016, for an academic paper at the Georgia Institute of Technology.
[2] Conversation with Ellen Dunham-Jones and Elizabeth Moule in Lancaster, CA, 13 July 2017.
[3] Joe Linton, "Lancaster's Livability: An Interview with Planning Director Brian Ludicke," *Streetsblog LA*, 12 July 2016: https://la.streetsblog.org/2016/07/12/lancasters-livability-an-interview-with-planning-director-brian-ludicke/.

completed quickly. The city hired Moule & Polyzoides, Architects & Urbanists, to do the plan in 2009.[4] Before construction started Caudle began drumming up developer interest in public-private partnerships for several of the properties fronting the corridor.[5]

Most road diets are part of a Complete Streets strategy where the focus is on shifting space in the public right-of-way away from car use and into sidewalks, bike lanes, and transit ways so as to reduce non-motorist injuries and fatalities. Moule & Polyzoides' design goes much further. Instead of simply trying not to maim or kill pedestrians, they looked at how to make the street itself an iconic welcoming space for gathering and strolling. Elizabeth Moule, lead principal on the project, says they used their "romantic imaginations" to propose a tree-lined rambla, inspired by Las Ramblas in Barcelona, one of the most pedestrian-filled sequence of spaces in the world.[6] Trees and lighting were a way to quickly transform the new median space, add beauty through landscape, and allow changes to the adjacent properties to be more incremental. Rows of sycamores and tall palms at the mid-block crossings also provide necessary shade from the desert sun and block the strong desert winds.

Surprisingly, the fact that the rambla is primarily used for parking rather than strolling does not detract from how much more inviting it is now to window shop and use the new mid-block crossings to go back and forth to support businesses on both sides. The design provides the new BLVD Association the flexibility to close off a block or two for the weekly farmers' market or musical performances, or the entire length for the massively popular BooLVD

(a)

(b)

(c)

(d)

---

[4] Vinayak Bharne ran project management on the project for Moule & Polyzoides. Additional services provided by David Schneider of FHS and Peter Swift of Swift & Associates.

[5] Los Angeles–based InSite Development has been the primary development partner with the Lancaster Redevelopment Agency and has been responsible for much of the new affordable housing, commercial, entertainment, and cultural facilities. See their website for details: www.insitedevelopment.com.

[6] Elizabeth Moule, "Lancaster Boulevard," lecture presentation at the KTH Royal Institute of Technology, Stockholm, 16 June 2016: https://youtu.be/tUeuNvgx5es.

Figure II.6-3 These simulations show the sequential transformation of the three center lanes into the 32-foot-wide rambla framed by streetlamps and trees and its use for parking or festivals. Source: Moule & Polyzoides, Architects & Urbanists.

(a)

(b)

Figure II.6-4 The rambla has many lives. It is typically used for parking (a). Two blocks are converted weekly into a farmers market (b). For holidays and festivals, the entire length becomes a parade and gathering space. Sources: (a) Moule & Polyzoides, Architects and Urbanists; (b) Photo by Ellen Dunham-Jones, 2017.

Figure II.6-5 A former grocery store turned furniture store with parking in front has been transformed by the addition of liner shops fronting the street. They back up to a twinkle-lit plaza for patrons of a popular restaurant, nightclub, and underground bowling alley that took over the former store and added some night life to The BLVD. Source: Photo by Ellen Dunham-Jones, 2017.

Halloween and Harvest Festival and annual go-kart Grand Prix. A truly multiuse space with permeable pavers, the rambla is designed to accommodate a proposed streetcar or, in a driverless car future, more pedestrians.

As award winning as the rambla is, and as skeptical as stakeholders were about the lane reductions, Caudle says the most controversial aspect of the project was the

removal of the seven traffic lights.[7] This is a city whose top-rated "thing to do" on Trip Advisor is visit the Musical Road, where intermittent grooves in the asphalt "play" the finale of the William Tell Overture when driven at 55 miles per hour. This is a city highly respectful of its aerospace engineer and military personnel residents. This is not a city particularly open to replacing the precision of traffic signals with ad hoc eye contact at intersections, although it helped having the city engineer provide reassurance it would be okay. Caudle managed outreach for the project by making it clear that the city was looking for input, not consensus, and kept to the tight schedule.

The entire streetscaping project was constructed in eight months at the relatively low cost of $11 million, largely because the design changes occurred without moving the existing curbs and gutters. The city invested an additional $30 million downtown in partnerships on nine new housing complexes with 800 affordable units; rehabilitation and construction of more than 110,000 square feet of commercial space; the 13.5-acre American Heroes Park; a new building for the Museum of Art and History; a new cinema on a former parking lot; and numerous programs to help tenants and property owners. In 2012, after barely two years of operation, the Redevelopment Agency calculated that their $41 million investment had yielded $273 million in economic output,

---

[7] Conversation with Jason Caudle, Elizabeth Moule, and Ellen Dunham-Jones in Lancaster, CA, 13 July 2017.

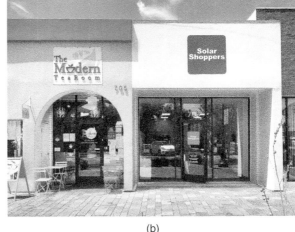

(a)   (b)

Figure II.6-6 Business owner Gabrielle Ratcliff (a) considered space at the mall, but instead chose to open the Modern Tea Room on The BLVD: "I preferred the vibe here. It's so much more locally focused." The solar panel shop next door (b) reflects the popularity of the locally run solar power utility, Lancaster Choice Energy. Source: Photos by Ellen Dunham-Jones, 2017.

37 new businesses, and over 1,900 jobs.[8] Six years after completion, counts of pedestrians had doubled and retail sales increased almost 60%.[9]

Despite all of the new activity on The BLVD—or because of it—public safety has dramatically improved. Total motor vehicle collisions are down 38% and pedestrian-involved collisions have plummeted by 78%.[10] Based on the behavioral changes he saw after the road diet, Ludicke introduced a Complete Streets Master Plan for the entire city in 2016.[11] The Antelope Valley Healthcare District also took notice and in collaboration with the city are planning to redevelop automobile-oriented properties surrounding the to-be-rebuilt hospital into a walkable, mixed-use, medical, commercial, residential district called Medical Main Street.

This lean and enriching project has more than lived up to the goals of economic development, increased public safety, and enhanced culture and arts. It transformed a windswept asphalt corridor into a beautiful, green Main Street. It also demonstrates the benefits reaped from reshaping the street as social infrastructure.[12] Caudle says it increased trust in local government's ability to deliver on its promises and he credits the success of The BLVD with the community's embrace of Mayor R. Rex Parris's ambitions for Lancaster to be the first net-zero energy municipality in the US.[13]

[8] For these figures and many more on the early fiscal performance of the project, see Lancaster Redevelopment Agency, "The BLVD Transformation Project," 2012 California Redevelopment Association Awards Submission: http://www .insitedevelopment.com/pdfs/BLVD_transformation_project.pdf.

[9] The Modern Tea Room owner, Gabrielle Ratcliffe, confirmed the growing activity on the BLVD in conversation with Elizabeth Moule and Ellen Dunham-Jones, Lancaster, CA, 13 July 2017.

[10] In addition to these statistics, for technical information on the project's process, ADT, and dimensions see Robert Steuteville, "From Car-Oriented Thoroughfare to Community Center," *Public Square*, 14 December 2017: https://www.cnu.org/ publicsquare/2017/12/14/car-oriented-thoroughfare-community-center.

[11] Linton, "Lancaster's Livability."

[12] For more on social infrastructure, see Eric Klinenberg, *Palaces for the People: How Social Infrastructure Can Help Fight Inequality, Polarization, and the Decline of Civic Life* (New York: Broadway Books, 2018).

[13] The city was the first in the nation to require all new homes to have solar. They've partnered with eSolar, SolarCity, sPower, and BYD and have set up a city-run solar utility company. See Felicity Barringer, "With Help from Nature, A Town Aims to Be a Solar Capital," *New York Times*, 8 April 2013.

TAXI
Denver, Colorado

Challenges Addressed:

- Compete for jobs
- Add water and energy resilience
- Leverage social capital for equity

Mickey Zeppelin refers to the River North (RiNo) area around TAXI as "urban fringe." Until recently, the former industrial riverfront, three miles from downtown Denver, was filled with aging mills and warehouses, several of them used as artist studios. It's a stretch to call it "suburban." But the former taxi dispatch yard for Yellow Cab that Zeppelin bought fits our criteria as suburban in its form (auto-oriented with a preponderance of paving) and we're glad to include its retrofit into TAXI. This eco, do-good, anti-corporate, creative office and family-friendly housing mix was designed with alternative design strategies for competing for jobs, building social capital, and increasing water and energy resilience. Its

embrace of RiNo's big, gritty scale through adaptive reuse and a bold aesthetic have resulted in a unique identity that both fosters interaction and innovation and is rooted in place. Whether seen as a reinvention of the office park or a modern take on conventional live-work-play environments, TAXI's success has triggered massive reinvestment throughout RiNo and has helped inspire its transit-oriented future.

Zeppelin has always been attracted to authentic old places and ahead of the curve. In the 1970s he collaborated with existing business owners and residents to lead development of a neighborhood plan for Denver's dowdy lower downtown, investing in its revitalization into the very popular LoDo. He did it again with Denver's Golden Triangle neighborhood, partly acting as community activist and partly as developer. Living with an artist and seeing their friends beginning to organize the RiNo Arts District, Zeppelin purchased the abandoned Yellow Cab property, a remediated 8-acre brownfield, in 2000, eventually expanding it,

Figure II.7-1 This 2018 view shows TAXI squeezed between the Platte river in the foreground and massive rail yards behind. Surface parking lots are incrementally being built on, but despite an internal bike share program, the addition of numerous trees and attention to stormwater, the site remains highly auto dependent—for now. Source: Google Earth, Landsat/Copernicus.

working with his son Kyle, to 28 acres.[1] Mickey Zeppelin thought there was an unmet market for antitraditional workspace beyond artist lofts. At the groundbreaking he lit an office cubicle on fire to make his point.[2]

The incremental growth of the site to nine buildings has proved his market intuitions right. The buildings have leased up quickly with over 100 creative maker businesses of all sorts: designers, big and small high-tech companies, as well as over 100 residences. The complex includes the expected coffee shop, fitness center, and conference rooms, but it also provides more unusual amenities deliberately designed as "catalyst(s) for collaboration and communication."[3] A heritage food incubator serves lunch. There's a swimming pool made from shipping containers, an outdoor cinema, an early childhood education center, playground, nursing rooms, organic community garden, and artist-in-residence open houses. These unusual amenities help foster interaction and a culture of innovation that distinguishes TAXI from most mixed-use office developments.

Design is extremely important at TAXI—both to communicate the company it keeps and to distinguish it from would-be competitors. Wincing at the suggestion that the site plan could be compared to a suburban office park, Justin Croft, VP of Development for Zeppelin, says they are "using design to desuburbanize the suburbs."[4] Architect Will Bruder's site plan deliberately avoids the conventional

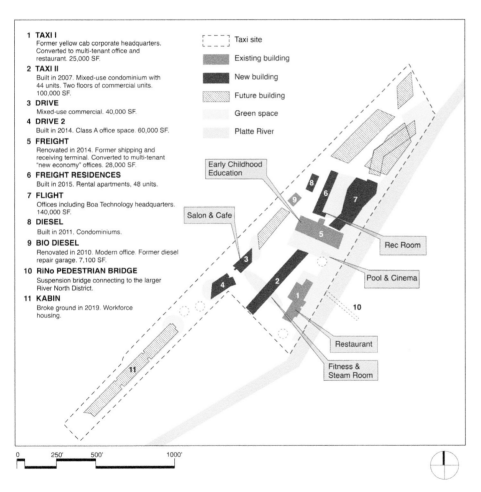

1 **TAXI I**
Former yellow cab corporate headquarters. Converted to multi-tenant office and restaurant. 25,000 SF.

2 **TAXI II**
Built in 2007. Mixed-use condominium with 44 units. Two floors of commercial units. 100,000 SF.

3 **DRIVE**
Mixed-use commercial. 40,000 SF.

4 **DRIVE 2**
Built in 2014. Class A office space. 60,000 SF.

5 **FREIGHT**
Renovated in 2014. Former shipping and receiving terminal. Converted to multi-tenant "new economy" offices. 28,000 SF.

6 **FREIGHT RESIDENCES**
Built in 2015. Rental apartments, 48 units.

7 **FLIGHT**
Offices including Boa Technology headquarters. 140,000 SF.

8 **DIESEL**
Built in 2011. Condominiums.

9 **BIO DIESEL**
Renovated in 2010. Modern office. Former diesel repair garage. 7,100 SF.

10 **RiNo PEDESTRIAN BRIDGE**
Suspension bridge connecting to the larger River North District.

11 **KABIN**
Broke ground in 2019. Workforce housing.

Taxi site
Existing building
New building
Future building
Green space
Platte River

Early Childhood Education
Salon & Cafe
Rec Room
Pool & Cinema
Restaurant
Fitness & Steam Room

0   250'   500'   1000'

Figure 11.7-2 New parcels and new buildings (in black) have been added to the site incrementally. Kabin, the long, skinny "future" building to the south, broke ground in 2019 to provide workforce housing. More is planned, including a long-discussed pedestrian bridge across the river. Source: Redrawn by authors from Zeppelin Development website.

1 Located within the Five Points and Globeville neighborhoods, with largely minority populations, the RiNo name originated in 2003, as a sub-neighborhood along the Platte River. The RiNo Arts District officially formed in 2005.

2 John Rebchook, "Taxi, Mickey Zeppelin's gritty vision," *Colorado Real Estate Journal*, 7 May 2018.

3 From the company's website.

4 Meeting with Justin Croft and Ellen Dunham-Jones at The Source, another Zeppelin project in RiNo, 13 February 2014.

(a)

Figure II.7-3 Lofts in both renovated old buildings and new construction attract residents and creative office tenants with their flexible spaces, roll-up glass garage doors, and ample use of recycled materials—including bowling alley floors as workstations and tempered glass hockey panels used as partitions. Sources: (a and b) Courtesy of Zeppelin Development; (c) Photo by Tim Davis.

(b)

(c)

spatial hierarchies of masterplans or downtown urbanism. Instead, it favors the long sightlines and more ad hoc organization of the industrial buildings and western vistas that have always given the area its character.[5]

The Zeppelins' motto is "don't create boring things" and they encourage the Western-based architects they hire to draw on the West's tradition of responding to the often harsh weather with innovative and bold architectural form. The resulting strong, nonconformist, look-at-me architecture

has been made both defiantly contemporary and part of a cohesive campus with explosions of color, enthusiasm for beveled cantilevers, seasonal gardens, and groves of trees (less formal than street trees). The old and new buildings are linked by the industrial materiality applied at TAXI and signature use of roll-up glass garage doors. In addition to flooding lofts with light and air, they're an extension of the garage doors in the original office-and-garage building on site. We can't help but see them as a knowing, anticorporate wink at the inoperable glass curtainwalls of typical office and condo buildings.

The landscape design also pays homage to the site's asphalt and concrete past, now infused with native or naturalized plantings in rain gardens. The landscape

---

[5] The master plan was designed by Will Bruder & Partners. The first new (rather than remodeled) building on the site, TAXI II, was recognized with an AIA Award to David Baker & Partners, Alan Eban Brown Architects, Will Bruder & Partners, and Harry Teague Architects.

Figure II.7-4 The award-winning TAXI II was the first new building on the site. The 550-foot long "land-scraper" establishes a prominent entry where it is spliced by guy wires to the retained taxi dispatch tower. Blurring the distinctions between living and working, the 50/50 mix of office and residential lofts are sheathed in rusted brown siding that match the railroad cars that pass immediately alongside the site. Source: Photo by Timothy Hursley.

architects at Wenk recognized that installation of conventional stormwater pipes and utilities underground would be costly on the almost perfectly flat site. Instead, despite a lack of public incentives, they convinced the Zeppelins to go without curbs and gutters and install the city's first green infrastructure: nine sand and compost bioretention depressions designed to treat the entire site like a sponge and maximize infiltration into the soil.[6] The system intercepts, infiltrates, or evaporates 80% of annual rainfall and has become a model for Denver.[7]

Zeppelin Development prides itself on fulfilling unmet needs and anticipating what's to come. It plays out in a father and son history of commitment to neighborhood revitalization and social activism. At the same time, it also positions them to serve new markets and pursue local partnerships and public funding.[8] While the rest of Denver fed a real estate boom with pricey apartments for the young and single, TAXI added Freight Residences, family-friendly lofts with up to four bedrooms.[9] In 2019 they broke ground on Kabin, 194 workforce units. The expectation is that employers—some onsite—will rent many of the units at market rates and lease them to service employees or younger workers at a 35–40% discount.

The opening of a light rail station in 2016 accelerated change in RiNo. Rezoned as a TOD (transit-oriented development), RiNo has attracted 18-story towers, class A office and "city within the city" proposals. TAXI is included in the TOD rezoning allowing for up to 12-story buildings if affordable housing is included. A pedestrian bridge over the Platte River would put TAXI within a 10-minute walk to the new station and the Zeppelins have offered to help fund it. Will that mean TAXI will soon see 12-story buildings? Perhaps.

In the meantime, RiNo is also getting a riverfront park on the Platte River and curbs and sidewalks on its main street, Brighton Boulevard, in part to better accommodate the cars expected from the $1.2 billion widening of Interstate 70 immediately to RiNO's north. Kyle Zeppelin has been a particularly vocal critic of the I-70 project and

6   Flight, a later LEED Platinum building on the site, added a green roof to further reduce runoff and gets 20% of its energy from solar panels.

7   See analysis of the first 6 acres in "TAXI II," Landscape Performance Series, by the Landscape Architecture Foundation: https://www.landscapeperformance.org/case-study-briefs/taxi-ii. See also Margaret Buranen, "Denver Models Good Stormwater Management," *Stormwater*, 29 Feb 2016.

8   For discussion of the $9 million in loans the Zeppelins received from Denver's Office of Economic Development and repaid from 2007 to 2015 and the Low-Income Housing Tax Credits they unsuccessfully sought to build Kabin, 300 units of affordable housing at 60% AMI (the largest such project in Colorado), see Ana Campbell, "Kyle Zeppelin Wants to Build a City of the Future. Is It All a Pipe Dream?" *Westword*, 29 January 2019.

9   They similarly broke with typical real estate practice when they prepared to host Beloved Community Village, a tiny home community for the homeless, until the city cited flood concerns to deny the permit.

(a)

(b)

Figure II.7-5   This pairing of the daycare center in "Freight," a renovated trucking terminal (a), and "Flight," a new building housing the corporate offices of BOA Technology (b), both designed by Stephen Dynia, shows how old is made new with the orange painted steel, while new picks it up and riffs on the old's use of cantilevers (even spelling out "Flight" on its underside in orange to mark the entry). Sources: (a) Photo by Tim Davis; (b) Photo by Ken Shroeppel.

the city not doing enough to support affordable housing. His work on social justice issues was recognized with an award from the Shorter Community AME Church. The contradictions between his rants against gentrification and his role profiting from it haven't gone unnoticed.[10] But it's important to recognize that many others beyond the Zeppelins are benefiting from their inclusive approach to redevelopment.

Figure II.7-6   The Fr8scape Plaza, designed by Plot, maintains connections to past and place by selectively restriping, depaving, and regreening a former parking lot. Recycled binblocks serve as benches, while a paved plaza reuses the removed concrete. Water from the Freight building's roof is directed to the central regreened strip for storage and infiltration. The stairs to the community swimming pool made from a shipping container are visible to the right. Source: Photo by Robert Charles Schmid, RCS Photo.

Figure II.7-7   When Kyle Zeppelin heard that a local nonprofit family resource center wanted to open a food incubator, he invited them to TAXI and built them a kitchen. Different crews eager to start businesses serve Syrian, Mexican, Argentinian, and Ethiopian dishes on different days of the week. *Food & Wine* magazine pronounced Comal Heritage Food Incubator Kitchen one of Denver's best restaurants. Source: Courtesy of Adam Larkey Photography.

---

[10] Ana Campbell, "Kyle Zeppelin Wants to Build…"

Guthrie Green
Tulsa, Oklahoma

Challenges addressed:

- Leverage social capital for equity
- Improve public health
- Increase water and energy resilience

By regreening asphalt into an actively programmed urban park, the creators of Guthrie Green in Tulsa, Oklahoma, jumpstarted an arts district. The transformation of the 2.7-acre truck yard and refueling station in a formerly industrial district adjacent to downtown integrates green technologies, is designed to promote public health, and has stimulated new construction and the reinhabitation of nearby vacant properties with businesses, restaurants, and arts-related activities.[1] In addition to winning several national awards, the downtown-adjacent project's success at building social capital for the arts community has inspired similar programmed parks on former parking lots in the Tulsa suburbs of Jenks and Owasso.[2] However, Guthrie Green's success has also fostered some fears of displacement of historic black businesses in the adjacent Greenwood neighborhood. Greenwood's John Hope Franklin Reconciliation Park provides a useful study in contrasts with Guthrie Green and the multiple roles of parks in revitalization.

Developed, owned, and operated by the George Kaiser Family Foundation (GKFF), Guthrie Green represents the growing role of philanthropy and nonprofits in retrofitting. Alongside investments in social programs, education, and care facilities for poor families, the foundation is committed to arts and civic enhancement in Tulsa. The construction of Guthrie Green, the ongoing operation of food truck Wednesdays, First Friday Art Crawls, fitness classes, school programs, concerts, movies in the park, and investments throughout the now-named Tulsa Arts District have enabled the foundation to merge their missions of social and physical improvement.[3]

Located just north of Tulsa's Central Business District, the 19-block arts district encompasses portions of the Brady and Greenwood neighborhoods on approximately 120 acres bounded by the BNSF rail lines to the south, Denver Avenue to the West, and Interstate-244 to the north and east. The Brady area retains many of the two- to three-story warehouses and mercantile buildings that developed around the railroad, as well as several active historic properties. The Brady Theater, known as "the Old Lady on Brady," and Cain's Ballroom, called "the Carnegie Hall of Western Swing," both date to the neighborhood's heyday in the early decades of the twentieth century.

Immediately to the east of Brady is what remains of the Greenwood neighborhood. Once home to what Booker T. Washington called "America's Black Wall Street," 35 square blocks of the once-thriving African American neighborhood were torched, with shameful assistance from the city police and the state national guard, during the 1921 Tulsa Race Massacre. Much was rebuilt and it became a hotbed of jazz and blues, only to be destroyed

---

[1] The list of primary consultants on the project includes Bing Thom Architects, SWA Group Sausalito, Project for Public Spaces, Creative Community Builders, Kinslow, Keith & Todd Architects, Schuler Shook (theater designers), Wallace Engineering, Flynt & Kallenberger, and Dr. James Bose of Oklahoma State University (geo-exchange design).

[2] See Michael Overall, "Jenks Breaks Ground on Park Some Locals Comparing to Guthrie Green," *Tulsa World,* 21 September 2016; and Art Haddaway, "City of Owasso Breaks Ground on Redbud Festival Park in Downtown District," *Owasso Reporter,* 24 May 2018.

[3] Routinely referred to on maps as the Brady District, the area was rebranded as the Brady Arts District in 2009. The area's business association changed the name to the Tulsa Arts District in September 2017 following revelations that its namesake, businessman Wyatt Tate Brady, was a member of the Ku Klux Klan.

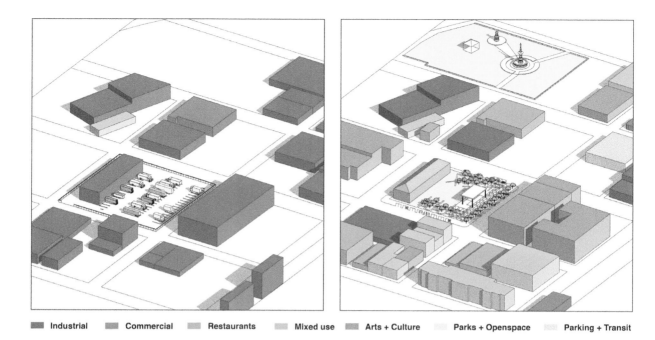

Industrial   Commercial   Restaurants   Mixed use   Arts + Culture   Parks + Openspace   Parking + Transit

Figure II.8-1   Before and after diagrams of the Guthrie Green block (at center) in the Tulsa Arts District and the John Hope Franklin Reconciliation Park (at the top). The introduction of the two parks on former parking lots triggered many reinhabitation retrofits of existing buildings, and some new infill construction with a range of new uses. The Tulsa Race Massacre Centennial Commission hopes to attract new development to neighboring Greenwood in association with the 100th anniversary in 2021. Source: Authors.

Figure II.8-2   Destroyed buildings on the 100 block of N. Greenwood Avenue, from "America's Black Wall Street" in Tulsa, photographed by the American National Red Cross after the race massacre and fires of June 1921. Source: American National Red Cross photograph collection (Library of Congress), LC-DIG-anrc-14739.

again by urban renewal and the construction of the I-244/US 75 highway interchange in the 1960s and 1970s, in the aftermath of the struggles for desegregation. By the early 2000s, vacancies were high in what was left of both neighborhoods; a two-block historic district in Greenwood; the Greenwood Cultural Center north of the highway, which had opened in 1995; a smattering of artists and businesses in lofts in Brady; and an abundance of parking lots and vacant sites owned through default by the Tulsa Development Authority.

The State of Oklahoma Tulsa Race Riot Commission set the stage for change in 2000 when it recommended "that restitution to the historic Greenwood Community in real and tangible form, would be good public policy and do much to repair the emotional and physical scars of this most terrible incident in our shared past."[4] While calls for reparations were denied, the state backed construction of the privately funded John Hope Franklin Reconciliation Park (and, significantly, in 2018 changed the Commission's

---

[4] The full report of the Oklahoma Commission to Study the Tulsa Race Riot of 1921 was released in 2001: http://www.okhistory.org/research/forms/freport.pdf.

name to the Tulsa Race Massacre Commission). Just two blocks from Guthrie Green, it broke ground in 2008 and opened in 2010. Ground was also broken in 2008 for a new minor league baseball stadium in the Greenwood historic district.[5]

Meanwhile, in 2007 GKFF saw an opportunity to boost the arts district by partnering with the Philbrook Museum of Art and Oklahoma University in their successful bid to retain the Adkins Collection of Contemporary Native American and Southwestern Art in Oklahoma. GKFF's contribution would be a new facility for the collection in the Brady neighborhood. George Kaiser invited architect Bing Thom to advise him on how to leverage the new collection to best help the arts district thrive. Thom's advice was to take advantage of the opportunity to buy up and renovate many of the old buildings and make the neighborhood attractive enough to create the critical mass needed to build a robust arts community.[6] GKFF then spent several years acquiring properties while Bing Thom Architects and SWA Group were hired to produce a plan for the area. It was adopted by the city in 2012 and centered on the gathering space that became Guthrie Green.

How does the regreening of a mere 2.7-acre lot build social capital across a 120-acre district and become a go-to

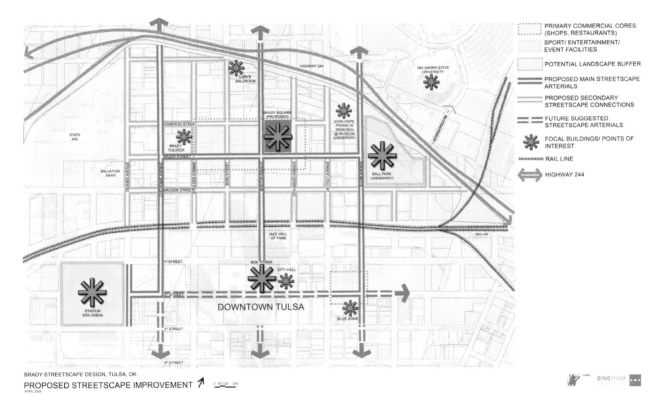

Figure II.8-3 As shown in the center of this early plan for streetscape improvements and focal points in the Tulsa Arts District, Guthrie Green was conceived from the beginning as an effort to revitalize the larger arts district and anchor a better-connected network across the highway to the north and the railroad to the south into downtown Tulsa. Source: Courtesy of SWA Group.

---

[5] The new ONEOK Field stadium was part of a deal between the city and the Drillers baseball team to keep them from moving to the suburbs and was financed largely by the city's 2003 one-cent sales tax increase. It was supported by the Greenwood Chamber of Commerce for its expected contribution to tourism and economic development in the area, expectations that are bearing fruit in terms of several new housing and hotel developments adjacent to the stadium.

[6] Stanton Doyle, senior program officer with GKFF, described this as the kernel of the Arts District revival in conversation with Ellen Dunham-Jones, 28 February 2017, in Tulsa.

Figure II.8-4 Guthrie Green's open-air stage, in the foreground, faces the gently sloped great lawn and the former truck dock that now houses restrooms and a café with solar panels on the roof. Note the ample, welcoming sidewalk entrances through the side gardens. Source: Courtesy of KKT Architects, Inc.

destination for the entire city? The answer lies in the combination of vigorous programming both within and adjacent to the park with a strategic emphasis on physical and social connectivity to the rest of the city. Guthrie Green punches above its weight class by design.

At the larger scale, the masterplan emphasizes improved physical connectivity between the city's two new entertainment anchors: the ballpark and the new BOK Arena. At the neighborhood scale, streetscaping with distinctive paving, LED streetlights, and new street trees enhance walkability and connections between local cultural destinations. Travel lanes were narrowed both to slow traffic and to allow the introduction of diagonal parking on major streets, lending support to new local businesses occupying previously vacant ground floors.

GKFF played a significant role in filling up the neighborhood's buildings, seeding the market for urban living and gathering a critical mass of arts organizations. Either as owner or with a long-term lease, they renovated older buildings into residences for artists and educators, and converted a long-abandoned warehouse into a home for

several area arts institutions.[7] New housing followed. But it's the legacy businesses and renovated older buildings with their refreshed ghost advertising signs that help connect new residents and uses with previous generations' sense of place.

GKFF recognized it wasn't enough to simply assemble more people and arts groups inside the district's buildings. They saw the need for a central gathering space. With community input through workshops led by Creative Community Builders and advice from Project for Public Spaces, the design for Guthrie Green morphed from its initial conception as a garden with interactive fountains into a town square, and finally into an open, unfenced, actively programmed urban park. Although owned and

---

[7] GKFF was proactive in partnering with Teach for America and creating the Tulsa Artist Fellowship program to populate the renovated buildings with residents for two-year stints. Similarly, their offer of custom-renovated space attracted the Philbrook Downtown, the Woodie Guthrie Center, 108/Contemporary, the Henry Zarrow Center for Art and Education, and space for the Tulsa Symphony. A new hotel and television station have since built buildings in the district.

operated by GKFF, the park is designed as a welcoming extension of the district's signature sidewalks, intended to enhance the public life of the street.

Named for Woody Guthrie, Tulsa's native son, the former truck dock now houses a restaurant, restrooms, and roofed viewing platform. A gradually sloped central lawn faces a covered stage and is flanked by fountains, and smaller gathering spaces with low walls that serve as informal seating. The small park accommodates casual visitors enjoying lunch in the park, families at the pop-up fountains, classes spread out over the lawn, or large groups watching a concert or movie. Color-changing lighting creates a nightly show on the stage roof enhancing nighttime usage and safety. But what makes the park most successful as a gathering space is the activation of the space by GKFF's commitment to daily programming of activities.

Unlike the great nineteenth-century Olmsted-designed urban parks that provide experiences of nature and solitude for an urban population, parks in or adjacent to suburban neighborhoods with abundant greenery and privacy serve a more community-building purpose. Smaller urban infill parks like Guthrie Green use active programming to provide opportunities for inclusive social interaction. This doesn't come cheap. GKFF has five full-time and two part-time staff members putting on all of the activities, in addition to providing maintenance and security. The investment has paid off handsomely in terms of revitalization. The district saw 20 new restaurants and bars open in the first two years and $150 million in public, commercial, and residential projects in the first four years. GKFF estimates that roughly 3,000 people use the park each week.

For all of their benefits to social life and wellness, Guthrie Green's programmable features escalated capital costs. The $10.5 million dollar "outdoor living room" has bathrooms, a café, interactive fountains, an irrigation system, stage lighting and projection equipment, amplifiers, and a generator. To better leverage all of these amenities and reduce operating costs, the design team sought grants for innovative energy and water features, including:

- 120 geothermal exchange wells are drilled to a depth of 500 feet below the depaved parking lot.[8]
- Solar panels above the dock power the geothermal pumps.
- All lighting uses low-wattage LED bulbs.
- Sloped bioswales on the east and west sides of the park catch surface runoff water, and slow and cleanse it through native plants and rocks before it is reused for irrigation or enters the sewers.
- Gridded gardens bridge the west-side bioswale and mirror the grid of the well field.
- Misting black granite cubes modeled after natural geothermal vents display the system's conversion of water to energy.
- Street trees provide a continuous shade canopy to reduce urban heat island effects, as part of an Oklahoma State energy grant.

GKFF is proud of Guthrie Green's contributions to environmental health, but it's the project's impact on public health that gets to the core of the foundation's mission: providing equal opportunities for poor families in Tulsa through investments in early childhood education, community health, social services, and civic enhancement. Oklahoma has one of the highest rates of obesity and lowest life expectancy in the US. Among GKFF's many programs, retrofitting a polluted site into Guthrie Green has proven to be a particularly effective way to promote healthier, active urban lifestyles—including for children. Events programmed for kids draw crowds, from running

---

[8] Using Rygan technology, the earth's temperature warms water in the wells to 66 degrees and feeds ground source heat pumps in two GKFF-owned buildings. The system generates 600 tons of heating and cooling, reducing costs for 120,000 square feet by 60%. The system was paid for with a $2.5 million ARRA Energy Demand Reduction grant and a $200k grant from the Oklahoma Department of Environmental Quality Brownfield Development. Additional funding of $975k from two EPA Brownfields Training, Research and Technical Assistance grants paid for soil remediation and removal of 12 fuel tanks discovered underground. Tom Wallace of Wallace Engineering recommended the geothermal exchange system after having great success with one under his firm's parking lot, kitty-corner to Guthrie Green. Interestingly, he proposed installing geothermal under all of the district's streets, a project that was technically but not financially feasible.

Figure II.8-5 On 8 July 2016, hundreds of Tulsans marched from Guthrie Green to John Hope Franklin Reconciliation Park, shown here, in a call for peace and love after a sniper killed two Dallas police officers during a protest over police shootings of Black men. Source: Photo by Daniel Jeffries, 2019.

races used to teach math to second and third graders, to dressing up for Superkids! Heroes and Villains Kids Day.

Guthrie Green won an Excellence Award from the Center for Active Design for its promotion of physical activity through these efforts and its "robust program of activities such as year-round fitness classes, bicycle races, farmers markets, musical events, and 'Tulsa Pulse,' a festival focused on health and wellness."[9] Since then GKFF has helped kickstart Tulsa's bikeshare program and embarked on an even more ambitious park project for the city called A Gathering Place on 100 acres on the Arkansas River.

There is much to learn from Guthrie Green's virtuous cycle where nonpolluting geothermal energy supports the nonprofit that provides the programming that supports public health and social capital, that supports reuse of the embodied energy in existing buildings and further reinvestment in walkable urbanism. Guthrie Green is much more than "just a park." It demonstrates how regreening, even of small parcels, can anchor the catalytic economic, social, and environmental infrastructure needed to revitalize a neighborhood. It helps that the Brady and Greenwood Districts already had a walkable street grid but more suburban areas could benefit just as well from how they peeled up the parking lots.

Guthrie Green also demonstrates the importance of the larger vision and masterplan—as well as the deep pockets sometimes needed to realize implementation. Obviously, few communities can rely on one of the country's largest community foundations to champion local change. But they can nonetheless learn from how GKFF orchestrated a large network of partnerships—from Teach For America to the University of Oklahoma—to broaden the number of organizations and individuals vested in its success.

Perhaps the most poignant design lessons are to be learned by comparing Guthrie Green to the nearby John Hope Franklin Reconciliation Park (JHFRP). Both are the result of efforts to revitalize neighborhoods and build social capital. Where Guthrie Green is open and lively, a space of activity integrated into the life of the city and its sidewalks, JHFRP is fenced and somber, focused inward and set apart as a space of reflection. Both rely on art and health to engage the community, but where Guthrie Green leans toward entertainment and physical health, JHFRP's powerful statues are designed to elicit emotional healing and catharsis. While Guthrie Green has generated more visits and more media attention with its ever-new programming and events, JHFRP reveals deeply painful memories and current cultural aspirations. Both kinds of regreened public spaces are very much needed to build social cohesion in communities traumatized by histories of violence.

---

[9] Center for Active Design website, 2015 Winners: https://awards.centerforactivedesign.org/winners/guthrie-green.

La Gran Plaza
Fort Worth, Texas

Challenges addressed:

- Leverage social capital for equity
- Compete for jobs

Many malls built for the mainstream have been reinhabited into ethnic malls, adding robust social programming to attract and nurture loyal customers. This growth caters to newer faces in suburbia, especially growing numbers of northern Americans with roots in Asia, Latin and Central America, the Caribbean, and Africa. Historically ignored by mainstream retailers because of reluctance to alter product lines and other rationales, the escalating buying power of these groups is increasingly recognized, especially by immigrant entrepreneurs themselves. Mexican-immigrant José de Jésus Legaspi has been particularly successful in retrofitting dying conventional malls into successful Hispanic-themed malls that serve as vital community centers. The properties he co-owns, manages, or has consulted on typically incorporate a space refitted as a *mercado*, filled with small booths and shops for Hispanic vendors selling goods and services—a signage and print shop, a tailor, party supplies, T-shirts, real estate and travel agents—much as one would find in a town or village market in Mexico or Guatemala. In addition to the *mercado*, the malls usually have a Spanish-speaking pharmacy, health clinic, cinema, nightclub, law offices, and even a Spanish-speaking radio or television station. Legaspi always includes a stage for frequent performances, such as quinceañera fashion shows, Mexican wrestling matches, pop star appearances, or the house mariachi band.

The largest mall his company manages, La Gran Plaza de Fort Worth, also includes two Baptist churches, a county health department immunization clinic, and dance studios

Figure II.9-1   A *lucha libre* professional wrestling match at La Gran Plaza de Fort Worth in June 2018. Where once there were fountains and ficus trees, now there is a stage for frequent Latinx-themed cultural events and entertainment. Source: Photo courtesy of Boxer Retail.

for Ballet Folklorico Azteca.[1] The three-level *mercado* at La Gran Plaza is a 120,000-square-foot former anchor department store filled with small businesses organized around an atrium. The mall, which now contains 1.1 million square feet, opened in 1962 as the open-air Seminary South Shopping Center at the corner of South Freeway and Seminary Drive on the city's outskirts. The shopping center, built on the drained site of Katy Lake, was the first completed project by the Homart Development Company, a subsidiary of mega-retailer Sears. At that time, the suburban neighborhoods of Fort Worth were largely white.

---

[1] The project team comprises David Hidalgo Architects, Boxer Properties, and the Legaspi Company.

Figure II.9-2 Fountains and families in a before view of the Seminary South Shopping Center, built as an open-air center on a drained lake in 1962 by the Homart Development Company, a subsidiary of Sears. Source: Photo courtesy of The Legaspi Company.

In the late 1980s the shopping center was enclosed, expanded, and renamed the Fort Worth Town Center. The renovated mall, however, eventually languished. The 2000 census indicated that 30% of Fort Worth's population identified as Hispanic or Latinx. Recognizing the potential in changed demographics, Houston-based developer Andrew Segal of Boxer Properties acquired the mall in the mid-2000s and partnered with the Legaspi Company to apply Legaspi's method, honed on smaller projects in and around Los Angeles. Architect David Hidalgo overhauled the generic "vanilla" look of the mall with design flourishes reminiscent of Spanish Colonial style: colonnaded arcades, bell towers, and vividly colored stucco. So far, La Gran Plaza has been an economic and social success, fully leased and attracting large crowds for frequent special events.

This reinhabitation-type retrofit is both unique and typical. The US and Canada have numerous Asian, Indian, Arabic, and deliberately global ethnic malls helping entrepreneurs, many of whom are immigrants themselves, cater to changing suburban ethnicities. In several media interviews, Legaspi has offered advice to developers. He suggests the enclosed mall development formula can still work if properties are explicitly repositioned to become akin to Latin American cultural or community centers, but with lots of shopping opportunities. He advises adding amenities that are attractive to the target customers, who tend to visit with family. Ample seating and large restrooms with changing areas help make the mall feel comfortable, like "tu casa."[2]

Joel Kotkin, ardent defender in print of low-density, auto-oriented suburbia with a few village-like characteristics, champions La Gran Plaza de Fort Worth as evidence that proclamations of the death of the mall in the United States—and by extension the end of suburbia—are premature.[3] But what is the credible argument that the twentieth-century mall development paradigm is still truly alive? Rather than vindicating Kotkin's "new suburbanism," La Gran Plaza's robust signs of life reveal profound, ongoing, irreversible changes. Reinhabited ethnic malls are like villages in their replacement of large generic national chain stores with small, local vendors, nonprofits, and community service providers. At the same time, they're actively connecting "the villagers" to broad global networks, building political clout and new local cultures that indeed mark the end of stereotypical suburbia as we knew it.

Will that local culture and La Gran Plaza last or will the mall evolve again as market demand and demographics continue to shift? Some ethnic malls have sputtered out. La Gran Plaza's chronology reproduces the typical 20- to 25-year life cycle between major renovations for regional shopping malls. And while the uniquely fostered cultural capital at La Gran Plaza suggests that it might have staying power, there is no guarantee that the current iteration will last any longer than previous cycles.

A similar story played out near Atlanta, in Dekalb County, Georgia, with a more pronounced political twist. The Buford-Clairmont Mall opened in 1968, far from

[2] See Krystina Gustafson, "Doubling down on the rebirth of the American shopping mall," *CNBC*, 8 June 2015; Bill Vourvoulias, "A Shopping Mall Developer is Mirroring 1950s Small-Town American for Latino Clientele," *Fox News World*, 27 May 2014; Miriam Jordan, "Mall Owners Woo Hispanic Shoppers," *Wall Street Journal*, 13 August 2013; and Amy Cortese, "At the Mall, Mariachi Instead of Muzak," *New York Times*, 20 May 2007.

[3] Joel Kotkin, "Mall's Washed Up? Not Quite Yet," *Daily Beast*, 7 June 2015: https://www.thedailybeast.com/malls-washed-up-not-quite-yet; Joel Kotkin, "It's A Mall World After All," *Forbes*, 24 November 2009: https://www.forbes.com/2009/11/23/malls-india-dubai-suburbia-columnists-opinions-joel-kotkin.html#8c783f53a4fb.

Figure II.9-3 A colonnaded arcade at La Gran Plaza de Fort Worth. In the mid-2000s, David Hidalgo Architects refaced the now enclosed but languishing mall in Spanish Colonial design garb. Source: Courtesy of David Hidalgo Architect.

Figure II.9-4 Large crowds gathered in September 2017 in La Gran Plaza de Fort Worth's parking lots for the annual celebration of Fiestas Patrias, Dia de la Independencia de Mexico. Source: Photo courtesy of Boxer Retail.

Figure II.9-5 Small booths and narrow aisles in the *mercado* at Plaza Fiesta in Chamblee, Georgia, originally the Buford-Clairmont Mall. Source: Photo by Phillip Jones, 2018.

Figure II.9-6 "A Day Without Immigrants" demonstrators assembled along the Buford Highway verge at Plaza Fiesta in Chamblee, Georgia, in February 2017. There are no sidewalks along the arterial roadway. Source: Photo by Dyana Bagby/Reporter Newspapers. Republished with permission.

downtown, along Buford Highway.[4] The arterial road, heading northeast, became lined over the next decade with strip malls and garden apartment complexes marketed to young white adults. After a wave of Eastern European immigrants moved into the apartments, followed by a wave from Asia, the mall was renamed Oriental Gardens. But it did not perform very well. In 2000, in response to the 230% increase in DeKalb County's Hispanic population over the previous decade, new owners Ram Development brought in Legaspi to consult. Potential profits from redeveloping the property with a big box store were compared to reinhabiting it with *mercado* booths. The *mercado* approach promised a higher rate of return on investment: a hundred small tenants, some operating several small booths, would pay more per square foot than one large tenant.[5] The economic analysis was convincing. Soon after, the center had a new name and identity: Plaza Fiesta.

Plaza Fiesta's community-building status goes well beyond tacos and western wear. In addition to the targeted retail, services, and events, the mall's management developed political muscle by agreeing to host a political rally in defense of immigrants in April 2006 that attracted 50,000 marchers.[6] The mall was chosen again in February 2017 as the symbolic location for the grassroots "A Day Without Immigrants" demonstration that bought hundreds carrying signs that they angled towards drivers on the highway.

---

[4] For discussion of an early 2000s urban design proposal for pedestrian-oriented improvements along the Buford Highway corridor, responsive to the needs of the greater-proportion of non-driving residents, see Dunham-Jones and Williamson, *Retrofitting Suburbia*, 89–91.

[5] Interview with Vincent Riggio of Ram Development, 30 March 2017, conducted by Georgia Tech students Rebecca Kim and Junteng Wang.

[6] Mary E. Odem, "Latin American Immigration and the New Multiethnic South," in Matthew Lassiter and Joseph Crespino, eds., *The Myth of Southern Exceptionalism* (New York: Oxford University Press, 2010), 234. See also Alyssa Abkowitz, "Plaza Fiesta! How a doomed strip mall became ground zero for a cultural revolution," *Creative Loafing*, 21 June 2006.

The Domain
Austin, Texas

Challenges addressed:

- Compete for jobs
- Disrupt automobile dependence

How do you retrofit a 300-acre corporate R&D campus into a second downtown for Austin? Bit by bit. The Domain, a developer-led project, has inserted chunks of walkable urbanism into a sprawling office park. The bits are anchored by familiar department stores but centered on well-designed pedestrian-oriented streets lined by loads of brand-name shops topped by loads more apartments. Bars and restaurants spill out into many of the popular public spaces. The developers have leveraged these urban interventions as an amenity to attract large-floorplate office tenants to renovated existing buildings and new taller ones, mostly on the existing, wider, faster, suburban streets. While detractors deride The Domain as "living in a mall," the strategy has been very successful at attracting the next generation of knowledge workers to approximately 10 million new square feet, twelve miles north of downtown Austin, Texas.[1]

The site was originally home to IBM's low-rise 2.5 million square-foot research and manufacturing campus for the Selectric typewriter (the epitome of high-tech design in its day). The property's eastern border is a five-minute walk from a light rail station connected to downtown, which opened in 2009, while its western border is immediately adjacent to a regional highway. As such, The Domain occupies a highly accessible sweet spot where downtown Millennials and Gen Zers can arrive at work by rail (as well as express bus) and suburban Boomers and Gen Xers can commute by car. Yet, it isn't as if the developers planned

from the start to develop what they later marketed as "Austin Continued."

When Endeavor Real Estate Group and their partners bought the property in 1999, their original plan was to build an updated suburban office park. They expected to capitalize on the IBM campus's abundant surface parking, the dot.com boom, and the site's proximity to Dell and other tech companies in what Austin promoters had started to brand as "Silicon Hills." Hence the name "Domain," a reference to internet domain names. When the boom went bust in 2001 the partners shifted their focus to retail. Impressed with the success of new urbanist town centers, Endeavor bet one would compete well in the otherwise completely auto-oriented, suburban market area. They requested and received a rezoning to allow for mixed-use, with the stipulation from the city that new construction achieve at least a one-star rating from the Austin Energy Green Building program.[2]

Fred Evins, redevelopment project manager in the city's Economic Development Department, credits Endeavor with seeing the potential for dramatic change. "That area wasn't on the city's radar particularly. Endeavor came to the city to see if the city would partner with them to do more than just 'suburban normal.'"[3] The mayor agreed that the area was ripe for redevelopment and was eager to capture sales tax dollars from the "Dellionaires" that were increasingly going to the neighboring northern suburbs.

In what became a highly controversial—and perhaps rushed—decision, the city agreed in 2007 to a $25 million tax incentive agreement for Domain I, its first and only subsidy for a local retail project. In addition to paying for

---

[1] Many firms consulted on the large, multiphase project. Primary credit for architectural and urban design goes to Nelsen Partners, Gensler, and JHP Architecture; Design Workshop for landscape architecture; and Stantec and Baker Aicklen for civil engineering.

[2] By comparison, three years later the City of Austin required development at Mueller to achieve at least three-star ratings for residential buildings and two-star ratings for commercial buildings.

[3] Telephone interview with Ellen Dunham-Jones, 7 May 2015.

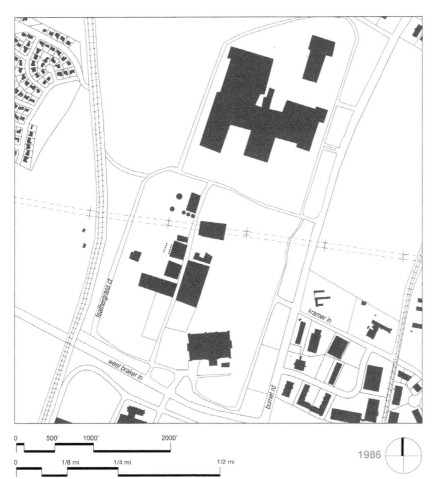

Figure II.10-1 1986 figure-field diagram. The site was built as an IBM Research and Development campus for the Selectric typewriter in 1966, 12 miles north of downtown Austin. Expansions followed in the 1970s and 1980s for production of the company's word-processing machines and early laptops. Overhead powerlines bisect the site's manufacturing plant to the north from the office buildings to the south. Source: Authors.

feathergrass ct

kramer ln

west braker ln

burnet rd

| 0 | 500' | 1000' | | 2000' |

| 0 | 1/8 mi | 1/4 mi | | 1/2 mi |

1986

upgrading the infrastructure to new urbanist standards, the city also required that the funds go toward the inclusion of local small businesses, green affordable housing, and a minimum of 1,100 permanent jobs.[4] However, those community benefits didn't stop an opposition group from filing a lawsuit and attempting to prohibit the city from providing incentives to retail projects.[5] Fred Evins feels the

tax incentive was justified to catalyze redevelopment and set a new, more urban, higher-quality—and more costly—standard. He admits, however, "we could have done a better job messaging what the community was investing in—parking garages for denser development and how that serves the public interest."[6]

The first phase, Domain I, was completed in 2007 on 57 acres with highway visibility, in partnership with mall owner Simon Property Group. It features a narrow, gently curving, walkable street lined by high-end retail. A small central plaza is surrounded by restaurants under preserved and relocated live oak and cedar elm trees. All of it is overlooked by three to four stories of office and apartments above the retail. It was a hit. Simon bought out Endeavor's stake in Domain I and built Domain II to the south, adding a great lawn gathering space to the mix.

[4] The city agreed to repay the developer 82% of the 1% sales tax revenue and 25% of the incremental property tax revenue the city receives from the site for the first five years. The percent drops to 52% for the next 15 years. The full details of the agreement are attached as an appendix to the *Domain Mixed-Use Development Compliance Report*, 1 October 2008, Year 1 of 20 for Chapter 380 Performance-Based Agreement. See also Richard Whittaker, "Are We Masters of Our Domain?" *Austin Chronicle*, 31 August 2007.

[5] Domain I has been in full compliance with the requirements and after five years netted the city $6.2 million after a $5.7 million rebate to Simon. See Shonda Novak, "Five Years In, Domain Living Up To City, Developers' Urban Village Vision," *Statesman*, 18 March 2012.

[6] Telephone interview with Ellen Dunham-Jones, 7 May 2015.

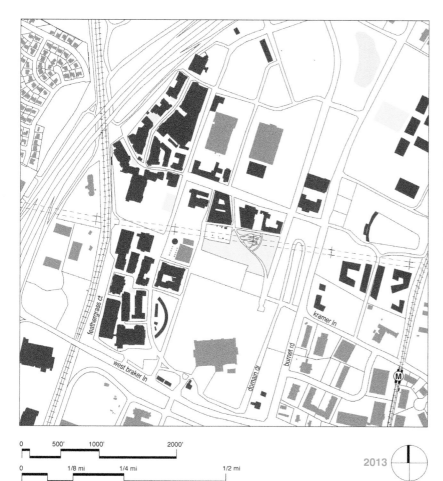

Figure II.10-2 2013 figure-field diagram. The North MoPac Expressway was completed in 1989 and the first phase of redevelopment, Domain I, backed up to it north of the powerlines. Domain II soon followed to the south, as well as a new park under the powerlines lined with new housing. In 2009 a light rail station opened off of Kramer Lane, lower right corner, attracting new housing nearby. Endeavor converted two portions of the manufacturing facility into loft offices and kept the onsite district heating and cooling plant, just west of the park. IBM retained the 1979 rotated rectangular office building to the south and its Broadmoor office campus east of Burnet Road, completed in 1992. Source: Authors.

| 0 | 500' | 1000' | | 2000' |

| 0 | 1/8 mi | 1/4 mi | 1/2 mi |

2013

Meanwhile, Endeavor worked on expanding the walkable framework on the remainder of the property and attracting new investment partners. They added their own "Domain Central Park" (under power lines where buildings couldn't go) and lined it with housing. In 2012 they demolished the center of the IBM plant, converted both sides into loft office buildings, and slipped Rock Rose in between, a narrow, walkable street with low-rise liner buildings full of restaurants and bars. Their third phase, Domain Northside, centers on narrow streets lined with a mix of office, housing, and anchored at opposite ends by high end stores. These walkable streets create what urbanists often refer to as the "A street" grid, inserted in between the "B streets" that have ground floors that tend to be less activated and, in The Domain's case, are more automobile oriented.

Despite the controversy at the time about tax subsidies, the move to establish connectivity and retail-anchored urbanism has succeeded in significantly increasing jobs, tax revenues, and property values. Not only was it successful despite the Great Recession of 2008, it became an amenity to attract the later, larger office phases. The Domain's urbanism provides employees with shops, restaurants, gyms, and green space that their employers do not need to provide internally, as well as residences and nightlife. The largely high-tech tenants also take advantage of the district cooling system and fiber infrastructure that the site inherited from IBM.[7] The office buildings are seen as such a good investment that TIER REIT, a Dallas-based real estate investment trust, has been buying them up at high prices.

---

[7] Austin Energy upgraded the Domain District Cooling Plant in 2013 with the addition of an innovative 92-foot-diameter by 48-foot-high thermal energy storage tank and associated pumps and monitoring equipment. The storage tank allows the plant to shift a major portion of the chilled water load from on-peak to off-peak over a four-hour period.

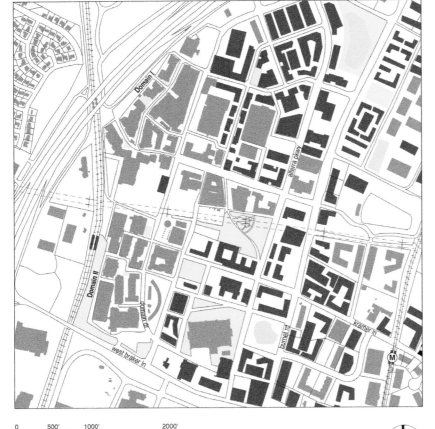

Figure II.10-3 Projected future figure-field diagram. Build-out includes Domain Northside (completed in 2016, center top), new housing on Kramer Lane connecting to the transit station, new office buildings along Alterra Parkway, as well as illustrative building footprints from the city's 2035 Conceptual Master Plan for the area (adopted in 2006). In 2019 redevelopment of the Broadmoor IBM campus east of Burnet Road (upper right) was approved for six million square feet of high density mixed-use and a new Capital MetroRail station. The retrofit of now more than 360 acres of suburban office park into a walkable, transit-oriented mixed-use jobs hub is well under way. Source: Authors.

FUTURE

By 2019 they owned 70% of the 3.4 million square feet of office built or under construction at Domain, including 12- and 17-story buildings leased to Amazon and Facebook.[8]

In some respects, the new high-end office buildings reconnect the development to the original dot.com "domain" vision—and not just because of their tenants. The newest buildings tend to be large, "object" buildings, set back from the street, with uniform skins wrapping large floor plates that reinforce the more suburban character of the wider B streets on which they're located. Yet, as part of a walkable, transit-served, amenity-rich environment, these new buildings are now able to compete for office tenants

with downtown Austin.[9] Endeavor's managing principal, Chad Marsh, acknowledges, "Downtown is more hip and cool and mixed-use. It gets a lot of the local entrepreneurs but more of the big employers are in northwest Austin. We compete very well with downtown on price, parking, bigger floor plates, and proximity to a dense employment base without having to drive downtown. The Googles of the world don't need to save $20 per foot and will still choose downtown. But for those who don't want to pay that premium, Domain is the next choice."[10]

The Domain certainly does offer plenty of parking. One of the premises of mixed-use is that planning for shared parking can reduce the number of spaces. Endeavor

---

[8] Lori Hawkins and Shonda Novak, "Tech's New Domain: Retail Came First, But Now the Domain Has Grown into a Hub for Tech Companies," *Statesman,* 3 May 2019.

[9] Brad Nelson, of Nelson Partners master-planned Phase 3 and notes that the landmass of the Domain is larger than downtown Austin and could eventually achieve a higher density. See Karrie Jacobs, "Say What?" *Metropolis,* January 2012.

[10] Telephone interview with Ellen Dunham-Jones, 8 May 2015.

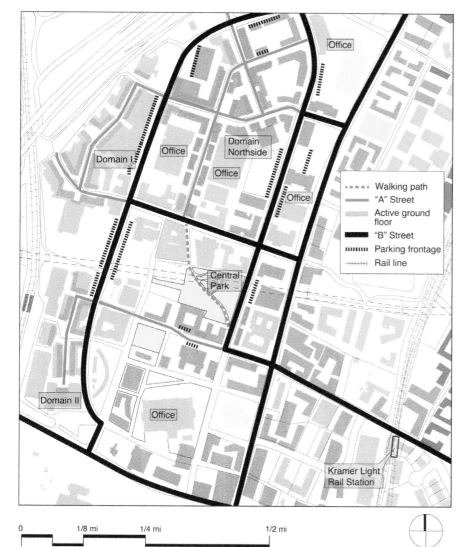

Figure II.10-4 To break up the blocks and create walkable nodes, the developers inserted narrow, walkable A streets with fine-grain active frontages in between the mostly existing auto-oriented and parking-fronted B streets. Source: Authors.

Legend:
- Walking path
- "A" Street
- Active ground floor
- "B" Street
- Parking frontage
- Rail line

Map labels: Office; Domain Northside; Office; Domain I; Office; Office; Office; Central Park; Domain II; Office; Kramer Light Rail Station

Scale: 0 — 1/8 mi — 1/4 mi — 1/2 mi

anticipated these savings, but given the size and complexity of the project, the number of their financial partners increased. Instead of agreeing on sharing a common garage, each of the partners' lenders required a clean exit strategy with four or more dedicated spaces per 1,000 square feet of office use. As a consequence, much of the B street frontage is taken up by dedicated parking decks or podium parking for each new office tower, encouraging automobile dependence rather than reducing it. In retrospect, Marsh says it might have made more sense to break up such a large development into five smaller projects.[11]

It's not surprising that a 300-acre project bisected by power lines breaks up into several smaller districts or that those districts are centered on the walkable A streets. It's also not surprising that the high-quality urbanism of those nodes has become the prime amenity attracting high-rent office tenants. The new office buildings bring much-welcomed tax revenues, jobs, and customers—but it is surprising to see them reinforce the suburban, car-oriented nature of the B streets. Does this mean that The Domain's transformational influence and walkable nodes are destined to be isolated from the surrounding neighborhood?

That answer likely lies with how soon the public sector implements its proposed retrofits to the streets and public

---

[11] Ibid.

(a)

(b)

Figure II.10-5 The new pedestrian-oriented streetscapes and public spaces of the "A streets" invite lingering under preserved trees in Domain I (a) and under a public art pavilion in Domain Northside (b). Both are in stark contrast to the existing car-oriented "B streets" of the rest of the office park and surrounding area. Source: Photos by Phillip Jones, 2019.

(a)

(b)

Figure II.10-6 Endeavor lured several of Austin's downtown hip restauranteurs to open sister locations on Rock Rose, meeting part of their community benefits agreement and creating a popular destination. Featuring more rooftop bars than residents, the intimate street of low-rise liner buildings was inserted between wings of the original IBM plant that have since been converted to creative loft space. Source: (a) Photo courtesy of The Dogwood, (b) Photo by Phillip Jones, 2019.

properties surrounding The Domain. These are called out in the ambitious 2,300-acre North Burnet/Gateway 2035 Master Plan adopted by the city in 2006. The plan envisioned significant transit-oriented development around the new light rail station three blocks east of The Domain and a possible new commuter rail station immediately southwest of the project. An accompanying regulating plan changed the area's base district zoning to encourage higher-density, mixed-use, and mixed mode neighborhoods, calling out maximum block sizes, and identifying several new street types, including converting Burnet Road, the eastern boundary of The Domain, into a transit

boulevard.[12] As of 2020, improvements are on their way, including two more MetroRail stations.

It is tempting to conclude that Austin's market is so strong that the public sector was able to let the developers take the lead, give them a financial boost and the flexibility they needed—and then try to leverage their success. Austin regularly ranks near the top in lists of cities with the highest job growth and most entrepreneur-friendly

---

[12] This was followed up by plans in 2013 for the 5-mile North Lamar/Burnet Corridor Development Program with improvements for bus stops and pedestrian crossings.

Figure II.10-7 Taller, fatter new office buildings and their parking podiums or decks are going up on the wider, faster "B streets," such as Alterra Parkway. Despite the bus stops and landscaped sidewalks, the result still feels like a conventional auto-oriented office park. This is an unfortunate trend. While retail and residential uses have successfully plugged into urban formats in mixed-use suburban redevelopments, integrating large-floorplate office buildings with large parking needs remains a challenge. Source: Photo by Phillip Jones, 2019.

Figure II.10-8 The 5,000 residential units permitted in The Domain are mostly housed in 4- to 5-story buildings with parking decks of similar height and dominate this view looking southeast at the Palm Way entrance off the MoPac Expressway and the backside of Domain I. A few of The Domain's office buildings jut up as high as 18 stories, while Downtown Austin's skyline can be seen poking above the horizon. Source: Photo by Phillip Jones, 2019.

environments. This makes it appear as if Austin is so unique that transformative projects like The Domain cannot be replicated elsewhere. In fact, there are over 200 office and industrial parks being retrofitted in various ways across the US, and they're not all high-tech hotspots. Nor did Austin's tech-boom happen overnight or by accident. The savings and loan crisis of the late 1980s left Austin with the fourth highest commercial real estate vacancy rate in the country. City and civic leaders at the University of Texas made a conscious effort to recruit high-tech companies and established the ATI business incubator in 1989. Communities facing high office park vacancies today can embark on a similar path, bit by bit.

Challenges addressed:

- Compete for jobs
- Increase water and energy resilience
- Disrupt automobile dependence

Educational activities are perhaps the most forward-looking uses that communities can bring to a dead or dying mall. Schools of all kinds have moved into obsolete big-box stores, strip malls, and malls, especially charter schools and community colleges, both of which have been growing in number.[1] ACC Highland is Austin Community College's 12th and largest campus. It is a particularly impressive example of an academic institution reinhabiting a dead mall, due in large part to strategic partnerships. What started as simply the reuse of a former department store at the Highland Mall quickly expanded to fulfill the neighborhood's desire for a "live-work-play" redevelopment and the city's aspirations for demonstration of a transit-oriented development (TOD) and form-based code along Airport Boulevard.

ACC ended up taking over the entire mall and plans to construct a few new buildings as well. The expanded scope was powered in large part by the partnership between ACC and RedLeaf Properties. Matt Whelan, principal of RedLeaf, acted as both middleman and master developer, transforming the mall's parking lots into a transit-served, walkable mix of uses and parks.[2] This allowed ACC to focus on its mission of affordable access to higher education and workforce training. In turn, their projected 21,000 students provide RedLeaf with a reliable population of visitors and a strong institutional anchor. The combination of students, walkable urbanism, and a new transit station

has attracted significant employers to the site who hire student interns as part of their lease agreements.

There are plenty of reasons why the Highland Mall was prime for redevelopment, not the least of which appear to be as a result of two other Austin-based retrofits. ACC Highland sits five miles northeast of downtown at the junction of two major highways. It's also one mile from the old airport, historically a damper on nearby real estate values. Since the airport started being redeveloped into a new mixed-use community called Mueller in 2000 and light rail came to Airport Boulevard in 2010, East Austin has been changing.[3] However, despite rising incomes, the 40-year old, 80-acre, 1.2-million-square foot Highland Mall went into foreclosure in 2010, blamed in part on

Figure II.11-1 A before aerial view of the Highland Mall in East Austin shows Airport Boulevard in the foreground, and department stores JCPenney to the north (left in the photo), Dillards to the south, Macys to the east, and Interstate-35 and Highway 290 in the background. More than three-quarters of the site was surface parking. Source: Photo by Ibai Rigby.

---

[1] See the retrofit of Surrey Place Mall into Surrey Central City for Simon Fraser University, discussed in *Retrofitting Suburbia* and an inspiration for ACC Highland.

[2] Whelan brought this expertise from his experience overseeing the Mueller retrofit (see Case Study II.12) as senior Texas executive at Catellus Development Group.

[3] Marie Albiges, "Highland's revival raises area home prices, spurs growth," *Austin Metro Community Impact Newspaper*, 27 February 2017.

(a)

(b)

(c)

(d)

Figure II.11-2 Before (a, c) and after (b, d) views of the JCPenney show the welcoming addition of a shaded colonnade at the entry and flexible seating inside. Daylighting the interior with a 170-foot- long skylight and harvesting roof rainwater and air-conditioning condensate in cisterns helped earn this phase of the project LEED Gold certification. Sources: (a) Courtesy of Barnes Gromatzky Kosarek Architects; (b, d) Photos by Casey Dunn; (c) Photo by Ibai Rigby.

competition from Domain, an extensive retrofit of an office park 6 miles to the northwest.[4]

ACC entrusted Barnes Gromatzky Architects to give the mall a new visual identity along with its new purpose.[5] In Phase One, they transformed the former JCPenney department store from a concrete, windowless bunker to an award-winning light-filled sequence of loft-like spaces. More like open-plan offices than traditional classrooms, these spaces have been conducive to effective tech-oriented modes of instruction. The ACCelerator Lab cut the attrition rate in math by more than half, particularly benefitting traditionally disadvantaged groups of students.[6] Phase Two's programming is further assisting students from

[4] "General Growth, Simon in Austin Drama," *Wall Street Journal* developments blog, 13 May 2010.
[5] Additional consultants on the project include McCann Adams Studio; Coleman & Associates; Laukgroup; Bury; MWM Design Group; and Datum Engineers.
[6] Virginia Tech pioneered the modular instructional system. See Paul Fain, "Texas-Size Math Lab," *Inside Higher Ed,* 20 March 2015.

diverse backgrounds with a Veterans Resource Center and large daycare center. The campus is also expanding high-tech resources with the first wetlab at a community college in Texas, a Health Sciences/STEM Regional Simulation Center, robotic equipment in the Regional Workforce Center, and an expansive and very well-outfitted Creative Media Program.

Companies have shown interest in locating near community colleges for targeted workforce training that they no longer wish to provide in-house. They also like to use them as recruiting hubs, especially for the growing number of hard-to-fill middle-skill, middle-wage jobs. Cloud-hosting company Rackspace (coincidentally headquartered in a reinhabitation of the Windsor Park Mall in San Antonio, Texas) planned to move 500 employees into the former Dillards department store at ACC Highland and hire ACC interns. But when a change in ownership in 2017 put the deal on hold, KLRU-TV, Austin's PBS-affiliate station, knocked on ACC's door. KLRU agreed to set up its offices and production facilities in the ground floor of the three-story building and offer paid internships and enhanced job training for ACC's arts, digital media, and communications students. RedLeaf hopes to attract up to 1.1 million square feet of similar office users to the "innovation district" campus.

The partnership with the neighbors and city has also worked well despite local real estate journalist Caleb Pritchard's story on the project likening efforts to redevelop *anything* in Austin to "a naked belly crawl through a fire ant-infested mesquite patch."[7] In 2002, three years after the nearby airport closed and as the mall was starting to struggle, the city organized a series of planning workshops with residents of the adjacent Highland and Brentwood neighborhoods. In 2004 the city adopted the Brentwood/Highland Combined Neighborhood Plan calling for three new "neighborhood urban centers," including one at the Highland Mall. A follow-up charrette in 2011, shortly after ACC's initial 18-acre purchase, confirmed the local support for approximately four-story build-out of the site and nearby redevelopments. In partnership with RedLeaf, this both emboldened ACC to purchase the rest of the mall and built support for the successful bond package they needed in order to do so. McCann Adams Studio produced a Design Book to guide the realization of ACC Highland and RedLeaf's master plan.[8] It was developed in close coordination with the City and Gateway Planning's innovative work on the 3-mile Airport Boulevard Form-Based Code Initiative.[9] Both were completed and adopted in 2014 and advance the goals of the city's 2012 comprehensive plan.[10]

[7] Caleb Pritchard, "The Plan to Turn Highland Mall into a Neighborhood," *Austin Monthly,* 19 July 2017.
[8] A form-based code for the project, the Design Book sets standards to coordinate the separately designed components into a cohesive whole. It designates street and frontage types linked to pedestrian-friendly priorities, building form and development standards, building design guidelines, streetscape design guidelines, and the review and approval process.
[9] To spur redevelopment on the corridor, Gateway Planning proposed a form-based code to provide what principal Scott Polikov calls "adjacent predictability" to landowners, a significant factor in underwriting; reconstruction of the right-of-way with wide sidewalks, bike lanes, and a planted median; and district-scale stormwater detention on the sites of the large property owners to greatly facilitate redevelopment of smaller parcels. See Sam Newberg, "Airport Boulevard Corridor: Where a Form-Based Code Advances Redevelopment," *Urban Land,* 29 February 2012. The form-based code was adopted in 2014. New sidewalks and bike lanes were approved as part of a larger Smart Corridor referendum in 2016 with promised implementation by 2024.
[10] For five years Austin's planning department worked to shift the entire city toward form-based zoning; however, the CodeNEXT project was canceled in 2018. ACC Highland, and a few other retrofits (Midtown Commons at Crestview and the Linc), continue to demonstrate the value of the Airport Boulevard form-based code as the area evolves.

Figure II.11-3   Instead of chopping the former JCPenney department store into individual classrooms, the 300-foot-long space was outfitted with 600 computer work stations and named the ACCelerator Lab. Students work through remedial math modules at their own pace while instructors in red or blue jackets roam the room and respond to visual signals to give assistance. Source: Photo by Casey Dunn, courtesy of Barnes Gromatzky Kosarek Architects.

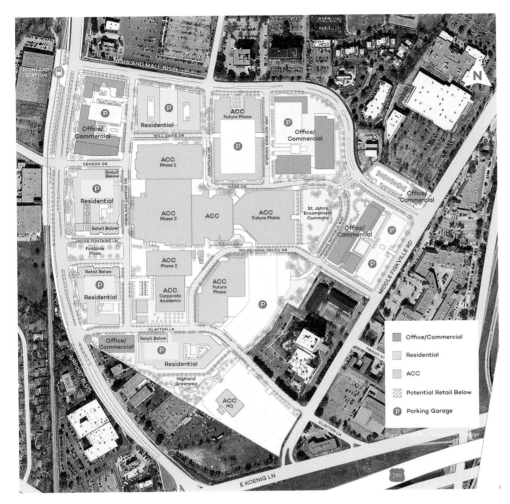

Figure II.11-4 This site plan from late 2018 shows ACC in the reinhabited mall with future additions and green quads for outdoor activities. The former parking lots are filled with "Texas donut" apartment buildings wrapped around parking and office/commercial buildings. A park and jogging trail surround the campus and connect to the new light rail train station on Airport Boulevard. Source: Courtesy of RedLeaf Properties and Austin Community College.

ACC Highland's master plan reduces automobile dependence with the introduction of new transit, urban form that promotes and encourages walking, partnerships with car share programs, and a reduction of the parking coverage of the site's surface area from 68% to 4%.[11] The master plan also improves overall environmental performance and achieved LEED Gold certification. Retaining the mall building saves its embodied energy—that is, the energy expended in manufacture and transportation of building materials and initial construction. However, new wastewater lines were installed and the building's outdated mechanical systems are being replaced with an underground district cooling system for the entire site. ACC is providing Austin Energy with a 30-year service agreement and lease on 35,000 square feet of land on which to build a 100-foot-diameter, 50-foot-tall thermal energy storage tank and phase in 7500 tons of chillers and cooling towers as the site gets built out.

The master plan calls for over 1000 new trees to mitigate heat island effect and reduce stormwater runoff. Most of them will line the new streets, but many will also shade the more than five acres of parks, connected by a 1.25-mile trail loop. In addition to the retained trees in the green quad off of Airport Boulevard, a new park is planned to the east of the former Macy's. To be called St. John's Encampment Commons, it honors the St. John's Industrial Institute and Home for Negro Orphans that graced the site

---

[11] Parking coverage calculations by Gita Khote and Melvin McLure as students at Georgia Institute of Technology, April 2014.

Figure II.11-5 In this view from early 2019 looking south, ACC is in the retrofitted JCPenney on the left while renovation is taking place on the rest of the mall. New housing has risen on the former parking on the right. Of the 1,200 apartments planned for the site, 120 will be designated affordable. The parking lots in the foreground are planned for new office and retail use. Downtown Austin is visible on the skyline. Source: Photo by Phillip Jones, 2019.

from post–Civil War Reconstruction circa 1870 until the 1940s. It will include an amphitheater and playground for the new daycare center and Veterans Resource Center. Further increasing the social and civic nature of this park, it will be fronted on the opposite side by a new home for Austin's planning and development office.

It's too soon to tell the full impact of the reinhabitation, redevelopment, and regreening of the Highland Mall on Austin's economy, the neighborhood's air and water quality, let alone the quality of its streets and public spaces. The combination of the three primary retrofitting strategies bodes well for connecting inhabitants, workers, and students to the past, the future, and to nature. However, we're concerned that at 4 spaces per 1,000 square feet, the project contains too much parking for a TOD.[12] We also wonder about an overreliance on "Texas Donut"–type

housing.[13] Austin's transit system is quite limited so it's understandable why the parking standards still assume that most residents and visitors will be arriving by car.[14] But we would like to see TODs and housing incorporate parking structures designed to be retrofitted to other uses in the

---

[12] See Smart Growth America and Department of City and Metropolitan Planning at the University of Utah, "Empty Spaces, Real Parking Needs at Five TODs," January 2017.

[13] **"Texas Donuts"** is the colloquial name for wood-construction residential units wrapped around concrete parking decks. They have become ubiquitous in development and redevelopment projects around the country and are today's cheapest way to build 200–300 units on 2- to 3-acre sites. They screen parking garages from public view, increasing walkability. However, their long facades can be monotonous, decreasing walkability and leading to unattractive attempts to break up the bulk with varied materials. Plus, there are concerns about their long-term viability. Which will last longer: their concrete parking decks, which may not be needed in the future, or their wood-framed, thinly-sheathed apartments? In moderation, we appreciate their contribution to affordability but would like to see more quality in their design. Moule & Polyzoides Architects and Urbanists' not dissimilar courtyard buildings reward the pedestrian eye inside and out with much more diversity of massing and detailing.

[14] In addition, ACC found that historically their campuses require more parking spaces than the City of Austin's standards. Too bad more of the apartments on campus aren't priced for students.

Figure II.11-6 Highland Greenway Park, on the left, is the first of three planned parks on the mall's former parking lots. It features a community garden, picnic areas, and a fitness trail that will eventually loop the entire site and is here shown wrapping Elan Parkside, a new apartment building. On the right, the former Dillards department store's cladding has been removed as it gets transformed into ACC classrooms and KLRU-TV office and production facilities. Source: Photo by Phillip Jones, 2019.

future. Not only does reduced parking reduce car trips, but it can also reduce the cost of living—always a challenge for students.

That said, we're extremely hopeful about the impact the project might have on ACC's graduates. Will they be intrigued by how the different systems—from paid internships to rainwater harvesting—increase resiliency? Will the project's transformation inspire them to seek changes to the status quo in their careers? More than 40% of current US high schoolers are projected to attend two-year community colleges. How many of them, let alone those in lower grades, might similarly end up studying in retooled shopping centers? We know that a lot of them already are. Studying in retrofitted buildings may be the best possible preparation for adaptable and resilient career paths.

Mueller
Austin, Texas

Challenges addressed:

- Improve public health
- Add water and energy resilience
- Disrupt automobile dependence
- Leverage social capital for equity

The redevelopment of underused public land is one of the great tactics for retrofitting suburbia. One of the largest and more ambitious examples is Mueller, an ongoing retrofit of a 711-acre municipally owned airport decommissioned in 1999. East Austin's neighborhoods were long considered the less desirable side of town because of the airport. After it closed, forward-looking Austinites wanted more density, not less, in the underinvested area. An award-winning, citizen-led plan for a sustainable community drove the tightly drafted public-private partnership agreement guiding its redevelopment.[1] While Mueller's progressive goals are sometimes mocked as utopian—and also sometimes criticized as imposing Stepford Wives–like controls on behavior—performance metrics on the new community are being closely monitored, allowing it to serve as a living research lab on designing compactly for improved public health, increased affordability, and water and energy resilience.

The decision-making process over closing the airport and what to do with it took over two decades. Ultimately, consensus formed around green urbanism, affordable housing, jobs, neighborhood form that supports community building, and environmental sustainability.[2] Stakeholder leaders continue to oversee the team responsible for making it all happen: the City of Austin, McCann Adams Studio (formerly ROMA Design Group), and Catellus

Development Group. They took on several tasks above and beyond the usual call of duty, including:

- The city rewrote its regulations to allow a mix of uses, narrow lots, and narrower streets, getting buy-in from the waste-management and emergency services departments. It set development requirements that 25% of all for-sale and all rental residential units be set aside as affordable housing (later raised to 35%) and that all new construction meet green building standards. And, like many other communities, they established a tax-increment financing district so that increased property and sales taxes reimburse the developer for upfront infrastructure costs.
- Catellus established the Mueller Foundation. Funded by real estate transaction fees, the foundation supports affordable housing at Mueller and quality education and sustainability throughout Austin.[3] Catellus also partnered with a local nonprofit to manage a shared equity program. It provides buyers meeting the affordability requirements with an interest-free second mortgage.[4]

---

[2] When the airport needed to expand in the 1970s, locals began arguing for its closure instead. Neighbors first proposed a dense, sustainable neighborhood for the site in 1983. The airport closed in 1999. ROMA's reuse plan was approved by the city council in 2000 but it took two years for the city to figure out how to change the regulations to allow it, conduct public outreach, select a developer, and craft an agreement with them to minimize the city's risk. The children's hospital was among the first buildings to break ground in 2004. The first residents moved in three years later.

[3] The foundation invested more than $21 million in its first nine years. It is supported by three sources: a fee added to all real estate transactions in Mueller in perpetuity of 0.25%, proceeds from the Shared Equity housing program, and donations.

[4] The Shared Equity program allows a homebuyer to pay less than market value, with the second mortgage making up the difference. In return, at the next time of sale the foundation pockets a percentage of the appreciated value and holds a purchase option to keep the home within the program.

---

[1] Robert Steuteville, "Former Airport Turns Into Complete Community," *Public Square* blog, 27 January 2020.

McCann Adams Studio produced the new urbanist master plan intended to balance approximately 13,000 residents and 13,000 workers over a walkable street network surrounded by 140 acres of parks. It is accompanied by the detailed *Mueller Design Book* illustrating the different neighborhoods and a wide range of diverse, compact building types and landscaping standards featuring native plants. Of all the communities they've worked with, the principals liked this one so much they joined the first round of residents and have continued to advise the plan's evolution.

To meet the agreed-upon goals, the plan dedicates 18% of the land to uses that generate employment in 4.5 million square feet of commercial space; 20% to green infrastructure and open space; and the rest to 6,200 residences of various types and sizes. To begin paying off the bonds, early phases concentrated on building houses in the south and revenue-producing strip retail in the north. The air traffic control tower and a hangar were adapted to public spaces, the aviation terminal became the visitor center, and the Austin Film Society took over several aviation buildings along East 51st Street, the northern boundary of the former airport, for film production.

According to Greg Weaver, executive VP of Catellus: "A big question is when do you build the town center. Does it come first, or do you wait? Instead of putting it in first as an amenity but at low density, we felt we could wait, sell homes, get the hospital in, and be able to build the town center later at higher density."[5] Construction of the children's hospital was a catalyst for the adjacent health research district, together providing over 5,000 jobs and justification for the decision to postpone the town center. It's a strategy counter to that employed at the nearby Domain retrofit. Home sales have continued to be brisk without it, but not without some grumbling from residents.

The project advances the twin goals of housing affordability and water and energy resiliency at multiple scales:[6]

- Buildings must adhere to both the LEED and the Austin Energy Green Building standards for energy and water efficient buildings.[7] Small residential lots minimize both land costs and private lawns.[8] Less lawn space lowers household water bills and improves air quality by

Figure II.12-1   The bright red Thinkery Children's Museum adds a playful civic presence to the town center at the southern end of Aldrich Street. It abuts Lake Park and a playground and reinforces the particularly family-friendly urbanism in Mueller. Source: Photo by Phillip Jones, 2019.

minimizing gas-powered landscape maintenance. Less private outdoor space is compensated for by ample shared yards and parks, irrigated with Austin's "purple pipe" reclaimed water.

- Residential lots and blocks are laid out to minimize heat gain from western frontages and maximize south-facing sloped roofs for solar panels, thus reducing both air conditioning needs and household energy bills while producing clean power. Porches are required on all detached houses, further reducing heat gain while inviting social interaction and increasing eyes on the street.

- Walking and biking, the cheapest and cleanest forms of transportation, are encouraged by the small block sizes, typically 220 feet wide by 350 to 450 feet long. Alleys keep garages and curb cuts from interfering with

5 Greg Weaver presentation at Mueller, 4 May 2015.
6 The 95-page *Mueller Green Resources Guide* by the Center for Maximum Potential Building Systems laid out the strategies and resources early on. In 2016 it was deemed the world's largest LEED ND Gold project.

7 Recognized at the 1992 UN Earth Summit, as the first of its kind in the world, Austin's Green Builder Program is now expected standard practice in the city. The program claims that as of August 2017, 1,375 homes at Mueller were rated and achieved a savings of 1.925 million kWh of energy savings.
8 In 2007, the design book included single-family house lots as small as 37' x 90 and live-work "shop house" lots at 25' x 55'. Lots have shrunk further since Catellus organized a two-day symposium on affordability by design in 2008. The 2017 version of the design book includes lots for row house paseos at 15' x 40', small lot row houses at 22.5' x 45', and zero-lot-line detached garden houses at 26' x 60'.

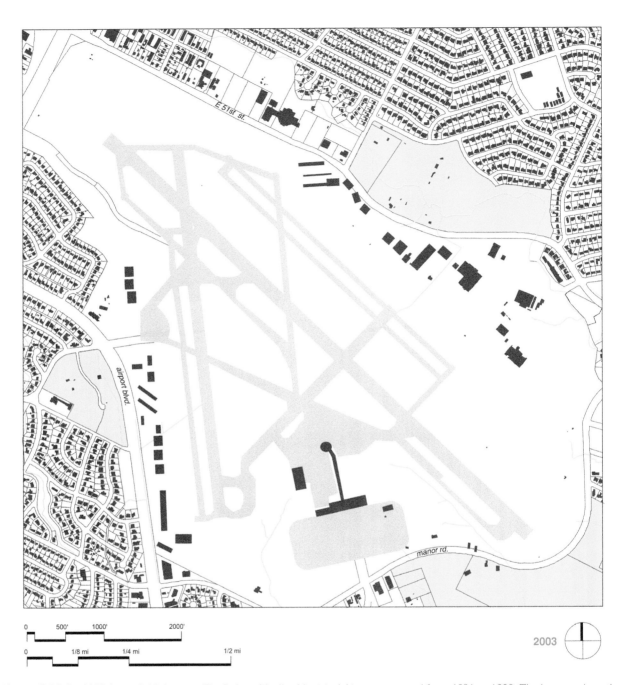

0   500'   1000'   2000'

0   1/8 mi   1/4 mi   1/2 mi

2003

Figure II.12-2   2003 figure-field diagram. The Robert Mueller Municipal Airport operated from 1931 to 1999. The hangars along the northeast side of the airport have since been converted into sound stages for film and production companies while the arched roof of the Browning Hangar to the south has been retained as a gathering space just south of the preserved 1961 control tower. The site continues to have direct access to I-35 (just visible in the upper left corner) from East 51st Street and Airport Boulevard. Source: Authors.

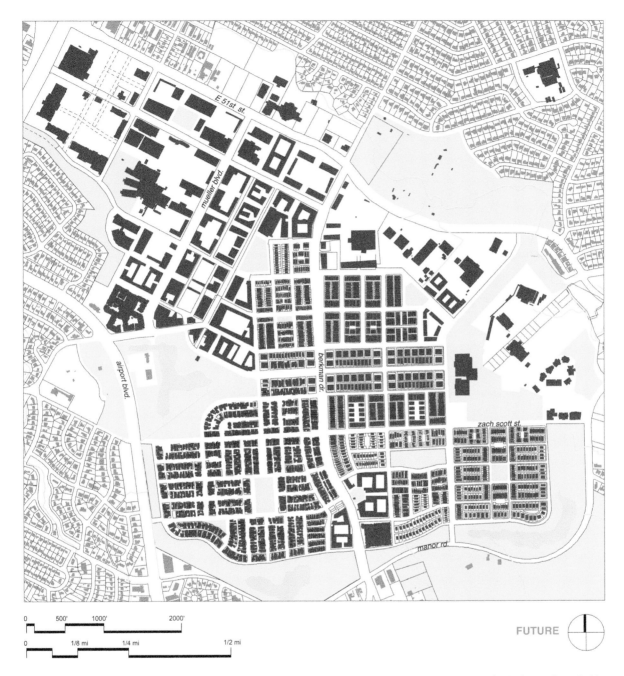

0   500'   1000'   2000'

0   1/8 mi   1/4 mi   1/2 mi

FUTURE

Figure II.12-3   Projected future figure-field diagram. At build-out, the 711 acres will comprise a series of linked, mostly walkable districts. Neighborhood parks anchor diverse housing types in the southern, mostly residential districts. The Dell Children's Medical Center (a large building with "fingers" of patient rooms) anchors the northwest commercial district and a grocery store and the Austin Film Society anchor the northeast commercial area. These districts were substantially complete by 2019. They converge at the final phase, Aldrich Street, two blocks east of Mueller Boulevard, envisioned as a lively Main Street and the community's town center. Dotted lines in the northwest commercial district parking lots anticipate future fine-grained redevelopment. A perimeter park system supports trails and provides stormwater retention. Source: Authors.

(a)

(b)

Figure II.12-4 Mueller contains a wide variety of compact housing types and styles in close proximity to each other, including alley-loaded detached houses fronting a shared garden court (a). Modern row houses (b) share an alley with traditional triplexes and share frontage on Branch Park with four-story apartments. Source: Photos by Phillip Jones, 2019.

the pedestrian experience and provide opportunities for second-unit carriage houses, which can be rented out.

■ Streets are designed with relatively narrow widths and frequent intersections and consistent sidewalks to reduce car speeds and encourage more walk and bike trips. Streets have rain gardens and light-colored

Figure II.12-5 One of several pocket parks, Paggi Square combines community-building activities with green infrastructure. It features a sunken gravel court popular for the game of pétanque, surrounded by live-work shop houses, casual seating, and rain gardens. The Mexican sycamores and cedar elm trees are just some of the 15,000 new trees. Source: Photo by Ellen Dunham-Jones, 2017.

concrete, and are lined with trees in 20 local varieties, aiming for 30% tree canopy coverage within public spaces, including the streets.

■ A necklace of landscaped greenways, neighborhood parks, and the 13-mile trail network interconnecting them provide district-scale "green" stormwater conveyance and detention, allowing individual lots and yards to be smaller and cheaper. The green infrastructure mitigates off-site flooding and cleanses stormwater before it is released into the natural stream system, and it serves as social infrastructure, hosting a range of activities from community gardens to sport facilities for Mueller residents and neighbors.

Affordability for lower-income households is provided by the Mueller Affordable Housing Program and the real estate transaction fees that go to the Mueller Foundation.[9]

---

9 In 2006, a household earning up to 80% of Austin's Median Family Income qualified to purchase a home for $140,000. Those making up to 60% MFI qualified for one of the greater number of rental units. As per the Master Development Agreement, the affordable units are scattered throughout the project and appear no different on the exterior than those that are market rate. Market-rate apartment houses are to include 10–15% affordable units. All will be guaranteed for 50–99-year affordability. Wildflower Terrace, a 55+ age-restricted mixed-use building, is the first predominantly affordable rental property in Mueller, with some units reserved for tenants at only 30% MFI.

However, Mueller's home values escalated enormously and squeezed out access by middle-income households.[10] In response, as of 2016 the program includes an additional 10% of homes targeted for households earning 80–120% of MFI (median family income). New lot and building types that are even more compact have been introduced to provide affordability by design and the city has allowed an increase in the total number of units.

Austin Energy and Pecan Street earn accolades as Mueller's innovative energy program partners. Austin Energy, a city-owned utility, is a national leader in district energy and renewable energy systems as means to improve regional air quality. Both are employed at Mueller. The Mueller Energy Center is a combined heating and power plant (CHP) that operates at twice the efficiency of a conventional central plant and produces half as many greenhouse gas emissions. It captures waste heat from power generation to provide both steam heat and chilled water. These are disseminated through a microgrid serving the children's hospital and others in the commercial district.[11] In residential areas Austin Energy operates a distributed generation system powered by solar panels, installed by one in three homeowners, that contribute excess capacity to the solar microgrid. In 2018 the Austin Energy SHINES project began tackling energy storage, one of the thorniest obstacles to reliance on solar power, with utility- and customer-scaled batteries.

One of the key partners on the SHINES project is Pecan Street, a consumer energy research and development nonprofit associated with the University of Texas that collects fine-grain energy consumption and generation data from volunteer Mueller homeowners, renters, and businesses.[12] Pecan Street has developed and distributed internet-connected devices to monitor water usage and detect leaks, and are monitoring the impacts to the power grid of electric vehicle charging and energy storage. Their consumer energy

(a)

(b)

Figure II.12-6 Whether along the strictly pedestrian Aldrich Street Paseo (a) or a slow residential street lined with quadplexes (b), Mueller's varied streetscapes invite walking, biking, and casual social interaction. All streets have sidewalks. Protected cycle tracks are provided on through-streets that allow higher driving speeds. Source: Photos by Phillip Jones, 2019.

---

[10] In 2019, three-bedroom row houses at Mueller started at over $600,000, while the Austin region's median home value was $323,000. This speaks to Mueller's desirability, but also to the region's rising home prices in the face of unprecedented population growth. According to data from the Austin Board of Realtors Market Statistic Reports, the area has seen a 67% increase in median single-family home values from 2010 to 2019.

[11] The CHP's efficiency and low emissions helped the Dell Children's Medical Center become the first LEED Platinum hospital in the world.

[12] As of 2019, Pecan Street is monitoring 250 solar homes and 65 electric cars in Mueller, in addition to over 1000 homes elsewhere. With funding from the Verizon Foundation, Pecan Street was able to equip 140 apartment units, including those of seniors and low-income residents, with the equipment needed to see which of their appliances were energy hogs. Testimonials abound from participants saying how the data enabled them to make simple changes and lower their bills.

(a)

(b)

(c)

(d)

Figure II.12-7   A January day in the parks found plenty of evidence of healthy physical activity for the whole family. Research findings show that residents walk and bike more, and travel less in cars, after moving to Mueller. Source: Photos by Phillip Jones, 2019.

database is considered the largest in the world. Research findings based on this data improve smart grid technologies, providing lessons for urban designers and architects. A widely distributed 2013 study upended conventional design wisdom, finding that west-facing solar panels produce 49% more electricity than south-facing ones during energy demand peaks in the late afternoon.[13] Importantly, this enables designers to integrate some west-oriented roofs into solar communities and better shape public spaces.

Mueller is also a test bed for research on the intersection of public health and "bridging" social capital. When development was 40% complete, a team of researchers at Texas A&M University began a series of pre-move and post-move comparative assessments. They used surveys to study changes in residents' physical activities, social interactions, and neighborhood cohesion.[14] Of the hundreds of respondents studied, the total mean average of minutes walked per week rose by half an hour, to a figure close to the recommended 150 weekly minutes of moderate physical activity. Reported weekly minutes spent bicycling rose from 12 to 22, while the time spent traveling in a private car decreased to three hours, a reduction of

[13] Katherine Tweed, "Are Solar Panels Facing the Wrong Direction?" *GreenTech Media*, 13 November 2013.

[14] Based on the 2013 study, the same team leaders have received funding for a longitudinal study where volunteers' activities will be measured. It will be interesting to see if the self-reports were exaggerated or whether walk and bike trips increase as Aldrich Street's commercial destinations get built out. A review in 2019 of over 93 comments on the Reddit social media site shows frequent complaints that until the town center is built, many residents feel that Mueller is not as walkable or bikeable as promised, especially given the location of the grocery store on East 51st Street, far from most Mueller residents.

Figure II.12-8 Future walkable urbanism? The strip shopping center and parking lot adjacent to I-35 were built as a temporary use to provide revenue to pay off the TIF bonds. Utilities were laid in locations that are anticipated to be new streets when the site is redeveloped at a higher density. The Mueller Energy Center, directly behind the awning-fronted strip, is also designed to expand as needed. Source: Photo by Phillip Jones, 2019.

more than one hour per week. Rates of social interaction with neighbors also rose significantly. The researchers found that physical activity increased significantly even for residents who didn't claim walkability as a factor in their decision to move to Mueller.[15]

Both pragmatic and forward-looking, Mueller's design and development structure is conceived in anticipation of future changes. A New Construction Council was established at the start to enable changes in response to new innovations or market changes.[16] The *Mueller Design Book* encourages designing for *future* retrofits at both the urban and building scales: "Each subarea should be planned with an existing and future network of streets that will allow a finer-grained pattern of development to emerge over time."[17] In addition to requiring homes to be "solar-ready," the design book encourages designs that enable aging-in-place by incorporating zero-step wheelchair access and stacked closets that could be converted to elevator shafts.

Recognizing how trends and desires evolve, Jill Fagan from Austin's Economic Development Department says,

"In 2002 when we were trying to get our transportation, waste management, and fire folks on board with the Mueller plan, our roads were deemed too narrow. Now they're seen as too wide."[18] While residents of Mueller love many aspects of their community, a frequent complaint expressed on social media is that Mueller is too suburban, with cars everywhere. It doesn't help that multiple transit options have been voted down or are in flux, and the pilot projects were not as popular as those at The Domain or Downtown.[19] Will that change when the town center on Aldrich Street finally gets built out? Will transit access improve and allow for even greater density? Will the retail parking lots then be redeveloped as anticipated? For now, the site of Mueller—where airplanes once parked, taxied, and took-off—remains reliant on automobiles. However, with the highest concentration of electric vehicles in the country, and many of them solar-home powered, this is a much less-energy-consumptive form of auto dependency.[20] The impacts are being monitored as yet another test case in Mueller's family-friendly, affordable, green urbanism.

[15] Xuemei Zhu, Chia-Yuan Yu, Chanam Lee, Zhipeng Lu, and George Mann, "A retrospective study on changes in residents' physical activities, social interactions, and neighborhood cohesion after moving to a walkable community," *Preventative Medicine* 69 (2014): 593–597. See also Xuemei Zhu, Zhipeng Lu, Chia-Yuan Yu, Chanam Lee, and George Mann, "Walkable communities: Impacts on residents' physical and social health," *World Health Design* (July 2013): 68–75.

[16] At the NCC's recommendation, the Planned Unit Development agreement adopted in 2004 was amended in 2009. The illustrative plan in the design book has gone through four iterations, primarily expanding the town center district.

[17] *Mueller Design Book*, 2017, 90.

[18] Conversation with Ellen Dunham-Jones at Mueller, 4 May 2015.

[19] See the results of the "Electric Last Mile" eight-month pilot project run by Pecan Street and Capital Metro in 2018: https://www.pecanstreet.org/work/transportation/elm/.

[20] Bryan Walsh, "Is this America's Smartest City?" *Time*, 26 June 2014. See also Mark Fischetti, "Electric Car Owners All Plug In at Once," *Scientific American*, 21 August 2012.

Promenade of Wayzata
Wayzata, Minnesota

Challenges addressed:

- Support an aging population
- Add water and energy resilience
- Disrupt automobile dependence

The Twin Cities of Minneapolis–St. Paul are famous in shopping mall history both for Southdale (1956), designed by architect Victor Gruen as the first enclosed and fully air-conditioned shopping center ever, and for the gargantuan Mall of America (1992). But what of the regions' other malls? In scenic Wayzata, Minnesota, on the shores of Lake Minnetonka west of Minneapolis, Presbyterian Homes & Services redeveloped the 14-acre former Wayzata Bay Shopping Center (1967). The Promenade of Wayzata, designed by LHB, Inc., is five blocks of mixed-use, mid-rise buildings on a deck built over underground parking and extensive stormwater management systems.

The program includes ground floor retail and office space, apartments, condominiums, a boutique hotel, and 326 residential units providing a variety of senior housing options directly connected to the walkable downtown.[1] The former one-story enclosed mall comprised 33 stores plus two buildings on outparcels, built over a creek that drained into the lake on paved over wetlands and polluted the lake for 50 years. The drainage problems at the mall became legendary—when flooded, a rowboat was required to navigate the crawlspace underneath! Wet conditions required a novel and highly complex set of water management solutions to redress them in the retrofit.

Wayzata was founded in 1854 and became a fashionable Victorian-era resort of hotels and summer cottages, optimally located at the terminus of a passenger rail line into the city and a launching point for steamboats. With the advent of the automobile age, the resort village was transformed into a commuter suburb. The regional shopping mall, as with so many others from the era, was a success for a while, and then it wasn't. The 1990s opening of I-395 and associated newer commercial competition contributed as culprits. Businesses along nearby Lake Street, Wayzata's downtown main street, suffered too. Intending to replace retail with retail, conventional attempts at redevelopment failed.[2]

Recognizing the importance of the prominently located site, and frustrated with the stagnant condition, the city of Wayzata created a downtown mixed-use district in 2008, granting "limited flexibility in building height and density in order to achieve desired outcomes of a walkable retail and residential center that incorporates public green space, and minimized environmental impacts on the site."[3] The plan squarely addressed two main challenges for suburban retrofitting: managing stormwater on a site that was once wetlands and had become grayfields, and reducing auto dependency by promoting walkability. Solutions to a third challenge, supporting an aging population, came about through the selection of Presbyterian Homes as master developer.

While Wayzata's growth rate over the past few decades was relatively modest, due to zoning and density controls and other factors, the age demographics of the population

---

[1] The total redevelopment cost of the retrofit is described as $342 million. Kelly Smith, "After 5 years and $342M, Wayzata set to end its largest redevelopment project ever," *Star Tribune*, 20 May 2017. InSite Architects designed the senior housing, while the Regatta Wayzata Bay and Hotel Landing buildings were designed by Cuningham Group.

[2] City of Wayzata, *City of Wayzata 2030 Comprehensive Plan*, 2010.
[3] Ibid., 3–6.

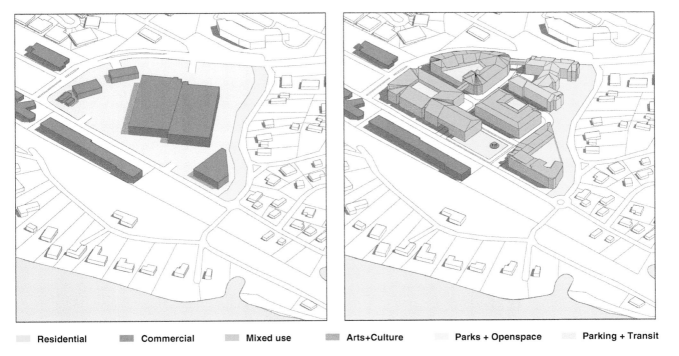

| Residential | Commercial | Mixed use | Arts+Culture | Parks + Openspace | Parking + Transit |

Figure II.13-1 The 1967 Wayzata Bay Shopping Center was built on 14 acres of filled wetlands on Lake Minnetonka. Fifty years later the site has been transformed into the Promenade at Wayzata, five mixed-use blocks that form an extension to the walkable downtown district. Source: Authors.

shifted considerably. From 1990 to 2010 the percentage of residents aged 65 and older grew from 16 to 22%, and the median age increased to 51.7 years, almost 15 years above the national median.[4] This shift redefined the community as a naturally occurring retirement community or NORC, of the "open" type. In "open" NORCs the older residents are spread throughout a residential neighbor-hood, while the classic "vertical" NORC is concentrated in one large building or complex.[5]

Nonprofit, faith-based developer Presbyterian Homes conceived the project to both meet the needs of residents who wish to age-in-community and downsize, as well as to attract new resident "perennial" downsizers. Planning began in 2007, construction commenced in 2012, and was completed in 2017, a ten-year process to opening of the final component, a one-acre public "Great Lawn" facing Lake Minnetonka. Also included in the last phase: a

92-room boutique hotel, the first hotel of any kind in more than half a century to be built in this once-fashionable former summer resort town.

The senior housing units, located in two of the five buildings, designed by InSite Architects and operated by Folkestone, are built as "55-plus" units, a controversial but legally protected, age-restricted category of housing in the United States that has become increasingly popular as the proportion of the population that is older increases. This type of housing may include a range of apartments for rent and for sale with a suite of amenities customized for residents who are older; assisted living units with supportive medical services; traditional skilled nursing care units; and memory care units for elders suffering from dementia. Folkestone at Wayzata includes all of the above, all within a short walk of a host of activities, services, and recreational areas. In high demand, the project was 87% preleased.

[4] 2010 US Census.
[5] Elinor Ginzler, "From Home to Hospice: The Range of Housing Alternatives," in Henry Cisneros, Margaret Dyer-Chamberlain, and Jane Hickie, eds., *Independent for Life: Homes and Neighborhoods for an Aging America* (Austin: University of Texas Press, 2012), 57.

(a)

(b)

Figures II.13-2 Street (a) and courtyard (b) views of senior housing by Folkestone at Wayzata. The entire development, including the surface streets and open spaces, is constructed over an elaborate stormwater management system designed for the once-wetlands site. Master plan by LHB, Inc., building design by InSite Architects for Presbyterian Homes. Source: Photos ©Dana Wheelock.

As part of the deal for tax-increment financing (TIF), the retrofit includes two significant public spaces: a landscaped children's play area and the one-acre Great Lawn. The Promenade has lived up to its billing, helping to revitalize the entire downtown area, bringing new visitors and economic activity. But it also brought traffic. In response, the city added bike lanes and a seasonal free trolley, while funds from the TIF were used to pay for a modest city-owned and constructed two-level parking structure on a nearby downtown surface lot, doubling capacity for car storage.

Some of the most significant innovations in suburban retrofitting at the Promenade of Wayzata are to be found beneath the surface. A different scenario might have resulted in more direct restoration of area wetlands hydrology by regreening this very, very wet site—subsidence of 50-foot-deep layers of swampy soils and fill had increased the head room in the crawl space under the old mall to standing height. But regreening by reconstructing wetlands was a path not taken. Instead, city council in the largely built-out suburb adopted a plan to concentrate growth and higher density on this specific downtown-adjacent site, design it for zero stormwater runoff, and contribute funds to a wetland bank instead.[6]

Consequently, an extensive civil engineering approach came into play. Over 3000 pilings were needed to stabilize the soil, described by the master developer as the "worst soil conditions" he had ever encountered.[7]

The team set a goal to far surpass local regulations by designing the site to mimic native wetlands conditions. How? By constructing a foundation that is in essence a "land bridge" of heavy concrete grade beams supported on the aforementioned 3000 steel driven pipe pilings. The concurrent approach to managing on-site storm water is three-pronged, comprising: an infiltration basin for 5 acres of the site, a filtration basin for another 5 acres, and an expanded and reinforced landscaped pond to handle the rest as well as surface run off from 20 acres of adjacent upland residential development. The infiltration and filtration basins are built under on-grade concrete street decks and are also slipped in between below-grade parking floors beneath each block.

For those with an engineering bent, more grainy details: the infiltration basin, 200 by 300 feet, was excavated up to 31 feet deep to reach existing sandy soil, lined with a 5-foot-thick clay dike, and filled with clean sand. There is also a second, smaller infiltration basin. The filtrated runoff recharges groundwater through the sand stratum. The filtration basin, 40 by 220 feet, is a precast

---

[6] Minnesota, "the land of lakes," has a statewide Wetlands Bank Program. See "Wetland Bank Credits and Fees," https://bwsr .state.mn.us/wetland-bank-credits-and-fees.

[7] Kelly Smith, "After 5 years and $342M."

Figure II.13-3 A free concert on the Great Lawn in the Promenade of Wayzata, summer 2018. Source: Photo by Jason Jenkins/Sun Sailor. Republished with permission.

concrete vault lined at the bottom with geotextile filter fabric. This water flows slowly to the lake after being filtered and cleansed.[8]

Elevated concrete decks on the residential blocks, forming central courtyards, are covered with over one acre of extensive green roof. The drainage pond, meanwhile, works to reduce surface run-off contaminants such as suspended soils and phosphorus, contributors to harmful algae blooms. Another feature, significant in wintry Minnesota, is 80 linear miles of hydronic snowmelt tubing in concrete street paving and sidewalks, eliminating on-site

use of road salts that pollute freshwater lakes with chloride. Lastly, the pilings double as a system for geothermal building heating and cooling.

The challenges in Wayzata are found elsewhere in the Minneapolis–St. Paul metropolitan region: stormwater drainage and runoff pollution problems due to the combination of a high water-table plus suburban sprawl; a population that is aging more rapidly than in many other northern American regions; and dying malls and strip centers built on imprudently filled land. In *Retrofitting Suburbia*, we profiled the distressed outlying St. Paul neighborhood of Phalen, where a strip center regreening retrofit produced a reconstructed wetland and lake, ringed with new affordable housing.[9] On a recent visit, one of us observed hawks at the lake, evidence of a healthy wildlife habitat. Pedestrians were there, too, some also observing

[8] Tiggelaar is an engineer with LHB, Inc., an urban designer, and a civil engineer for the retrofit. James W. Tiggelaar, "Transforming What Was Wet and Wasted in Wayzata," *Informed Infrastructure* 5 April 2015: https://informedinfrastructure.com/14117/transforming-what-was-wet-and-wasted-in-wayzata/; James W. Tiggelaar, "Storms on the Promenade," n.d.: http://www.minnehahacreek.org/sites/minnehahacreek.org/files/Plans_Promenade%20of%20Wayzata.pdf.

[9] Dunham-Jones and Williamson, *Retrofitting Suburbia*, 72–75.

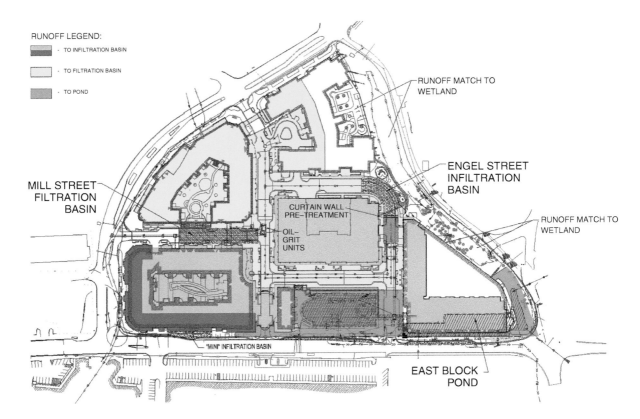

RUNOFF LEGEND:
- TO INFILTRATION BASIN
- TO FILTRATION BASIN
- TO POND

MILL STREET FILTRATION BASIN

CURTAIN WALL PRE–TREATMENT

OIL-GRIT UNITS

"MINI" INFILTRATION BASIN

RUNOFF MATCH TO WETLAND

ENGEL STREET INFILTRATION BASIN

RUNOFF MATCH TO WETLAND

EAST BLOCK POND

Figure II.13-4 LHB, Inc. engineered three primary systems to handle the extensive stormwater management demands of the filled wetlands site: infiltration, filtration, and a below-grade pond. Source: Courtesy of LHB, Inc.

the hawks. Due east, in the St. Paul suburb of Oakdale, the smaller Oakdale Center mall was demolished in 2011 and the site retrofitted into Tartan Crossing. The project includes a large grocery store, senior housing, and a small park for stormwater comprised of a series of cascading, stepped biofiltration ponds on the edge of the property.

Even the storied Southdale Mall in Edina is being retrofitted with new apartment housing and a hotel on its outparcels. These projects speak to the seriousness with which public and private entities in the Twin Cities region are taking up the challenges of aging demographics, housing need, and ecological degradation.

Maplewood Mall and Living Streets
Maplewood, Minnesota

Challenges addressed:

- Add water and energy resilience
- Improve public health
- Support an aging population

We have long recognized suburban commercial developments, such as shopping malls, as wellsprings of runoff due to their vast acres of parking lots. Maplewood Mall, a 70-acre enclosed regional mall a 10-minute drive from St. Paul, Minnesota, was fingered as a major contributor to the phosphorus contamination of nearby lakes due to decades of high-volume stormwater runoff. Partnering with the city of Maplewood, Ramsey County, and the mall's then-owner, Simon Property Group, the local Ramsey–Washington Metro Watershed District (RWMWD) took the innovative approach of enhancing the mall and improving its environmental performance by transforming 35 acres of impervious asphalt grayfields with tree trench islands, rainwater gardens, and areas of permeable paving. After the project was completed in 2012, more than 65% of the property's runoff was captured, filtered, and infiltrated, up from only 3% before the regreening retrofit.[1]

Designed by Barr Engineering Company, the scheme was installed in phases over four years. While 55 rain gardens, 6,700 square feet of permeable pavers at the mall's entrances, and a 5,700-gallon cistern are the most visible elements of the project, the primary workhorse is a series of rock-lined tree trenches with 200 trees. Collectively one mile in length, they ring the property.

Stormwater is detained below ground before being sucked up by the trees or slowly draining to the sewer. Adopting a design developed in Sweden to minimize compacting of soils in areas of heavy traffic, the engineers chose the trenches as the method that would result in the fewest lost parking spaces. Together, these elements are designed to remove up to 50 pounds of phosphorus and 5 tons of sediment from stormwater falling on the mall property each year. The designers expect further improvement in measured run-off reduction as the hundreds of trees mature and grow.[2]

Some pushback resulted from the public's funding of the project's $6.5 million budget, through grants, loans, and levies. Strict agreements are in place for the mall owner to maintain the improvements and thus reap significant public benefit over time to the watershed from the expenditure.

Meanwhile, Sears, one of four anchors at the Maplewood Mall, closed its doors permanently in summer 2018, as did two other large retailers nearby. A planning study is underway for the mall district's economic future; this presents an opportunity to address two additional challenges: to improve public health and to support an aging population. Early indicators point to breaking up the site into smaller blocks, and adding health care, wellness, and medical office uses, following trends we've observed elsewhere, as well as more multi-unit housing. We expect the plans to recommend improvements and enhancements to transit options and walkability. The new housing would serve lower-income families as well as older adults,

---

1   Ramsey-Washington Metro Watershed District website, Maplewood Mall Retrofit project page, n.d.: http://www.rwmwd.org/projects/maplewood-mall-retrofit/.

2   Clifton Aichinger and Erin Anderson Wenz, "Retrofitting a Major Retail Mall for Stormwater Volume Reduction," *Land and Water*, September–October 2012: 8–14; Taylor Griggs, "Three steps to pollution reduction at a mall: Maplewood, Minnesota," Build a Better Burb website, n.d.: http://buildabetterburb.org/three-keys-to-stormwater-management-at-a-suburban-mall/.

Figure II.14-1 Rain gardens cut out of parking lot asphalt, a prominently located cistern for collecting stormwater runoff from the roof, and an environmental conservation-themed mosaic mural frame the main entrance to Minnesota's Maplewood Mall. Source: Courtesy of Ramsey-Washington Metro Watershed District.

Figure II.14-2 Schoolchildren studying *Rainy Day*, the mosaic mural designed and installed by Tessera Mosaics. Source: Photo by Sage Passi, 2014, courtesy of Ramsey-Washington Metro Watershed District.

demographic segments that are growing in Maplewood. Already, a two-story Days Inn motel on one of the mall's outparcels was retrofitted into Maple Hill Senior Living, with 115 apartments for assisted or memory care living.

And now 35 acres at the mall site are significantly improved for stormwater. But this is just a drop in the proverbial bucket. What about other impervious surfaces throughout the suburban city of Maplewood? Maplewood, population 40,000, has a remarkably forward-thinking history of sustainability projects, especially in the area of soft or green infrastructure. It was one of the first in Minnesota, known as the "Land of 10,000 Lakes," to begin installing rainwater gardens as a routine part of street improvements, such as resurfacing or water main replacement, so as to reduce stormwater runoff into the sewer system and prevent pollutants such as phosphorus from reaching water bodies. Since the first installation in 1996, the city now maintains an inventory of over 700 home rain gardens in the planted strip between sidewalk and roadway along residential streets, and 60 rain gardens on city-owned property. The city's Natural Resources Office in the Planning Department freely shares ten standard designs, from "Butterfly and Friends" to "Minnesota Prairie," adaptable to a range of site conditions.[3]

How did they do it? Success with early installations led Maplewood, back in 2003, to set up an Environmental Utility Fund to finance an ambitious Storm Water Management Program. The fund collects a fee from all properties, including tax-exempt uses; there is a flat fee for residential property, and for commercial and industrial uses the fee is based on area of land covered with impervious surfaces. This provides incentive for property owners to replace impervious surfaces with permeable ones to qualify for a substantial reduction in the annual fee. Residential owners receive a 30% credit each year for a properly installed and maintained rainwater garden, confirmed with a yearly inspection—hence the impressive cumulative inventory of 700 examples.

Maplewood's next step was an official Living Streets Policy, adopted in 2013.[4] The policy, which has proved a

[3] City of Maplewood website, Rain Gardens page, n.d.: https://maplewoodmn.gov/1032/Rain-Gardens.

[4] Michael Thompson, P.E., *City of Maplewood, Minnesota Living Streets Policy*, 2013: http://maplewoodmn.gov/DocumentCenter/View/8955/Living-Streets-Policy-Final-Version.

Figure II.14-3 Raindrop ripples are stenciled into new sidewalks at each rainwater garden in the Bartelmy/Meyer Living Streets Demonstration Project in Maplewood, completed in 2012. The project's success led to the adoption of a city-wide Living Streets Policy. Source: Courtesy of Ramsey-Washington Metro Watershed District.

model for other area municipalities, was finalized following the successful implementation the previous year of the Bartelmy/Meyer Living Streets Demonstration Project. Technical and funding assistance came from RWMWD, the same regional watershed district that initiated the Maplewood Mall regreening. Commenters lauded the demonstration project for forging partnerships, as well as for the groundbreaking—or should we say *pavement*-breaking—efforts to incorporate improvements fulfilling ambitions of both the Complete Streets and the Green Streets movements.

Rainwater gardens and street trees remove pollutants from stormwater through filtering before the water enters area lakes, thus improving lake quality. In nearby Burnsville, Minnesota, an experiment in the early 2000s monitored 18 rain gardens on a 1980s-era residential street with 25 houses to test their performance relative to a similar neighboring street. Monitoring over 48 rain events showed the rain gardens reduced runoff by 90%.[5] Maplewood was thus confident of results. Narrowed streets plus new trees can also calm vehicle traffic, creating a safer environment against crashes. The addition

of sidewalks makes it easier for neighbors, many of whom are aging-in-place in vintage late-twentieth-century residential subdivisions, to exercise by walking and connect socially with one another.

The Living Streets Policy explicitly calls for streets to be narrowed, freeing space for other uses. In the Bartelmy/Meyer neighborhood, the roadway was uniformly narrowed from 30 to 24 feet wide. Even with the addition of sidewalks, the overall area of impervious paving was reduced by a full acre, spread over two miles of residential streets. The project included one and a half miles of new sidewalks, 32 rainwater gardens, and one larger regional basin, and 200 trees. Now, only 10% of the water in a storm event runs into the sewers; the rest is filtered, infiltrated, or evaporates. Significantly, project costs only increased slightly, boding well for the new policy's continued success.[6]

These efforts speak to the importance of repairing landscape ecology. Many states could benefit from looking at the policies and programs of the particularly proactive watershed districts in the "Land of 10,000 Lakes."

5 Barr Engineering Company, "Burnsville Stormwater Retrofit Study," June 2006: http://www.ci.burnsville.mn.us/DocumentCenter/Home/View/449.

6 Ramsey-Washington Metro Watershed District website, Maplewood Living Streets project page; Metropolitan Council website, Living Streets Maplewood page, n.d.: https://metro-council.org/Handbook/Local-Planning-Highlights/Living-Streets-Maplewood.aspx.

Case Study II.15

Baton Rouge Health District
Baton Rouge, Louisiana

Challenges addressed:

- Improve public health
- Disrupt automobile dependence

How do you transform a congested suburban medical corridor into a coordinated walkable, mixed-use health district? More than a dozen leading heathcare, academic, and research anchor institutions located at the intersection of two interstate highways in Baton Rouge, Louisiana, have been actively grappling with this question. The area, developed from the 1970s, hosts more than 17,000 parking spaces, servicing drivers traveling to and between 11 million square feet of disconnected development. Only 22% of the streets had sidewalks on either side. Local leaders were made acutely aware of the scope of their challenge by a 2014 study that ranked Baton Rouge worst among medium-sized US cities in measures of sprawl—such as degree of separation of uses, low levels of density, and street network disconnection.[1] The Baton Rouge Area Foundation engaged the design firm of Perkins & Will to devise a cure.

Released in late 2015, the resulting plan document examines the Baton Rouge medical corridor like a patient, using medical metaphors accessible to a principle stakeholder audience steeped in healthcare language.[2] The planners propose a series of "diagnoses" by outlining chief complaints, key symptoms, vital signs, and providing assessments. The plan for "treatment" comprises priority interventions, prescriptions, follow-up tests, and expected outcomes.

"Heathy Place" and "Heathcare Innovation" are two main topics in the plan. In the area of Healthy Place, the chief complaint is acute congestion on arterial roads, while symptoms include an inefficient transportation network, weak alternatives to the car, low intersection density, and generally sprawling conditions. Treatments include infilling the street network and adding a 7.4-mile walking and biking trail ("Health Loop Trail") to improve efficiency and choice in the transportation network. The follow-up tests include metrics on travel speed, bicycle and pedestrian counts, and surveys of employee travel behavior. The area of Healthcare Innovation addresses the chief complaint that healthcare focus is on acute care rather than on population health management. Notably high rates of the preventable—and costly—chronic diseases of diabetes and obesity and a low ranking in the supply of primary care physicians in Louisiana are the weak "vital sign" readings. The primary treatment is to establish an innovative diabetes and obesity center. Promoting healthy living beyond hospital walls is the goal of these and other treatments in the district plan.

The 1,000-acre Baton Rouge Health District is conceived as both a place and an organization. It is formed to best treat the "ailing patient"—to extend the healthcare metaphor—through an unusual tactic of asking competing institutions to put aside some differences in order to form a joint nonprofit umbrella entity. The emphasis on weighing place equally with organization admirably reflects recent research findings about the significant role that environmental factors play in influencing behaviors, such as diet and physical activity, that together account for up to 70%

---

[1] The original study, conducted by Reid Ewing and Shima Hamidi at the Metropolitan Research Center at the University of Utah, was supported by the National Institutes of Health and the Ford Foundation. Report, *Measuring Sprawl 2014*, Smart Growth America (April 2014): https://smartgrowthamerica.org/resources/measuring-sprawl-2014/.

[2] Baton Rouge Area Foundation and Perkins & Will, *A Master Plan for the Baton Rouge Health District: Treatment Plan* (October 2015): https://www.braf.org/braf-research/2016/2/29/health-district-master-plan.

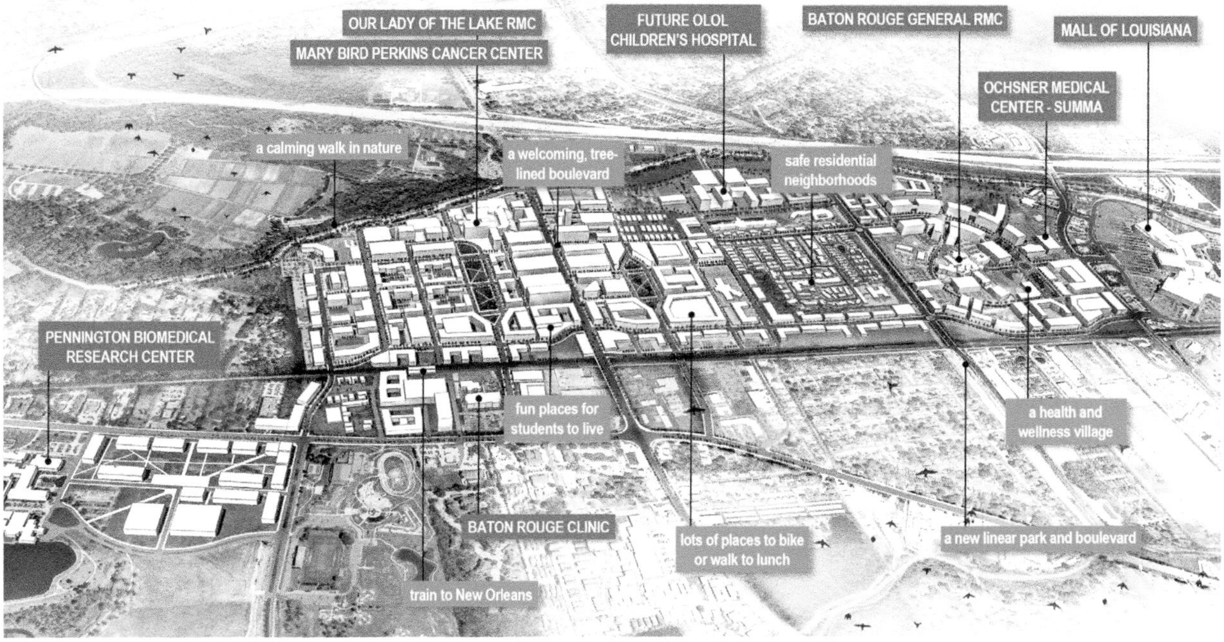
OUR LADY OF THE LAKE RMC
MARY BIRD PERKINS CANCER CENTER
FUTURE OLOL CHILDREN'S HOSPITAL
BATON ROUGE GENERAL RMC
MALL OF LOUISIANA
OCHSNER MEDICAL CENTER - SUMMA
a calming walk in nature
a welcoming, tree-lined boulevard
safe residential neighborhoods
PENNINGTON BIOMEDICAL RESEARCH CENTER
fun places for students to live
a health and wellness village
BATON ROUGE CLINIC
lots of places to bike or walk to lunch
a new linear park and boulevard
train to New Orleans

Figure II.15-1 Perkins & Will's visualization of potential future transformation of the Baton Rouge Medical District, currently an auto-oriented, congested corridor stretching from the Pennington Biomedical Research Center to the Mall of Louisiana. Source: Courtesy of Perkins & Will.

of overall health outcomes in the United States.[3] How can Baton Rouge's major medical centers claim to be providing high-quality healthcare when they can't even provide decent, continuous sidewalks and adequate crosswalks?

The report asks us to "imagine if the area surrounding a hospital were actually hospitable: a place where it's easy to walk between medical offices, parks, restaurants, and shops, or to escape to a quiet, natural setting for some fresh air."[4] What if the main hospitals were turned inside out, clustering public open spaces and activities around the main entrances? What if they linked up to one another with a 7.5-mile creek-side trail, usable by patients, employees, and visitors alike?

Implementation began right away, with formation of the Baton Rouge Health District as a coordinated nonprofit entity, appointment of an executive director, fast-tracking by local authorities of a complete streets project for the district's most congested and pedestrian-unfriendly arterial corridors, and construction of new segments on the "Health Loop Trail." Four miles of additional sidewalks and trails will be added in the next years. Other implementation activities since the plan's adoption include construction of a new wellness-focused hotel to serve patient families, and key population initiatives between the partners to address the acute opioid addiction crisis.[5]

[3] Ibid., 12. Supported by the Bipartisan Policy Center's Nutrition and Physical Activity Initiative report, "Lots to Lose: How America's Health and Obesity Crisis Threatens our Economic Future" (2012): https://bipartisanpolicy.org/wp-content/uploads/sites/default/files/5023_BPC_NutritionReport_FNL_Web.pdf.

[4] Ibid., 13. See also Basak Alkan and Tatiana Guimaraes, "Setting the Foundation for Healthy Living," *Healthcare* Design, 26 May 2016: https://www.healthcaredesignmagazine.com/trends/perspectives/setting-foundation-healthy-living/.

[5] Email from Basak Alkan of Perkins & Will, April 2019.

Only time will tell on the success of the full treatment plan. For right now, however, the prognosis for Baton Rouge seems fair to good. And the cure is spreading. Hospitals around the country are increasingly recognizing that their ambulance sirens, extensive parking, ambitious building expansions, and so forth have contributed to the decline of adjacent areas. Many have begun to invest in neighborhood physical improvements as a means to improve public health, while preserving their nonprofit status.

As of late 2019, 46 health systems (many of which are the largest private sector employers in their states and represent about 20% of the nation's hospitals) have joined the Healthcare Anchor Network's commitment to leverage hiring, purchasing, and place-based investments to build more inclusive and sustainable local economies. In addition to investments in walkability infrastructure, grocery stores in "food deserts" (areas that lack access to healthy food choices), child care centers, and minority- and women-owned businesses, the network encourages members to direct at least 1–2% of their investment portfolios to affordable housing. Network members have begun to leverage their land holdings to establish land trusts.[6] As the neighborhoods revitalize, the land trusts can help to maintain the long-term affordability that is needed so that the most vulnerable low-income populations get to reap the array of long-term health benefits of Health District retrofits.

---

[6] The Maggie Walker Land Trust, funded largely by Bon Secours Mercy Health, in Richmond, Virginia, is a good example. See Carey L. Biron, "'Good Neighbors'? U.S. Hospitals Invest in Land, Housing to Treat Crisis," *Place*, 21 November 2019.

Case Study II.16
Uptown Circle
Normal, Illinois

Challenges addressed:

- Improve public health
- Add water and energy resilience
- Disrupt automobile dependence

There's nothing "normal" about the water-cleansing roundabout in Normal, Illinois, and its impact on revitalization of this town of around 55,000 people. In the town's central business district, adjacent to the train station, a large, awkward, asphalted five-way intersection was transformed in 2010 into Uptown Circle, a roundabout with an innovative landscape design. The circle tames traffic, improves air and water quality, and creates a safer environment for pedestrians, bicyclists, and motorized vehicles.[1] It also creates a lively central place for people to gather, where before there had been only a surfeit of vacant land and parking lots. It quickly became a valued placemaking anchor for the new Uptown District, an area defined in a downtown renewal planning effort, led by architects and urban designers Farr Associates, launched in Normal a decade earlier to curtail sprawl and bring people together.

A second master plan, Uptown 2.0, expanding the district to adjacent areas, including an adjacent town-owned 9-acre area south of the railroad tracks, was completed by Farr Associates in 2015. The new plan calls for meeting the rigorous standards of the Living Community Challenge, for net-positive energy and water systems.[2] The ongoing revitalization of downtown promises to continue to contribute to the improvement of public health by providing more places for residents in Normal to engage in everyday physical activity.

The roadway infrastructure investment improves access to the Constitutional Trail, a 45-mile walking, running, and biking path, as well as to newly improved rail service. It soon bore fruit as a catalyst to infill redevelopment. Three significant new buildings now frame the 135-foot diameter circle: a multimodal transit station for Amtrak and connecting bus lines, a children's museum, and a mixed-use building. A fourth building facing the circle is in the planning stages. As a reminder of how new and different pedestrian-oriented, compact, mixed-use development still seems in Normal, the lede of a local news story on the latest proposal describes the four- to five-story-tall building as "high rise."[3]

The award-winning Uptown Circle itself was designed by Hoerr Schaudt Landscape Architects and Clark Dietz Engineers as a marvel of stormwater management.[4] Rainwater flows from neighboring streets through new tree wells into an obsolete brick storm sewer converted into a large detention cistern, 700 feet long and 5 feet in diameter, capable of holding 76,000 gallons. It is pumped into two circular surface channels. In the outer channel, the water flows through a series of four wet planted areas, called "filtration bogs," which cleanse it to a "touchable" standard. It then flows over a textured surface and fountain, which also functions as a seasonal wading pool. Excess filtered water is held in an irrigation cistern, where it

1 The roundabout design has 75% fewer points of conflict than a conventional four-way intersection and is expected to reduce traffic accidents by 35%. Landscape Architecture Foundation, "Uptown Normal Circle and Streetscape," Landscape Performance Series, n.d.: https://www.landscapeperformance.org/case-study-briefs/uptown-normal-circle-and-streetscape.

2 Douglas Farr, *Sustainable Nation: Urban Design Patterns for the Future* (Hoboken, NJ: Wiley, 2018), 59-62.

3 Derek Beigh, "Town Considers Another New Building on Uptown Circle," *Bloomington Pantagraph*, 6 January 2018.

4 The project garnered two major awards: the US EPA's National Award for Smart Growth Achievement for a Civic Place in 2011, and a Transportation Planning Excellence Award from the Federal Highway Administration and Federal Transit Administration in 2012.

Figure II.16-1 Uptown Circle in Normal, Illinois. A pathway connection from the roundabout to the regional Constitution Trail is flanked by two new buildings: Uptown Station (upper right in photo), which also houses City Hall, and a children's museum (upper left). Source: Photo by Scott Shigley, courtesy of Hoerr Schaudt Landscape Architects.

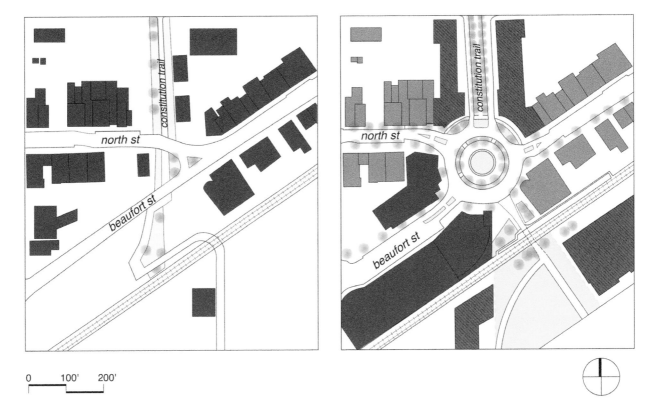

Figure II.16-2 An awkward five-way trail and road intersection (left) was replaced with a lushly landscaped roundabout that also functions as a valued civic space (right). New and proposed buildings will soon provide a complete 4- to 5-story streetwall around the circle. Source: Authors.

can be pumped back through the fountain. Remarkably, almost all of the stormwater runoff evaporates or is used for landscape irrigation, and almost none is discharged into the storm sewer. During dry spells, the fountain and pools run dry, conveying a sustainability narrative to the public about the interconnectedness of green infrastructure systems to the high-quality civic space.[5]

Three final landscape elements complete the composition. First, an outer lawn, with a mountable curb,

Figure II.16-4 The fountain and wading pools at Uptown Circle have become a major civic attraction in Normal. Source: Photo by Scott Shigley, courtesy of Hoerr Schaudt Landscape Architects.

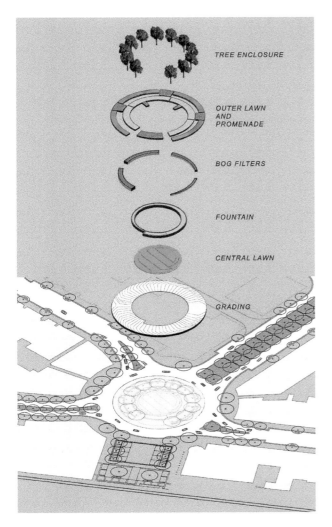

TREE ENCLOSURE

OUTER LAWN AND PROMENADE

BOG FILTERS

FOUNTAIN

CENTRAL LAWN

GRADING

Figure II.16-3 The roundabout is designed as a series of concentric elements, connected by flows of stormwater and people, with traffic tamed and kept to the periphery. Source: Courtesy of Hoerr Schaudt Landscape Architects.

comprises a safety apron that can accommodate large trucks and emergency vehicles while keeping the roadway "skinny," thus mitigating a common objection to converting intersections to roundabouts and traffic circles. Second is an enclosure of trees, planted in Silva Cells to prevent soil compaction and encourage healthy tree canopy growth. A full canopy helps separate the occupiable central spaces of the circle from surrounding traffic, and better mitigates urban heat generation by providing maximal shade. And finally, there is a central lawn with a slight slope for casual comfortable sitting. This contrasts with other roundabouts that feature a central object, such as a statue or sculpture—think Columbus Circle in Manhattan, or the Addison Circle retrofit near Dallas.[6]

On its own, the roundabout is a marvel of landscape and civil engineering design, but it is also a key element in the larger transformative planning effort to transition Normal from an auto-dependent past to a multimodal mobility future, encouraging use of passenger trains and buses, bicycles, and walking, in place of driving, for many trips. This approach not only reduces auto dependency by increasing options, but also promises to improve people's health by encouraging residents to be physically active while downtown.

5 Jay Landers, "Illinois Traffic Roundabout Collects Storm Water for Use in Fountain," *Civil Engineering,* 80:10 (October 2010): 32–35.

6 Dunham-Jones and Williamson, *Retrofitting Suburbia,* 180–182.

One Hundred Oaks Mall
Nashville, Tennessee

Challenge addressed:

- Improve public health

One Hundred Oaks Mall is a pioneering example of the turn to medical clinics to breathe new life into moribund retail centers on life support.[1] The 56-acre property a few miles south of downtown Nashville had once been the site of a spacious log home, surrounded by dozens of graceful oak trees, the base of operations for a popular local catering business. As a family member recalled, "There were 98 oaks there when my mother bought the property. She planted two acorns and named it Hundred Oaks."[2] By the early 1960s, the land was surrounded with encroaching commercial development, including a Pepsi bottling plant (the sugary American elixir, a contributor to top burdens of disease). It was time to sell.

In the often-repeated story of suburban development, the trees were bulldozed and replaced with a two-story enclosed shopping mall—replete with 60 stores, a twin-screen movie theater (a novelty at the time), and parking for 4000 cars. Then, in what journalist Joel Garreau somewhat famously described as a standard real estate practice, the mall developers named it for the flora and fauna they had just eradicated: One Hundred Oaks.[3]

The 1967-vintage One Hundred Oaks Mall had seen much better days when, forty years later, Vanderbilt

|(a)|(b)|

Figure II.17-1 Views of the main second level entrance to One Hundred Oaks, before (a) and after (b) a reinhabitation-type retrofit into the Vanderbilt Health Medical Center. To realize the project, Vanderbilt Health worked with developers ATR Corinth Partners and the architecture firm Gresham Smith. Source: (a) Courtesy of Gresham Smith; (b) Photo by Bob Schatz.

---

[1] Project credits include Vanderbilt University Medical Center, developer ATR Corinth Partners, and the architecture firm of Gresham Smith.
[2] Wayne Wood, "When Hundred Oaks Was Home," *House Organ*, the magazine of the Vanderbilt University Medical Center, December 2008–January 2009.

[3] Joel Garreau, *Edge City: Life on the New Frontier* (New York, Doubleday, 1991).

(a)   (b)

Figure II.17-2   Interior views of the entry lobby, before (a) and after (b). The retrofit design aimed for the ambiance of a hotel lobby. Source: (a) Courtesy of Gresham Smith; (b) Photo by Bob Schatz.

University Medical Center (VUMC) chose to move some of its outpatient services from a crowded, parking-challenged, midtown Nashville campus into the mall's vacant second floor. The first floor had already been converted to outward-facing discount box stores in a mid-1990s "Hail Mary pass" renovation. The mall offered 450,000 square feet and ample parking. And a new marketing tagline: "'Convenience' is about to become a medical term. Take Exit 79, then left."

Gresham Smith's 2009 gut renovation introduced warm colors and furnishings that dramatically changed the feel of the interior to something akin to a hotel lobby. A new facade with grand entrances and ample perimeter windows and skylights welcomes patients from well-organized parking lots partially regreened with hundreds of new trees, including oaks, of course, rain gardens, and other site navigation and stormwater management improvements. Cyril Stewart, then director of facility planning at VUMC, cited increased patient follow-up visits at the mall location.[4]

On arrival, patients sign in at an electronic kiosk and are given pagers, freeing them to visit the shops at ground-floor level or grab a bite while waiting for appointments. The focus is on the ease of the patient experience. The floor plan for the medical center is laid out as if the 22 different clinical groups, including heart health, surgical weight loss, imaging, and women's health, are inline stores. Each has its own waiting area along the daylit, high-ceilinged public corridor and transitions back to the most private spaces along the exterior wall.

In the decade since completion, the project has been repeatedly profiled in the press, joining the dozen other enclosed shopping malls that have been substantially converted to healthcare and inspiring imitators. University medical systems in Dallas, Atlanta, and Charleston, South Carolina, are working with developers to convert former Sears and JCPenney mall anchor stores.[5] Healthcare isn't only moving into malls. Our database contains over 30 examples of healthcare uses moving into former big box stores and strip malls, seven of them alone in the state of Minnesota.

And why not? Since 2010 US healthcare providers have themselves "gone shopping" for more consumer-friendly locations by which to compete for the 30 million new medical customers created by the Affordable Care Act. The retail health clinics have been so successful that efforts to repeal "Obamacare" haven't slowed the trend down. By one estimate there was 47% growth in healthcare retail

[4] Cyril Stewart, "Vanderbilt Health at One Hundred Oaks: Transforming Architecture, Healthcare and a Community," presentation at the American Institute of Architects convention, Denver, Colorado, 19 June 2013. See also Todd Hutlock, "The Ultimate Recycling Project: Vanderbilt Health One Hundred Oaks Outpatient Clinic Mall," *Healthcare Design,* 12 January 2012.

[5] Maria Halkias, "UT Southwestern's move is a trend breathing new life into big, empty department stores," *Dallas Morning News*, 12 December 2019; Patrick Hoff, "Citadel Mall redevelopment progressing," *Charleston Business Journal*, 1 November 2018; Raisa Habersham, "Emory Healthcare to Anchor Northlake Mall," *Atlanta Journal Constitution*, 24 October 2019.

Vanderbilt Health One Hundred Oaks

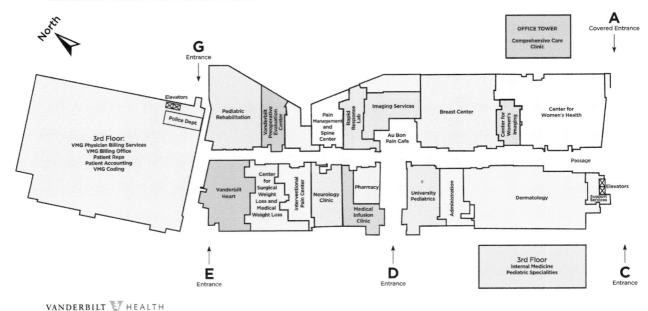

Figure II.17-3 The floor plan for the VUMC, on the second floor of the One Hundred Oaks Mall, laid out as if the different clinical group areas are stores. While all of the original wall partitions and storefronts were removed in the gut renovation, the new configuration evokes the old, but instead of buying goods, patrons are "shopping" for their health. Source: Courtesy of Vanderbilt University Medical Center.

clinics from 2015 to 2018 and the number of retail locations could double by 2022.[6]

Improving access to healthcare in the suburbs is a good idea. The sedentary lifestyle of driving and sitting, associated with the era of mass suburbanization and suburban form built during the second half of the twentieth century, is a proven major contributor to the risk factors for premature death and disability in northern America. These risks threaten to stall the immense gains made over the twentieth century in longevity and compression of morbidity, while contributing to many of the serious health conditions treated with convenience at the VUMC.

---

[6] Natalie Dolce, "How to Incorporate Healthcare Services into Retail," *GlobeSt.com*, 24 May 2019.

Historic Fourth Ward Park
Atlanta, Georgia

Challenges addressed:

- Add water and energy resilience
- Compete for jobs

Can the regreening of 17 acres of parking lots into a stormwater park trigger award-winning redevelopment, reinhabitation, and trail building on a grand scale? That's the case that can be made by Atlanta's decision to address its combined sewer overflow (CSO) problem with a $23 million stormwater park instead of a $40 million underground tunnel. The park attracted the first major investment to support the Atlanta BeltLine, an ambitious 22-mile long rails-to-trails project that's also hoped to be a future transit loop. As such, Historic Fourth Ward Park proved the viability of the BeltLine to be the catalyst for change that it's since become. And by solving the site's recurring flooding problems, the park enabled the renovation of a large vacant Sears distribution warehouse into Ponce City Market, a highly successful mixed-use complex with a popular food hall. Rents for creative office space there were the first in the city to breach $50 per square foot.

The ripple effects can be seen in the ever-expanding new office and apartment buildings flanking both the park and the BeltLine. Contrary to previously accepted popular opinion, the transformations have proven that Atlantans quite love to walk, bike, and gather in well-designed public spaces. So much so that some of the nearby lower-income residents the park was intended to serve have been displaced. Further away the project has inspired an explosion of new trails, several stormwater parks, more redeveloped parking lots, and the reinhabitation of many vacant buildings to similar uses throughout Atlanta's suburbs.

The confluence of the park, Ponce City Market, and the BeltLine appears to be the result of a well-laid masterplan. In fact, they're linked more by topography, water, and history. In the 1860s an Atlanta physician christened the "healthful" waters at the low-lying junction of two creeks the "Ponce de Leon Springs" and it became a popular attraction. The Ponce de Leon Amusement Park opened on the site in 1903, soon followed by the Ponce de Leon Ballpark (built on top of a drained lake, and eventually replaced by the Midtown Place strip shopping center in 1999).

In the early 1920s, Atlanta learned that Sears was looking for a site in the southeastern US outside of a downtown with both railroad access and space for ample parking. To entice the company, the City of Atlanta buried the two creeks in culverts and agreed to extend North Avenue to meet the site. In 1926 Sears built a multistory warehouse for goods sold by catalog, along with a large retail store, above the junction of the culverts. An existing rail line on a ridge to the east provided freight access, while paved parking lots stretched far to the south. By the mid-1960s, Sears was the largest retailer in the US and their Atlanta building had expanded to 2 million square feet. But their catalog business slowed in the 1970s and they vacated the building in 1987. The city bought it in 1990 and used the lower floors as City Hall East and the parking lots to store municipal vehicles. Utility vehicle parking for various companies extended the parking lots further south.

By the 1990s, heavy rains and runoff from all those parking lots contributed to frequent flooding in the area. Like many northern American cities, Atlanta has a combined sewer system, collecting rainwater runoff and sewage in the same pipes. In storms, these systems can overflow, releasing untreated sewage into the Chattahoochee River; this was happening up to 70 times a year. In 1999 EPA hit the city with a $2.5 million penalty and negotiated two consent decrees requiring elimination of overflow events by 2007. The city has complied largely by constructing large underground stormwater storage tunnels deliberately designed to have no impact on the neighborhoods above them.

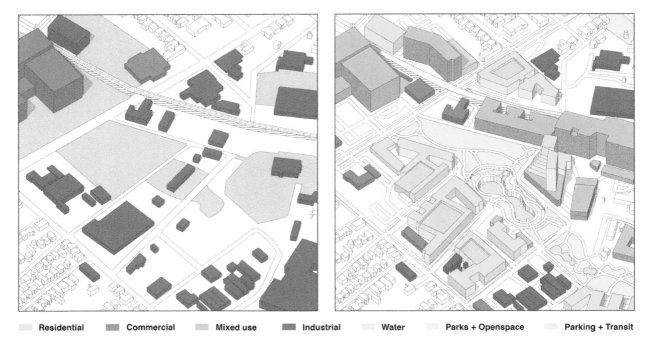

Residential   Commercial   Mixed use   Industrial   Water   Parks + Openspace   Parking + Transit

Figure II.18-1 These before-and-after diagrams looking northeast show the former parking lots regreened into Historic Fourth Ward Park adjacent to the BeltLine trail. The stormwater park has since attracted new development along its sides and is anchored to the north by the massive former Sears warehouse, since reinhabited with the mixed-use Ponce City Market. The park's sports field and skatepark are beyond this view, further south along the BeltLine. Source: Authors.

Figure II.18-2 In 1953 the Sears building was serviced both on its third floor by the railroad up on the ridge, by its truck dock below and retail store facing Ponce de Leon Avenue and the baseball field. Its parking lots extended even further south on the low-lying land than shown. Source: Kenan Research Center at the Atlanta History Center.

This strategy was proposed in 2003 for the City Hall East parking lots. Instead, local engineer Bill Eisenhauer and architect Markham Smith began rallying support for a stormwater park that would be an amenity to the neighborhood and could trigger redevelopment of the underused area.[1] They pointed out that the Old Fourth Ward neighborhood had the highest number of public housing residents and the least amount of park space, and that their open-air solution would cost half as much as the underground tunnel.

Designed by HDR like a heavily landscaped bathtub on top of a natural spring, the 2-acre detention pond holds up to 4 million gallons of stormwater from a 300-acre subdrainage basin.[2] To avoid overflows,

---

[1] For more details on the process and discussion of other stormwater parks, see *City Parks, Clean Water: Making Great Places Using Green Infrastructure*, a report by the Trust for Public Land, March 2016.

[2] Additional organizations involved in the planning and design include, for the park, the Trust for Public Land, Wood & Partners, Inc.; for the Fourth Ward masterplan, TSW; for Ponce City Market, S9; for the BeltLine, Perkins & Will.

Figure II.18-3 The land was excavated and sloped down to create an attractive stormwater pond and park that has attracted much new development around it, including new housing, 12-story office buildings, and, in the distance, the renovated brick Ponce City Market. The remaining parking lot is approved for a grand staircase connecting the park and the BeltLine and more tall buildings. Source: Photo by Phillip Jones, 2018.

Figure II.18-4 The Eastside Trail Gateway in the foreground opened in 2014 making a direct connection between the low-lying stormwater park on the left and the 6,000+ visitors a day on average on the BeltLine, the multiuse trail on the ridge to the right. Both infrastructural amenities have attracted new development. Credit: Photo by Phillip Jones, 2018.

this water is gradually released after a storm.[3] However, unlike other detention ponds, this one was designed in response to community input to invite the public

30 feet below street level to walkways lined with native plants. Visitors hear the sounds of chirping, quacking, and the splashing of flowing water. Atlanta-based artist Maria Artemis designed granite slab and boulder features at the inlets to transform box culverts into fountains, a 35-foot tall step channel and a 40-foot long waterwall. The design enhances water quality by the increased aeration and exposure to ultraviolet light; however, it is mostly appreciated for its aesthetic and biophilic qualities. The amphitheater is frequently rented out for weddings—high marks for a stormwater facility!

Community input also informed the design of other components of the Historic Fourth Ward Park: a lawn/festival space east of the pond and a playground to the south with a series of very popular splash pads for kids. Soon after, designers leapfrogged the park southeast to regreen a 5-acre abandoned trucking company site beside the BeltLine into sports fields and Atlanta's first skatepark. Local skateboarders who were already using the former truck dock for their sport consulted on the park, helping it win it a coveted construction grant from the Tony Hawk Foundation (a retired professional skateboarder, Hawk is one of the pioneers of modern vertical skateboarding).

At the same time that Eisenhauer and Smith were talking up the crazy idea to turn a sewer tunnel project into a public park, planner and architect Ryan Gravel was drumming up support for the

---

[3] The pond has succeeded in reducing area flooding and is estimated to be reducing peak stormwater flow by 9.6% in trunk sewer flows for a ten-year storm. Rachael Shields, Jon Calabria, Brian Orland, and Alfie Vick, "Historic Fourth Ward Park, Phase 1 Methods," *The Landscape Performance Series* (Landscape Architecture Foundation 2018): https://doi.org/10.31353/cs1381.

Atlanta BeltLine.[4] As he's fond of saying, no one needed the 14-foot wide abandoned rail line turned into a multiuse trail and transit line. But 45 abutting neighborhoods had fallen in love with the idea of a trail loop connecting them to each other and to public parks. When the Trust for Public Land, a national nonprofit, began acquiring crucial parcels for the Historic Fourth Ward Park in the mid-2000s, the ability of the BeltLine concept to spark investment was validated.[5] In 2006 the city established Atlanta Beltline Inc. (ABI), which made plans for the addition of 1,300 acres of new greenspace, including the Historic Fourth Ward Park, which opened in 2011. The BeltLine's Eastside Trail followed in 2012, and the former Sears warehouse reopened as Ponce City Market in 2014.

Figure II.18-5 The first of many examples of bike-oriented development along the BeltLine, the entry to Ponce City Market from the BeltLine at 9 am leads to the free bike valet for visitors and extensive secure bike parking for residents and employees. Source: Photo by Phillip Jones, 2018.

The former Sears building had been vacant since 2010 and the mayor tried to sell it to Jamestown Properties, the Atlanta-based developer behind Chelsea Market in New York City. That food hall–anchored adaptive re-use project helped popularize the neighborhood where the High Line linear park was built. Jamestown saw the potential to similarly reinhabit Atlanta's large historic warehouse with a food hall–anchored, mixed-use project. But they refused to complete the purchase until the flooding problem was solved. When the stormwater park opened they signed the contract and began converting the property into Ponce City Market, an award-winning example of bike-oriented development that has attracted record rents for creative office space, crowds to its restaurants, and a long waitlist for its 259 apartments, 20% of which are designated affordable.[6]

The $23 million public infrastructure sewer project has provided abundant returns: a $250 million investment in Ponce City Market, plus $2 billion worth of additional private investment in the six blocks adjacent to the park.[7]

In many respects, the park has returned to its roots as a place to visit healthful waters and engage in amusement park–like entertainment. Enormously popular, the park and the BeltLine are improving both the physical and mental health of the growing number of visitors each year.[8] However, there is increasing concern that the benefits of the park are reaching fewer and fewer of the lower-income, disadvantaged population they were most intended to serve. In the mid-2010s, home values rose more than twice as much in areas within a half-mile of the Eastside Trail than elsewhere in the city, leading to property tax increases and displacement of residents in the Old

---

[4] We discussed the BeltLine in Dunham-Jones and Williamson, *Retrofitting Suburbia*, 93–94.

[5] The city council approved Tax Allocation District funding for the BeltLine Redevelopment Plan in late 2005. Georgia's Tax Allocation Districts (TAD) operate similar to what many states call Tax Increment Financing (TIF). Upon its designation as a TAD, the BeltLine was expected to result in an approximately $20 billion increase in the tax base over 25 years. By 2012 the TAD was collecting double the revenue anticipated. Between 2005 and 2018, over 50 projects representing more than $1 billion in private investment have occurred within the TAD, most of them clustered near the Eastside Trail and Historic Fourth Ward Park.

[6] It has plenty of parking as well, including Atlanta's first paid parking for retail and restaurant visitors.

[7] From 2009 to 2016, median property tax revenue in the park's census tract (17) increased 56% and occupied housing units increased 60%, compared to a 27% decrease in tax revenue and 8% increase in housing units for Fulton County as a whole. Shields et al., "Historic Fourth Ward Park."

[8] In 2018, 1.9 million people accessed the BeltLine's trails. An intercept survey of 71 users at the park in 2018 found that 44% live in a zip code within a 15-minute walk and 88% of that group visit the park more than twice per week. Shields et al., "Historic Fourth Ward Park."

Figure 11.18-6 In addition to numerous daytime festivals and sporting activities, the Lantern Parade on the Eastside Trail has become a new tradition, bringing neighbors with handmade lanterns out at night to enjoy the trail and park. The always well-lit skatepark is in the background. Source: Photo by John Becker, 2017, Atlanta Beltline Partnership.

Fourth Ward.[9] Now, in addition to being recognized as an exemplary stormwater park, Historic Fourth Ward Park is also seen by some as an example of "eco-gentrification."

Is the lesson learned that we shouldn't invest in great design that integrates stormwater solutions into beautiful parks? Hardly. But we recommend that municipalities planning similar green infrastructure upgrades should anticipate the potential for displacement and get ahead of it.[10] They would do well to look at recent efforts to increase and preserve affordable housing along other sections of the BeltLine.[11] These include the Anti-Displacement Tax Fund Program set up by a nonprofit specifically focused on the Westside, the city's and ABI's contributions to the Atlanta BeltLine Affordable Housing Trust Fund, collaboration with the Atlanta Land Trust, and ABI's programs to provide information on resources to existing renters and homeowners.

---

[9] Between 2011 and 2015, while City of Atlanta homes more than half a mile from the BeltLine rose 17.7% in value, those on the Eastside Trail rose 40%. These figures are for the NE segment of the BeltLine, which is dominated by the Eastside Trail. Further analysis claims that homes in the NE segment appreciated 17.9% more than homes more than ½ mile from the BeltLine. See Dan Immergluck, Tharunya Balan, "Sustainable for whom? Green urban development, environmental gentrification and the Atlanta Beltline," *Journal of Urban Geography*, vol 39, 2018, issue 4.

[10] There were early warnings of the potential for displacement along the BeltLine but in 2017 ABI was severely criticized for failing to meet the TAD's requirement for 20% affordable housing units. See Catherine Ross, "Atlanta BeltLine, Health Impact Assessment," Center for Quality Growth and Regional Development, Georgia Institute of Technology, June 2007. See also Willoughby Mariano, Lindsey Conway, and Anastaciah Ondieki, "How the Atlanta Beltline Broke its Promise on Affordable Housing," *Atlanta Journal-Constitution*, 13 July 2017.

[11] Atlanta Beltline Inc., "ABI Affordable Housing Working Group Final Report," August 2018: http://beltlineorg-wpengine. netdna-ssl.com/wp-content/uploads/2018/08/Affordable-Housing-Working-Group-Report-v14-Single-Pages-ABI.pdf.

Technology Park
Peachtree Corners, Georgia

Challenges addressed:

- Improve public health
- Disrupt auto dependence
- Compete for jobs

Can lower-density suburbs effectively reduce and disrupt auto dependence with multiuse walking and biking trails and autonomous vehicles (AVs)? Can an aging 500-acre office park leverage such amenities to attract the next-generation hipster and "creative class" workers its tenants want to hire? Peachtree Corners is giving it a try with housing designed for Millennials and Gen Zers, an expanded trail system so they can bike to work, and a high-tech test AV track to connect to a new town center development.

Figure II.19-1 The manicured and heavily wooded landscape of Technology Park, the heart of the "Central Business District" of Peachtree Corners, obscures the fact that 55% of the land in the district is impermeable to rainwater due to building footprints, roads, and 400 acres of paved parking lots. Source: Photo by Ellen Dunham-Jones, 2018.

Peachtree Corners is an affluent community of 40,000 residents in Gwinnett County, Georgia, 20 miles north of Downtown Atlanta. Master-planned in the 1960s and built over the ensuing three decades, the 500-acre Technology Park forms its core. But vacancy rates began to increase in the 2000s as newer technology-oriented clusters formed around the region, making it harder to recruit the next generation of employees. Following incorporation as a city in 2012, officials in the new municipality eagerly started planning upgrades. A 2015 Livable Centers Initiative study (LCI), under the aegis of the Atlanta Regional Commission (ARC) for the purpose of reducing automobile dependence, identified projects in Peachtree Corners eligible for ARC implementation grants. After extensive community input, recommendations included developing a new walkable town center with public gathering spaces, enhanced pedestrian infrastructure to improve public health, and revitalization of the aging Technology Park as an Innovation Hub within the 1,450-acre "Central Business District."[1]

These are all important steps and are underway. They are, however, unable to change the area's fundamental urban morphology of very large, irregular-sized blocks and curving, looping streets on hilly terrain into walkable urbanism. Instead, Peachtree Corners aims for bikeable urban form by overlaying the existing urban morphology with a network of multiuse trails. The plan was led by urban designer Marco Ancheita of Lord Aeck Sargent, lead consultant on the LCI study, and planner Diana Wheeler, the city's community development director. Ancheita is a

---

[1] As a newly incorporated city, Peachtree Corners set property taxes at zero. Public revenue is entirely based on business taxes, so the city is extremely interested in Technology Park's success. While the office park had relied on upscale housing subdivisions and the reputation of its public schools to attract tenants, the discussion in 2015 focused more on lifestyles, livability, shops, and housing, according to Marco Ancheita, presentation at Georgia Institute of Technology, 19 April 2016.

Millennial and avid cyclist, while Wheeler has extensive experience implementing a greenway in nearby Alpharetta, Georgia.

The multiuse trail system they designed connects the largely hidden green spaces and lakes inside the office park both to an existing regional bike trail and to core commer-

cial areas primed for redevelopment outside of Technology Park. What a welcome change from the more typical admonitions *against* walking or biking though the private landscaped open spaces of office parks!

In residential areas, the trails are widened sidewalks within the existing public street right-of-way.[2] In commercial

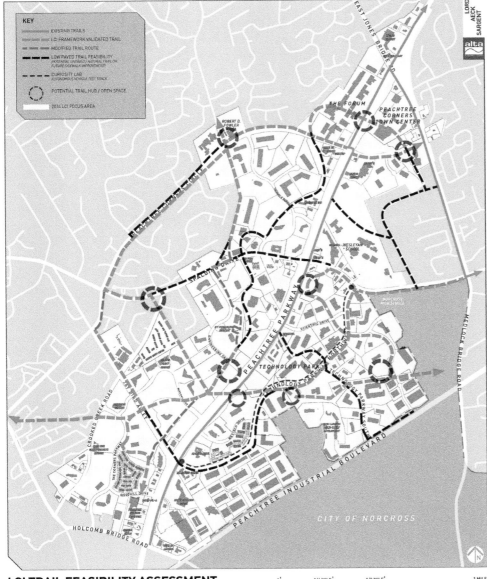

LCI TRAIL FEASIBILITY ASSESSMENT
Technology Park Trails Master Plan
Prepared for The City of Peachtree Corners by Lord Aeck Sargent | Map Revised 10.24.19

Figure II.19-2 The Technology Park Trails Master Plan connects existing trails (solid line) to new trails (thick dashed lines) in Technology Park and Peachtree Corner's larger "Central Business District." Many of the trail hubs (circled) target sites for revitalization and infill development, including a town center to the north. The thinner dashed black line shows the first phase of the Curiosity Lab Autonomous Vehicle test track. Source: Courtesy of Lord Aeck Sargent, A Katerra Company.

[2] It's worth noting that the Georgia Department of Transportation allows trails to be added to interstate rights-of-way that might otherwise be unusable. This is the case with PATH400, a 5.2-mile trail alongside GA-400 connecting the Atlanta BeltLine through the Buckhead neighborhood to Sandy Springs, GA.

Figure II.19-3 Cortland Peachtree Corners (built as Echo Lakeside) contains 295 apartments in six buildings, replacing two 38-year-old office buildings. What it lacks in urban form it makes up for with active recreational spaces: the new bike trail, a cabana-lined pool, a dock on the lake, and a dog park. Source: Photo by Phillip Jones, 2018.

areas, the trails are aligned with existing easements for sewer and gas infrastructure, around stormwater retention lakes, and in flood plains along creeks.[3] Wheeler recognizes that locating much of the trail on land unsuitable for new buildings makes it easier for her to encourage property owners to donate land to the trail or create a conservation easement, and to redevelop buildable land at higher density.[4] The trails ordinance she wrote allows owners to stop paying taxes on land they can't build on while receiving an amenity for office workers that enhances the property's appeal to new tenants. Plus, they receive a "density credit" allowing construction of thirteen new residential units per acre of land contributed to the trail, approximately three times what underlying zoning allows. The credits can be sold to other property owners in the district.[5]

A well-designed and connected trail network can both enhance public health and reduce car dependence by encouraging residents and office park workers to bike rather than drive. But can it spur investment and redevelopment? It can in Metro Atlanta. The popularity of the BeltLine in the City of Atlanta has proven the market for both urban multiunit housing and attractive "creative loft" office use along its trails and parks. Suburban municipalities and business improvement districts throughout Metro Atlanta are now seeking to replicate that success.[6] In 2018, Gwinnett County approved a master plan for a 320-mile, $1 billion trail network. While assessment of the results of that investment is a long way off, Peachtree Corners is already seeing traction.

The first leg of 11.4-miles of multiuse trails was built on land donated in conjunction with construction in 2018 of the Cortland Peachtree Corners apartments (built as Echo Lakeside), the first residences inserted into Technology Park.[7] Retrofits of office buildings to attract creative and new technology businesses have also begun. After completing nine such projects on the Atlanta BeltLine, Parkside Partners purchased four outdated low-rise office buildings located on Peachtree Corners' new trail. Remodeled into "loft suites" with exposed brick walls and high ceilings, the offices surround a new one-acre park. Parkside Partners is one of a growing number of Atlanta developers adapting their intown playbooks to locations on the suburbs' new office park trails.[8]

To complement enhancements to walking and biking infrastructure and zoning allowances for mixed land use, the suburb allocated $2 million to retrofit Technology Parkway with Curiosity Lab, a 1.5-mile test track for autonomous and connected vehicle technology. It is hoped that the track will eventually form a complete loop

3 The 2015 Livable Centers Initiative plan was conducted by Lord Aeck Sargent with Bleakley Advisory Group and Stantec Consulting, https://www.lordaecksargent.com/assets/documents/ PeachtreeCorners_LCI_Plan.pdf. Lord Aeck Sargent and Alta Planning did the follow-up 2016 trails study: https://www. peachtreecornersga.gov/government/community-development/ city-projects.
4 Wheeler successfully used a very similar strategy to get land donated to 6 miles of the Big Creek Greenway in Alpharetta, GA. In that case, developers received relief from impact fees. Phone call between Ellen Dunham-Jones and Diana Wheeler, 14 October 2019.
5 See Ordinance 2015-11-59, City of Peachtree Corners.

6 Discussing the priority list made by the members of the Perimeter Community Improvement District, Executive Director Ann Hanlon said, "The most compelling thing about the list is that trails rose to the top as a priority. There used to be such an emphasis on roads and bridges, intersections, and signal times, but now the pendulum has definitely swung in the other direction." Cited by Greg McKillips, "Expanding Trail System Provides Transportation, Recreation," *Atlanta Business Chronicle*, 9 November 2019.
7 Echo Lakeside was designed by Niles Bolton Associates with landscape architecture by HGOR.
8 See also the trajectory of Novare Group from in-town projects to suburban retrofits, from Sky House residential high-rises in numerous downtowns to SouthLawn in 2018, a mixed-use redevelopment on a bike trail and new town green in the heart of Lawrenceville, the seat of Gwinnett County.

throughout Technology Park. The lab's focus is twofold: transportation innovations at street-level, and tests with drones flying up to 400 feet high. According to Mayor Mike Mason:

> The emphasis will not be on the shuttle or ridership but the track itself, which will be used for designing and testing new AV technology. While some communities have chosen to invest in the autonomous vehicles, Peachtree Corners recognizes that the vehicles themselves will become obsolete as new versions emerge. Instead, Peachtree Corners is investing in the development of the test track, the environment in which innovation can occur over and over again, regardless of the end product.[9]

Outfitted with 5G wireless technology and smart traffic signals, Curiosity Lab has already succeeded in attracting a wide range of technology company partners.[10]

Early on, Curiosity Lab attracted a partnership with The Ray, a project testing concepts to make "net zero highways": zero deaths, zero waste, zero carbon, and zero impact.[11] The Ray is using an 18-mile stretch of Interstate 85 in rural Troup County as a test ground for various "first-in-the-US"-type pilot projects, including a solar highway, a drive-through tire safety station, and new planting approaches to carbon sequestration and stormwater infiltration. It expects to provide one of the first high-speed road corridors to test AVs and connected vehicle technology. Leaders of The Ray and Peachtree Corners see their high- and low-speed settings as complementary, mutually beneficial to realizing the efficiency potentials of new mobility technologies.

The rapid implementation of Peachtree Corners' ambitious goals is impressive. In addition to the new

Figure II.19-4 In 2019, Peachtree Corners opened Curiosity Lab, which it claims is the first 5G-equipped "vehicle-to-everything" smart test track in the US. It kicked off with a three-month pilot of an Olli autonomous shuttle bus. Narrowing driving lanes to 10 feet made room for the dedicated AV track and exemplifies how collector streets in office parks, which tend to be wide, are prime candidates for installing dedicated lanes for multimodal mobility. Source: Courtesy of City of Peachtree Corners.

housing and AV track in the office park, the 21-acre town center development opened with a concert and drone show on a new town green just six years after land purchase.[12] But connecting these investments to each other and to adjacent, more automobile-dependent areas in the suburb will be key to enabling more active, less car-dependent lifestyles. Wheeler is optimistic that the trail system will be completed within ten years. Her advice to planners in other communities is to expand beyond thinking about trails as simply recreational amenities. Think of them as transportation and align them strategically with your demographics and land-use goals.

[9] Mike Mason, "Viewpoint: Why Peachtree Corners is investing in autonomous vehicle technology," *Atlanta Business Chronicle*, 7 September 2018: https://www.bizjournals.com/atlanta/news/2018/09/07/viewpointwhy-peachtree-corners-is-investing-in.html.

[10] The first phase is anchored by Prototype Prime, a new city-funded incubator. The 5G is provided by Sprint.

[11] The Ray is named for Ray Anderson, founder of the carpet company Interface and a noted advocate for sustainable manufacturing. Georgia Tech architecture students, working with Perkins and Will and the Georgia Conservancy, helped kick off the Ray with their designs for it as a Mission Zero Corridor: https://www.georgiaconservancy.org/blueprints/missionzero.

[12] The town center's plan was designed by Pieper O'Brien Herr Architects and town green was designed by TSW Planners, Architects, Landscape Architects.

Case Study II.20

Walker's Bend
Covington, Georgia

Challenges addressed:

- Leverage social capital for equity

Responding to the heavy hit to the suburban housing market associated with the 2008 Great Recession and its aftermath, the developers of a number of stalled retrofitting projects pivoted to address the needs of suburban and exurban lower-income families and older adults. In some cases, the public sector stepped up to take a leading role, expanding the retrofitting suburbia toolkit to encompass the negotiation of complex and innovative public-private partnerships.

The case of Walker's Bend illustrates how the public sector can leverage its patient capital and assume the role of master developer to acquire and replat land within a failed "zombie" subdivision. It shows the value of public-sector led strategic partnerships that qualify for various forms of public financing. It also shows how an exurban town can use the role of master developer to improve the quality not just of affordable housing, but also of affordable living in a mixed-use, mixed-income community.[1]

Located 35 miles east of Atlanta, Covington is the county seat of Newton County, Georgia, graced with an intact courthouse square in its walkable, historic downtown. Covington served as the small Southern town setting for films and television shows, including *In the Heat of the Night* and *The Dukes of Hazzard*. Like many other places in the exurban periphery of US cities, Covington saw expanded development and rapid, diversifying population growth throughout the 1990s and early 2000s, which then came to a screeching halt in 2008.[2] Unlike most other municipalities, the city government in Covington intervened as master developer to retrofit foreclosed property after the private developer of a partially built subdivision just a mile from the historic downtown declared bankruptcy. As a result, Walker's Bend today features a more diverse mix of uses, shared green spaces, housing types, and housing tenure options.

This outcome has a back story. Concerned about how to preserve small-town fabric and predominantly rural landscapes in the face of sprawl, the Georgia Conservancy selected Covington in 1997 as the inaugural site of its Blueprints for Successful Communities program. The resulting workshop led by Georgia Tech faculty and students brought environmentalists and members of the business and development community together around then-emergent ideas of new urbanism and smart growth to examine five greenfield sites. For the 280-acre site that includes the area that became Walker's Bend, the workshop team proposed walkable traditional neighborhood development.[3] Soon after, in 2000, a team led by Duany Plater-Zyberk & Company (now DPZ CoDesign) arrived to

---

[1] This case study is informed by Ellen Dunham-Jones and Wesley Brown, "The Public Sector Steps Up—And Retrofits a Zombie Subdivision," in Emily Talen, ed., *Retrofitting Sprawl* (Athens, Georgia: University of Georgia Press, 2015), 139–156. See also Alana Semuels, "What to Do with a Dying Neighborhood," *The Atlantic*, 14 January 2015; Kaid Benfield, "From Town to City: Can Grassroots Planning Facilitate the Transition?" *Smart Cities Dive* blog, 2011: https://www.smartcitiesdive.com/ex/sustaina blecitiescollective/can-grassroots-planning-save-whats-best-rapidly-suburbanizing-community/32333/.

[2] Between the 2000 and 2010 US Census, Covington's population became "majority-minority," with 58% identifying as not-white, and 25% living below the poverty line.

[3] The Blueprints reports are available at: https://www.georgia conservancy.org/blueprints/communities/?rq=blueprints. See also Ken Edelstein, "Covington: The First Blueprints Workshop": https://www.georgiaconservancy.org/blueprints/covington.

Figure II.20-1 1987 figure-field diagram of the southeast quadrant of Covington, Georgia, with the town square in the upper right. The once-sleepy, quintessential Southern town was beginning to sprawl. Concerned planners organized efforts in the 1990s to plan developments on greenfield sites informed by emergent new urbanist and smart growth principles. Source: Authors.

conduct a ten-day charrette and produce a more detailed master plan to guide compact future neighborhood development near to the downtown, and thus avoid both residential and commercial sprawl.[4]

   To shepherd the vision to reality, the city made zoning changes that encourage, but do not require, a mix of uses and smaller lots.[5] As is often the case in such situations, the results are a mixed bag. One of the sites, just a half mile from downtown, was developed as a very attractive demonstration project called Clark's Grove. The first houses became available in 2003 and build-out is nearly complete.[6] That same year, a different group created a plan for 249 owner-occupied dwellings on the central 50 acres of another of the studied sites and called it Walker's Bend.

---

[4] The Covington charrette team, led by DPZ Principal Galina Tachieva, was sponsored by the Arnold Fund and the City of Covington and included Gibbs Planning Group, Hall Planning and Engineering, and Home Town Neighborhoods.

[5] This was paralleled by the addition of institutional capacity for directing growth in Newton County. In 2002, the Center for Community Preservation and Planning was founded as a neutral place for discussions between citizens and elected officials. It was followed in 2005 by the establishment of a leadership collaborative to help the city and county work together. In 2007, the two organizations produced an ambitious county-level comprehensive plan.

[6] Construction on Phase 2 was suspended in late 2008 with 90% of the infrastructure in place. New construction resumed in 2017 on new houses and the Swann Building, an 11-unit, three-story brick-clad condominium building.

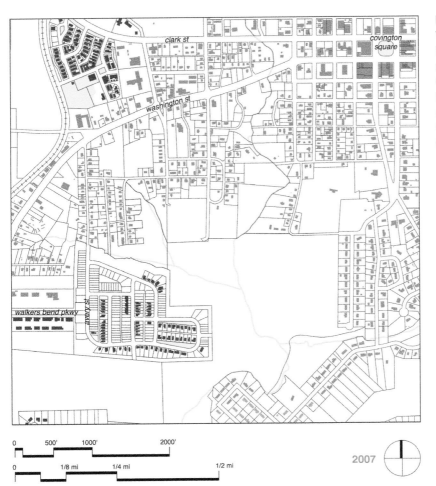

Figure II.20-2 2007 figure-field diagram. Walker's Bend, at lower left, with narrow lots and no dead-end streets, is less than a mile, within walking distance, of Covington's downtown. Only one-third built when the Great Recession hit, it devolved into a "zombie" subdivision. Clark's Grove, west of downtown (upper left), fared better. Source: Authors.

Although the subdivision plat for Walker's Bend included narrow lot frontages (55 feet or less) and proposed a mix of dwelling types (detached and attached houses as well as fee-simple townhouses), the street plan is a more regularized grid, less artful and with fewer connections, terminal vistas, and enclosed communal spaces than the DPZ plan. The land fronting the adjacent state road, designated a "village center" during the charrette, was instead inauspiciously sold for light industrial buildings, in conformance with preexisting zoning. In 2008, with 79 houses and townhouses constructed, about a third of the total, and only 50 sold, the development team filed for bankruptcy. Walker's Bend became a "zombie" subdivision, with many of the new owners "underwater" on their mortgages, meaning the market resale value had fallen below the mortgaged amount. Unsold houses and lots were destined for the auction block.

Fearful that the subdivision failure would have a widespread impact on property values throughout the town, the Covington City Council decided to intervene. Relying upon Georgia's Urban Redevelopment Act, enabling legislation dating back to 1955 for urban renewal, in 2009 the city established the Covington Redevelopment Authority (CRA) and passed an Urban Redevelopment Plan. The city expanded its ability to qualify for state and federal financing by designating certain areas as blighted. To gain control of enough of Walker's Bend to redirect its future, the city council loaned the CRA about $570,000 and allocated the entire $428,070 grant received from the federal Neighborhood Stabilization Program (NSP), for a total budget of $1 million for purchasing vacant houses and undeveloped lots. The strategy: to refine the original design and finish the development as a mixed-use, mixed-income community of housing built to high

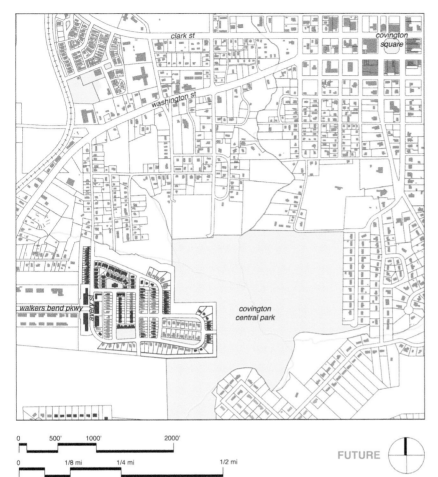

Figure II.20-3 Projected future figure-field diagram. By 2020 Walker's Bend was largely completed as a mixed-use, mixed-income, walkable neighborhood with more shared green spaces and a greater range of residential types and housing tenure models than originally anticipated. A new park broke ground and trails will expand connectivity to nature, healthy activities, and other neighborhoods through fields and creekside trails. Source: Authors.

FUTURE

environmental performance standards.[7] The tactics: to purchase key clusters of lots in order to replat and reposition the property.

This task fell to Randy Vinson, a landscape architect and Covington's director of planning and zoning. Having previously served as town planner and project manager for Clark's Grove, and as one of the professional leaders on the 1997 Blueprints team, Vinson had experience as a new urbanist developer and familiarity with the site to bring to the city's new role as master developer. Vinson soon found himself trawling online auction foreclosure websites to find and purchase lots that had been dispersed to various owners. Many of the auctions are managed through the US Federal Deposit Insurance Corporation (FDIC), a process with a steep and cumbersome learning curve. A sign posted in October 2009 announcing an FDIC auction for a key parcel at the entrance to the neighborhood created a sense of urgency. At the time no funding had been approved, let alone a checking account. In order to prevent the initiative from failing before it had even begun, Vinson used personal funds to secure the parcel, which he then sold back to the city at cost.[8]

---

[7] Randy Vinson, interview in his office with Ellen Dunham-Jones and Wesley Brown, Covington, 17 July 2012. Vinson explained that because the city's revenues are largely based on utilities usage, not property tax, Covington was somewhat cushioned from recessionary cutbacks. This helped to explain why the city council was able to loan funds to the CRA at a time when many other cities would not.

[8] Ibid.

Figure II.20-4 The charrette plan from 2000 for a neighborhood to be called Parker Pasture by Galina Tachieva of DPZ CoDesign, author of *Sprawl Repair Manual*. The upper portion of this plan became Walker's Bend, with a substantially different, and less compelling, street and lot configuration. Source: Courtesy of DPZ CoDesign.

While the city's decision to assume the role of "master developer" generated local controversy, the elected officials persisted. Initially drawn to the city because of Covington's legacy of planning, Vinson, who retired back to private practice in 2017, has said, "The citizens expect [the city] to continue to achieve this plan."[9]

The city did forge on. By 2011, it had assembled 92 lots from six different banks and the FDIC. The CRA assembled partnerships with key allies. By 2010 Habitat for Humanity had placed families in the eight never-occupied townhouses. The local housing authority and health services board each operate a multiunit building of supportive housing. One building houses residents transitioning from homelessness and the other developmentally disabled adults, together comprising 50 units. Affordable Equity Partners used federal Low-Income

Housing Tax Credits (LIHTC) to replat a block of 28 empty lots into a subsidized rental community called the Village at Walker's Bend, consisting of 32 small houses plus a common green and clubhouse. But the path has been bumpy. As of this writing, plans have fallen through for a new seniors housing project on lots flanking the entry road. The project would have included 60 units, 90% of them designated affordable, available to residents over 62 years of age. In 2019 the CRA transferred the remaining lots to the Covington Housing Authority to seek grants to complete the build-out.[10] A bright spot is the 2019 groundbreaking of a large new park immediately to the east, promising extensive trail access to healthy recreation and several other neighborhoods.

In the role of master developer, coordinating these and other partnerships and initiatives, the CRA was helped enormously by having a strong vision based on the planning work previously completed for the site. A targeted replatting effort restored many of the traditional neighborhood features of the DPZ scheme, including provisions for common spaces and multi-unit housing, albeit now for a much leaner economy and through use of substantial subsidies. The revised master plan allowed the CRA to direct partners to focus their efforts on differing housing needs on targeted clusters of lots. At the same time, it linked each piece of the redevelopment together around a sequence of distinct shared places: community meeting rooms, a green, a playground, and a park.

The master plan is complemented by the controls of the overlay zoning ordinance. After it was adopted in 2010, the CRA no longer continued to acquire the remaining lots. Vinson said that at that point they were happy to get out of the way and let the market take over.[11] In return for its initial loan to the CRA, Covington received over $30 million in capital investment in green, affordable housing built to high performance standards for green building, most of it from private sources. In addition, the sale of the city-owned lots is going to support redevelopment initiatives in other neighborhoods in Covington.[12]

[9] Ibid.

[10] Larry Stanford, "City Transfers Walker's Bend to Housing Authority," *Rockdale Citizen*, 19 March 2019.

[11] Vinson, interview.

[12] Amount stated by the chair of the CRA at the time, Nita Thompson, in Crystal Tatum, "Redevelopment investment totals $30M," *Rockdale Citizen*, 13 May 2012. EarthCraft, a green home building standard developed for the southeast region of the US, was used.

Figure II.20-5 When the developer of Walker's Bend declared bankruptcy in 2008, several built townhouses were unsold, the yards gone to seed. The Covington Redevelopment Authority used Neighborhood Stabilization Program funds and a partnership with Habitat for Humanity to quickly clean up and place owners in the homes. Source: Photo by Randy Vinson, 2009.

The CRA's timely intervention rescued Walker's Bend from an indeterminate fallow future, retrofitted it back into a mixed-use and (somewhat) mixed-income traditional neighborhood development (TND), and improved the quality of affordable housing options in the city for a range of ages and levels of need, while helping to realize the city's long-term plans to accommodate growth in ways that boost the downtown area instead of furthering sprawl. Vinson believes his city gained a fuller appreciation of both the value and the pace of community building, as well as a renewed understanding that a good community requires more than an accumulation of detached houses.

Not every exurban zombie subdivision should be reinhabited and redeveloped. In rural places like Teton County, Idaho, where subdivisions were excessively approved during boom years, many are now being regreened and having their entitlements vacated.[13] Nor should every city take on the task of master developer in order to stimulate suburban retrofits, although the approach is also being used in strong markets like West Valley City, Utah.[14] Nor is Walker's Bend likely ever to be as connected or as attractive as its nearby cousin Clark's Grove. Nevertheless, the retrofit of Walker's Bend presents valuable lessons for other communities that struggle with zombie subdivisions and increased need for affordable

Figure II.20-6 The housing at Walker's Bend is more mixed, and more affordable to lower-income residents, than originally planned. The Village at Walker's Bend comprises 32 small rental houses around a common green and clubhouse. Source: Photo by Phillip Jones, 2018.

---

[13] Jim Holway with Don Elliott and Anna Trentadue, "Combating Zombie Subdivisions: How Three Communities Redressed Excess Development Entitlements," *Land Lines*, January 2014, 4–13: https://www.lincolninst.edu/publications/articles/combating-zombie-subdivisions.

[14] Will Macht and Christopher S. Blanchard, "City as Master Developer," *Urban Land*, December 2012: http://urbanland.uli.org/Articles/2012/Dec/MachtMasterDeveloper.

Figure II.20-7 Two three-story buildings provide supportive housing for residents transitioning from homelessness and adults with developmental disabilities. Source: Photo by Phillip Jones, 2018.

and supportive housing, especially in the face of the ongoing dramatic rise in suburban and exurban poverty rates.[15]

The Walker's Bend case study reinforces the crucial importance of having both a strong vision—provided by the good new urbanist plans that Covington invested in over several years—and strong champions. Committed individuals and organizations who persevere through the political, financial, and societal challenges that retrofitting inevitably confronts, make the difference between pretty projects on paper and realized change. As the public sector continues to step up its role in retrofitting suburbia, there will be just as much need for visionary planning and rezoning as there will be for savvy implementation, including understanding the role of the city as master developer.

---

[15] Elizabeth Kneebone and Alan Berube, *Confronting Suburban Poverty in America* (Washington, DC: Brookings Press, 2013); "American Poverty Is Moving from the City to the Suburbs," *Economist*, 26 September 2019.

Challenges Addressed:

- Compete for jobs
- Disrupt automobile dependence
- Support an aging population

Like many other retrofits of suburban office parks, Downtown Doral is introducing a walkable mix of uses. Unlike others, instead of focusing on housing and nightlife targeted at young, mostly single Millennials and Gen Zers, Downtown Doral is focused on building civic amenities and attracting families. It has successfully reimagined suburbia's conventional market drivers—family-friendly housing and public school reputation—to create a diverse new downtown with a growing number of jobs out of an aging office park.

Located 10 miles northwest of downtown Miami, the area was swampland until 1958, when Doris and Alfred Kaskel drained some of it for a golf course resort that they christened "Dor-al," an amalgam of their first names.[1] Across the road, Ira Koger, one of the pioneers of suburban office park development, began construction in the 1970s of the 120-acre Koger Executive Center, now the site of Downtown Doral.[2]

The rest of Doral started filling up in the 1980s with single-family house subdivisions, many of them gated, and densely packed low-rise warehouses for the booming import-export businesses that took advantage of the area's proximity to Miami's airport and Free Trade Zone status.

When Doral incorporated as a suburban city in 2003, the median household income was more than 50% higher than in Miami-Dade County but it lacked upscale shopping and dining options, let alone a downtown. At the time, "city hall" was rented office space in the Koger office park—but not for long.

Codina Partners, a local father-daughter team with a respected track record in high-quality mixed-use development, acquired the office park and worked with the municipality to reenvision the site as a mixed-use downtown with a well-designed civic realm. They brought in urban designer Richard Flierl of Cooper Carry for early concepts, followed by Elizabeth Plater-Zyberk and Xavier Iglesias of DPZ CoDesign to "create a framework for a flexible masterplan that would create a "downtown" that felt organic and not overly planned."[3] Uses are loosely clustered into a retail and high-rise district to the west, civic and office use in the center (which includes four 1990s office buildings that provide the project with a sustaining revenue stream), and more housing both to the east and to the south, on a former golf course. (So many golf courses!) The plan stitches these areas and the existing road infrastructure into a more connected grid, with new sidewalks and on-street parking.

A decision to retain existing roads resulted in the retail-fronted blocks being 12 acres in area, considerably larger than the 1- to 4-acre small blocks generally preferred by new urbanists for improving walkability. Instead, DPZ's design at Downtown Doral incorporates superblocks in a test of their "lean urbanism" concepts for emphasizing horizontal rather than vertical mixing of uses on a block. In the aftermath of the 2008 Great Recession, reflecting on a well-known shopping center retrofit in San Jose, California,

---

[1] The resort now has five golf courses and is the 800-acre Trump National Doral Miami Resort, renovated in 2011.
[2] The Koger company was very successful building economical office parks often for low-rent government agencies. Armando Codina argues that this changed after September 11, 2001, when governments were pressured to make themselves less subject to attack by decentralizing. Quoted in Ina Paivia Cordle, "Downtown Doral, A Codina Partners development brings city flair to the suburbs," *Miami Herald*, 15 December 2013.

[3] Stated by Ana-Marie Codina Barlick, CEO of Codina Partners, in a presentation to the CNU Sprawl Retrofit Council in Miami, 19 March 2016.

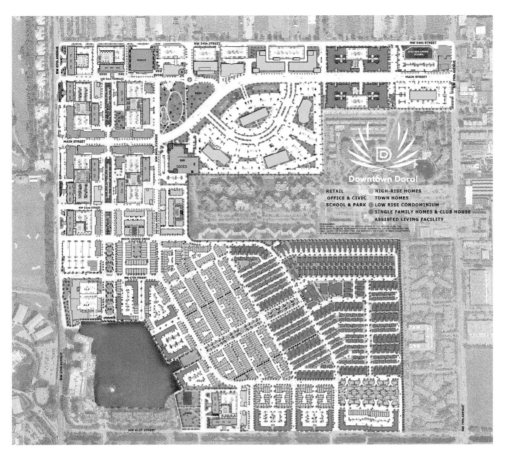

Figure II.21-1 The top half of this 2019 master plan shows the original retrofit of the office park. Main Street is an east-west spine (retail use in lavender) that passes the city park, flanked by the elementary school (in orange) and city hall, before curving past new and existing office buildings, 4-story condominiums and the upper grade school. Paseo Boulevard is a north-south linear parkway linking high-rise apartment buildings, town houses, and an assisted living facility (pink). The lower half of the plan shows the more recent expansion onto a former golf course with a lake and much more housing. Source: Courtesy of Codina Partners.

Figure II.21-2 This view looking east shows the "lean urbanism" version of Main Street mixed-use superblocks. Uses are mixed horizontally so they can be operated independently and adapted to market changes more easily. Residential high-rises face Paseo Boulevard and back onto parking garages decked on top with amenities. The garages are wrapped on two fronts with one-story retail buildings. Source: Photo by Tony Tur, courtesy of Codina Partners.

Figure II.21-3 Downtown Doral Park replaced a low-rise office building and parking lot and is fronted by city hall (top center). In addition to hosting the usual park activities, the park was a site for demonstrations in response to unrest in Venezuela, where many area residents have roots, living up to its intended civic purpose. Source: Photo by Tony Tur, courtesy of Codina Partners.

Figure II.21-4 The Downtown Doral Charter Elementary School was designed by Zyscovich Architects to have a civic presence. In its first year of operations, the English, Spanish, and Portuguese school had the highest math scores in the district and quickly developed a long waitlist for its 770 seats, half of which are reserved for Downtown Doral residents. Source: Courtesy of Zyscovich Architects.

that her firm had an early hand in planning, Plater-Zyberk said, "We worried that the Santana Row superblock had a limited future."[4]

In Doral, continuous fine-grained retail and restaurant frontage on Main Street encourages walking, although housed in cheaper-to-build one-story liner buildings.[5] Not tucking them into the ground floors of high-rise residential buildings limits risk to investors should either use fail. Similarly, the high-rises are independent structures from their parking decks. This allows greater economies during construction, future flexibility, and better placement and configuration of towers to maximize views and minimize shadows on the amenity sundecks on the roofs of the parking structures. On a tour of the project, Armando Codina proudly pointed out how the urban design solution

enabled him to construct the flat-plate concrete parking decks at relatively low cost while avoiding complaints from apartment tenants about noise and smells from restaurants below—a common occurrence for him while managing Mizner Park in Boca Raton, the first dead mall-to-downtown retrofit.[6]

While mindful of costs, Codina Partners doggedly pursued creative ways to finance the civic components. Through a series of deals involving discounted land sales in exchange for development rights and donation of land in lieu of impact fees, they were able to anchor Downtown Doral with a stand-alone city hall, public library, three-acre city park and public art pavilion, and two charter schools.[7]

The investment in high-quality, high-performing public charter schools has proven to be catalytic to the project,

4 Telephone interview of Elizabeth Plater-Zyberk by Ellen Dunham-Jones, 20 February 2019. She is referring to the compact vertical stacking of mixed-uses at Santana Row, a retrofit in San Jose, CA, discussed in Dunham-Jones and Williamson, *Retrofitting Suburbia*, 78–80.
5 Bike share, a free shuttle, and a trolley to nearby Florida International University further reduce auto dependence.

6 The cost of parking was $15,000 per space, as stated by Armando Codina during a tour of Downtown Doral to the CNU Sprawl Retrofit Council, 20 March 2016. For a description of Mizner Park see Dunham-Jones and Williamson, *Retrofitting Suburbia*, 123–125.
7 William Macht, "From Suburban Office Park to a New Downtown in Florida," *Urban Land Magazine*, 27 July 2016.

Figure II.21-5 Similar to new buildings in cities like Toronto and San Francisco, the high-rise apartments at Downtown Doral are supportive of family households with children. In addition to including three-bedroom units, this building by Sieger Suarez Architects includes a kids' activity room next to the fitness center. Source: Photo by Ellen Dunham-Jones, 2016.

although complex to implement.[8] Demand for larger residential units with more bedrooms, appealing to households with school-age children, has risen accordingly. Codina Partners outbid the Trump Organization to purchase the 130-acre golf course to the south for residential expansion, much of it intended to be suitable for large and multigenerational households.[9]

The Marin family is a good example. Jorge Daniel and Gabriela Marin first lived in a high-rise apartment, then a townhouse in Downtown Doral when their children were toddlers, and they found both to be family friendly. They were attracted by the short walk to the grocery store and community events at the park. Jorge Daniel particularly enjoyed the five-minute walk to the office he shares with his father, Jorge Lorenzo Marin.

Jorge Lorenzo and his wife, Felicia, soon traded in his 45-minute driving commute to join their son's family and both households moved into the same four-story apartment building. The grandkids love being able to run upstairs and knock on their grandparents' door. Jorge Daniel and Gabriela love being able to walk to restaurants and bars for date nights while his parents watch their kids. And Jorge Lorenzo loves heading downstairs each morning to walk his grandson to school before returning to his apartment and having breakfast with Felicia.[10]

Should more suburban redevelopment retrofits include new schools? Downtown Doral proves the value of schools to the growing cohort of Millennials with children and their extended families who also want walkable urbanism and proximity to good jobs. But getting suburban school districts to allow new schools on parcels smaller than 10 acres remains a challenge. Plater-Zyberk credits the Codina family as a whole, and CEO Ana-Marie Codina Barlick in particular for adamantly pursuing the schools as well as for translating their own multigenerational family-focused lifestyle into a project that integrates schools into the master plan. Unlike developers with a more corporate outlook, the Codinas, as Plater-Zyberk describes them, are true "town founders" who seek to leverage the value of long-term investment in a robust and carefully designed public realm.[11]

Codina Barlick, for her part, credits much of the success of the project to DPZ's flexible regulating plan and pattern book based on massing and form rather than uses and quantities.[12] That flexibility allows them to make changes to the project, such as adding units with more than two bedrooms once the school proved successful. It also allows a mash-up of ultra-modern and neo-traditional styled buildings, anchored by the park, paseo boulevard, and palm trees—a mix that is true to the diverse population and aesthetic sensibility of Miami.

---

8 Codina Partners donated the 3.5-acre site to Miami-Dade County Public Schools in lieu of school impact fees. The school system leased the site to the Downtown Doral Charter Elementary School (DDCES), a nonprofit whose president is Ana-Marie Codina Barlick, CEO of Codina Partners. As a nonprofit, DDCES was allowed flexibility in the design of the school and issued $21.85 million in bonds for construction before hiring the school district to provide education services. Codina Partners negotiated with the school district to keep the average class size to 20, add one hour to the school day, hire nonunion teachers on yearly contracts, commit to dual-language instruction in English-Spanish and English-Portuguese, and reserve 50% of the slots for residents of Downtown Doral. The upper grade school opened in 2019 with similar conditions.

9 Codina Partners went back to Richard Flierl, now with Katalyst, to masterplan the expansion and accommodate growing residential demand. Downtown Doral has been particularly popular with Venezuelans seeking a more stable situation for their extended families. The new extension includes a 105-unit assisted living facility, independent living, and an express care health facility as part of the entitled 2,709 residential units, 800k square feet of office, and 300k square feet of retail.

10 Based on email correspondence with Brian Falk, director of the Center for Applied Transect Studies and grandson-in-law to Jorge Lorenzo and Felicia Marin.

11 Telephone interview with Elizabeth Plater-Zyberk by Ellen Dunham-Jones, 20 February 2019.

12 Telephone interview with Ana-Marie Codina Barlick by Ellen Dunham-Jones, 18 March 2019.

Collinwood Recreation Center
Cleveland, Ohio

Challenges addressed:

- Improve public health
- Leverage social capital for equity
- Support an aging population

It is vital to have numerous places in all communities to support those who wish to engage in any kind of physical activity, for all ages, at a range of times, and in any type of weather. Public health research supports the recommendation that engaging in 150 minutes a week of physical activity—which doesn't have to be a workout; it can simply be walking around—can have a transformative effect on a person's health.

Many suburban areas were designed around the car and many people who do exercise choose to drive cars to designated locations (i.e. gyms) to do so. Consequently, one retrofitting tactic that supports the public health goal to increase everyday physical activity in communities dominated by suburban form is to encourage building retrofits programmed with new uses that explicitly promote fitness and exercise. A number of vacant big box stores, shopping center anchor stores, and suburban office boxes have been reinhabited with wellness centers, medical office, and recreational gyms. In shopping centers this has the double benefit of providing an activity that you cannot get online. A 2019 study found that as a result, the number of gyms in retail centers had increased 23% since 2010 and expects the segment to continue to grow, especially in mixed-use centers.[1]

One exemplary retrofit is in the Collinwood neighborhood at the northeast tip of Cleveland, Ohio. A former Big Lots store has been converted into the Collinwood Recreation Center, a LEED Gold–certified, award-winning public gym and community center, financed through general obligation city bonds and completed in 2011. Paul Volpe of City Architecture designed the project using a brightly colored, playful idiom along with several sustainability features.

In the reinhabitation-type retrofit, the original big box store building was downsized from 68,000 to 45,000 square feet and features an indoor "Main Street" corridor, connecting the different program areas. Directly adjacent are public playing fields.[2] An underground cistern collects rainwater from the roof for irrigation. The showers are heated with solar hot water heaters and a new rain garden captures and filters run-off from the site's 200-space parking lot, reducing contaminants entering Lake Erie mere yards away.

A few states away, in South Dakota, a dead 70,000 square foot Walmart store was reinhabited in 2008 into the Spearfish Rec & Aquatics Center, a public facility. The retrofit was funded with a penny municipal sales tax and is programmed with a gymnasium that includes two full basketball courts, two walking tracks, one suspended, as well as various fitness rooms, and a childcare center. Two acres of the parking lot were converted to an outdoor water park.[3]

Both Collinwood Recreation Center and Spearfish Rec & Aquatics Center are primarily programmed for the physical activity needs of children and their parents. Older Americans have differing needs for physical activity to promote wellness and assist with rehabilitation from disease and injury, as well as prevention.

---

[1] Al Urbanski, "There Are 23% More Gyms in Retail Centers Today Than There Were in 2010," *Chain Store Age,* 14 October 2019.

[2] Steven Litt, "City Architecture design for Collinwood recreation center scores green points," *Plain Dealer*, 16 October 2009; Amara Holstein, "Recycling the Big Box: Collinwood Recreation Center," *Build a Better Burb* website, n.d.: http://buildabetter burb.org/recycling-the-big-box-collinwood-recreation-center/.

[3] Spearfish Rec & Aquatics Center: http://spearfishreccenter.com/.

(a)

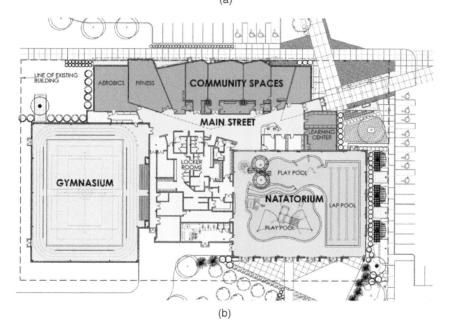

(b)

Figure II.22-1 While the basic structure of the old building was retained, new spaces were grafted onto it, including a gymnasium, natatorium, and an array of community spaces. "Before" aerial view of the former Big Lots big box store and parking lot (a), and floor plan as converted into the Collinwood Recreation Center (b). Source: Courtesy of City Architecture.

For an example, look east to Fitness & Wellness Professional Services, a project of the Robert Wood Johnson healthcare system. Robert Wood Johnson established ten centers, nine in New Jersey suburbs and one outside Philadelphia, intended specifically as wellness alternatives to commercial gyms.[4] The initiative is a response to national calls to curb healthcare spending with preventive care, and is supported by provisions in the 2010 Affordable Care Act (aka Obamacare). Patients with heart disease and other ailments, many of whom are older adults, are prescribed sessions at the wellness gyms.[5]

By reinhabiting vacant buildings, these retrofits are also boosting community economic health. For one wellness center, in Scotch Plains, New Jersey, Jarmel Kizel Architects adaptively reused a nondescript 50,000-square-foot

---

[4] Fitness & Wellness Professional Services: http://www.fitness andwellness.org.

[5] Beth Fitzgerald, "Not Just for Sick and Injured Any Longer, Hospitals Make Splash with Fitness Clubs," *NJ Spotlight*, 4 June 2012.

(a)

(b)

Figure II.22-2 The Collinwood Recreation Center features a central spine labeled "Main Street" (a) and a natural light-filled natatorium (b) with play pools and a lap pool. Source: Photos by Scott Pease, 2011, courtesy of City Architecture.

1960s-era one-story office building. A former Grand Union grocery store in north Princeton, New Jersey, was converted into another. An 82,000-square-foot defunct Ames Department Store, anchor of the Clover Square strip shopping center in nearby Mercerville, New Jersey, was converted to the RWJ Hamilton Fitness & Wellness Center, and now boasts solar panels, huge workout areas, a large pool, meeting rooms for wellness classes, and physical therapists on site. Unfortunately—and indicative of the scope of the general public health challenge—other tenants of Clover Square run the gamut of fast food chains: Five Guys, Dunkin Donuts, Burger King, Taco Bell, and Smoothie King.

The Mosaic District
Merrifield, Virginia

Challenges addressed:

- Disrupt automobile dependence
- Improve public health
- Leverage social capital for equity

How does a retail development company with an unrivaled 50-year history of building grocery-anchored suburban strip malls retrofit itself in the face of rising vacancies, online competition, and market preferences for urbanism? This was the question that Jodie McLean, CEO of Edens, strategized with her team after being appointed president in 2002. Their answer is the Mosaic District, built on the 31-acre site of a dead multiplex theater in an affluent suburb of Washington, DC, just outside the Beltway. The result is a compact "mosaic" of uses lining highly walkable streetscapes and an active town green anchored by a new arthouse cinema.[1] Instead of strip malls designed to speed up transactions, Mosaic demonstrates the value of designing green mixed-use town centers for lingering and social experiences you can't get in the surrounding burbs or online.

For McLean, the business case revolves around how to best serve her customers' changing needs. She knows precisely how much their discretionary income and time have declined and the advantages these give to e-commerce.[2] She's fighting back by creating welcoming physical places that foster engagement and attract people out of their homes, fending off social isolation and the "loneliness epidemic."[3] As McLean sums it up, "The people we are trying to serve have less money, less time, but a bigger need than ever to feel part of a community. . . . We are successful if we can drive our customers to make 3.5 trips here a week and 5 hours of dwell time."[4] To do that, she has to build places that are

(a)

(b)

Figure II.23-1   In addition to serving onsite residents, Mosaic is a popular destination for parents to get out of the house and bring their kids to the splash fountain or social activities in Strawberry Park. Strollers abound throughout the project but especially in this shared "front yard" surrounded by ground-level eateries and shops. Source: Photos by Phillip Jones, (a) 2014, (b) 2018.

---

[1] The initial build-out for the Silver LEED-ND certified project called for 500,000 square feet of retail and restaurants, 73,000 square feet of office, a 148-key hotel, and 1,000 residences. Principal design firms involved include RTKL, Nelsen Partners, House & Robertson, Mulvanny G2, Fred Dagdagan, and Law Kingdon.

[2] RE Insight podcast interview of Jodie McLean by Scott Morey, http://reinsight.com.

[3] Interview of Jodie McLean by Ellen Dunham-Jones, 29 October 2018, at the Mosaic District, Merrifield, VA.

[4] RE Insight podcast.

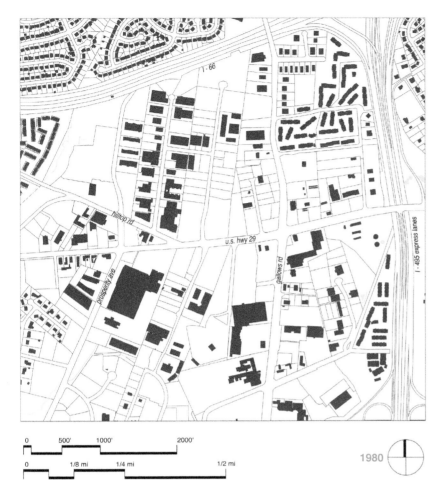

Figure II.23-2 1980 figure-field diagram. Merrifield's commercial district southwest of the intersection of I-66 and I-495, the Washington Beltway, featured large blocks and a mix of small office and industrial buildings, some garden centers, and a few apartment complexes. Much of what would become the Mosaic District centers on the wedge-shaped site that was a drive-in theater built in 1954. It sat south of US Hwy 29 and west of Gallows Road, west of the Fairfax Plaza strip mall. Source: Authors.

extremely convenient and successfully engage customers in a community that makes them feel great—two goals that are very hard to do simultaneously.[5]

Can we combat loneliness through physical spaces designed to facilitate stronger communal ties? McLean had her team read Ray Oldenburg's theories about "third places," authentic local gathering places like pubs, coffee shops, and post offices that often serve as the centers of community life.[6] They then visited all of the new mixed-use town centers to see what they could improve on with their first experiment, the Mosaic District.

In 2006 Edens purchased the failing multiplex and some adjacent properties in the center of Merrifield's 1.3-square-mile commercial district.[7] With over 100,000 square feet of office space bordered by major highways and commuter rail transit, the area had a largely degraded public realm yet was in an affluent county eager to provide incentives for redevelopment. Fairfax County had a new comprehensive revitalization plan and, eventually, a willingness to back the project with tax increment financing (TIF).[8] Mosaic was something of a test case on the use of public-private partnerships for

[5] Such "experiential retail" deemphasizes the cash register but builds brand awareness and customer satisfaction. It is increasingly recognized as the primary role for physical stores in collaboration with ecommerce. One of many possible references is Christina Binkley, "The Man Who Could Save Retail," *Wall Street Journal*, 17 September 2018.

[6] See Ray Oldenburg, *The Great Good Place* (1991) and *Celebrating the Third Place* (2000).

[7] At the time of purchase, Edens had two other partners, which it subsequently bought out.

[8] Barbara Byron, then director of Fairfax County's Office of Revitalization, credits the task force that started visioning exercises with stakeholders in 1998 with "setting the stage for everything you see today." See David R. Millard, "The Mosaic District: Urban Village Grows from Suburban Wasteland," *Development Magazine,* Fall 2013.

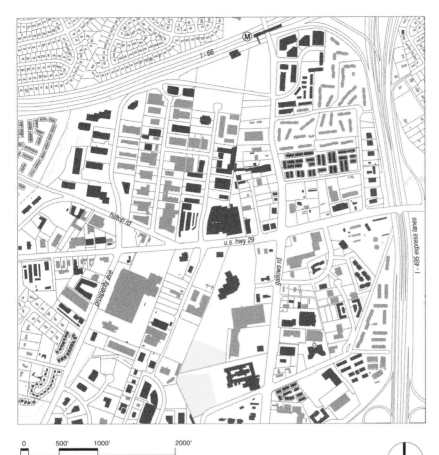

Figure II.23-3 2000 figure-field diagram. The drive-in theater went to seed after a 14-screen multiplex was built closer to US 29 and lasted 25 years (1984–2009). The Dunn-Loring Metrorail station opened in 1986 in the center median of I-66, straddling Gallows Road, with a park-and-ride lot to the station's south. A pair of mid-rise office buildings arose east of the park-and-ride, each with their own large parking decks; the rest of the area developed piecemeal, in a car- and parking-oriented pattern. Source: Authors.

the 60-times-larger retrofit of nearby Tysons Corner. And it was an opportunity to deliver something stylistically distinct from the neotraditional look of the numerous new town centers popping up around Washington, DC.

Bill Caldwell, managing director and lead urban designer on the project, said, "Why design nineteenth-century brick facades if they're going to be poorly detailed with cheap, thin panels? We have to use contemporary building techniques and materials so we wanted to spend our money on what really matters: the ground and the first 20 feet up."[9] In search of a fun and distinctive creative

identity, Edens sprinkled references to the Beatles and the Grateful Dead into the street names and deliberately hired non-DC-based design firms. They challenged them to ensure that the well-detailed storefronts and small businesses were not dominated by all the big boxes (a discount department store, speculative offices, cinemas, and parking decks).[10]

The individually designed storefronts add great visual interest and walkability to the already highly walkable street network and well-sized blocks. Edens' choice to maintain private ownership of the streets allows flexibility to close them for festivals and the weekly farmers market,

---

[9] Telephone interview of Bill Caldwell by Ellen Dunham-Jones, 31 May 2016.

[10] Telephone interview of Tom Kiler, former VP of Development at Edens, by Ellen Dunham-Jones, 18 May 2016.

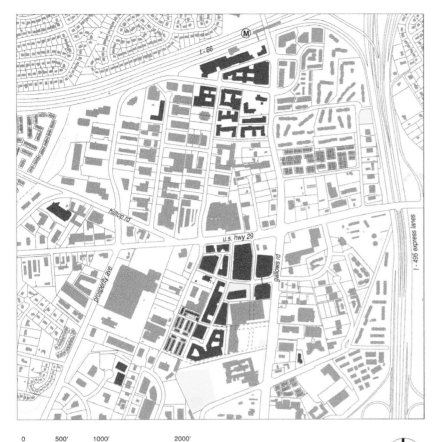

Figure II.23-4 Future figure-field diagram. The Mosaic District Phase 1, a walkable, mixed-use town center with 2 million square feet organized around Strawberry Park and the Angelika Film Center, opened in 2012 and was completed in 2018. Phase 2 will extend the street grid through the to-be demolished Fairfax Plaza strip mall (dashed lines). Since Mosaic opened, the Metrorail station's park and ride and several other properties were redeveloped with mixed-use apartments. We expect the mile-long walking corridor between Mosaic and the station to be enhanced by the county's plans for further redevelopment and enhanced connectivity. Source: Authors.

| 0 | 500' | 1000' | | 2000' |
| 0 | 1/8 mi | 1/4 mi | | 1/2 mi |

FUTURE

Figure II.23-5 At the outset, Edens had difficulty interesting residential developers. So they started by making a gathering place, Strawberry Park between the theater and the Target building. By insisting on managing those buildings' ground-floor retail and parking (thereby reducing risk for the office and residential developers), Mosaic was then able to build out the project with the small park as its heart. Credit: Photo by Phillip Jones, 2018.

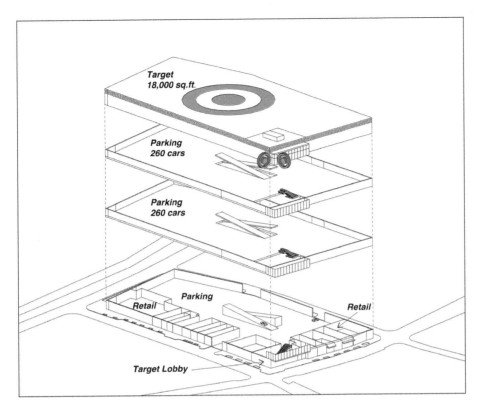

Target
18,000 sq.ft.

Parking
260 cars

Parking
260 cars

Parking

Retail

Retail

Target Lobby

Figure II.23-6 Similar to the way that grocery stores try to encourage a "destination shopper" to become an "impulse buyer" by placing the milk at the rear of the store, Mosaic's commercial buildings place large-floor plate uses (cinemas, office, and large retailers) above ground-level boutique retail and restaurants. The Target building is lined with small shops at ground level on its two walkable street frontages, has two levels of parking above, and a Target discount department store at the top, serviced by highly visible escalators at the prime corner. Source: Authors.

privileging the pedestrian more than cars.[11] The grid establishes much-needed connectivity to the area and will be extended in Phase 2 through the redevelopment of the neighboring strip mall.

However, even with this connectivity and the mile walk to the Dunn Loring Metro station, how much is Mosaic reducing automobile dependency? For now, the project's walkability is highly internalized, presenting mostly blank walls at the perimeter frontage to the bounding highways.

This will likely change if the county realizes its ambitions to convert US Highway 29/Lee Highway into a tree-lined boulevard.[12] In the meantime, Mosaic's mix of uses allows a reduction in car trips—including for the residents of the new apartments that have popped up between Mosaic and the station. Biking is popular and Mosaic provides shuttle service and recently received approval for the state's first self-driving shuttle.[13] But, at present, because Mosaic is providing the only programmed communal urban

[11] Bill Caldwell helped write the design guidelines for the redevelopment of Tysons Corner but failed to convince the county to take ownership of the streets away from the state. He said, "It's resulted in property owners creating individual fiefdoms that are inadequately stitched together by a truly walkable public realm. We wanted much more control of that at Mosaic. We put in stop signs to slow traffic that VDOT would not have allowed on public streets." Interview of Bill Caldwell by Ellen Dunham-Jones, 29 October 2018, at the Mosaic District, Merrifield, VA.

[12] Plans include continuous "Main Street" frontage along Eskridge Road, converting Gallows Road into a boulevard and connecting the area's perimeter streets into a continuous ring road. Fairfax County Comprehensive Plan, 2017 Edition The Merrifield Suburban Center, Amended through 9-24-2019, n.d.: https://www.fairfaxcounty.gov/planning-development/sites/planning-development/files/assets/compplan/area1/merrifield.pdf.

[13] Brian Trompeter, "Supervisors OK Autonomous-vehicle Pilot program in Merrifield," *Inside NOVA,* 30 June 2019.

Figure II.23-7 Unlike most suburban retail frontages that are designed as signs to be read at 50 miles per hour, storefronts and streetscaping at Mosaic provide pedestrian-oriented texture and details. Strolling and engagement are invited through varied fine-grain storefronts, sidewalk signboards, street trees, and plantings with uplighting. Varied seating is everywhere—even at Target—where it encourages people watching and chance conversations. Source: Photo by Phillip Jones, 2018.

Figure II.23-9 Tall ground floors in parking garages are designed to be infilled with more shops if parking demand diminishes over time. The open but covered parking in this case provides convenient access to the grocery store across the street and feels much safer than an enclosed, low-ceiling, parking garage. Source: Photo by Phillip Jones, 2018.

gathering space for miles around, it is largely functioning as drive-to walkability for residents of nearby communities. To accommodate them conveniently, Mosaic has ample parking in garages at its edges, located to ease visitors' access while keeping walk distances to the theater and restaurants within a 17-minute "seat-to-seat" window.

The many activities programmed in the park may not cure loneliness, but they enable people to choose to be social around other people instead of online. McLean knows she's providing this, but points out, "the biggest challenge is inspiring conversation."[14] Toward that end, she partnered with a local artists association on a pop-up art gallery and art performances, and integrated murals and art display cases into Mosaic's streetscapes. Visitor statistics show that Edens' attention to placemaking creates a destination that many people want to experience.[15]

Caldwell urges every community and every developer to start by creating a gathering place, no matter how small. It might just be twinkle lights over picnic tables between two small businesses. If designed well, it can be the spark. This is where he feels retail developers really excel. He also emphasizes that communities must work

Figure II.23-8 Design matters! The redevelopment at the Dunn Loring Metrorail Station shown here has urban apartments fronting walkable streets with ground-level retail in parking decks. Yet, despite being further from transit, Mosaic commands a 20% rent premium. Most likely this is due to its more attractive invitations to residents and visitors to linger in street side seating or attend the many programmed activities. Source: Photo by Ellen Dunham-Jones, 2018.

[14] Jodie McLean interview, 2018.
[15] When social distancing requirements in 2020 severely limited gatherings, management at the Mosaic got creative, returned to the site's roots, and started a drive-in movie series on the roof of one of the parking garages.

Figure II.23-10   The park's most innovative feature was an afterthought. "Lucy" is a 22- by 38-foot LED screen attached to the side of the movie theater. Whether used to lead yoga classes, show movies or sports, or broadcast the local Boy Scout troop's awards ceremony, "Lucy" is used in programming free daily events at different times of day to bring people out of their private worlds and into a communal space. Source: Photo by Neil Arnold.

with developers to do what they can afford. Mixed-use neighborhoods are inherently complex and the cost of place management, security, and operations are significant. Regardless, as of this writing the Mosaic District is both an environmental and a fiscal success by many measures.[16]

---

[16] Walkability and transit access contributed to Mosaic receiving silver certification in LEED for Neighborhood Development, a green ratings system. Construction of underground vaults with sand filters to restore the site's stormwater holding capacity to predevelopment standards garnered points. One is under the one-acre Strawberry Park. As the community space for both informal hanging out and actively programmed activities, it also helps meet LEED-ND's "human experience" criteria." Other sustainability features include a green roof on the theater, the purchase of energy from renewable sources for all Edens-owned streets and spaces, ample street trees, and tenant sustainability guidelines. In terms of fiscal performance, the fourth-floor Target store is one of the best performing in the region. The residential units have wait lists, and the county's workforce housing affordability requirements are being met. And as of 2019 Mosaic was ahead of schedule in paying back the $66 million TIF financing it received from the county.

Social success is harder to measure than the fiscal capital performance. Might the Beatles' Eleanor Rigby have overcome her loneliness at Mosaic? Can a development that is privately owned and managed evolve into an authentic community? Or are visitors, employees, and residents simply consuming a carefully curated experience? Jane Jacobs might appreciate the mixing of big and small uses, day and night activities, residents and workers, while Ray Oldenburg might find the programming too scripted for casual interactions. Nevertheless, we are impressed by Edens' charting of a new path—under McLean's conscious leadership—away from a history of building grocery-anchored suburban strip malls.

South Dakota Avenue and Riggs Road
Fort Totten, Washington, DC

Challenges addressed:

- Disrupt automobile dependence
- Leverage social capital for equity
- Support an aging population

Many communities have underused publicly owned land that can and should be put to better use. Overly large intersections are a good place to look, as in the example where South Dakota Avenue crosses Riggs Road in Washington, DC. The 1950 Comprehensive Plan for Washington prepared the US capital city for a primary inner ring road, an "express parkway" that would cut a broad swath through the newest neighborhoods on the outskirts of the District of Columbia. Thankfully, the winds of change shifted, and funding for the Inner Loop Expressway was redirected to building a commuter mass transit system extending into the suburbs instead, the Washington Metrorail. One of the earliest stations in Metrorail, which began operations in 1976, was Fort Totten, servicing the Lamond-Riggs neighborhood in northeast Washington near the Maryland border, on the Red Line to Silver Spring. Designed with park-and-ride lots abutting the park system, pedestrians had limited access to the station.

Despite fixed rail transit service, the primarily African American, working- and middle-class neighborhood of neat 1950s brick duplexes, row houses, and garden apartment blocks suffered over decades from a lack of private and public investment and attention. "Like a way station in Siberia. . .it is in the city, yet, incongruously, it is remote," proclaimed an article lede in the *Washington Post* on the occasion of the station opening. The reporter quoted a municipal planner: "The opportunity for redevelopment is there. . .but I am not aware of any great rush by developers."[1] Ten years later, in 1988, another reporter

characterized the neighborhood as "scrappy" and described a pervasive "feeling of having to fight for services in Riggs Park."[2] Would conditions ever change? When and if they finally did, would long-time lower-income Black residents risk displacement?

Change did finally start to come in the first decade of this century. So far, the transformations have been relatively low-key, especially when compared to booming development conditions nearby. But maybe this is just the sort of under-the-radar suburban retrofit process that succeeds in avoiding some of the social penalties of gentrification.

One significant impediment to progress was the highway-style, large radius turning lanes and lack of crosswalks at the intersection of South Dakota Avenue and Riggs Road, smack in the middle of the neighborhood. The roads, engineered to feed the never-built express parkway, were aggressively "pedestrian-hostile." The District Department of Transportation (DDOT) finally responded to pressure, from Harriet Tregoning, then director of the District Office of Planning, and others, and rebuilt the intersection between 2009 and 2013 to remove sweeping turn lanes, while adding sidewalks, crosswalks, benches, on-street parking spaces, and improved lighting. No longer can drivers make unimpeded right turns, imperiling the lives of pedestrians. A series of posts from 2009 on the *Greater Greater Washington* blog authored by blog founder David Alpert tracks community efforts to improve the walkability of the DDOT's initial proposal.[3] Alpert's advocacy helped transform the design to include four new crosswalks, rather than only three. In early 2019, the South Dakota and Riggs Road Main Street program kicked off,

[1] Paul W. Valentine, "Fort Totten," *Washington Post*, 1 February 1978.

[2] Ed Bruske, "D.C.'s Riggs Park: Scrappy, Down-Home Neighborhood," *Washington Post*, 10 December 1988.

[3] See, for example, David Alpert, "Fort Totten development plans pedestrian street," *Greater Greater Washington* blog, 26 January 2009: https://ggwash.org/view/1123/fort-totten-development-plans-pedestrian-street.

Figure II.24-1 The approach to the rebuilt, more pedestrian-friendly intersection from the southwest, on Riggs Road, shows new sidewalks, on-street parking, street trees, and crosswalks. The eastern quadrant of "liberated" public land, ready for town house development, is at right. A "desire line" walking path marks the former right turn lane. Source: Photo by Phillip Jones, 2018.

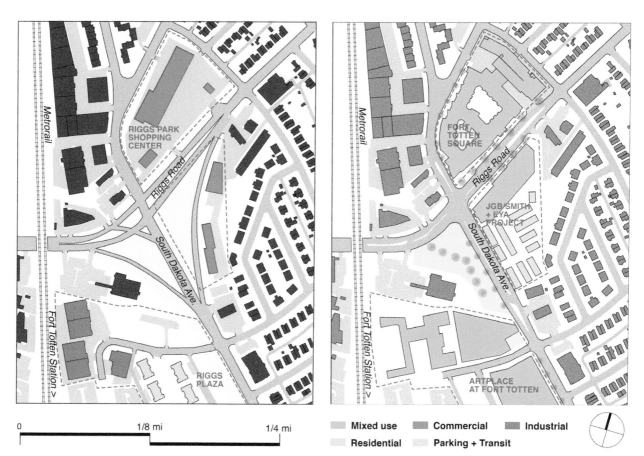

Figure II.24-2 "Before" and "future" building footprint, land use, and roadway diagrams of the intersection of South Dakota Avenue and Riggs Road in northwest Washington, DC. Source: Authors.

intended to promote both new and legacy small and local businesses.

The intersection reconstruction liberated acres of wasted city-owned land and made it useable for infill buildings not far from transit. Two major new mixed-use developments in the neighborhood followed: Fort Totten Square and the Modern at ArtPlace. More infill projects are to come, including phase two of ArtPlace, scheduled to open in 2022, finally realizing the location's long-dormant potential for transit-oriented infill development. Each of these projects includes a community benefits package negotiated with the Lamond-Riggs Citizens Association (LRCA) to include major public space improvements, as well as an array of small grants and scholarships, in fulfillment of the initial planning agreement.[4]

Lowe Enterprises and the JBG Companies partnered on Fort Totten Square, opened in 2015, on the north quadrant of the South Dakota/Riggs intersection, a redevelopment retrofit of the automobile-oriented Riggs Park Shopping Center. The strip shopping center was once central to daily life in Lamond-Riggs, with a supermarket, drug store, hardware store, jewelers, savings and loan, barber shops, and beauty parlors. But it had long since ceased to serve.

On an 8.6-acre site, the retrofit, designed by Hickok Cole Architects, includes an "urban format" Walmart of 120,000 square feet, with a full-service grocery. The Walmart level is a podium for 345 moderately priced rental apartments (20% designated affordable), organized around courtyards that feature such amenities as a pool with sundeck and an indoor/outdoor yoga studio. The architects took advantage of the grade change on the site—the land slopes up 20 feet in elevation from Riggs Road to the north—to tuck parking levels and the bulk of the big box into the hill. The project was the third of six planned DC Walmart stores in the new format. The architects were worried about Walmart's signage standards, and the challenge of threading residential plumbing down through the big box podium, but neither proved an unmanageable problem.[5]

The liberated 3.9-acre plot of public land at the east quadrant of the intersection was acquired in 2017 by developers JBG Smith and EYA; together they plan to build 80 to 100 for-sale town houses and 60–80 rental apartments for seniors, with some street-level retail. Some portion of the town houses will be sold below market rate to income-eligible buyers.

Three blocks to the south along South Dakota Avenue, closer to the Metrorail station, the nonprofit Morris and Gwendolyn Cafritz Foundation is gradually redeveloping a 16.5-acre site into a multiphased mixed-use project called ArtPlace at Fort Totten. In the 1950s, Morris Cafritz, a prolific builder in the DC area, developed the property into Riggs Plaza, a red brick garden apartment complex of 232 units in fifteen low-rise buildings. Six decades later, Cafritz's heirs, under the umbrella of their charitable foundation, are implementing ambitious redevelopment retrofitting

Figure II.24-3 Relatively low-key Walmart signage at Fort Totten Square. The mixed-use redevelopment replaced an auto-oriented strip shopping center, connecting affordable retail and affordable housing to affordable transit. Source: Photo by Belma Fishta, 2018.

plans: four phases of construction, master planned by Ehrenkrantz Eckstut and Kuhn, are to be completed by 2030, including over 900 rental apartments, 300,000 square feet of retail, and over 200,000 square feet of cultural and arts space, including the Explore! Children's Museum and the first East Coast location of famed Santa Fe, New Mexico, arts collective Meow Wolf. (Meow Wolf's first bootstrap endeavor, the wildly successful *House of Eternal Return*, was installed in a reinhabited strip mall bowling alley off Cerrillos Road.)

In the first phase, the Modern at ArtPlace with 520 apartments, designed by Shalom Baranes Architects (SBA), opened in 2017. One quarter of the apartments are designated affordable, and fifty of these were allocated to elderly residents displaced from their longtime Riggs Plaza homes. Are the rehoused residents happy with their new apartments? Anecdotal evidence suggests a mix of responses. Some are in awe of the new units, and all the amenities in the Modern at ArtPlace available for their use—rooftop pool, arts studio and classes, bocce ball courts—while others miss the multiroom layouts and cross-ventilation of their old garden apartments. The new apartments are just as large in area, but are differently configured, and therefore unfamiliar.[6]

---

4 Lamond-Riggs Citizens Association: https://lrcadc.org/.
5 Fort Totten Square description from Lowe Enterprises website: https://lowe-re.com/buildings-beyond/fort-totten-square/. See also Amanda Kolson Hurley, "Walmart Scales Down and Branches Out," *Architectural Record*, 16 April 2014.

6 Anecdotal evidence provided by an on-site rental agent in informal conversation with June Williamson, 27 July 2018.

Figure II.24-4 The exterior face of the Modern at ArtPlace, the first phase of an ambitious retrofit of Riggs Plaza apartments, where it meets South Dakota Avenue. Source: Photo by Phillip Jones, 2018.

Figure II.24-5 The entry court of the Modern at ArtPlace. Source: Photo by Belma Fishta, 2018.

Figure II.24-6 Some of the remaining garden apartment blocks of Riggs Plaza, awaiting eventual demolition and redevelopment in later phases of the Cafritz Foundation's ambitious, multiphase, nonprofit ArtPlace redevelopment. Source: Photo by Belma Fishta, 2018.

The second phase is expected to be complete by 2022, with 270 additional apartments, including 30 affordable artists units and ground-floor studios, and an ambitious Family Entertainment Zone (FEZ), with the aforementioned children's museum and arts collective space as well as a food hall. Exterior amenities include pedestrian plazas and a much-needed dog park. The architecture team is Perkins Eastman and Studio Shanghai.

While Lamond-Riggs is still not and may never be considered a hot and happening neighborhood in

Washington, DC, despite all the new redevelopment, that is for the best. The gradual changes there, catalyzed by the transformation of a key intersection, promise new life for existing residents, especially older Black residents who stuck it out through difficult decades, and ample opportunities for new residents to arrive, thrive, and put down anchoring roots.

White Flint and the Pike District
Montgomery County, Maryland

Challenges Addressed:

- Disrupt automobile dependence
- Add water and energy resilience

t's one thing to retrofit a single parcel into a node of drive-to walkability. It's altogether another thing to get multiple property owners to agree to build public streets on their private land in order to create a walkable street network intended to cut the percentage of automobile trips in half. It's hard enough to build support to do this on 430 acres. It's harder still to extend the model for 4 miles of sprawling development along Rockville Pike, an 8-lane state road, 14 miles northwest of downtown Washington, DC.

Entities from both the public and private sectors have collaborated surprisingly well on this ambitious, large-scale retrofit. Strong champions and partnerships on both sides argued for the value of leveraging existing Metrorail stations to anchor multiple new transit-oriented developments (TODs). Together, they came up with unique financing and staging mechanisms for establishing the finer-grain street network, increasing the tree canopy, installing stormwater management, and gradually shifting trips from the highway to the transit line.

Montgomery County (MoCo) has a long history of inventive, progressive urban planning. It was among the first (regrettably) to employ urban renewal funds to replace much of downtown Rockville with a window-less concrete shopping mall, since retrofitted into Rockville Town Center. It was the first (admirably) to institute inclusionary zoning. And it has a strong legacy of regional planning in coordination with the Maryland-National Capital Park and Planning Com-mission (M-NCPPC), including the notable two-county "On Wedges & Corridors" general plan of

1962.[1] As a result of that plan, more than a quarter of the land in the county remains in the largest agricultural reserve in the US, at 93,000 acres, while green "wedges" of unbuilt land are preserved around stream valleys. However, the rest of the county's acreage was largely built out at low densities and when DC Metrorail's Red Line was extended through the center of the county in the 1980s, the stations were built with large park-and-ride lots.

In 2008, to reduce encroachment on the agricultural reserve, the county established a Building Lot Termination program (BLT) where landowners are compensated for permanently foregoing residential development. Developers purchase BLTs as density bonuses in the areas where the county is incentivizing growth. For MoCo Planning Director Rollin Stanley, the means to protect the agricultural reserve *and* accommodate growth called for reconsidering—and reinventing—the concept of "corridor cities" from the 1962 plan.[2]

The White Flint Sector Plan is one of several county efforts to do just that.[3] It proposes the construction of a walkable grid of public streets on private land within three-quarters of a mile from the White Flint Metrorail Station (most of which is paid for by an additional 10% tax

---

[1] The plan advocated for green "wedges" between "corridor cities" along rapid rail transit lines in parallel with the National Capital Transportation Act's proposal of 83 miles of new lines. When two-thirds of the lines were curtailed, the "On Wedges & Corridors" plan went through revisions in 1964 and 1968.

[2] Rollin Stanley, "Wedges & Corridors: The Country's First Sustainable Growth Plan?" *Greater Greater Washington* blog, 4 November 2011: https://ggwash.org/view/11293/wedges-corridors-the-countrys-first-sustainable-growth-plan.

[3] The 2006 Shady Grove Sector Plan, the 2010 Great Seneca Science Corridor Master Plan, and the additional plans along Rockville Pike are part of a coordinated effort by MoCo and M-NCPPC to transform single-use commercial or industrial auto-oriented areas into mixed-use, urban environments with dense housing to balance the heavy concentration of jobs along I-270.

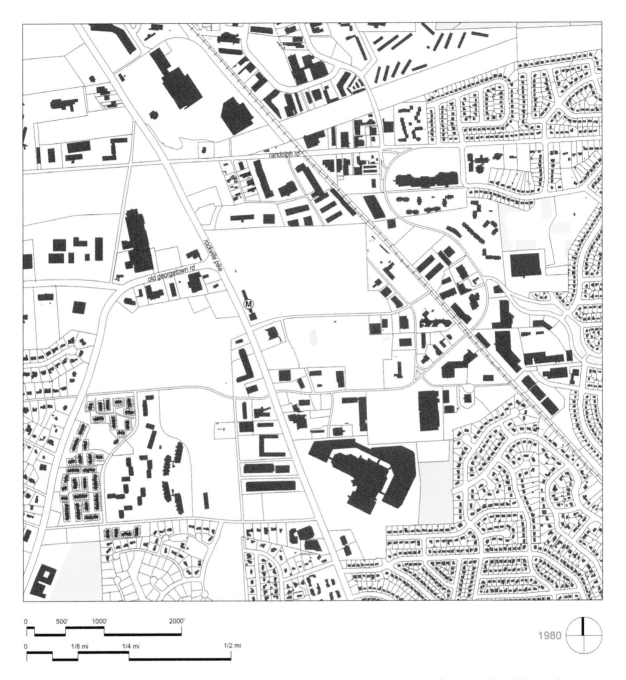

0   500'   1000'   2000'

0   1/8 mi   1/4 mi   1/2 mi

1980

Figure II.25-1   1980 figure-field diagram. Older, low-rise industrial and commercial buildings flank the railroad line. Little remains from the time of the trolley that served farms between Rockville and Georgetown from 1890 to 1935. They were replaced in the 1960s and 1970s with strip malls, motels, and the White Flint Mall on Rockville Pike (lower right) to serve residents of new residential subdivisions between Rockville and Bethesda. The soon-to-open White Flint Metrorail station is under construction. Source: Authors.

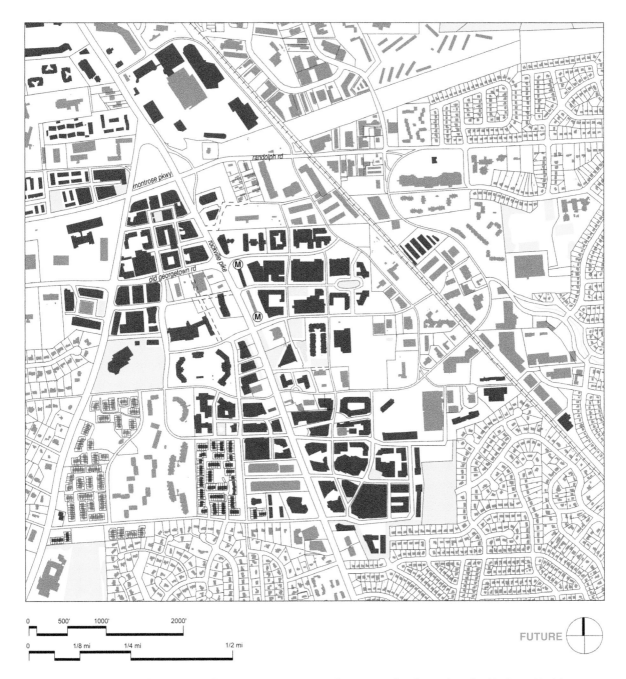

Figure II.25-2 Future figure-field diagram. The plan to transition to a finer-grain urban form of smaller blocks and buildings was approved in 2010. This view shows the approved sketch plans as of 2018, some of them already constructed, particularly Pike & Rose between Montrose Parkway and Old Georgetown Road. It does not yet show many of the expected redevelopment plans for parcels in the nearby 2018 White Flint 2 Sector Plan. Source: Authors.

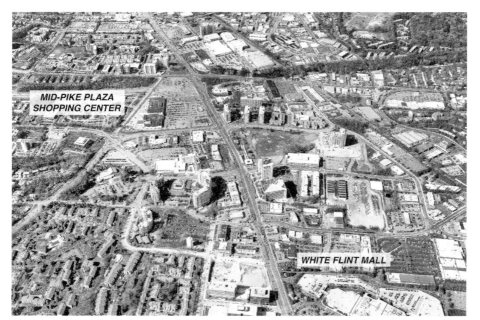

Figure II.25-3 Regulations from 1978 and 1992 encouraged density near the Metro station but resulted in piecemeal tall buildings with little relationship to each other and plenty of parking lots and under-used landscaping, as visible in this aerial from 2012. The Mid-Pike Plaza Shopping Center is upper left, since redeveloped into Pike & Rose. White Flint Mall is lower right. Source: Courtesy of Federal Realty Investment Trust.

on commercial property owners), rezoning to quadruple residential and double nonresidential density, and conversion of Rockville Pike from a "stroad" into a boulevard.

The proposal was largely developed by the commercial property owners themselves. The JBG Companies triggered interest in redevelopment after they received permission to build North Bethesda Market, a 24-story apartment tower, plaza with restaurants, and a Whole Foods grocery store in an urban format in exchange for including additional moderately priced units. Executives at Federal Realty Investment Trust (FRIT) were well aware of the higher rents they were receiving at Rockville Town Square and Bethesda Row, two suburban retrofit redevelopments a few Red Line Metrorail stops in either direction.[4] The developers started meeting among themselves, with county officials and community groups. All were concerned about the corridor's traffic problems and the need for a masterplan to accommodate growth.

In 2008, the White Flint Partnership (made up of six of the area's major developers) hired Glatting Jackson, new urbanist transportation planners, to conduct a charrette with various stakeholders. The resulting plan calls for a new

walkable street network centered on Rockville Pike reconfigured as a tree-lined boulevard with wide sidewalks and bus rapid transit running down the median. Over the course of some 200 meetings between 2006 and 2010, The White Flint Partnership and the Friends of White Flint (predominantly residents but supported by the developers) built consensus that the plan's walkable urbanism with higher density but more green space was preferable to the status quo.[5]

Under Rollins's direction and with the support of the County Planning Board and County Council, county staff developed the proposal, new commercial-residential zoning and incentives, and the county planning board adopted the White Flint Sector Plan, its financing, and staging in 2010.[6]

---

[4] The first phase of Rockville Town Square's redevelopment of a strip mall into mixed-use urbanism opened in 2007. At numerous community meetings prior to 2010, FRIT executive Evan Goldman was able to show residents and county staff Rockville Town Square and ask if they'd like something like that on the Mid-Pike Plaza strip mall site. County staff encouraged him not to create an island of walkability and he helped encourage the rest of the property owners to collaborate and create the new street network.

[5] The beginnings of the plan are well described by Louis Peck, "In Like Flint," *Bethesda*, 26 February 2012. The authors would like to thank Margaret Rifkin, Nkosi Yearwood, and Atul Sharma of the Montgomery County Planning Department and Dan Reed of the Just Up The Pike blog for their additional input.

[6] The plan gives developers permission to build up to 300 feet high in locations close to the corridor and with the purchase of BLTs. However, they will pay 75% of the $601 million in infrastructure improvements ($280 million for construction of public streets on their private land and $169 million through a Development Impact Tax), an *ad valorem* property tax of 10.3% (later raised to 11.5%) for schools. County-issued bonds based on that revenue stream cover the rest of the cost of new infrastructure. Early on, the developers favored using Tax Increment Financing, but county officials vetoed it because of the uncertainty of revenues to repay the bonds—especially on a project being carefully staged. Tanya Snyder, "How Value Capture Financing Will Revitalize White Flint," Streetsblog USA, 20 October 2011: https://usa.streetsblog.org/2011/10/20/how-value-capture-financing-will-revitalize-white-flint/.

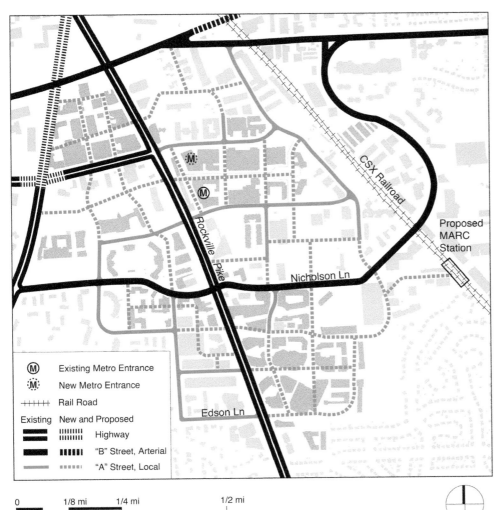

Figure II.25-4 The approved plan adds ten additional east-west streets and six additional north-south streets, allowing local trips to use local streets instead of all trips being funneled onto Rockville Pike and Old Georgetown Road. Some are designated "business streets" for higher traffic counts, while others are more local, sometimes private. The target speed for all of them is 25 mph. Source: Redrawn by authors based largely on Glatting Jackson plan.

While the bulk of the new streets will be paid for by the private sector, the public sector also committed to several street realignments, improving the pedestrian, bicycling environment, and the reconfiguration of Rockville Pike with bus rapid transit (part of a new 22-mile route to connect the county's major employment centers). Strict staging requirements ensure that affordable housing, a jobs-to-housing balance, and new infrastructure (including a new publicly-funded civic core and other privately funded civic uses throughout the eight neighborhoods) is constructed in

pace with new development in three stages.[7] Additional goals include increasing the tree canopy from 10.5% to

---

[7] To proceed from Stage 1 to Stage 2, the area has to achieve a 34% non-auto driver mode share. To go from Stage 2 to 3, 51% of trips have to be non-automobile. Similarly, at each of these points, the planning board has to assess progress on achieving a better jobs-to-housing balance and adequate affordable housing. For details of the staging requirements and calculation of the mode share splits for residents and employees, see Montgomery County Planning Department, *Midtown on the Pike: White Flint Sector Plan Implementation Guidelines,* July 2011.

Figure II.25-5 This view of Pike & Rose from 2018 shows development focused along Grand Park Avenue, a new street connecting a new park (not visible behind the tall buildings) to the planned town green to be built across Old Georgetown Road on the parking lots in the foreground. Residential buildings are concentrated to the west, while the frontage along Rockville Pike, to the right, is expected to be built up with dense, mixed-use office buildings once Rockville Pike itself is retrofitted. Source: Courtesy of Federal Realty Investment Trust.

Figure II.25-6 The master planners, landscape architects, and environmental graphic designers devoted close attention to the design of the public realm at Pike & Rose. Eye-catching textures and details, plantings, seating, undergrounded utilities, and coordinated but individualized storefronts create a strong sense of place and invite pedestrians to linger—in great contrast to the former strip mall. Source: Courtesy of Clinton & Associates, PC.

20%, improving stream quality, and reducing 2005 carbon emissions 80% by 2050.

Staging allocation charts on the MoCo Planning Department website and Biennial Monitoring Reports enable everyone to see progress on the infrastructure, building permit approvals, and goals. The 2019 Biennial Monitoring Report proudly reported meeting the Stage 1 goal of 34% non-auto driver trips for the third year in a row (up from 20% in 2010). It also reported completion of all Stage 1 triggers. This allows Stage 2 to proceed with slightly over a quarter of the 13,400 residential units and 8.8 million square feet of nonresidential use that have already been approved by the planning board. The rest will have to wait until the next phase of infrastructure is installed.[8]

The first development allocation for Stage 1 went to Pike & Rose, FRIT's mixed-use redevelopment of the

1960s-era 24-acre Mid-Pike Plaza strip mall. So far, its transformation bodes well for the feasibility of the larger plan. The new grid of public streets designed by Street-Works Studio divides the former superblock into nine squarish blocks at a very walkable dimension of around 300 feet per side. Streets are narrow with wide, lushly streetscaped sidewalks and richly textured storefronts, especially on Grand Park Avenue.[9] A bike-share station and bike infrastructure improvements to abutting streets further invite ditching the car. Nonetheless, despite the proximity to the Metro station, a conventional suburban parking ratio of approximately four parking spaces per 1000 square feet is planned for the mix of uses.[10]

Pike & Rose's green roofs are the first line of defense in slowing and cleansing stormwater. Planting strips at ground level drain the stormwater to an extensive array of Silva Cells under the wide sidewalks. Likened to large milk crates, the cells support the sidewalks structurally,

---

[8] The 2010 White Flint Sector Plan was written to recognize that a learning process would occur and revisions would be needed from time to time. In 2018 the implementation guidelines were revised to clarify the procedures for switching from Stage 1 to Stage 2 and the development allocations were revised upward.

[9] FRIT hired nearly 100 consultants on Pike & Rose so as to foster a visually diverse environment. Those with a major role include Street-Works Studio, WDG Architecture, Design Collective, Foreseer, and Clinton & Associates Landscape Architects.

[10] Build-out is expected to contain 1,600 dwelling units, over one million square feet of office and 470,000 square feet of retail, restaurants, cinema, and a performing arts and jazz club.

Figure II.25-7 Pike & Rose's roofscapes are mostly put to good use as tenant amenity space, a 260-watt solar array, and ample green roofs. Uptop Acres, a 17,000-square-foot rooftop farm just visible in the upper right corner, provides fresh veggies for its sold-out CSA membership. Source: Photo by Phillip Jones, 2018

allowing less compaction of the soils and more voids for water storage and healthy tree roots. The county estimates Pike & Rose has cut polluted run-off into storm drains and streams by 77%.[11] An independent academic study credits much of this to the almost tripling of tree canopy area and the five times increase in percent of permeable surface area.[12]

In keeping with the larger plan goals, Pike & Rose met the county's inclusionary zoning requirements for

subsidized residential units, while receiving a density bonus for contributions to the BLT program. The project has won major urban planning awards and became the first by a publicly traded developer to achieve LEED for Neighborhood Development Gold certification.

Is the public sector similarly living up to its promises? FRIT CEO Donald Wood didn't think so in 2018 when he fired off a letter to the Montgomery County Executive and County Council. He complained that the road upgrade projects were behind schedule, progress was sluggish on creating parks and civic spaces, and the county had not been receptive to FRIT's push for financial incentives for a new office project at Pike & Rose. MoCo's Chief Administrative Officer replied that market forces, decisions of private property owners, and strict state policies have reined in the pace of White Flint's transformation.[13]

Nonetheless, MoCo and M-NCPPC have proceeded not only with design studies for the retrofit of Rockville Pike, but with several more Sector Plans expanding the finer-grained street network, the percentage of non-automobile trips—and revenues—further north. Collectively, the 4-mile length is being branded as the Pike District and new special tax districts have been proposed to fund bus rapid transit. In Stage 1, the county received a 2.3 to 1 return on public investment in new property tax revenue, and projects a return of 7 to 1 or more from Stage 2.[14]

There are several hundred corridor retrofit projects in the works around the US, but few that aspire to the level of "corridor cities." Is the stroad-to-street network model equally replicable elsewhere? Clearly, it helps to be in a real estate development market where the desire for urban living has already been proven. It helps to have a rail transit system in place. It helps to have just enough property owners buy in to multiply the benefits of investing in the public realm, but not so many as to make it difficult to

11 Casey Anderson, "The Environmental Benefits of New Suburbanism," The Third Place: A Montgomery County Planning Department Blog, 18 December 2018: https://montgomeryplanning.org/blog-design/2018/12/the-environmental-benefits-of-new-suburbanism/.

12 The study also found an 89% decrease in average block size, 133% increase in intersection density, 242% increase in linear feet of sidewalk, a 248% increase in gathering space, and estimated a 114% increase in site energy demand but a 39% decrease in energy use intensity. While the bar was pretty low to begin with, this kind of performance data is important to assessing the longer-term impacts of retrofits. Yeinn Oh, Jun Wang, Nevedita Sankaraman, Osvaldo Broesicke, Alexandra Maxim, Yilun Zha, John Crittenden, and Ellen Dunham-Jones, "The SuRe Gap: Bridging the Gap Between Idealized and Attainable Infrastructure Sustainability and Resilience," research poster, the Brook Byers Institute of Sustainable Systems, Georgia Institute of Technology.

13 Bethany Rodgers, "Federal Realty Considers Moving Employees Out of County Amid Frustrations with Local Officials," Bethesda, 24 July 2018.

14 Jay Corbalis, Development Associate, FRIT, presentation in session, "The Good, Bad and the Undiscovered: An Insider's Look into Successful Public-Private Partnerships across the Country," New Partners for Smart Growth Conference, Baltimore, 29 January 2015.

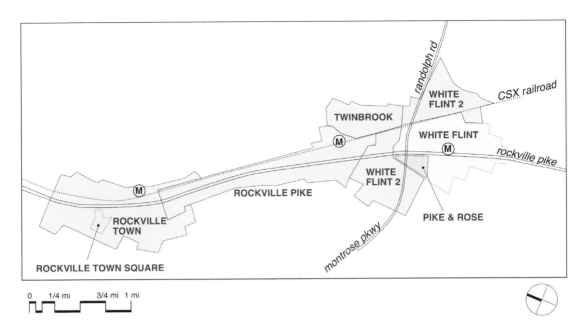

0   1/4 mi   3/4 mi   1 mi

Figure II.25-8   MoCo and M-NCPPC are now extending the basic goals and methods of walkable densification employed in the White Flint Sector Plan (shown on the right) up Rockville Pike for four miles. The Rockville Pike Plan's corridor city should enable a regional-scale transfer of more car trips from the highway to the planned rapid transit bus and the Metro rail stations while accommodating significant growth in the renamed Pike District. Source: Authors.

reach consensus.[15] And it really helps to have a strong public-sector planning department with the capacity to coordinate and stage such a complex public-private partnership.

Could smaller-scale bus transit instead of rail and lower-density development still finance new street networks at the scale of targeted "nodes" on a corridor instead of a full-blown "corridor city"? Increasingly, the answer is yes. More and more bus-oriented TODs are under development in northern America and around the world. These projects are more likely to connect suburban nodes together than to radiate from a central downtown. All could benefit by learning from White Flint and the Pike District how to integrate multiple partners to reduce automobile dependence while adding much needed new housing and improving stormwater management at the scales of the street, the project, the corridor, and the region.

---

[15] The six major property owners in the White Flint Partnership are the JBG Companies, Federal Realty Investment Trust, Saul Centers, Inc., Gables Residential, Lerner Enterprises, and the Tower Companies. Their partnership and commitment both reduced the individual risk of investing in walkability without knowing if your neighbor would continue the network, and increased the returns they expect to receive from a truly walkable environment.

The Blairs District
Silver Spring, Maryland

Challenges addressed:

- Improve public health
- Reduce automobile dependence
- Add water and energy resilience

Planners have long understood the value to urbanized areas of ample open space, and northern American suburbs, developed at low densities, have generally had it in abundance. Increasingly, attention is directed to the *quality* of the open spaces: do people have access, and can they use them? It is one thing to have garden apartment buildings and residential towers set in a park, but what if much of the "park" is actually parking, and the remaining green space is largely ornamental and unprogrammed, replete with "keep off the grass" signs?

Enter the Blairs District in Silver Spring, Maryland. Over a 20-year build-out, a 27-acre superblock site will be gradually retrofitted into a walkable, urbanized node, laced with a network of highly programmed small park and plaza spaces. The property has been owned by the Tower Companies for over 70 years; they have pledged that these spaces will be open to the public, providing lively, accessible, direct connections to the nearby commuter rail.[1]

The property, a short distance south of the Silver Spring Metrorail station, was once the Falkland estate, built by prominent members of the Blair family with antebellum roots.[2] The mansion was destroyed in a "controlled burn" in 1958 (providing training practice for fire fighters!) and replaced in 1959 with the Blair Plaza Apartments, a collection of four cruciform-shaped, mid-rise apartment buildings, and Blair Shops, a neighborhood shopping center anchored by a large supermarket, extolled as the epitome of "modern" in its day.[3] Tall residential towers soon followed. The sloped site was regraded into two levels, separated with a steep retaining wall, forming a formidable barrier across the superblock; there was no easy way to navigate between the levels on foot.

The Tower Companies is run by the Abramson brothers, who grew up in a house across from Falkland, which their father purchased and developed in their youth. The brothers engaged architect Bing Thom of Vancouver and landscape architect Alan Ward of Sasaki Associates to

---

[1] The specific language in the Montgomery County Planning Department report states, "All record plats that include public use space must include a note that all public use spaces as illustrated on the certified Site Plan(s) must be maintained in perpetuity by the property owners and access must be provided to the general public." The Blairs Master Plan, Montgomery County Planning Department Staff Report, 24 October 2013, 11.

[2] Robert E. Oshel, *Home Sites of Distinction: The History of Woodside Park, Silver Spring*, The Woodside Park Civic Association, 1998.

[3] Jerry A. McCoy, "147th Anniversary of the Burning of Falkland Mansion," Patch.com blog, 13 July 2011. For more on downtown Silver Spring, its significant role in the history of the suburbanization of shopping, and recent struggles around asserting a "right to the suburb" in suburban spaces of urban renewal, see June Williamson, "Protest on the Astroturf at Downtown Silver Spring: July 4, 2007," in Christopher Neidt, ed., *Social Justice in Diverse Suburbs* (Philadelphia: Temple University Press, 2013), 54–69.

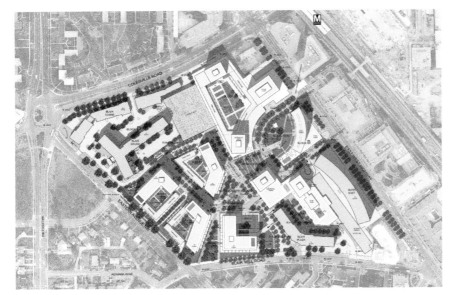

Figure II.26-1 Redevelopment plan for the Blairs District, approved in 2014, dividing up the superblock with a publicly accessible network of new streets, small parks, and plazas. Ten new "point" towers will eventually be built, over podiums of parking, wrapped with program. Existing residential towers on Colesville Road and East-West Highway will remain. Source: Courtesy of Sasaki Associates

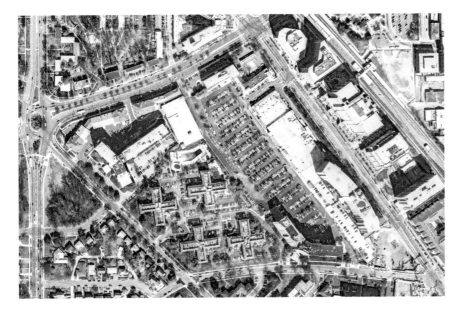

Figure II.26-2 A "before" 2008 orthophoto of The Blairs shows it largely unaltered from construction in the late 1950s and early 1960s. A few street-oriented buildings from the 2000s contrast with the original stand-alone X, Y, and V-shaped high rises. Source: Montgomery County GIS.

design a retrofit master plan.[4] The plan, approved by Montgomery County in 2014, proposed doubling the overall number of residential units, to 2800, tripling the commercial space, with retail, office, and a hotel, while adding five acres of connected spaces to the walkable public realm—20% of the site area.

Sadly, Thom, designer of the fabulous additions to the Surrey Central City mall in Canada (and consultant to Guthrie Green in Tulsa, Oklahoma), passed away in 2016. The commission was passed to the Design Collective of Baltimore to design the first two new buildings. The Pearl will eventually comprise four buildings, up to 14 stories tall each, with 1140 apartments, replacing the original 257 units in the Blair Plaza Apartments, more than quadrupling the unit density on the property.

Sustainable design features are emphasized through-out, as if to make amends for the previous auto-oriented

---

[4] Bing Thom retrofitted Surrey Central City mall near Vancouver. Alan Ward collaborated with RTKL, now CallisonRTKL, on the design of Addison Circle Park. Both projects area featured in Dunham-Jones and Williamson, *Retrofitting Suburbia*, 136–138, 180–182.

Figure II.26-3 Public realm landscapes at The Blairs: an urban farm (a), playgrounds (b), and curbside tree planters with bio-filtration (c). Source: Photos by Belma Fishta, 2018.

conditions on the site: the older towers were renovated and updated in the early 2000s, the newest buildings are LEED Platinum–certified, and the landscaping incorporates all the latest best practices for green site design: curbside tree planters with bio-filtration, green roofs, climate-sensitive plantings. The site currently includes a dog park, a children's playground, an adult fitness area, and a community urban farm. These elements are all temporary and will be reproduced in some fashion in the final site design. That won't be realized until the grocery-anchored strip mall on the upper level of the escarpment is redeveloped, sometime after the conclusion of the store's lease in 2024.

Jeffrey Abramson of the Tower Companies asserts, "the key element is that people are looking for wellness in their life, they are looking for balance. . .to support their health." The building and site design features in the Blairs District are selected to emphasize values of health and wellness.[5] Tower has leveraged considerable community social capital thus far with The Blairs. It remains to be seen, however, as local planner and influential Silver Spring–based blogger Dan Reed reminds us, if they will fully follow through with all that has been promised for a healthy, connected, fully accessible public realm.[6]

---

[5] Jeffrey Abramson, interview with USGBC, published March 2017 on YouTube.

[6] We hope that they do, justifying inclusion in this book. A series of thoughtful posts on The Blairs by Dan Reed can been found on the *Greater Greater Washington* blog: https://ggwash.org/.

La Station – Centre Intergénérationnel
Nuns' Island, Verdun, Quebec

Challenges addressed:

- Support an aging society
- Add water and energy resilience

Populations in developed economies are experiencing the "longevity dividend" produced by a lifetime of access to good nutrition, advanced medicine, and an array of cultural changes. Increased life expectancy increases needs for community facilities that cater to the social needs of "perennials," or older adults. In the planned community of Nuns' Island in Verdun, a 60,000-resident suburban area dating from the early 1960s that was incorporated into the City of Montreal as a borough in 2002, Les Architectes FABG realized an innovative reinhabitation-type retrofit in 2011. The architectural world took interest in the aesthetically compelling and historically significant project, and so did we.[1]

The master plan of Verdun, made possible by the completion of the Champlain road bridge to the mainland in 1962, was high modern, Canadian style, including both garden apartment complexes and apartment towers. Shortly before his death in 1969, renowned modernist architect Ludwig Mies van der Rohe, working with local architect Paul H. Lapointe, designed for Esso a model gas station on Nuns' Island. Two sleek, low-slung buildings, constructed of buff-colored brick, glass, and steel elements painted black or white enamel, flanked a gasoline-pump island. Bare fluorescent tubes provided stark lighting. One building was for sales and the other for servicing

Figure II.27-1 "Before" view of the iconic Mies van der Rohe–designed gas station taken in May 2006, shortly before it closed. Source: Photo by Bas Kegge, Architect, Rotterdam, NL.

automobiles and a flat roof covering the pump island connected the two.

The station, elegantly designed but functionally obsolete, ceased operations in 2008.[2] Because of its architecturally significant heritage it was soon landmarked by the City of Montreal. The Nuns' Island community has evolved into a "horizontal" or "open" NORC (naturally

---

1 "Conversion of Mies van der Rohe Gas Station / FABG," *ArchDaily* blog, 7 March 2012: https://www.archdaily.com/214540/conversion-of-mies-van-der-rohe-gas-station-les-archi-tectes-fabg/. See also Dave LeBlanc, "Mies's Montreal gas station gets new lease on life," *Globe and Mail*, 7 July 2011: https://beta.theglobeandmail.com/life/home-and-garden/architecture/miess-montreal-gas-station-gets-new-lease-on-life/article625701.

2 Between increased vehicle fuel efficiency standards and the shift to electric cars, the number of gas stations in operation has dropped significantly. While removal of the underground gasoline storage tanks can be a hurdle if leaks are found, hundreds have been retrofitted. The most popular reinhabitation-type retrofit in our database seems to be restaurants with patio seating under the canopies. Less frequent uses include urgent care clinics or redevelopment into housing or gyms. In addition to La Station, a few of our favorites are: Larkinville Square in Buffalo, NY; 2802 Pico Housing in Santa Monica, CA; Bloc 10 in Winnipeg, Canada; and Sport and Culture House, Prismen, in Copenhagen, Denmark.

Figure II.27-2 Exterior (a) and interior (b) views of the spaces after renovation by Les Architectes FABG. The minimalist architectural elements were preserved and renovated, while the functional equipment and systems were replaced and updated. Source: Photos by M. Steve Montpetit, courtesy of Les Architectes FABG.

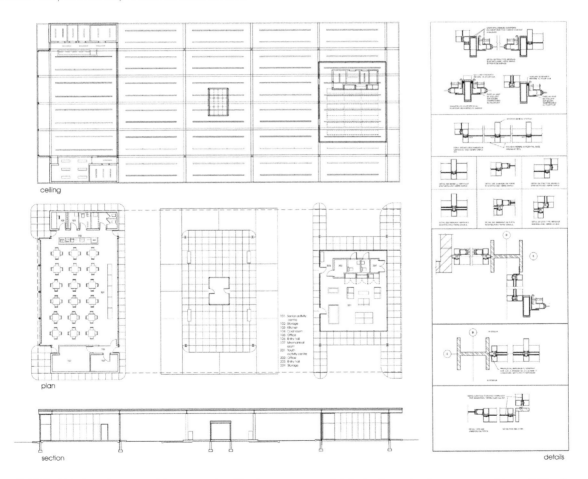

Figure II.27-3 Working drawings of the renovation. The largest space, at left in the floor plan, is programmed for activities for seniors, while the smaller space at right is the "Black Lounge" for the teenagers. The former cashier's booth, in the middle, was converted to a vitrine for displaying art. Source: Courtesy of Les Architectes FABG.

Figure II.27-4 Carrefour, a 2013 artwork by Francis Montillaud, commissioned by the City of Montreal, is installed in the former cashier booth. It features five bronze busts, expressive gestural portraits of three older residents and two teenagers from the neighborhood, placed on stainless steel bases. Source: © Francis Montillaud, photo by Guy L'Heureux, 2013.

occurring retirement community), in which a large percentage of residents are over 50, not because they've moved to the community as empty nesters or after retirement, but because they have stayed put in their houses and apartments over time. The city determined that the neighborhood was in need of a multigenerational activity center, serving youth and seniors.[3] The existing gas station building would suit: the larger service shed for seniors, a group of about 60 regulars, and the smaller volume for teens.

FABG received the commission to both restore and reuse the buildings. In the larger 3000 square foot room, painted white with white furnishings, members pay a nominal 15 CAD fee to enjoy a daily weekday schedule of exercise, language, and crafts classes, play games like bridge, and attend lectures. In the smaller 1000 square

foot room, dubbed "the Black Lounge" and finished accordingly, teens have a community-based third space for hanging out on weekends and evenings, playing table tennis, computer games, and piano, listening to music, and organizing group outings. The spaces are relatively small and the design minimalist, but when in use, the rooms are filled with reinvigorating life-affirming activities.

To reduce energy demand in the colder northern climate and minimize the size of roof-mounted equipment, geothermal wells were sunk under asphalt on the site. The old gas pumps were replaced with stainless steel facsimiles that function as air intake and exhaust vents for the system. In various ways this site of a former auto-oriented use has been elegantly repositioned to serve new modes of mobility, without negating its architectural lineage of "modern" living and the mid-twentieth century promise of the automobile-enabled "good life." The location is accessible by bus, and the parking area stores car share vehicles. All in all, La Station is a nifty reinhabitation retrofit to community-serving uses, and away from a built environment dependent on fossil fuels.

---

[3] Elinor Ginzler, "From Home to Hospice: The Range of Housing Alternatives," in Henry Cisneros, Margaret Dyer-Chamberlain, and Jane Hickie, eds., *Independent for Life: Homes and Neighborhoods for an Aging America* (Austin: University of Texas Press, 2012), 57.

Bell Works
Holmdel, New Jersey

Challenges addressed:

- Compete for jobs
- Support an aging population

In 1962 Bell Labs built a spectacular telephonics research facility on a pristine landscape in the affluent suburban Township of Holmdel in Monmouth County, New Jersey. Reinhabited as Bell Works, it is a new model for the twenty-first-century suburban workplace, and also a model for sensitive adaptive reuse of landmark twentieth-century works of architecture.

The building, designed by famed modernist architect Eero Saarinen, opened a year after his untimely death at age 51. Saarinen is known also for the iconic St. Louis Arch as well as suburban research campus buildings for mid-twentieth-century corporate giants IBM and General Motors. The black-mirrored glass box, 1.9 million square feet, six stories high, and a quarter of a mile long, with full-height, skylit atriums, is surrounded by a landscape of ornamental lakes and acres of asphalt parking lots, configured in an artful oval form by equally famed landscape architect Hideo Sasaki.[1] In its day it epitomized the sylvan corporate campus as the ideal environment for deep thought and research.

It worked. Bell Labs, now Alcatel-Lucent, was a storied place of innovation where scientists and inventors made many of the groundbreaking discoveries that undergird the telecommunications revolution, from the Nobel prize–worthy discovery of the cosmic microwave background, to the development of the touch-tone phone, UNIX, digital cellphone technology, and fiber-optic cables. *Fortune*

Figure II.28-1 The atrium at Bell Works is one quarter mile long and six-stories high. When tenants occupy leased space, the gallery partitions walls are replaced with glass, affording views into the atrium. A massive translucent photovoltaic array installation on the sawtooth skylights provides 15% of the energy for the common spaces. A 186-room boutique hotel will be built on the roof. Source: Photo by Belma Fishta, 2018.

magazine dubbed it the "best-funded and most successful corporate research laboratory the world has ever seen."[2] By 2006 the flagship facility was vacant, victim to a slow unraveling after the breakup of Bell Telephone's monopoly in the United States and the shifting of innovation in

---

[1] Karrie Jacobs, "The Bargain That Revived Bell Labs," *Architect*, 23 May 2016: http://www.architectmagazine.com/design/culture/the-bargain-that-revived-bell-labs_o.

[2] Chris Matthews, "The Reincarnation of Bell Labs," *Fortune*, 2 February 2015: http://fortune.com/2015/02/02/bell-labs-real-estate-revival/.

Figure II.28-2 Eero Saarinen–designed Bell Labs was a fabled center of telecommunications technology innovation. Teams of white-shirted engineers, inventors, and research scientists once roamed its orderly fluorescent-lit halls. Source: Photo © Ezra Stoller/Esto.

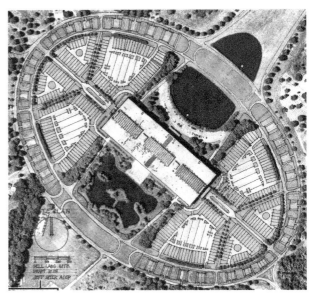

Figure II.28-3 The first site plan for retrofitting the site, a 2008 proposal to infill parking lots with town houses while maintaining the original Sasaki ornamental landscape, was by Jeff Speck. The property currently has around 5,000 surface parking spaces. Source: Image courtesy of Speck & Associates LLC.

communications technology to other locales. It became known as the largest empty building in the world.

It sat vacant for several years, as schemes to redevelop the property were hashed out with the local government of Holmdel, an exurban township containing mostly large residential estates, with a median resident income more than four times the national average. Despite the residents' wealth, the substantial tax income once generated by the labs facility was sorely missed in the local government budget.[3] While NIMBY-minded neighbors worried about the usual concerns—the impact of increased density on traffic and local schools—a coalition of preservationists and scientists joined forces to oppose demolition.[4] In 2013, after five years of negotiation, Somerset Development acquired the property with a scheme to reinhabit the

building, with a zoning allowance in place for building 225 new residential units on the property, the majority restricted to the older adult ("fifty-five-plus") market.[5]

Ralph Zucker, president of Somerset, has become a dynamic force for change in New Jersey, promoting the concept of transforming corporate white elephant campuses into "metroburbs." Zucker defines the term—his coinage—as a redevelopment format for creating a vibrant urban core in a great suburban location: "In a metroburb you can have the urban cool and the urban convenience, and yet you don't have to drive two hours or live in a little box to get it."[6]

The first site plan Zucker commissioned for the Holmdel property, designed by urbanist Jeff Speck in 2008, shows 300 rowhouse lots arrayed around the lab behemoth, and a ring of apartment villas, confined to the oval

---

[3] The facility is reported to have generated roughly $4 million in local taxes a year, around 25% of the total budget, but that amount was reduced to $400,000 by 2008. Matthews, "The Reincarnation of Bell Labs." See also Eillie Anzilotti, "Can We Create a New Kind of Downtown in Abandoned Suburban Offices?" *Fast Company*, 16 January 2018: https://www.fastcompany.com/40513730/can-we-create-a-new-kind-of-downtown-in-abandoned-suburban-offices.

[4] A first scheme for scraping the site and subdividing the property into large-lot estates proposed by Preferred Real Estate Investment was the target of the initial ire. Matthews, "The Reincarnation of Bell Labs."

[5] While it would seem to make more sense for the housing to be geared to employees rather than retirees, communities are often hesitant to allow any new housing that might increase the number of school children and local taxes to support them. This is particularly true in New Jersey, often frustrating planners' and developers' efforts to attract and retain younger members of the workforce.

[6] Interview of Ralph Zucker by June Williamson, 23 July 2018.

grayfield footprint of the parking lots. The plan envisioned apartments in the main building, with the atrium conceived as the community's mixed-use Main Street. The township rejected the plan as too dense, and Zucker went back to the negotiating table.

Zucker's implementation team includes New York–based architect Alexander Gorlin, who was awestruck upon encountering the vacant space. "We walked around, and it was completely abandoned," Gorlin recalled. "It was like coming into the Baths of Caracalla."[7] In his mind's eye Zucker envisioned a busy commercial street, albeit one covered with a skylit roof. As it happens, the atrium is one hundred feet wide, equal in dimension and proportion to the "urban canyon" of a typical north-south avenue in Manhattan and other northern American center cities. To communicate this vision, the team staged an open house in September 2009, early in the negotiation process. The potential of the town center concept was mocked up at full scale, with vendor stalls, a café, wine bar, and library with seating, planting, and other furnishings. The tactical approach worked.

The implemented renovation scheme for the main facility updates the common spaces with a playful design vibe, opening up the leasable spaces to atrium views by replacing Saarinen's white metal partitions with glass walls. Photovoltaic panels added to the sawtooth skylights handle 15% of the electrical load for the common spaces.[8] Rather than providing a setting for (mostly male) scientists to have epiphanies in isolation staring at nature, the redesign encourages the bubbling of new ideas through serendipitous, diverse social interactions. Instead of one business tenant, there are dozens.[9] On the ground floor, a Montessori daycare and preschool sits next to a new 17,000-square-foot public library for Holmdel. The county library system enjoys a perpetual free lease agreement with Somerset.[10]

(a)

(b)

Figure II.28-4 Rebranded a "metroburb," the atrium is beginning to bustle with energy in its new reincarnation as Bell Works. Some of the regular events include morning yoga, happy hour drinks, and a farmers' market (a), seen here during set up. In the popular ground-floor food hall, a vintage phone booth (b) is a ghostly reminder of a once-ubiquitous element in the urban streetscape and an homage to the Bell Telephone Company. Source: Photos by Belma Fishta, 2018.

[7] Jacobs, "The Bargain That Revived Bell Labs."
[8] The property was acquired for $27 million. The renovation budget was $200 million. Michael L. Diamond, "Bell Labs to Bell Works: How one man saved the historic site and made it a tech mecca," *App.com*, 15 November 2017: https://www.app.com/story/news/local/redevelopment/2017/11/15/bell-labs-bell-works-tech-jobs-holmdel/337632001/. See also Anzilotti, "New Kind of Downtown."
[9] Diamond, "Bell Labs." The going rent in November 2017 was $30–35 per square foot, around 20% over the state average.
[10] Joseph Sapia, "Coming to Bell Works in Holmdel: A Town Library," *Two River Times*, 2 January 2017: http://tworivertimes.com/holmdel-township-library-to-be-housed-at-bell-works/.

(a)   (b)

Figure II.28-5 Bell Market (a) draws customers from throughout the area. Holmdel Library (b), a branch in the county system, occupies 17,000 square feet of ground-level space. Source: Photos by Belma Fishta, 2018.

In the housing part of the project, new residential units are built on the periphery of the campus, on 103 acres that were sold to national homebuilder Toll Brothers. While Toll Brothers is a huge national real estate investment trust (REIT), the project manager has roots in Holmdel. In suburban retrofitting, local ties and local knowledge can be significant factors in building community trust. The 185 age-restricted units are attached town houses ("carriage houses" in Toll Brothers parlance), clustered around a clubhouse. The other forty units are more usual exurban subdivision fare, large houses on one-acre lots. While not directly adjacent to the central building, the housing is within easy walking distance; a separate connecting pathway is planned, as are rideshare discounts and bus shuttles to the nearest New Jersey Transit station, five miles away.

Following the success of Bell Works, Somerset is enthusiastically repeating the concept in Hoffman Estates, Illinois, on a 150-acre former AT&T corporate campus. The second "metroburb," called City Works, will have a similar amount of office space to lease to multiple tenants, with ground level retail in the atrium spaces. Preliminary plans prepared by Torti Gallas & Partners show new multiunit housing—apartments and town houses—directly adjacent. Zucker is optimistic that yet more housing might eventually be built on the Bell Works property, perhaps by building on the parking lot oval as envisioned in Jeff Speck's early site plan. If this happens (and we think it could), Bell Works might become the liveliest retrofitted "millennials plus

Figure II.28-6 View of the rooftops of the Toll Brothers "Regency" carriage houses at Bell Works, with the signature Bell Labs water tower in the background. The housing is screened from view with trees and a landscaped berm. Source: Photos by Belma Fishta, 2018.

perennials" community in New Jersey, living up to its promising name.

What is happening elsewhere in New Jersey? Retrofitting office parks in the Garden State often requires both public financing and clever leveraging of existing assets, as with Bell Works.[11] When pharmaceutical giant

---

11 See J. Hughes & J. Seneca, Reinventing the New Jersey Economy: New Metropolitan and Regional Employment Dynamics, *Rutgers Regional Report* (2012): 331-12.

Roche announced closure in 2012 of its 114-acre Nutley/ Clifton campus—a one-time employer of 10,000—it inspired New Jersey State legislators to propose the Corporate Disinvestment Property Tax Relief Act to financially assist municipalities after losing a large tax ratable. Although then-governor Chris Christie vetoed the act, he did participate in the press conference that announced a commitment to reinhabit a 14-acre portion of the site with the first new private medical school to open in the state in fifty years.

Tax benefits have since helped attract a bio-tech firm to make the reverse move from Brooklyn, New York. Prism Capital Partners was attracted to the site for its location (only nine miles from New York City), for its highly efficient district energy CHP plant, and for its tall buildings with skinny floorplates that provide all employees with ample access to light and views, a good recruiting tool for

future tenants. The site has been branded ON3, a reference to Route 3, a limited-access highway that borders the campus. Preliminary masterplans by Perkins Eastman integrates biotech, hotel, retirement housing (age-restricted), and research and development office use along a section of Bloomfield Avenue/First Avenue, envisioned as a walkable "main street." In addition, the schemes call for reversing the concrete channelization of a portion of Springer Brook and restoring the natural stream.[12]

To educate neighboring communities about the approved project and to build support for rezoning to allow market-rate and student housing on the site, Prism Capital held a series of Suburban Revitalization Forums featuring experts on economic development, demographic shifts, and retrofitting suburbia. Like Somerset, Prism is very much a New Jersey focused developer. Prism founder

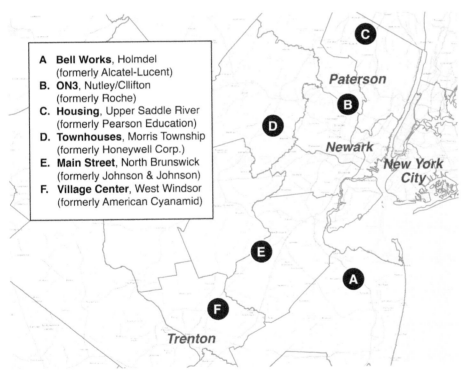

A **Bell Works**, Holmdel
   (formerly Alcatel-Lucent)
B. **ON3**, Nutley/Cllifton
   (formerly Roche)
C. **Housing**, Upper Saddle River
   (formerly Pearson Education)
D. **Townhouses**, Morris Township
   (formerly Honeywell Corp.)
E. **Main Street**, North Brunswick
   (formerly Johnson & Johnson)
F. **Village Center**, West Windsor
   (formerly American Cyanamid)

Figure II.28-7 During the late twentieth century, R&D and industrial campuses for prominent corporations were built through-out New Jersey. In the early twenty-first century, many are being retrofitted. Source: Authors.

---

[12] The latest developments at the former Roche site at the time of publication are available online at the City of Nutley's website: http://www.nutleynj.org/roche; and the ON3 website of Prism Capital Partners: https://on3nj.com/vision/.

Eugene Diaz leveraged his connections and commitment by opening the second forum, saying, "We aren't just looking for a quick investment flip. We're here to stay." He then cited native son Bruce Springsteen's lyrics to "My Hometown":

> Now Main Street's whitewashed windows and vacant stores
> Seems like there ain't nobody wants to come down here no more
> They're closing down the textile mill across the railroad tracks
> Foreman says these jobs are going boys and they ain't coming back
> To your hometown
> Your hometown
> Your hometown
> Your hometown

Larger corporate campus owners with fewer local ties have been less willing to stick around and invest the time it takes to produce high-quality mixed-use urbanism. They have recognized the value of their land for housing, but with a few exceptions (such as the Howard Hughes Corporation's plan for the former American Cyanamid site in West Windsor), instead of integrating living and working, they are simply selling off chunks of land for housing—usually high-end types. As at Bell Works, this is often due to community resistance and too often what appears to be a process of default design by lawsuit.

In Upper Saddle River, the Mack-Cali Realty Corporation won its lawsuit against the borough for refusing to hear its rezoning request to redevelop the former Pearson Education 47-acre office building site with over 500 residential units, claiming discrimination against lower-income people of color under the state's Fair Housing Act. The settlement agreement permits half that amount, with 47 units designated affordable. With these entitlements in place, Mack-Cali sold the property to a housing developer.[13]

In Morris Township, a citizens' group lost its two-year lawsuit to overturn approval of Honeywell Corporation's request to subdivide and rezone what it argued were underused portions of its 147-acre corporate campus to allow construction of hundreds of town houses. Citing uncertainty due to the lawsuit, Honeywell then sold the rezoned land and moved 1,000 jobs to three newly built but never occupied Johnson & Johnson buildings in Morris Plains on a more compact 40-acre site.[14]

In the meantime, Johnson & Johnson's vacated 212-acre site with over 1 million square feet of enclosed space between Route 1 and the Northeast Corridor rail line is being redeveloped into a transit-oriented development (TOD). New Jersey Transit has agreed to build a new station for the Main Street North Brunswick development.[15] If done well (and the first phase's Costco and Target on Route 1 are not that promising), the project could become a much-needed home base for Millennials and Gen Zers seeking "urban" living in the suburbs, along with downsizing older "perennials."

[13] Miles Ma, "Developer to build luxury homes on former Pearson site," *NJ.com*, 13 April 2016. http://www.nj.com/bergen/index.ssf/2016/04/developer_to_build_luxury_homes_on_former_pearson.html.
[14] Louis C. Hochman, "Judge knocks out lawsuit over Honeywell HQ development – but another still to be heard," *NJ.com*, March 2013. http://www.nj.com/morris/index.ssf/2013/03/honeywell_property_rezoning_ru.html.
[15] For updates on the Main Street North Brunswick TOD see: http://www.ourtowncenter.info/index.html.

Wyandanch Rising
Town of Babylon, New York

Challenges addressed:

- Leverage social capital for equity
- Improve public health
- Add water and energy resilience

How does a retrofitting project get started in an economically distressed community? The story of Wyandanch Rising, a multifaceted suburban renewal project in a small, long-overlooked unincorporated hamlet in the Town of Babylon, a suburb of New York City on Long Island, provides an instructive case study.[1] Named for Chief Wyandanch, a mid-seventeenth-century sachem of the indigenous Montaukett people, the hamlet's revitalization demonstrates the important role of new "chiefs" to champion on behalf of local voices. The effort began in 2000, when Wyandanch was identified by the Suffolk County Planning Commission as the most economically distressed place in the county.

Two decades later, the hamlet can boast a rebuilt boulevard and extension to the nearest sanitary sewer district two miles away, an impressive new rail station and new commuter parking structure, and, most significantly, two five-story apartment buildings with 177 apartments framing a public one-acre green plaza, with several additional new mixed-use buildings in the works, in place of surface parking lots, all within a short walking distance of the station. By 2016, the project had leveraged $1.74 million in state brownfields planning grants to over $131 million in public and private financing, an astonishing

Figure II.29-1 The first phase of Wyandanch Rising features two new mixed-use buildings, four stories of apartments over retail, flanking a public plaza. After decades of neglect, the Long Island Rail Road invested heavily in the area, with a large new commuter parking structure and an extensively enhanced station building. New water mains and an extension to the nearest sewer district were required to support the higher-density, transit-oriented retrofit. Source: Photo by Phillip Jones, 2018.

rate of return on investment of 75 to one, with the potential for millions more.[2]

---

[1] Contributors to the planning, design, and development of Wyandanch Rising, many years in the making and still ongoing, include the Town of Babylon, NY; the Albanese Organization; AKRF, Olin Studio; Speck & Associates, LLC; Sustainable Long Island; Torti Gallas and Partners, Inc.; VHB; BHC Architects; Keller Sandgren Architects; and Merrill, Pastor & Colgan Architects.

[2] The chronology of the project up to 2016 is well documented in Town of Babylon, Office of Downtown Revitalization, *Wyandanch Rising: A Community's Transformation*, April 2016: https://townofbabylon.com/index.aspx?nid=139. For news reports on the first decade of the project, see Will James, "Wyandanch Rising Tries to Undo Long Fall," *Wall Street Journal*, 4 April 2013, and C.J. Hughes, "In a Long Island Hamlet, a Downtown Is Being Built From Scratch," *New York Times*, 30 September 2014.

(a)

(b)

Figure II.29-2   Orthophoto taken in 2007 shows the "before" conditions (a) in the focus area for Wyandanch Rising, once characterized by surface commuter parking lots, a small strip center, and underutilized industrial buildings, a small train station, and less than a third of an acre of public open space. The adopted masterplan (b) by Torti Gallas and Partners, shown here as developed in 2013 by BHC Architects for the Albanese Organization, is being implemented in phases, starting with the parcels directly north of the train station. Source: (a) NYS Digital Ortho-imagery Program, 2007; (b) Courtesy of BHC Architects.

A significant part of the story is the ongoing effort to gain, and keep, the trust of local residents, who harbored, and continue to harbor, reasonable fears of displacement. These fears are deep seated in past experiences of race-based discrimination in access to housing and the provision of services.[3]

In 1950s Wyandanch, developers built and sold 400 Cape Cod saltbox houses in two FHA-insured, non-racially restricted subdivisions—a rarity at the time. The two subdivisions, Carver Park and Lincoln Park, led the growth and transformation by 1960 of Wyandanch from a mostly white working-class area to a majority African American community of homeowners. Current census figures track the hamlet's 11,600 residents (down from a 1970 peak of 16,000) as over 90% Black and Hispanic, with a higher poverty rate than nearby places with similar housing stock. Today, a disproportionate number of residents rent their houses from absentee landlords.

In 2000, a series of round-table events by local philanthropists and activists led to the formation of Sustainable Long Island (SLI), a nonprofit environmental justice organization. The group identified five focus communities to begin engagement, including Wyandanch. Vanessa Pugh, one of the organization's first hires, went straight to work. In Wyandanch, she knew residents would be distrustful, and alienated by the planning jargon of sustainability efforts—terms like "zero-lot line housing" and "density"—when they wanted to talk about hunger, food scarcity, and the need for jobs.[4] She proposed a community planning process based in methods of the Gamaliel Foundation, founded to empower ordinary people to effectively participate in the political, environmental, social, and economic decisions affecting their lives, thus uniting people of diverse faiths and races. Gamaliel's roots are in the 1960s effort of the Contract Buyers League

---

[3] Andrew Wiese, "Racial Cleansing in the Suburbs: Suburban Government, Urban Renewal, and Segregation on Long Island, New York, 1945–60," in Marc Silver and Martin Melkonian, eds., *Contested Terrain: Power, Politics, and Participation in Suburbia* (Hofstra University, 1995): 61–69. See also Q&A with Wyandanch publishing activist Delano Stewart, Thomas Clavin, "Offering News From a Black Perspective, *New York Times,* 19 January 1997.

[4] Interview of Vanessa Pugh by June Williamson, 4 January 2018.

to protect African Americans on Chicago's West Side, who, unable to obtain bank mortgages due to racial discrimination, had purchased homes from realtors at inflated prices on specious contracts.[5]

With SLI, Pugh was able to connect with local clergy from 25 churches and other school and civic leaders over many months of regular meetings to help bring over 600 residents out for a five-day visioning charrette in June 2003. (A charrette is an intensive planning session where citizens, designers, and others collaborate on a future vision.) During the charrette, Dan Burden of Walkable Communities was invited to come and lead walking audits of the hamlet's many wide and dangerous roads, brownfield properties, and surface parking lots.

The outcomes were formation of a Wyandanch Rising Implementation Committee comprised of a core group of clergy and civic leaders, adoption of a Wyandanch Hamlet Plan drafted by SLI for the Town of Babylon, and creation of a town Office of Downtown Revitalization.[6] The new office was charged with seeking grants for planning studies and marshalling funds for assembling "blighted" property for revitalization. Pugh explains that all of the lots around the train station, approximately 300 properties, qualified as brownfields, both because of real physical contamination with industrial pollutants and also due to *perceived* contamination, a legacy of racial discrimination and avoidance or "othering" of the hamlet and its residents over many decades. Pugh eventually transitioned from SLI to working in the Office of Downtown Revitalization, for then-town supervisor Steve Bellone. Bellone became a huge champion of the initiative and has continued to nurture it since his election to the higher office of Suffolk County Executive. By the end of 2017 the Town of Babylon had spent $27 million to purchase 48 parcels, a dozen of them by eminent domain.[7]

As planning proceeded, a number of specific obstacles came to light. Environmentally, a high water table (Long Island depends on an aquifer for fresh water), a lack of sanitary sewer infrastructure, and the preponderance of brownfields all needed to be redressed before the land could support higher-density redevelopment. On the regulatory front, restrictive and outdated single-use zoning coupled with a costly and lengthy review and approvals process needed reform. A series of experienced urban design and planning consultants produced increasingly refined retrofit schemes for a central transit-oriented development (TOD) area: AKRF, Speck & Associates, and Torti Gallas and Partners each produced successive master plans.

AKRF worked with SLI and the Town of Babylon to fulfil the terms of an initial 2007–2008 planning grant from the New York State Brownfield Opportunity Program. They identified strategic sites around the train station, proposed an intermodal hub concept, and produced a draft environmental impact statement. Speck & Associates led the original urban design vision plan and assisted the town in selecting Torti Gallas and Partners to produce a full master plan.

Erik Aulestia of Torti Gallas led the next phase of work, funded by a further round of state brownfield funding, to conduct another charrette, refine the master plan, write a detailed form-based code, and, with Speck, assist in procuring a master developer. The Torti Gallas team included detailed architecture standards in the code to guide the building architects, once they were selected. The standards are informed by measured drawings of notable nearby precedents, including the Tudor-style buildings of Forest Hills Gardens in Queens, New York, handsomely designed by architect Grosvenor Atterbury in the 1910s following tenets of the garden city movement.[8]

The town commissioned landscape architect Olin Studio of Philadelphia to design a one-acre green and plaza, a delightful centerpiece to the revitalization. The Delano Stewart Plaza at Wyandanch includes a seasonal outdoor ice rink and fire pit, a kiosk used for skate rental, terraced seating, a pavilion, and a palette of plantings that evokes Long Island's "geologic vocabulary" of terminal moraine, beaches, and meadows.

The Albanese Organization, the selected developer, engaged Beatty Harvey Coco Architects to design two five-story buildings comprising apartments over retail to

5 "Inside the Battle for Fair Housing in 1960s Chicago," *The Atlantic*, 21 May 2014: http://www.theatlantic.com/video/index/371360/the-story-of-clyde-ross-and-the-contract-buyers-league/.

6 Sustainable Long Island, *The Wyandanch Hamlet Plan: Wyandanch Rising*, 2004: http://townofbabylon.com/DocumentCenter/View/16.

7 Denise M. Bonilla, "Wyandanch Rising project to take off next year, officials say," *Newsday*, 10 December 2017.

8 Interview of Eric Aulestia by June Williamson, 27 July 2018. See also Torti Gallas and Partners and Joel Russell, consultants, *Code of the Town of Babylon: Chapter 213, Article XLII Downtown Wyandanch and Straight Path Corridor Form-Based Code*, August 2014: http://townofbabylon.com/index.aspx?nid=139.

Figure II.29-3 Street view along Station Drive of the new mixed-use buildings, developed by the Albanese Organization. The master plan and pattern book created for the Town of Babylon by Torti Gallas and Partners informed designs for the buildings by BHC Architects. Source: Photo by June Williamson, 2017.

(a)

(b)

Figure II.29-4 The Delano Stewart Plaza at Wyandanch, designed by Olin Studio, named for a longtime African American community activist. On opening day in 2018, dozens of local kids learned to ice skate on the seasonal rink, a focal point of the plaza. Source: Photos by Phillip Jones, 2018.

flank the plaza. A majority of these apartments are designated affordable. The apartments filled quickly, with a high proportion of female-headed family households, suggesting unmet demand from this demographic group. The retail spaces are filling more slowly. The building facades are better proportioned and feature more detail than we have typically observed in recent Long Island TOD infill developments.

One notable innovative aspect of the construction process is that the master development agreement included a labor requirement for all subcontractors to hire first from a pool of local residents, trained through the local Wyandanch Community Resource Center. The Center, opened in a temporary trailer building across the railroad tracks in late 2009, runs programs that have successfully provided employment and union membership to over two dozen trainees.[9] One of them was Erica Prince, a mother of three living in a shelter when she applied for training. She excelled, becoming a working member of Carpenters Local 290 union.[10]

As of this writing, the Albanese Organization, in partnership with the Community Development Corporation of Long Island (CDCLI), is constructing a further 124 apartments, all designated affordable, a small new building for the Wyandanch Community Resource Center, as well as a larger mixed-use building in a prominent location just adjacent to the station that will house a YMCA, a relocated health and wellness center, and other community-serving programs. Another parcel will be developed as 100 subsidized seniors apartment housing.[11]

Two primary infrastructural components of the retrofit are water and transit. First, water. As is true in too many northern American suburbs, sewers reach only 30% of the 1.5 million residents of Suffolk County. The rest rely on backyard septic and cesspool systems, incompatible with higher-density housing types. Wyandanch was among the last communities in the county to receive piped water, rather than relying on wells. To support Wyandanch Rising, thousands of feet of additional water mains and a sewer pipe extension along the main commercial boulevard, Straight Path Road,

were installed. In 2019, voters approved funding to expand the nearest sewer district northward, expanding coverage to residential areas in Wyandanch within the Carlls River watershed.

The site of Wyandanch Rising surrounds the Wyandanch Long Island Rail Road station on the Ronkonkoma Branch of the Main Line. One of the first transformations was the construction of a large parking structure, featuring a stair tower with stained glass windows, designed by Jeff Speck, to free up land that had been used for surface commuter parking and to ease pressure for commuter parking at other, land-constrained stations elsewhere in the Town of Babylon.

Figure II.29-5 Speck & Associates designed a striking stair tower for the new commuter parking structure, featuring stained glass public art. The tower not only forms a landmark, but it also encourages patrons to walk the stairs rather than taking an elevator. Source: Photo by Sid Tabak, 2015.

---

9   Town of Babylon, Office of Downtown Revitalization, *Wyandanch Rising: A Community's Transformation*, April 2016, 31.
10 Carrie Mason-Draffen, "Once homeless and unemployed, woman lands construction job," *Newsday*, 17 July 2014.
11 Bonilla, "Wyandanch Rising."

Figure II.29-6 The gracious new Wyandanch Station, designed by Keller Sandgren Architects, opened in 2018, forms a focal point at the end of Delano Stewart Plaza. The station building features Terrazzo tile floors, a wood-paneled ceiling, chandeliers, bike racks, benches, and free Wi-Fi. It's a significant upgrade from the previous cheaply constructed station structure. Source: Photo by Phillip Jones, 2018.

The next major project was the building of two modernized platforms, with an elevator-served pedestrian overpass, and an ADA-accessible, amenity-rich new Wyandanch Station for 4,200 daily LIRR riders.[12] Fitting the master plan, the station was imagined as a civic amenity, placed on axis with the Plaza at Wyandanch. The new station is the fourth built in this location. The first, a wood-framed structure dating to 1875 when the railroad was mostly used for freight, had been a shooting location for movie Westerns in the pre-Hollywood era.[13] It was replaced by a nondescript concrete masonry unit box in 1958, and by a slightly larger but equally nondescript station building in 1987, after a scheme to eliminate the stop and bypass the community altogether was defeated. Finally, in 2018, Wyandanch could boast a dignified station structure worthy of the community's residents.

It might be said that the process of Wyandanch Rising is akin to a traditional barn-raising, its success dependent on the participation of many sturdy hands, all working in concert together. It is a potent case study of how an engaged community process, designed to build resident trust and leverage social capital, can advance goals for increasing equity, brownfields cleanup, improving public health, and enhancing water and transit infrastructure. It not only mitigates the effects of decades of systemic race-based segregation and discrimination in housing and public investment, but it is a much-needed example of building resilience to future economic and environmental disruptions for the most vulnerable suburban populations.

---

[12] Wyandanch Station Enhancement project page, New York Metropolitan Transportation Authority, Long Island Rail Road Modernization Program blog: http://www.amodernli.com/project/wyandanch-station-enhancement/.
[13] "Historic L.I.R.R. Station is Razed," *New York Times*, 11 June 1958.

Meriden Green
Meriden, Connecticut

Challenges addressed:

- Add water and energy resilience
- Leverage social capital for equity
- Disrupt automobile dependence

t's curious what happens when complex arguments are abbreviated to shorthand. Some commentators on our *Retrofitting Suburbia* book reduced our careful documentation of a full range of strategies for retrofitting dead shopping centers to just one: demolition and redevelopment with a higher-density, mixed-use, walkable, compact town center.[1] Where the location and market are amenable, higher-density redevelopment works, adding resilience, economic and otherwise, to suburban municipalities that despaired when the mall died, as at the Belmar retrofit in Lakewood, Colorado.[2] Overlooked were the many other examples we included demonstrating combinations of all

three primary retrofitting strategies: redevelopment, reinhabitation, and regreening.[3]

In a stellar example of regreening of a retail site, a new park called Meriden Green, thoughtfully designed and engineered, replaced a dead enclosed shopping mall built over a culverted portion of a flood-prone brook.

The park features the daylit brook, one and a half miles of walking paths and pedestrian bridges, an amphitheater with canopied stage, and provisions for a regular farmer's market.[4] The land was extensively regraded into a park landscape that functions as a stormwater basin capable of detaining up to 60 acre-feet of water—an area equivalent to thirty Olympic-sized swimming pools—thus removing 227 properties in Meriden's historic downtown core from the 100-year flood plain including its train station. The retrofit efforts also upgrade and increase the stock of quality affordable housing nearby the now enhanced transit center. All these changes contribute to revitalizing an economically distressed town.

Located at the halfway point between the Connecticut cities of New Haven and Hartford and thus within commuting distance of both, Meriden was once known as Silver City because of the prodigious output of fine cutlery and other goods manufactured there by the International Silver Company. Fourteen acres of land once used by the silver and other industries is located on the low-lying banks of Harbor Brook, a waterway that meanders through on its way to the Quinnipiac River and Long Island Sound.

---

[1] For an example, see the 2009 review by Aaron M. Renn, now a senior fellow at the Manhattan Institute, on his widely read *Urbanophile* blog, in which he summarizes our approach as "how to make the suburbs more urban," mischaracterizes it as "one-size-fits-all," and then goes on to suggest alternative approaches that are, in fact, discussed in our book: http://www.urbanophile.com/2009/01/10/review-retrofitting-suburbia/. More recently, a review of Meriden Green suggests that the project presents an alternative to the "instant architecture" lifestyle center mall conversions of recent vintage. While the argument has great merit, from our experience it seems likely that Meriden might have welcomed just such a redevelopment approach, had it been deemed feasible. The article also glosses over the 3 acres yet to be developed with new construction that will replace a significant percentage of the square footage that was demolished. Olivia Martin, "One Connecticut town swaps a derelict mall for a 14.4-acre, community-centered green space," *Architect's Newspaper*, 17 January 2017: https://archpaper.com/2017/01/meriden-green-mall-connecticut/#gallery-0-slide-0.

[2] Dunham-Jones and Williamson, *Retrofitting Suburbia*, 154–171.

[3] Ibid., 51–52, 70–75, 119–122.

[4] Credits for Meriden Green: owner/developer: City of Meriden; design and construction team: Milone & MacBroom, AECOM, La Rosa Construction, U.S. EPA, FEMA, Army Corps of Engineers, State of Connecticut (DECD, DEEP, DOT), and the Meriden Flood Control Implementation Agency.

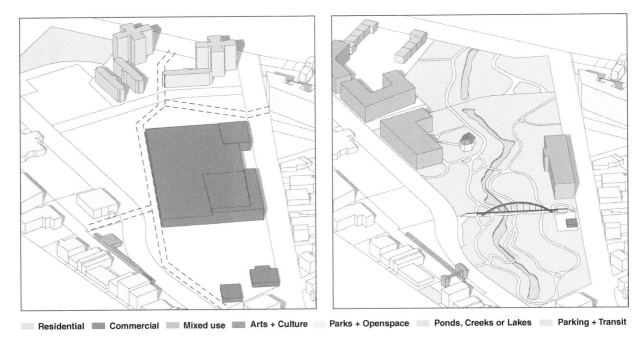

Figure II.30-1 Before retrofitting, the urban renewal–era Meriden Hub mall sat squat in a parking lot, over a culverted brook (dashed lines in diagram). After retrofitting, the mall site is regraded into Meriden Green, with new housing, relocated subsidized housing, and a sophisticated piece of green infrastructure including a daylit brook and stormwater park. Source: Authors.

The land was cleared, assembled, and filled in the 1960s for urban renewal, which arrived in 1970 in the form of the 250,000 square foot, one-story enclosed Meriden Hub mall.[5] It was an ill-conceived venture from the start: a second competing mall located closer to exits on the nearest interstate highway opened in Meriden the following year, the anchor store chain W. T. Grant went bankrupt in 1976, the industrial jobs base of Meriden declined even further, and the downtown location developed a reputation for seediness. To add insult to injury, the property was subject to regular flooding from the inadequately controlled Harbor Brook, including two catastrophic incidents in 1992 and 1996 that resulted in $30 million in damages and drove away the last remaining major tenant, a corporation that was occupying a large portion of the mall for offices.

After the second major flood, the city retained engineers and landscape architects Milone & MacBroom,

Figure II.30-2 Entrance canopy to the vacant Meriden Hub mall, built in 1970, photographed shortly before the building was demolished in 2007. Source: Photo courtesy of Nicholas DiMaio.

Inc. to create a flood-control plan for the 15-square-mile Harbor Brook watershed. Less than a decade later, in 2005, following recommendations by twenty stakeholders and findings from an EPA-funded report on vacant and

---

[5] The property was originally called the Meriden Mall. It was later renamed the Meriden Hub to reduce confusion with a second development, called the Meriden Square Mall, that opened nearby in 1971.

(a)   (b)

Figure II.30-3 Before and after view of the demolition of the Harbor Brook conduit (a) and its daylighting in Meriden Green (b), as documented by project design engineers Milone & MacBroom, Inc. Source: Photos courtesy of Milone & MacBroom, Inc.

underused sites, the municipality took over the mall by eminent domain. It became the centerpiece of the emergent flood-prevention strategy.

After a further decade of planning, demolition, and brownfields remediation, funded with $2.9 million in federal and state funds, and $14 million in new construction financing with state and local bonds, the 14-acre site was reborn as Meriden Green with a grand opening in September 2016. Mindful of economic development goals to leverage public bond funding into jobs, the project was built with 100% small business contracting and 25% women and minority-owned contractors.[6] The project required one of the most complex regulatory permits ever approved through the State of Connecticut.[7]

Eleven acres are devoted to the flood-control park, which slopes down to the meandering daylit creek. The 300-foot-long Silver City Bridge spans across the park and links up to the newly upgraded Meriden Transit Center. The bridge is elevated, designed to provide an evacuation route in the event of another major flood. Early schemes for the park show several surface parking lots. The final design includes none. Areas of grass in the park are structured with a subsurface reinforcement layer to accommodate market stalls and trailers for programmed seasonal events. The remaining three acres will be mixed-use buildings on two separate parcels, adding 170 apartments over ground floor retail, to be developed by Philadelphia-based Pennrose Properties and the Cloud Company, LLC.[8]

[6] City of Meriden website: http://www.meriden2020.com/Things_ To_Do/meriden-green-/.
[7] As reported on the Milone & MacBroom website: https://www .miloneandmacbroom.com/work/meriden-green.

[8] These units will be 80% market rate and 20% affordable, priced below 80% AMI.

Figure II.30-4 Signage in Meriden Green includes a reminder of the primary purpose for public investment in regrading and regreening the mall site into a park. Periodic flooding is a feature, not a bug. Source: Photo by June Williamson, 2016

The entire area was rezoned as a transit-oriented district (TOD) in 2013, capitalizing on the new New Haven–Hartford-Springfield commuter rail line, a partnership between the Connecticut Department of Transportation, Connecticut Rail, and Amtrak. Enhanced service began running in June 2018, providing commuters with lower fares, opening up a vast jobs shed to residents living downtown, where poverty is concentrated and unemployment is high, relative to other parts of Meriden.[9] The service is intended to relieve traffic congestion on the Interstate 91 corridor. The old Amtrak station was replaced with the new $20 million intermodal Meriden Transit Center, for trains, buses, and rideshare vehicles.

Meriden Green, designed not only for hydrologic function but also to encourage walking and biking, will be extended to the north, along Harbor Brook, where another covered section of the creek will be opened up. That section is part of the Mills Memorial Apartments site, where 140 units of public housing, built in 1962 and—like the adjacent mall—subjected to frequent flooding, will be demolished. Redevelopment is proceeding under the HUD

Choice Neighborhoods Transformation program.[10] Every single apartment will be replaced in project-based voucher units and all "lease-compliant" Mills Apartments residents retain a right of return to new replacement units (with the same number of bedrooms) located outside the 100-year flood plain. If the tenant wishes it, their new residence must be within walking distance of the Mills project.[11]

It is an impressive public housing replacement scheme. While some might argue that a better scheme is keeping the housing, in this case repairing the existing buildings is untenable, given the flood-prone site. While old news reports suggest that gang activity once thrived in the Mills, the apartments are now reported to be calm; it is the risk associated with the *physical* site conditions that is not tolerable.

The first new housing, called Meriden Commons I, is built on a parcel to the west of the Mills, on a former municipal parking lot regraded to a higher elevation. The four-story building, U-shaped in plan, was developed by Pennrose, the same developer selected for the Meriden Green parcels, and designed by Wallace Roberts & Todd, LCC. It sits at the northwest corner of Meriden Green.

The building contains 75 units: 26 replacement units for residents displaced from the Mills making below 30% of the area median income (AMI), 60 affordable units (for those making between 30-60% AMI), and 15 market rate units. It is part of a larger phased plan that will bring over 650 new units, many designated affordable, to the TOD.[12] Where the public housing buildings once stood, another culverted portion of Harbor Brook will be daylit, and an additional 2.2 acres will be landscaped as an extension of Meriden Green.

Meriden's transformation from small, gritty industrial city to affordable, walkable, transit-served commuter town, in the US state with the second highest level of income inequality, has been painfully gradual.[13] But just as the water in Harbor Brook is now exposed to daylight, there is good reason to anticipate bluer skies ahead.

[9] In census tract 1701, where Meriden Green is located, the poverty rate was 34%, compared to 7% in Meriden as a whole; the unemployment rate was 8% versus 4.66%. 2017 American Community Survey 5-year estimates.

[10] Together with master developer Pennrose Properties, LLC, WRT served as grant writer, planning coordinator, master planner, and architect to the Meriden Housing Authority.

[11] Meriden Choice Neighborhoods Transformation Plan, City of Meriden website:http://www.meriden2020.com/Downtown-Redevelopment/meriden-choice-neighborhood/.

[12] Ibid.

[13] Analysis based on the Gini coefficient from the 2012–2016 American Community Survey, Zippia (2018).

Cottages on Greene
East Greenwich, Rhode Island

Challenges addressed:

- Leverage social capital for equity
- Add water and energy resilience

Retrofits can be large, and they can be small. Retrofits of varied sizes and types each contribute to a larger vision of "incremental metropolitanism," where each retrofit contributes to a cumulative, metropolitan-scale transformation, realized over time.[1] Cottages on Greene, in the affluent Providence, Rhode Island, suburb of East Greenwich, is a case in point. One block from the town's Main Street (a portion of famed US Route 1, extending from Miami to Maine), there used to sit an automobile repair shop, with a paved yard filled with cars, with a single detached house on one side and a circa-1960 mini strip shopping center on the other. Now the combined lot, less than one acre in size, supports a compact cottage court or pocket neighborhood development with fifteen two-bedroom units of housing.[2]

The small project packs a big punch in demonstrating how a housing project that is relatively dense can be seamlessly introduced into a suburban residential neighborhood, if designed in a manner that is compatible with the existing context. In this case, it is a neighborhood of street-facing detached houses, with rear garages. The retrofit also incorporates exemplary site design strategies

Figure II.31-1 Pedestrian paths flank the central linear green of Cottages on Greene, a retrofit that replaces an auto repair shop on a 0.85-acre lot with fifteen cottage units. The paths provide access to each unit, as well as a connection from Greene Street to the dead-end Olson's Way at the rear. Source: Photo by Nat Rae, courtesy of Union Studio Architecture & Community Design.

for managing stormwater, while adding to the town of East Greenwich's long-term affordable housing stock.[3]

---

[1] Dunham-Jones and Williamson, *Retrofitting Suburbia*, 9–12.
[2] For background on cottage courts and pocket neighborhoods, see Ross Chapin, *Pocket Neighborhoods: Creating Small-Scale Community in a Large-Scale World* (Newtown, CT: Taunton Press, 2011).

[3] HUD User, "East Greenwich, Rhode Island: Cottages on Greene's Innovative Approach to Infill," US Department of Housing and Urban Development, 2012: https://www.huduser.gov/portal/casestudies/study_07022012_1.html. See also Union Studio, "Cottages on Greene" project: http://unionstudioarch.com/projects/cottages-on-greene/.

(a)

(b)

(c)

Figure II.31-2 Sequence of diagrams illustrating (a) the "before" condition; (b) a conventional massing approach for an apartment building; and (c) the cottage court or pocket neighborhood configuration that was built as Cottages on Greene. Both (b) and (c) have the same density and number of units. Source: Courtesy of Union Studio Architecture & Community Design.

One conventional way to add this number of new two-bedroom units on a lot of this size is to propose a three-story apartment building with a central staircase and four to six units on each floor. Such a configuration is likely to be met with objections that it is "incompatible" with the adjacent detached houses. Instead of a single building, the project is a cottage court configuration of differing unit types—a mix of detached houses, side-by-side duplexes, and a three-unit townhouse structure—arranged around a small central linear green running perpendicular to the street. This massing arrangement visually maintains the neighborhood building scale, and when viewed by passers-by, appears to be a "compatible" row of detached houses.

Buildings in the court are distinguished from one another architecturally with gabled roofs, front porches, and picket fences. Cottages on Greene cleverly illustrates the "missing middle" approach to infill housing design that can be inserted into any similarly sized and proportioned lot, as long as zoning and fire safety code requirements do not preclude it.[4]

A missing middle approach to housing design can be an effective means to introduce multiple smaller housing units onto conventional lots in existing lower-density residential neighborhoods. Not only do the smaller homes tend to reduce costs, but the reduced amount of land per home also contributes to affordability. In the case of Cottages on Greene, designed by Union Studio Architecture & Community Design with civil engineer Jonathan Ford, PE and landscape architect Diane Soule & Associates for 620 Main Street Associates, five of the fifteen units, all sold as condominiums, were designated affordable. They were sold to income-eligible applicants with deed restrictions limiting appreciation gains for a period of at least 30 years, meeting the standards of Rhode Island's Low- and Moderate-Income Housing Act (LMIH). The law was passed in 2004 with the intent of increasing the stock of long-term affordable housing in communities throughout the state to a minimum threshold of 10% of supply. Many suburban towns, including pricy East Greenwich, do not meet this standard, exacerbating the trend of an increasing housing affordability gap for the

---

4 "Missing Middle" was coined by Daniel and Karen Parolek of Opticos Design, Inc. in 2010 to define a range of multiunit or clustered housing types compatible in scale with single-family homes that help meet the growing demand for walkable urban living. See Daniel Parolek, *Missing Middle Housing: Thinking Big and Building Small to Respond to Today's Housing Crisis* (Washington, DC: Island Press, 2020).

Figure II.31-3 This view of the on-site contouring for bioswales and rain gardens, spanned with small bridges at Cottages on Greene soon after construction, illustrates the low-impact development or LID approach to managing stormwater on site. The plantings have since matured. Source: Photo by Jonathan Ford, PE, 2010.

state's residents.[5] While housing advocates might debate whether 30 years of affordability is "long-term," this project helps in an incremental manner. In addition, it introduced these units into the walkable heart of the town through a redevelopment retrofit, rather than in an out-of-the-way location.

The other retrofitting innovation to highlight is the approach to managing stormwater. The cottage court site plan doesn't yield a large area for a conventional single retention pond. Also, the site is in a low-lying area, just a few streets away from a vulnerable coastline, and has a high water table. The project's designers assertively pursued a low-impact development (LID) approach. The landscaping features surface bio-retention in swales and rain gardens, providing small bridges and boardwalks for the residents to cross the many small ponds and spillways. The parking lot paving is permeable, with a below-ground infiltration layer below (24 inches of crushed stone reservoir) that eventually recharges the groundwater.[6]

As we often point out, design matters! Cottages on Greene's design introduces affordability and sustainable features at the relatively high density of over 17 units per acre. And does it very attractively. By maintaining the scale and features of neighboring houses at the street frontage, the project fits into the context. Such strategies are often especially useful in established neighborhoods.

[5] HousingWorks RI, *2017 Housing Fact Book,* Roger Williams University (2017): https://www.housingworksri.org/.

[6] Jonathan Ford, "Rhode Island Stormwater Solutions," *Rhode Island Stormwater Solutions,* University of Rhode Island, Fall 2010, http://web.uri.edu/riss/cottages-on-greene/.

Assembly Square
Somerville, Massachusetts

Challenges addressed:

- Leverage social capital for equity
- Improve public health
- Compete for jobs
- Disrupt automobile dependence

Somerville is a small, densely populated inner suburban city outside Boston, Massachusetts.[1] Formerly industrial, by the 1990s it had come to rely on property taxes for three-quarters of its budget. At that time, eager to capture more sales tax revenue, city officials slated a large brownfield site on the Mystic River, much of it vacant or underused for many years, for clean-up followed with new big box retail. The drawn-out, 20-year

planning and redevelopment process that unfolded on this site abetted a political shift in the City of Somerville, as an "old ethnics" power base rooted in patronage politics gave way to a new coalition between two "newcomers" groups: educated professionals with an activist bent and more recent immigrant residents, including refugees, many of whom are people of color.[2]

Two decades later the cleaned-up site boasts Assembly Row, a high-density destination district of walkable streets and blocks developed by mixed-use developer Federal Realty Investment Trust (FRIT); a new rail transit station; bike paths and a waterfront park; a large healthcare office building; and much more infill redevelopment to come.

(a)

(b)

Figure II.32-1 Located north of downtown Boston, the Assembly Square area in Somerville, Massachusetts, was once largely accessible only by car, cut off from neighboring areas by highways. Before (a) and after the first phase (b) aerial views show how the growing mixed-use and walkable district is now served by an added stop on an existing fixed rail transit line. Source: Photos courtesy of Federal Realty Investment Trust.

---

[1] Somerville encompasses 4.1 square miles, with 80,000 residents, resulting in a high population density of approximately 20,000 residents per acre.

[2] See Susan Ostrander, *Citizenship and Governance in a Changing City: Somerville, MA* (Philadelphia: Temple University Press, 2013).

Assembly Square is made up of 145 acres of filled salt marsh, now cut off from the rest of Somerville by two highways, Route 28 and Interstate 93. Major industrial employers included the Ford Motor Co., which from 1926 to 1958 occupied a then-state-of-the-art assembly plant designed by renowned industrial architect Albert Kahn; and First National Stores, which built a grocery manufacturing and distribution center, and later occupied Ford's buildings until 1976. Most other industrial businesses in East Somerville were shuttered by the late 1970s, with dire consequences for the tax base. In "patronage politics" deals, city officials eased permits throughout the city to convert buildings to apartments, leading to a significant imbalance in the housing to jobs ratio.[3]

Circa 1980, developers converted Kahn's buildings for Ford into the 340,000-square-foot Assembly Square Mall and a Loews Theater. Additional big box uses followed, accessible by car from the elevated highway. Vehicle exhaust shed particulate matter on adjacent blocks,

contributing to elevated rates of asthma for nearby residents. Officials unearthed barrels and barrels of polluted liquids taken from the Ford plant buried on a former employee's land in New Hampshire. His property became that state's most contaminated Superfund site.[4] Back in Somerville, however, regulators deemed the riverfront brownfield site suitable for conventional soil cleanup methods.

People took to deriding Somerville, calling it "Slummerville," a place of diminished municipal services but cheap rents for those working or studying elsewhere. The parking lots at Assembly Square Mall became known for some of the highest rates of vehicle theft in the region, associated with notorious organized crime rackets. What to do?

Early in 1998, a local development group bought the moribund 26-acre mall site (for $18.8 million), with plans to demolish and rebuild it as a big box "power center." Ikea purchased the 17-acre parcel to the east for their first New England store. Meanwhile, a State Representative from Somerville heard architect and Rhode Island School of Design architecture professor Anne Tate speak about new urbanism and the nascent concept of Smart Growth at the Massachusetts State House. He invited her to present at "SomerVision," an event held that April. Tate spoke about Assembly Square, and the proposed big box redevelopment, to be called "Riverside," as misnomers. You can't "assemble" at Assembly Square, while "Riverside" would not provide access or even a "view" to the Mystic River, she told the audience. Members of the audience were galvanized, and immediately afterward formed a citizens' advocacy group to push for a different scheme, naming themselves the Mystic View Task Force (MVTF).

MVTF soon came up with a plan for a walkable mixed-use town center and developed a "30-30-30" vision: 30 acres of new waterfront park space, 30,000 new jobs, and $30 million in new net tax revenue.[5] Their alternative scheme would provide the density to support a new transit stop on the Massachusetts Bay Transit Authority (MBTA or "T") Orange Line that crossed the site

Figure II.32-2   Interior view of the historic Ford Assembly Plant in Somerville, Massachusetts, by famed Detroit architect Albert A. Kahn. The innovative butterfly skylights are preserved in the building's current incarnation as a big box power center. Source: *Architect's Journal*, 22 August 1928. Public domain.

[3] William Shelton, "Assembly Square, the back story," *Somerville Times*, 22 June 2012. Reprint of a series of columns by William Shelton that appeared in the *Somerville News* between 13 April 2005 and 15 August 2006: http://www.thesomervilletimes.com/archives/39645.

[4] John Glass, "Ford's Somerville legacy bubbles up in N.H.," *Boston Business Journal* 11:19 (1 July 1991): 7, ISSN: 0746-4975.
[5] Ellen Dunham-Jones, a Somerville resident at the time, participated in the first MVTF charrette. Wig Zamore led many of the further discussions between MVTF and the city to agree on the 30-30-30 goals.

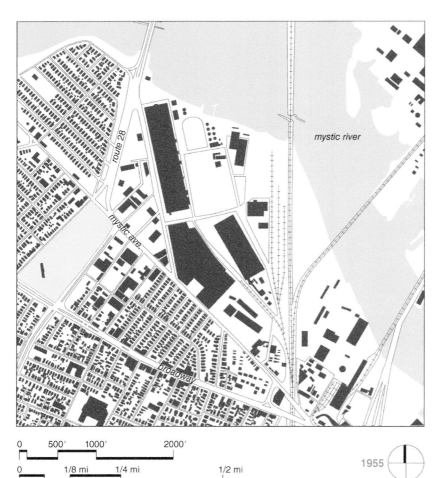

but did not stop in Somerville. In an unusual and perhaps unprecedented process, these citizen activists called for a YIMBY or "Yes In My Backyard" scheme for *more* density at the industrial redevelopment site of Assembly Square, rather than the NIMBY or "Not In My Backyard" objections that are more typically associated with community groups in changing suburbs.

Soon after, MVTF started filing lawsuits. They argued that the city's approval of the developer's plans were in violation of the protection of health, safety, and welfare, citing induced traffic and increased air pollution to result from the planned purely auto-oriented uses, rather than the walkable, transit-oriented ones their alternate vision advanced.[6] This had the effect of gumming up the works,

slowing negotiations between developers and the city.[7] In October 2001, after the city approved Ikea's auto-oriented plans, Anthony Flint, a land use scholar and reporter for the *Boston Globe* wrote, "Assembly Square has become a test case: Can a community stay committed to 'smart growth' development in tough times that demand the more immediate economic returns of suburban-style growth?"[8] For a time, stalemate ensued, and it seemed that nothing might get built on the site.

The electorate became restless. In early 2004 a new mayor took office, Joseph A. Curtatone. Somerville-born,

---

[6] Doug Brugge, professor at Tufts University, was invited to provide expert opinion on the air quality impacts of the city's versus MVTF's schemes. He describes his assessment in his book *Particles in the Air: The Deadliest Pollutant is One You Breathe Every Day* (Springer International, 2018).

[7] William A. Shutkin, "A river (and $5 billion of transportation infrastructure) runs through it: Sustainability slouches toward Somerville's waterfront," *Boston College Environmental Affairs Law Review* 28:4 (Summer 2001): 565–581.

[8] Anthony Flint, "Somerville: Test case for growth city in spotlight after IKEA deal," *Boston Globe,* 29 October 2001, B1. See also Anthony Flint, "The Density Dilemma," in *This Land: The Battle over Sprawl and the Future of America* (Baltimore: Johns Hopkins University Press, 2006), 206–207.

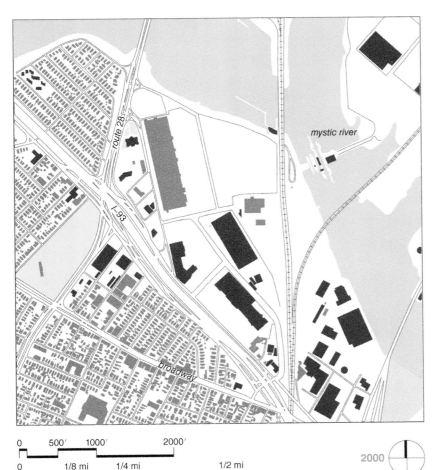

Figure II.32-4 2000 figure-field diagram. By the turn of the millennium, the Ford plant had been converted to a shopping mall, already dying. Other parcels in the district were redeveloped with other big box, automobile-oriented uses, easily accessed from Interstate 93, which had cut Assembly Square off from the adjacent neighborhoods. Source: Authors.

much younger than his predecessors, and a childhood asthma sufferer, Curtatone quickly announced plans to speed up redevelopment by proceeding with rezoning. He stated unequivocally that he was prepared for battle and "making unpopular decisions."[9] The next year, Maryland-based Federal Realty Investment Trust (FRIT) purchased the mall property, executed a land swap deal with Ikea, and announced the mixed-use, pedestrian-oriented "Assembly Row" plan, following on the retrofits the firm had built at Bethesda Row in Maryland, and Santana Row in San Jose, California.[10] Anticipating the deal, $25 million in federal transportation funds were set aside for the new "T" station. By the end of that year Assembly Square Mall reopened, bringing in a revenue stream to help finance the adjacent redevelopment.[11] Two MVTF lawsuits remained unresolved.

In January 2007, a final deal was inked between the City of Somerville, MVTF and FRIT. Sociologist Susan Ostrander characterizes the three-way agreement as a notable example of local governance sharing with a voluntary civic association. Her thesis is that a lack of a strong commercial base in the wake of deindustrialization opened "a space for civic engagement, allowing civil society associations and organizations to obtain greater influence and power," especially around urban develop-ment, in the transformation of a once-declining community to a place celebrated for diversity, arts scene, restaurants, and progressive planning, with bike lanes, and so on.[12]

[9] Donovan Slack, "Incoming mayor plans shakeup in Somerville," *Boston Globe*, 3 January 2004, B.1.

[10] Dunham-Jones and Williamson, *Retrofitting Suburbia*, 78–80.

[11] Interview of Don Briggs of Federal Realty Investment Trust by June Williamson, 30 August 2016.

[12] Ostrander, *Citizenship and Governance*, 6–7, 37.

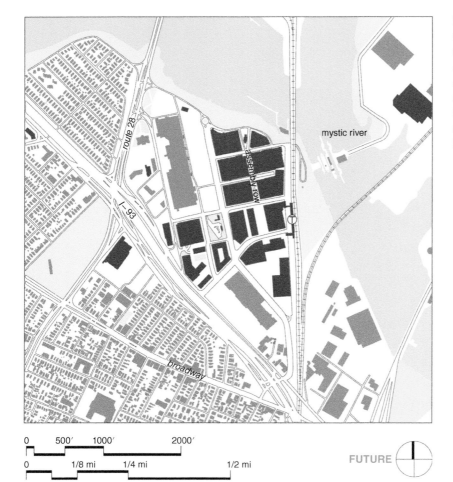

Figure II.32-5 Projected future figure-field diagram. Gradually, the area is undergoing transformation into a compact, mixed-use, walkable district comprising a grid of new streets and mid-rise buildings, with park access to the Mystic River waterfront and a shiny new T stop on the existing MBTA Orange rail line. Source: Authors.

In 2012, after delays caused by the Great Recession of 2008, construction began on the first apartments in Assembly Row. Two AvalonBay buildings contain 448 rental units. In accordance with Somerville's inclusionary housing regulations, 56 of the units (12.5%) are designated affordable.[13] Full build-out is expected to include more than 800,000 square feet of retail space, about 1.75 million square feet of office use, and more than 2,000 apartments. FRIT then acquired Ikea's 12-acre parcel. The outlet shops of Assembly Row opened soon afterwards, arguably the first example of outlets clustered in a non-exurban, mixed-use location.[14] When Assembly Station opened, it was the first new stop added to existing lines in Boston's transit system since 1987.

Somerville's planners—professionals recruited to the city by Mayor Curtatone, seasoned by Assembly Square battles, and now involved in an array of progressive planning projects around the city—rezoned seventy-three acres of adjacent land, parcels closest to the highway, for higher density. A 300-foot buffer from the highway excludes new residential uses, to protect against auto-related air pollution. A 2014 study by the Community Assessment of Freeway Exposure and Health or CAFEH group, entitled "Improving Health in Communities Near Highways," explicitly measured particulates adjacent to

---

[13] Then Somerville Director of Planning George Proakis credited Assembly Square with producing more inclusionary housing units in two years than the city's entire inclusionary housing program in 18 years. Interview in Somerville by Ellen Dunham-Jones on 13 April 2015.

[14] Don Briggs interview.

East Somerville highways and informed the rezoning effort.[15] While project head Don Briggs of FRIT didn't give much credit to the public health arguments advanced in MVTF lawsuits, seeing them more as tactical instruments of delay than as fully supported science, he's stated that he does accept that high-vehicle-miles-traveled corridors like highways compromise air quality and elevate health risks.[16]

As Mayor Curtatone said when asked about health impacts of development and the importance of careful urban planning:

> The CAFEH study which we did near and around highways shows that the closer you live to highways, the higher rates you have of heart disease, respiratory illness, lung disease, premature death. We are the most densely populated city in New England, we have more than 200,000 vehicle trips per day in the city, we know the impacts on our health, we know how the lack of planning has curtailed our ability economically, we know that the disparate ratio in our tax base between residents paying a greater share of the tax burden than the commercial side. So, all those things, all that data, pushes people to say, well we need to change this narrative, we need a new paradigm for the future.[17]

At full build-out the FRIT project is likely to contain proportionately more retail and less office use than called for by MVTF's 30-30-30 vision. Even so, Assembly Row successfully landed a new, consolidated headquarters for PartnersHealthcare, resulting in a 13-story, 825,000-square-foot building for 4,500 workers.[18] In addition to those employed in retail, an additional 950,000 square feet of office use approved for development on neighboring parcels in the XMBLY project could add another 5,000 workers to Assembly Square.

(a)

(b)

Figure II.32-6   For Assembly Row, FRIT followed their previous successes, building office and residential use over ground-floor retail, with storefronts facing handsomely designed and well-proportioned sidewalks and plazas (a). One difference is in the retail leasing approach: Assembly Row includes big box retailers, premium outlet stores, and "tactical" pop-up markets of reused shipping containers (b). Source: Photos courtesy of Federal Realty Investment Trust.

[15] The CAFEH study was funded by the Kresge Foundation. See D. Brugge, J. Durant, A. Patton, J. Newman, and W. Zamore, "Improving Health in Communities Near Highways: Design Ideas from a Charrette," *Community Assessment of Freeway Exposure and Health*, November 2014; and D. Brugge, A.P. Patton, A. Bob, E. Reisner, L. Lowe, O-J.M. Bright, J.L. Durant, J. Newman, and W. Zamore, "Developing Community-Level Policy and Practice to Reduce Traffic-Related Air Pollution Exposure," *Environmental Justice* 8:3 (2015): 95–104.
[16] Don Briggs interview.
[17] Interview of Somerville Mayor Joseph A. Curtatone by June Williamson, 30 August 2016.
[18] Priyanka Dayal McCluskey, "Somerville to be new home base for Partners HealthCare," *Boston Globe*, July 13, 2016, C.4.

Figure II.32-7 The new Assembly Station stop on the MBTA Orange Line provides convenient regional transit access to workers, shoppers, and residents from points north and south to the emergent Assembly Square district, where construction is ongoing. Source: Photo by Phillip Jones, 2019.

When asked to reflect on the lengthy, complex, contested public processes of retrofitting Assembly Square over the decades, from automobile assembly plant to auto-oriented shopping mall and big box stores to its current, emergent incarnation as a cleaned-up, walkable, transit-served, mixed-use, waterfront-oriented district, Anne Tate is emphatic:

> This site has spawned the discussion of inner belts, spawned the discussion of Union Square, the whole culture of the comprehensive plan, the hiring of the planning staff. All that stuff came out of the energy that was produced and the expectations that were produced citywide by this.. . . The community group created the pressure that allowed the politicians to support it and to go for it. And at times the city and the community group were at odds, because the mayor really wanted something to happen much earlier than it did, but when their interests could align you had a very powerful push. You had people who knew how to do the planning, the engineering, the economics, and the politics.[19]

When asked about Assembly Square as a retrofitting case study, Somerville Director of Strategic Planning and Community Development George Proakis echoed and amplified Tate's claim:

> It is one of the few studies in the country where you will find an activist community group that demanded *more* development and stopped a project because it wasn't dense enough. They took massive steps to stop a project because the un-dense project was going to have community impacts that were far greater and far more negative than building quality, well-built, integrated density could produce.[20]

---

[19] Interview of Anne Tate by June Williamson, 30 August 2016.
[20] Interview of George Proakis by June Williamson, 30 August 2016.

(a) (b)

(c) (d)

Figure II.32-8 Elements of the public realm at Assembly Square are designed to support walking, biking, and transit use. Upcoming phases of the build-out are expected to add more enhancements, especially to access under the highway. Source: Photos by June Williamson, 2016.

An outcome of a concerted, proactive effort to leverage social capital in the form of civic activism, the Assembly Square retrofit not only adds an attractive new mixed-use, walkable, transit-served district to a key Boston inner suburb, but also contributes to improved health outcomes on the site itself and in surrounding neighborhoods, and positions the inner suburban City of Somerville to continue the work of redressing the severe jobs-housing imbalance that resulted from late twentieth-century processes of deindustrialization. Yes, it has taken two decades to realize, and it has been worth the time and effort.

INDEX

NOTE: Page references in *italics* refer to figures.

COVID-19 pandemic, 16, 18, 58, 97
dementia care, 37, *37*, 39
emotional health and biophilic design, 26–27
emotional health and community engagement, 19
Global Burden of Disease, overview, 17–18
loneliness and, 27
measurement and evaluative tools, 22–23
obesity rates in United States, *20*
physical activity, obesity and chronic disease, 18
physical activity and physical design, 19–23, *21*
reducing impact of polluted air, soil, water, 27–28
safety and, 24–26, *25*
suburban retrofitting patterns and, 16–17, 28
vehicle crashes and likelihood of being killed/injured, 19
See also individual case studies
Pugh, Vanessa, 224–225
Purl, Elizabeth, 108

Q

Quality Urban Energy Systems of Tomorrow (QUEST), 78
Quebec. *See* La Station - Centre Intergénérationnel (Nuns' Island, Verdun, case study)

R

Rainwater
case studies, *106, 109,* 125, *139, 143,* 154–156, *156, 157*–159, 163, 169, *174,* 189, 235
harvesting, 71, 80, 83
See also Water and energy resilience
Ramsey–Washington Metro Watershed District (RWMWD), 157, 159, *159*
Ratcliff, Gabrielle, *115*
The Ray, 177
RBF Consulting, 112
Reed, Dan, 213
Regreening, viii, ix, 31, 43, 61, 64, *66,* 70, *120,* 121, 126, 154–155, 157, 169, 229, *232*
Reinhabitation, viii, ix, 34, 43, 52, *66, 68,* 98–99, 101–103, 121, 128, 142, *166,* 169, 189, 214
Replacement units, 108, *109,* 232
Resilient Cities (Newman, Beatley, and Boyer), 42–43
Retrofitting
defined, 4
social infrastructure and, 42
See also Aging population; Automobile dependence; Case studies; Job competition; Public health; Social capital for equity; Water and energy resilience
Retrofitting Suburbia (Dunham-Jones and Williamson), 4, 36, 73, 155, 229
Rhode Island. *See* Cottages on Greene (Cottage court, East Greenwich, Rhode Island, case study)
Ride-hailing services, parking impacted by, 10–11
Right to the city concept, 53
RiNo. *See* TAXI (Denver, Colorado, case study)
Riverview Gardens (Appleton, Wisconsin), 67–68
Roads, streets, and stroads
automobile dependence and, 4–6, *5*
Complete Streets movement, 12, 18, 53–54, 89, 113, 115, 159, 161

housing and (*See* Aging population)
LIT lanes (light individual transport), 13
road diet, 8, 15, 76, 111–115
road widening, 7
roundabouts, *25*
stroad example (Buford Highway, Atlanta, Georgia), *12*
stroad example (Rockville Pike, Montgomery County, Maryland), 206
See also individual case studies
Robert Mueller Municipal Airport, *146*
Roberts, Emily, 40
Robert Wood Johnson, 190, 191
Roche, 80, 221
Rockaway Village (Queens, New York), *51*
Rockville Centre (New York), parking in, *10*
Rome, Adam, 27–28, 70n3
Rose Center for Public Leadership, 90
Roundabouts, *25*
See also Uptown Circle (Normal, Illinois, case study)

S

Saarinen, Eero, 217, *218*
Sacramento, California
Design 4 Active Sacramento example, 21, *21*
Phoenix Park Apartments (case study), 101–103, *102, 103*
WALKSacramento, 21–22
Safe Drinking Water Act (1974), 72
San Fernando, Growing Together Project, 50
San Francisco. *See* Parkmerced (San Francisco, California, case study)
Santa Fe (New Mexico), water resilience in, 76
Santana Row (San Jose, California), *62*
Sasaki Associates, 211–212
Schultze, Leonard, 105
Schupbach, Jason, 42
Schwartz, Harold, 33
Sears, 112, 127, *128,* 157, 169, *170,* 172
Security, design for, 48
Seneca, Joseph, 61
Sewers. *See* Water and energy resilience; *individual case studies*
Shalom Baranes Architects (SBA), 201
Shirley, Aaron, *24*
The Shoe Bar, *67*
Shoreline (Washington). *See* Aurora Avenue North (Shoreline, Washington, case study)
Shoup, Donald, 9–10
Silva Cells, 165, 208
Silver Spring (Maryland). *See* The Blairs District (Silver Spring, Maryland, case study)
Simon Property Group, 132, 157
Skidmore, Owings & Merrill (SOM), *105,* 106, 107
Small businesses. *See* Job competition
Smart Growth America, 51
Social capital for equity, 42–55
as benefit to all, 55
conceptual frameworks for increasing equity, 43–45, *44*
demographic trends in suburbs, 45–47, *46*
design and social diversity, 47–48